Writing History

Also in the *Writing History* series

Published:

Writing Gender History, 2nd edition
Laura Lee Downs

Writing Postcolonial History
Rochona Majumdar

Writing the Holocaust
Edited by Jean-Marc Dreyfus and Daniel Langton

Writing the History of Memory
Edited by Stefan Berger and Bill Niven

Writing History
Theory and Practice

Second edition

Edited by

Stefan Berger, Heiko Feldner
and Kevin Passmore

BLOOMSBURY
NEW DELHI • LONDON • OXFORD • NEW YORK • SYDNEY

First Published in India 2017
This edition published in 2010 by Bloomsbury Academic

Bloomsbury Academic
An imprint of Bloomsbury Publishing Plc
Bloomsbury is a registered trade mark of Bloomsbury Publishing Plc

This edition published with permission from Bloomsbury Publishing Plc
50, Bedford Square, London, WC1B3DP

British Library Cataloguing-in-Publication Data
A catalogue record for this book is available from the British Library.

ISBN: 978-93-86643-19-3
10 9 8 7 6 5 4 3 2 1
For sale in the Indian subcontinent only

Bloomsbury Publishing India Pvt. Ltd
Second Floor, Building No. 4
DDA Complex LSC, Pocket C – 6 & 7
Vasant Kunj, New Delhi 110070
www.bloomsbury.com

Exclusively Distributed in India by:
Manohar Publishers & Distributors
4753/23, Ansari Road
Darya Ganj, New Delhi 110002
Tel.: 23284848, 23289100
Email: sales@manoharbooks.com, manoharbooks@gmail.com

Printed and bound in India

Contents

Notes on Contributors

Stefan Berger is Professor of Modern German and Comparative European History at the University of Manchester, where he also directs the Manchester Jean Monnet Centre of Excellence. He is the author of numerous publications on comparative labour history, national identity and the history of historiography. His most recent books are *The Contested Nation* (Palgrave, 2008), edited with Chris Lorenz, and *Narrating the Nation* (Berghahn, 2008), edited with Linas Eriksonas and Andrew Mycock. Between 2003 and 2008 he directed a European Science Foundation programme entitled 'Representations of the Past: The Writing of National Histories in 19th and 20th Century Europe'.

Laura Lee Downs is a directeur d'études at the Ecole des Hautes Etudes en Sciences Sociales in Paris. She is the author of *Manufacturing Inequality: Gender Division in the French and British Metalworking Industries, 1914–1939* (Ithaca, NY: Cornell University Press, 1995); *Childhood in the Promised Land: Working-Class Movements and the Colonies de vacances in France, 1880–1960* (Durham, NC, 2002); *Writing Gender History* (London, 2004; 2nd ed. 2009) and, with Stéphane Gerson, *Why France? American Historians of France Reflect on Their Enduring Fascination* (Ithaca, NY: Cornell University Press, 2006).

Geoff Eley is the Karl Pohrt Distinguished University Professor of Contemporary History at the University of Michigan, Ann Arbor. The author of *Forging Democracy: The History of the Left in Europe 1850–2000* (2002), he has published widely in German history of the 19th and 20th centuries, including books on the German Right between Bismarck and the 1920s, and the idea of the *Sonderweg* in German history. His most recent publications include *A Crooked Line: From Cultural History to the History of Society* (2005) and (with Keith Nield), *The Future of Class in History: What's Left of the Social?* (2007). He is a finishing a new book on the German Right to be called *Genealogies of Nazism: Conservatives, Radical Nationalists, Fascists in Germany, 1860–1945.*

Heiko Feldner is senior lecturer in modern German history and co-director of the Centre for Ideology Critique at Cardiff University. His publications include *Das*

Erfahrnis der Ordnung (Frankfurt am Main 1999), *Žižek Beyond Foucault* (Palgrave 2007, with Fabio Vighi) and *Did Somebody Say Ideology? On Slavoj Žižek and Consequences* (CSP 2007, ed. with Fabio Vighi).

David Gentilcore is Professor of Early Modern History at the University of Leicester. As a historian he has explored the complex relationship between beliefs and practices, with a focus on early modern Italy. His most 'anthropological' monographs are *From Bishop to Witch: The System of the Sacred in Early Modern Terra d'Otranto* (Manchester 1992) and *Healers and Healing in Early Modern Italy* (Manchester 1998). He is also the author *Medical Charlatanism in Early Modern Italy* (Oxford 2006), and is currently exploring the reception and assimilation of New World plants like the tomato, the potato and maize in Italy, from the 16th century to the modern day.

John Harvey is associate professor of European history at St. Cloud State University, located in central Minnesota. His research interests are in comparative historiography and transnational intellectual history. He has authored studies on the *Annales*, the transatlanticism of German conservative historiography, and the development of European historical writing in modern American universities.

Pat Hudson is retired professor of History at Cardiff University.

Glenn Jordan is Reader in Cultural Studies and Creative Practice at the University of Glamorgan and Director of Butetown History & Arts Centre in Cardiff, Wales. His books include *Cultural Politics* (with Chris Weedon) and *Somali Elders: Portraits from Wales*. He is currently working on two exhibitions and books combining portrait photography and life stories: *Mothers and Daughters: Portraits from Multi-Ethnic Wales* and *A Sikh Face in Ireland*. He is also writing *Birth of the Black Subject* – an analysis, influenced by Foucault, of the development of Black subjectivity during the middle passage, slavery, racial violence and the New Negro movement in the USA.

Peter Lambert lectures in Modern European History at Aberystwyth University and is the author of a number of essays and articles on historiography and on 20th-century German history. His recent publications include (with Stefan Berger and Peter Schumann, eds.) *Historikerdialoge* (Göttingen, 2003), a collection of essays on Anglo-German historiographical relations, and (with Phillipp Schofield, eds.), *Making History: An Introduction to the Practices of a Discipline* (London, 2004).

Jon Lawrence is senior lecturer in Modern British History at the University of Cambridge and a fellow of Emmanuel College. He has written widely on the social, political and cultural history of modern Britain, and is the author of *Speaking for the People: Party, Language and Popular Politics in England, 1867–1914* (1998), *Electing Our Masters: The Hustings in British Politics from Hogarth to Blair* (2009) and, with Miles Taylor, *Party, State and Society: Electoral Behaviour in Britain since 1820* (1997).

Matthias Middell is Professor for Cultural History and Acting Director of the Global and European Studies Institute at the University of Leipzig and Director of the Graduate Center for Humanities and Social Sciences at the same university. His recent publications include *Historische Institute im internationalen Vergleich* (2001), *Weltgeschichtsschreibung im Zeitalter der Verfachlichung und Professionalisierung 1890–1990* (3 vols, 2005) and *Transnational History as Transnational Practice* (2009). His research interests include global and transnational history, the history of historiography in the nineteenth and twentieth centuries and processes of cultural transfer between France and Germany.

Kevin Passmore is Reader in History at Cardiff University. He is a specialist on modern French history, and has authored 'The gendered genealogy of political religions theory', *Gender and History*, vol. 20, no. 3 (2008), pp. 644–68, and 'History and Social Science since 1945', in Daniel Woolf and Axel Schneider (eds), *The Oxford History of Historical Writing*, vol. V: *1945* (Oxford: Oxford University Press, 2010).

Miles Evan "Milla" Rosenberg is an independent scholar. He holds a master's in the humanities from The Ohio State University. His research interests include the history and historiography of race, and how discourses shape and code possibilities for action. He is currently a master's candidate in the School of Computing at DePaul University, Chicago, Illinois.

Beverley Southgate is Reader Emeritus in History of Ideas at the University of Hertfordshire. His recent publications include *Postmodernism in History* (London, 2003), *What is History For?* (London, 2005), and *History Meets Fiction* (Harlow, 2009). He is currently working on the relationship of contentment and aspiration.

Garthine Walker is Senior Lecturer in History at Cardiff University. She is the author of *Crime, Gender and Social Order in Early Modern England* (Cambridge, 2003), editor of *Writing Early Modern History* (London, 2005) in this series, and co-editor of *Gender and Change: Agency, Chronology and Periodisation* (Oxford, 2009).

John Warren is Senior Lecturer in History and Professional Studies at Birmingham City University. His published works include *Elizabeth I: Religion and Foreign Affairs* (London, 2nd ed., 2001), *The Wars of the Roses and the Yorkist Kings* (London, 1995) and *The Past and its Presenters* (London, 1998). His research interests lie in the field of Victorian intellectual history, with particular reference to radical and denominational periodicals.

Thomas Welskopp is Professor for the History of Modern Societies at Bielefeld University. Recent publications include (co-edited) *Der Migros-Kosmos. Zur Geschichte eines außergewöhnlichen Schweizer Unternehmens* (Baden 2003), *Das Banner der Brüderlichkeit. Die deutsche Sozialdemokratie vom Vormärz bis zum Sozialistengesetz* (Bonn, 2000) and (edited) *Geschichte zwischen Kultur und Gesellschaft. Beiträge zur Theoriedebatte* (Munich, 1997). His present research focuses on a social and cultural history of the United States during National Prohibition, 1919–1933.

Preface

Like it or not, historians cannot avoid theory. Indeed, the idea that history could and should be a separate field of academic enquiry – now taken (largely) for granted – depended, as the first chapter of this book demonstrates, upon shifts in 18th-century understandings of the very nature of knowledge. Even if they do not explicitly use theory themselves, the writing of historians is subtly informed by theoretical assumptions. Geoffrey Elton, the great anti-theorist, might have argued that training in the techniques of historical research, coupled with fidelity to the documentary record, would permit the accumulation of objective accounts of the past. But his own work assumed the theoretical primacy of politics, and he presented a view of history in which the development of the British state was paramount. Some contemporary historians dismiss as jargon expressions taken from literary criticism such as 'discourse', just as their early 20th-century predecessors turned up their noses at modish psychological concepts such as 'unconscious motivations'. Soon, 'discourse' too will pass into common sense, and it will cease to be regarded as a theoretical term. Actually, none of the concepts used by historians are innocent. Each has its history.

Writing History: Theory and Practice is the first book in a series – *Writing History* – designed to introduce students of history at university level to the theoretical ideas – conscious and unconscious – that have moulded the discipline of history, largely in the west. This particular volume surveys the competing 'schools' of theoretical reflection which have underpinned the study of history, and the empirical method is treated as one among several ways of doing history. The book provides succinct critical introductions to the ideas, techniques and institutional practices which made possible the establishment of history as an autonomous discipline. It surveys the major bodies of theoretical knowledge which have been used to explain the past, and explores the impact of these ideas upon real examples of historical writing and upon certain fields of historical study.

This is not a book about the 'philosophy of history'. It is not directly concerned with abstract issues relating to epistemology, causation, the question of whether history is a science or art, or the use of laws in historical explanation. Knowledge of these matters is, nevertheless, essential to the practicing historian, and they figure indirectly in many of the chapters of this book. The interested reader will be able to follow such themes through the book with the aid of the index.

Neither is this book about 'historiography' or the 'history of history'. It does not provide a comprehensive survey of the development of the historical profession in its political, social, cultural and institutional context. The complete separation of theory from this context is, of course, impossible. The empirical-scientific-professional mode of historical writing, as the first three chapters in the book demonstrate, was closely tied to the establishment of history as an autonomous discipline, and the legacy of this founding moment continues to structure the discipline today – so much so that theoretical innovations often appeared to challenge the disciplinary autonomy of history and therefore even the very possibility of objective knowledge of the past. Most recently, poststructuralism seems to some like a devilish plot by literary critics to destroy the discipline, and by extension objectivity and the whole social order. Important as these issues are, they are not at the centre of this book.

The goal of this book is to explore the ways in which theory has informed *practical* historical writing. *Writing History* is based on the recognition that students often find it difficult to see how abstract discussions of the philosophy of history or histories of the discipline, relate to their own practice as historians. Each of the chapters combines explanation of essential concepts with critical discussions of the ways in which such concepts have informed works by practicing historians. Students would be well-advised to combine their reading of this book with sampling of the authors discussed in it.

Of course, the range of theories used by historians is too large to cover everything in a single volume. Our decision was to include those methods, theories, and objects of enquiry which students are most likely to find in their reading for 'normal' history courses, and thus enable them to recognize the assumptions that structure individual works and fields as a whole.

The book's structure is tripartite. The three chapters in the first section examine the intellectual and institutional conditions in which professional history developed. It explains the intellectual innovations which made possible the emergence of history as a 'scientific' discipline in Germany in the late 18th century; the spread of Rankean historical methods from 19th-century Germany to the rest of the world; and the diversification of method since the late 20th century and challenges to 'western ways' of writing history.

Part Two of the book introduces approaches to history which purport to be applicable to all periods and fields of history. The Marxist, social scientific and Annalistes approaches dealt with in Chapters Four, Five, and Six are all explicitly totalising explanations of history. Their theoretical insights and concepts have been applied to all fields of historical enquiry, and each object of study is fitted into a general explanation of history, or a 'metanarrative'. In recent decades all of these approaches have witnessed attempts to eliminate more teleological and determinist features. This has led to some convergence between them and to a certain loss of specificity as theories.

Although poststructuralism provided much of the force behind this critique metanarratives, it is included in part two because it proposes a method of critical analysis that is meant to be applicable to all of the objects studied by historians. Likewise, psycho-history is included in Part Two because Freudian psychoanalysis provided a set of concepts which allegedly explained all aspects of human behaviour, from individual motivations to the origins and nature of wars, in terms of infant relations with parents. More recently psychoanalysis has come under the influence of poststructuralism, and this has not reduced its broad ambitions. Finally, comparative history is treated in Part Two because it claims to be a universally applicable method, which does explicitly what all historians do implicitly.

The chapters in Part Two of *Writing History* deal with single theoretical traditions, those in Part Three consider the impact of a diverse range of theories in a single field of history. They often assume knowledge of the particular theories discussed in the previous section. Readers must, of course, bear in mind that theories are rarely applied in a 'pure' form to specific objects of study. More frequently historians have combined elements from a range of theories.

The decision to include a given chapter in Parts Two or Three might seem somewhat arbitrary. Gender and race historians, for example, have argued that *all* history can – and must – be re-written in accordance with their concepts. But for two reasons chapters on these topics have been included in Part Three. First, the authors of these chapters have treated gender and race as *objects of study* onto which a number of theoretical traditions have been brought to bear, rather than as *methods*. Secondly, much contemporary gender and race theory can be seen as methodologically derived from poststructuralism.

Indeed, Part Three of *Writing History* reflects the extent to which engagement with poststructuralism has shaped historical writing in recent years. Historians of politics, societies, ideas, gender, race and the economy have all, in differing degrees, shifted their attention from underlying causes to histories of meaning and identity. Whatever their fields, contemporary historians concern themselves increasingly with cultures.

At the time of writing, structuralism and poststructuralism have been with us for two decades or more, and its 'cutting-edge' status is somewhat attenuated. Several chapters suggest the need for reconciliation of the poststructuralist preoccupation with culture into a method which takes more account of social structure and inequality and which is able to account for change. Chapter Four argues that the new cultural histories need to be related to 'a bigger picture of society in general'. Chapters Seven, Eight and Fifteen suggest that Bakhtinian methods might suggest a way forward, while Chapter Nine advocates the fusion of poststructuralist-influenced cultural transfer with a socially grounded method. Chapter Ten urges the fusion of cultural with elite and social approaches to political history, and Chapter Thirteen advocates Quentin Skinner's approach to the history of ideas as a socially contextualised method which possesses the strengths but not the weaknesses of poststructuralism. Chapter Fourteen calls for gender historians to re-consider the relationship between language, body and psychology. Chapters Five and Twelve suggest that economic and cultural approaches have much to learn from each other. Whether these tendencies are seen as positive or as attempts to blunt the critical edge of poststructuralism by incorporating it into established methods is an open question.

Kevin Passmore, Stefan Berger, Heiko Feldner 11 September 2009

Part One

1

The new scientificity in historical writing around 1800

Heiko Feldner

'Schorske is not so foolish as to declare the death of history,' Steven Beller concedes in his review of Carl E. Schorske's *Thinking with History*:

> but Clio has certainly, in his view, fallen on hard times. The queen of the sciences in the mid-19th century, she is now in much straitened circumstances, reduced, in Schorske's phrase, to going on 'dates' with any discipline that will have her. This sense of history having suffered a fall from grace is overly pessimistic. History never had quite the pre-eminence Schorske ascribes to it, except perhaps in Germany.[1]

Beller's critique refers to a number of issues that form the backdrop of the following chapter. To begin with, there is the idea that history is a science and, subsequently, the uncertainty as to what exactly that means; second, the assumption that there was a golden age of history which, if it ever existed, was in 19th-century Germany; and finally, the endeavour to endow the academic discipline of history, in one way or another, with a distinctive biography. Underlying these issues is the question of what constitutes historical science (French *science historique*, German *Geschichtswissenschaft*) and its claims to objectivity, validity and truth, a recurrent theme that gives rise to controversial debates, particularly in times of paradigm shift.[2]

Part and parcel of these debates is the discussion about the *emergence* of scientific order in historical writing.[3] It is obvious that historiography as a cultural practice and true representation of the past is much older than the academic discipline of history. Even so, until the 18th century no serious attempt was made to claim for historical writing a scientific code of practice. In fact, within the premodern order of knowledge, *historia* and *scientia* were mutually exclusive.

However, what had seemed a contradiction in terms to the English philosopher Thomas Hobbes (1651), the German scholar Christian Wolff (1712) and, as late as 1751, the French editors of the *Encyclopédie*, d'Alembert and Diderot – namely that historiography could be viewed in science-like terms – was to be the point of departure for Johann Gustav Droysen's theory of historical science (*Historik*) only some hundred years later, in 1857.[4] Were 19th-century scholars, like the historian and Hegel-pupil Droysen, more astute than their seventeenth- and 18th-century counterparts? Did they detect some untapped potential in the writing of history that their predecessors had overlooked?

There is no such thing as historical science, and this is a chapter about its beginnings. Asking how it became possible to conceive of history as a science, it explores the rise of the new scientificity claimed, discussed and practised in historical writing around 1800. Since, we are usually told, it was at German universities that modern historical science took off, the German case looms large in this chapter, although this will not prevent us from reflecting on developments elsewhere and drawing some broader conclusions about history writing as a whole.

1.1 *Experientia aliena*

In *Leviathan* (1651) Hobbes introduces his system of knowledge by declaring emphatically that '(t)here are of knowledge two kinds, whereof one is knowledge of fact: the other knowledge of the consequence of one affirmation to another ... The later is called Science ... The register of knowledge of fact is called History.' Whereas science relates to 'reasoning' and 'contain(s) the demonstrations of consequences of one affirmation, to another', history represents 'nothing else but sense and memory', that is 'the knowledge required in a witnesse'. History consequently does not appear in Hobbes' table of sciences.[5]

A lot of time has passed since Hobbes wrote these lines. And yet, even to the present day it is almost impossible for a historian to speak of history as a science without provoking a smile, since whenever the topic under discussion is philosophy of science, history of science or quite simply science, historians are very likely to be the only ones to assume that their discipline belongs there too. Worse still, historians themselves have made heavy weather of this and have been at issue over whether to treat history as soft science, quasi-science, science *sui generis* (of its own kind), or even not as a science at all but as an art.[6]

While this line of questioning has its merits, it is not going to concern us here. I do not want to explore whether scientificity (acting along the lines of scientific rationality) is an attainable goal for historical practitioners. Nor do I intend to ask whether scientificity and its attendant categories of objectivity and truth really exist, and if they do, whether that is something desirable. This chapter is not concerned with problems of existence and legitimacy but with those of history. In fact, what it means 'to do things scientifically' has changed quite dramatically over the past three centuries. The traces of this change can still be seen in our current usage of the word scientific. We glide, for example, with ease from ontological assertions about the ultimate structure of historical reality (the objective truth of a scientific claim) to statements about the procedures that ensure the validity of our empirical findings (scientific methods) and to claims about the scientific ethos of a true scholar (self-distancing, detachment, impartiality, self-effacement, or simply: objectivity). Our notion of scientificity, a blend of essentially different meanings, points to differing and often conflicting histories, which in turn refer to different intellectual traditions, cultural practices and social contexts of origin in which the various images and ideals of scientificity acquired their respective meanings. What I want to do here is to trace some aspects of this history and relate them to the history of historical writing.[7]

It is safe to say that from the time of the Reformation in the 16th century the array of diverse genres and practices we refer to as historical writing was firmly established in Germany, if not as *scientia* then nonetheless as an important part of *eruditio* (erudition or learned education). *Historia* figured prominently as a distinct discourse, with corresponding groups of practitioners, norms and institutions. The first *lectio historica* had already been established in 1504 at the University of Mainz. Constituting a fourth form of knowledge besides *scientia*, *prudentia* and *ars*, *cognitio historica* was recognized as *experientia* or *cognitio empirica* – that is, empirical knowledge. As such, historical knowledge was seen as an indispensable component of most branches of learning, to the extent that these branches were not only based on axiomatic principles but also on empirical concepts developed by process of induction. Within this context, history achieved particular significance as *experientia aliena*, as alien experience. Expanding the horizons of personal experience by drawing exemplary lessons from the past, history was valued as a store of moral and political maxims for the guidance of present conduct. For all its importance, however, within the epistemological framework of Aristotelianism, which was prevalent in Germany and indeed across Europe until far into the 18th century, history as a science was in principle inconceivable. How can we explain this?[8]

Roughly speaking, the Aristotelian theory of knowledge is predicated on two principles. For one thing, only the universal and abstract can be known with certainty, while the particular and concrete allow merely for statements of probability. For another, certainty can be achieved only about constant and essentially immutable entities, whereas that which keeps changing without rules permits merely probable statements. The first category includes the universal and perennial qualities of all being and nature, covered most notably by those branches of knowledge that were grounded in mathematics and logic. The second category refers to 'man and his actions'. The metaphysical prerequisite of these principles is the assumption that ontological necessity (the quality of following inevitably from logical, physical or moral laws) and epistemological truth (the quality of being a verified or indisputable fact, proposition or theory) are inseparable. Within this framework, the notion of science implies absolute certainty. It means knowing the necessity of why something is so and not otherwise, i.e. the exploration of causes, aimed at the universal and perennial qualities of what exists.

What is important with respect to our question is the fact that historians were precluded from practising science, as it were, on two grounds. On the one hand, history was incompatible with science inasmuch as it explored the concrete realities of particular facts and circumstances. On the other hand, it was incompatible with standards of science inasmuch as it sought to capture the shifting ground of human affairs, an effort conspicuously flawed by the imponderables of human agency and free will.

My argument in this chapter is a triple one. To start with, I shall argue that *cognitio historica* became conceivable as historical science in Germany in the wake of a fundamental de-hierarchization of the edifice of scholarly knowledge, a process set in motion in the 16th century and accelerated during the seventeenth and eighteenth centuries by the two intellectual revolutions known as the Scientific Revolution and the Enlightenment. In other words, we have no reason to assume that at a certain historical juncture historiography successfully crossed the threshold of scientificity – an immutable, monolithic ideal – by developing certain methods that were, at long last, adequate to the study of history. Scientificity (French *scientificité*, German *Wissenschaftlichkeit*) is not a transhistorical given. Like any other concept it has itself a history.

Second, the levelling of scholarly knowledge forms was accompanied by an erosion of the plausibility and acceptance of interpretative frameworks associated with Aristotelianism. This occurred in the German setting during the second half of the 18th century, i.e. considerably later than in Britain and France. The philosophical agenda of Aristotelianism was eclipsed and in large measure superseded by other types of scientific rationality that a range of historians embraced and put to good use in the writing of history.

Third, the background of the dwindling plausibility of some modes of scientific rationality on the one hand, and the rise of new ones on the other, consisted of broad European changes in attitude towards knowledge in general, and the relations between knowledge and social order in particular. The environment for these changes was the crisis and fundamental transformation of European societies during the century between 1750 and 1850, which has often been portrayed as a 'dual revolution'. The Industrial Revolution, however, was not only accompanied by a revolution in political practices, as embodied in the French Revolution of 1789 and its democratic legacy. The 'dual revolution' was paralleled, and in some measure reinforced, by profound changes in *epistemic* practices, i.e. practices by which knowledge was secured, assessed and communicated.[9]

The outgoing 18th century witnessed a particularly tense debate about historical writing and its role in securing and subverting social order. The existing debates over method assumed greater significance as the capacity of historical knowledge to ensure certain desirable values and, in consequence, right conduct was thought to have a considerable impact on the outlook of society. Historical practitioners had to address some ticklish questions. What exactly was proper historical knowledge? Who was authorized to hold it and on what conditions? What degree of certainty was it appropriate to expect of it? Could differing groups of people be made to believe the same things and, if so, how could this be achieved? The recourse to notions of scientificity was to play a key role in answering these and other questions.[10]

I want to illustrate my argument with a brief survey of the shift from Aristotelian towards experiential conceptions of knowledge during the seventeenth and eighteenth centuries, in order to establish the exact implications of this for the province of history. Of the many aspects that a more comprehensive account would include, I have selected three main elements. I first examine the rise of useful knowledge and how that changed the map of knowledge. I then turn briefly to what the Dutch historian E.J. Dijksterhuis once called 'the mechanization of the world picture', to show what impulse historical thinking derived from this. From there I take a look at the rise of the experiment as a knowledge-making practice and consider how this affected the case for empirical historical studies. Finally, I conclude with some thoughts about how the above three elements had helped change the understanding of scientific knowledge by the end of the 18th century. In doing so, I shall clarify the notion of scientificity in historical writing, which I want to leave diffuse at this point, allowing its sense and implications to emerge as the inquiry proceeds.

1.2 The rise of useful knowledge

Perhaps the single most astonishing feature that a medieval intellectual like Umberto Eco's Franciscan William of Baskerville would have registered in early-modern Europe was the revaluation of knowledge produced to achieve practical ends. Broadly speaking, the aspiration to shape society according to rational principles placed intellectual practices increasingly in the service of practical objectives. 'Thinking', in Hannah Arendt's words, became 'the handmaiden of doing as it had been the ... handmaiden of contemplating divine truth in medieval philosophy.' With the rise of useful or practical knowledge (of trade, for example, or production processes), the contemplation of eternally given truth was to lose its epistemological prerogative. As a result, 'scientific and philosophic truth have parted company'.[11]

The belief that knowledge ought to be useful was not a free-floating idea, however; it was an integral part of the formation of early-modern states and the concomitant politics of knowledge. In fact, the practice of government in early-modern Europe was increasingly predicated on the systematic collection of information arranged for practical purposes such as public finances (*économie politique* or, in Russia, *kameralnaja nauka*), the mapping of the state territory (cartography) and the welfare and surveillance of the governed ('political arithmetic', statistics and, in Germany, *Polizeiwissenschaft*). Not without good reason did the sociologist Max Weber describe the rise of bureaucracy, one of the key factors in the development of early-modern states, as the 'exercise of control on the basis of knowledge'.[12]

The rise of useful knowledge found a variety of expressions. The burgeoning book markets, for instance, were swamped with publications like Thomas Bray's *An Essay toward promoting all Necessary and Useful Knowledge* (1697) and Johann August Schlettwein's *Von den nützlichen Würkungen einer Universität auf den Nahrungsstand des Volkes* (1776). The Electoral Academy of Useful Sciences in Erfurt (1754), the Mining Academy in Freiberg (1765) and similar societies in Philadelphia (1758) and Virginia (1772) are but a few examples of the numerous institutions set up to promote knowledge of crafts and trades. Designed as *Staatsdienerschulen* (schools for public servants), the newly founded universities in Halle (1694) and Göttingen (1736) promoted in large measure 'useful' subjects. 'Mechanical arts' like engineering and agriculture were playing an increasingly prominent part in best-selling encyclopaedias such as Ephraim Chambers' *Cyclopaedia: or, An Universal Dictionary of Arts and Sciences* (1728) and Heinrich Zedler's *Universal-Lexicon aller Wissenschafften und Künste* (1732–54) while, a little later, the French Academy of Sciences began producing its *description des arts et des métiers* (1761–88), thus underlining the importance it had come to ascribe to the useful or practical branches of knowledge.[13]

Even the scholastic curriculum of European universities did not escape unscathed. Although the system of the four faculties remained by and large intact – the liberal arts (including philosophy) were still followed by the three higher faculties of medicine, law and theology – its order and inherent hierarchy was increasingly challenged by a growing range of new disciplines like chemistry, political economy and, not least, history. The ascent of history as an academic discipline during the 18th century was inextricably linked with its usefulness for the training of the growing number of lawyers, 'politicians' (to use a convenient anachronism) and administrators. Good knowledge of international history, for example, was deemed imperative for the training of diplomats at such universities as Paris and Strasbourg. The institution of the Regius chairs in history at the universities of Oxford and Cambridge at the beginning of the 18th century had a similar background.[14]

By the mid-18th century, useful or practical knowledge had finally become respectable. The extent to which the traditional order of knowledge had been remapped can be seen in Diderot's 'Prospectus' (1750) and d'Alembert's 'Preliminary Discourse' (1751) to the *Encyclopédie*. D'Alembert, for example, gave particular prominence to mathematics whereas theology, once queen of the four faculties, was presented as but an offshoot of philosophy. That the intellectual flagship of the French *philosophes* should allocate such an important position to the trades in general and to state-of-the-art technologies indicated; moreover, the increasingly problematic ranking of scientific and hitherto non-scientific forms of knowledge. Equally important is the fact that the entries in the *Encyclopédie* were arranged in alphabetical order, which paralleled and underpinned the general trend away from traditional hierarchies of knowledge. Francis Bacon's earlier attack on the Aristotelian classification of knowledge – his *New Organon* of 1620 was meant to replace Aristotle's *Organon* once and for all – had eventually borne fruit.[15]

1.3 Making and knowing: the world as a machine

This leads me to the second element. The revaluation of useful knowledge was connected with the increasing use of mechanical metaphors for imagining the world. The 'mechanization of the world picture', to use the title of Dijksterhuis's classic, played an important part in the shift away from Aristotelian physics. Construing matter as essentially active and motion as having developmental character, Aristotelian physics ascribed design and purpose to material nature. What is important in our context is that the historically triumphant attempts to establish an alternative theoretical framework, collectively known as mechanical philosophy, modelled nature on the characteristics of a machine. 'Disenchanting the world' (Max Weber) by construing matter as inert and nature as a causally specifiable machine, mechanical philosophers as different as René Descartes, Robert Boyle and Isaac Newton were convinced that they had found an intelligible metaphor that allowed one to understand nature and its components without having to invoke such 'occult powers' as soul-like qualities (animism) and the capacities of purpose and intention (teleology). In fact, it was a widely held belief in the seventeenth and eighteenth centuries that humans could reliably know only what they had made themselves, either manually or intellectually.[16]

The mechanical metaphor and its attendant conviction that humans could know only what they constructed themselves did not remain restricted to the study of nature; it pervaded all branches of knowledge, as the following passage from Thomas Hobbes exemplifies:

> Geometry therefore is demonstrable, for the lines and figures from which we reason, are drawn and described by ourselves; and civil philosophy is demonstrable, because we make the commonwealth ourselves.[17]

The epistemological implications of this for the conceivability of a historical 'science of man' become apparent in Giambattista Vico's *Scienza Nuova* (1725/44). Expecting secure knowledge exclusively from things that owed their existence to man, the Italian professor of rhetoric turned his attention away from the study of nature to history. He reasoned that since it was God who created the natural world, only God could comprehend it. Man himself, however, could expect secure knowledge only from the study of the 'civil world', for the latter was the product of human creativity in the same sense that nature was the creation of God. Although Vico's notion of a new science did not attract much attention at the time, it indicates that, on purely epistemological grounds, the historiography of human affairs could be imagined as a science.[18]

The degree to which the mechanical metaphor had penetrated the tradition of Aristotelianism by the beginning of the 18th century can be seen from the case of the leading German Aristotelian Christian Wolff. In his theory of knowledge from 1712 he demands that history 'be written in such a way that where men's deeds are measured against their circumstances, one can learn the rules of divine governance therefrom'. The study of history should allow us to observe the great clockmaker in the act of clockmaking, as it were, so that we can understand the mechanics of His clockwork. 'I understand the nature of a clock,' Wolff specifies, 'when I grasp clearly what kind of wheels and other accessories it is composed of, and how each is related to the other.' Employing the clock as the favourite mechanical metaphor of his era, Wolff calls for a kind of historiography that is both didactic and useful in that it reveals history's hidden causal structure (pragmatic historiography).[19]

But the use of the clock analogy has yet another side. 'One understands the nature of a thing,' Wolff's passage on clocks emphasizes, 'only when one grasps clearly how it has become what it is, or by what manner and means it is possible.'[20] At this point, Wolff's notion of determining the nature of a thing through intellectual reconstruction of its constituent parts and structure turns into a genetic explanation of its coming into being. In fact, the latter is to complement the former, as is the case in Wolff's system of knowledge where each individual discipline is divided into an abstract-rational part and an empirical-historical one. Wolff was seconded by the Erlangen theologian Johann Martin Chladenius. In his *Allgemeine Geschichtswissenschaft* of 1752 – the German counterpart of Lord Bolingbroke's *Letters on the Study and Use of History* (1752) – Chladenius claimed:

> The main event of a moral being [such as a state] is the origin of the same; which is all the more remarkable, since it supplies the reason for the subsequent events, without which these will not be understood.[21]

The search for regular configurations, developmental patterns and laws ('rules of divine governance') was a well-established theme throughout the 18th century. The *Ordre Naturel* of the French physiocrats, the *Staatswissenschaften* (sciences of the state) in Germany, and the rise of conjectural history in Britain are prominent examples of this.

The clock analogy thus illustrates two things. On the one hand, it shows that the emergence of a new historical consciousness in early-modern Europe owed one of its greatest impulses to the use of the mechanical metaphor and its attendant belief that humans could know securely only what they produced themselves. On the other hand, the analogy reveals the limitations of the mechanical metaphor, which confines the notion of history to the process of coming into being. Once the clockwork is in place, it is a more or less stable end product. Mechanical analogies did not lose their metaphorical appeal until the last third of the 18th century when they were superseded by other, mainly organicistic, metaphors.

1.4 The rise of empirical knowledge

The third element that had a profound impact on attitudes to knowledge was the rise of the experiment as a legitimate knowledge-making practice, epitomized in Francis Bacon's dictum of 'putting nature to the question'. The plausibility of the experiment as a knowledge-making activity owed much to the view discussed above that humans could comprehend only what they had made themselves. From the same view the conviction followed that, for reliable knowledge of things that were not man-made, one had to imitate or reproduce the processes through which these things had come about. Indeed, it is the nature of the experiment that it itself produces the phenomena that are to be observed. 'Give me matter,' the German philosopher Immanuel Kant exclaimed in his theory of the origin of the universe (1755), 'and I will build a world from it, that is, give me matter and I will show you how a world developed from it.'[22] Kant's words highlight the mélange of making and knowing that was so characteristic of the time. They allow us to catch a glimpse of the awareness that still existed of the link between 'fact' and 'manufacture', two words that were to become (almost) antonyms by the end of the 18th century as 'fact' drifted towards 'datum', i.e. something that is given rather than made.

The critical point in our context here is the belief that lay at the heart of experimental philosophy (and early-modern empiricism more generally), namely that proper knowledge was and had to be derived from direct sense experience. This was an assault on yet another pillar of the Aristotelian tradition. Robert Boyle's experimentation with the air-pump, which was arguably the most prolific fact-making machine of the era, is emblematic of this attitude. Did Aristotelians fail to grasp the importance of sensory experience? Not at all. They gave, however, a different answer to two crucial questions. What part can experience play in the constitution of reliable knowledge? And, second, what kind of experience is thus to be sought? Suspicious as it was of the reliability of our sensory experience, the Aristotelian tradition privileged a type of experience that testified to general views of the workings of nature rather than providing the basis for those insights. Experience, while deemed important, was ultimately subordinated to securing an already established knowledge of a general and indubitable nature. In the Baconian tradition of experimental philosophy, by contrast, direct sense experience was to form the foundations of proper scientific knowledge. The purpose of experimentally constituted experience was thus not to illustrate some general point; instead of serving general philosophical reasoning, it was to control it. This type of experience, however, was not to be misconstrued as the mindless collection of data that Bacon likened to the activity of the ant. Rather, it was the result of the combined efforts of both collecting and digesting, as symbolized by the bee. The proposed method of inquiry was therefore inductive and empirically grounded – that is, one was to start out from observational and experimental facts ('particulars') and then rise step by step to causal knowledge and general conclusions.

Yet the experience sought in the experiment was not that of the spontaneous senses of the uninitiated ('old wives' tales'). Experimental philosophers from Christiaan Huygens to Robert Hooke held firmly to the belief that the workings of nature could be fully understood only if the constitution of experience was guided and disciplined by correct rules of method. The 'interrogation' of nature, as it were, was to be carried out 'as if by machinery' (Bacon). To put it another way, the rise of the experiment as an acceptable knowledge-making practice went hand in hand with aspirations to mechanize the production of knowledge itself, i.e. to discipline the procedures of knowledge-making through methodological directions designed to remove or, at least, control the effects of human passions and interests.[23]

Although experimental methods of scientific inquiry could only be applied to some branches of knowledge, their triumphant advance throughout the 18th century gave a strong impulse to empirical studies in many fields, including history. Just as the Protestant Reformation insisted on each Christian engaging directly with scripture (without having to rely on the readings of priests), and just as experimental philosophers from Bacon to Newton urged their contemporaries to study the 'divine book of nature' for themselves (without relying on time-honoured interpretations), so late 18th-century historians increasingly expected of each other that the authority of secondary works should be resorted to only when experiential access to things was impossible. Historical writing was increasingly to be based on what we have come to call the study of 'primary sources' – that is, on empirically grounded research.[24]

The success story of historical empiricism was partly written in the streets of Paris, though not necessarily by historians. Just as Gutenberg's invention of printing with movable type facilitated the Protestant demand to read the Bible for oneself; and just as the use of the telescope and microscope turned the rhetoric of individualistic empiricism ('Read the book of nature for yourself!') into a practicable idea, so 'the forcible opening of some of Europe's once secret chanceries and archives'[25] in the aftermath of the French Revolution lent impetus to the historians' call for the critical study of primary sources.

The status of the historical experience that could be derived from the study of primary sources was, however, more than precarious. The epistemology of Immanuel Kant, one of the most prominent philosophers in late 18th-century Europe, was, for instance, incompatible with the very idea of archival records being the 'primary sources' of what we could know about the past.[26] What is more, the study of documents with the aid of historical-critical methods is skilled reading. It requires special training that teaches us what sorts of things to 'read' in a document and what to disregard. Yet lasting institutions for the professional training of historians that would enforce correct reading were nowhere in sight before 1800.[27] In fact, only in the mid-19th century were the practitioners of historical writing in a position to establish what could be sifted and evaluated from the records ('historical facts') as sufficiently reliable foundations of our knowledge of the past. In this process, the historical works of Leopold Ranke came to act both as awe-inspiring accounts of the past and as gauges to discipline the historiographical practices of others.[28]

On the whole, however, Ranke's contribution to the rise of empirically grounded, critically researched and objectively written historiography should not be overrated. He was neither the originator of objectivity in historical writing, nor did he invent the historical-philological method of source evaluation.

> In order to write and present [history] in such a way that the historical truth is not distorted, the historian must be personally impartial, must portray the events without preconceived ideas of his own, must not have a preference for any form of government, or any state; likewise, he must not regard any of the existing forms of government as the best one . . . nor draw up an ideal one and compare the existing ones with it; rather, with self-effacement and strict neutrality he must only tell what happened and how it happened (bloß erzählen, was und wie es geschehn ist).[29]

Although the above is reminiscent of his famous credo, it was not Ranke who wrote this but the Prussian medievalist Karl Dietrich Hüllmann, whom posterity has taken less seriously. Ranke had just been born when, in the spring of 1796, Hüllmann published his essay on the history of the European states, which contained these rules of conduct. The ideal of impartial or impersonal knowledge, and how to achieve it, had been hotly debated throughout the 18th century. Codes of impartiality and disinterestedness prevailed in many areas, ranging from legal practices of testimony evaluation to natural philosophy.[30] The rhetoric of perspectival flexibility (impartiality that rises above all particular viewpoints) appears in tracts on moral philosophy as well as historical theory. Adam Smith, for example, demanded in his *Theory of Moral Sentiments* (1759) that 'the selfish and original passions of human nature' must be transcended and things be viewed 'with the eyes of a third person ... who judges with impartiality'.[31] Indeed, transcending individual points of view in deliberation and action appeared to many moral philosophers an important recipe for a harmonious and just society. Lorraine Daston has called this attitude to knowledge 'aperspectival objectivity', i.e. the attempt to 'escape from perspective' by eliminating individual and group idiosyncrasies in the name of public knowledge and universal communicability.[32]

What was symptomatic of the historiographical debates in the second half of the century was the heightened sense that viewpoint and partiality were in fact unavoidable attributes of the historian as such, which had to be dealt with effectively rather than bemoaned.[33] To try and eliminate the effects of perspectival distortions by calling on the historian's moral integrity was, however, increasingly considered inadequate. The emphasis was shifting from moral notions of personal impartiality (ethical imperatives) towards a type of aperspectivity and impartiality to be guaranteed by impersonal rules of method (methodological imperatives). In Chladenius' *Allgemeine Geschichtswissenschaft* it reads:

> Should not historical truth enjoy the same right ... of also being formulated in rules, since now almost all the motivating forces of human reason in the discovery of general truths ... lie explained before our eyes?[34]

Not only were formal methodological directions to ensure the metamorphosis of the historian into a disembodied epistemological subject that rose above all particular viewpoints; the empirical credibility of 18th-century historians as a whole depended increasingly on their methodological expertise. If historical writing was to be based on an inductive and empirically grounded procedure, this groundwork had to be secure. It was in this context that the historian's ability to sort out the genuine from the fabulous became paramount and considerations of textual criticism took centre stage. Finally, the triumph of inductive methods in historical writing was inextricably linked to the rise of the 'footnote'.[35] The practice of giving reference to one's sources was in many respects the equivalent of the minute report on an experiment, as it was meant to enable the reader to repeat and verify the process through which the knowledge in question was constituted. This was held to be an indispensable feature of scientific rationality. The extent to which footnoting had become entrenched practice in historical writing during the 18th century can be seen from the fact that, in 1758, David Hume felt obliged to apologize for the lack of proper references in his *History of England*.[36]

To sum up, the discussion of specific historiographical rules of method had been well under way before history writing became a profession in the 19th century. However, in practice, formal rules of method were often far less important in 'sifting and evaluating' historical records than a good knowledge of what counted as acceptable and proper, i.e. the social codes of truth-telling that did not need to be spelled out. What kind of historical experience was to ground historical writing? Whose experience should count as authentic historical experience that could provide the proper foundation of historical knowledge? What exactly constituted a credible primary source? Was it the oral testimony of popular tradition or the written testimony of the elites? Answering questions like these implied judgement about where to draw the line between the genuine and the fabulous, the historical and the philosophical, the literary and the scientific, the vulgar and the sublime. In the eighteenth, no less than in the 19th century, the methodicization of historical knowledge implied a map of the social order.

1.5 History as human science

The shift from Aristotelian towards experiential attitudes to knowledge had many other facets that had equally important implications for historiography and its conceivability as a science. The Newtonian conception of linear and uni-directional time, for example, according to which time was an absolute, real and universal entity that was experienced by everyone, everywhere, in the same way, had a dramatic impact on the convergence of historical and scientific modes of inquiry. It also facilitated the notion of time being a progressive and homogeneous continuum and, by extension, the emergence of the idea of the past being and having 'history'. The idea of history (in the singular) as a distinct and coherent form of reality that could be analysed in entirely this-worldly and rational terms only finally crystallized in the discourses of the 18th century.

Another strong impulse to historical writing came from what – in the wake of the French historian Michel Foucault – has been called the 'anthropological turn' in the second half of the 18th century and the attendant rise of the 'life sciences' (such as anthropology, biology and psychology).[37] One can hardly overestimate the importance of the new paradigm of 'vitalism' for the aspirations to conceptualize history as a human science. Peter Hanns Reill, for example, has shown the particularly vigorous impact of the appearance in 1749 of the first three volumes of the French natural historian Georges Louis Leclerc de Buffon's *Histoire naturelle* (1749–1804).

Buffon championed a notion of scientificity that distinguished between abstract truths (such as mathematical proofs) and real physical truths. While the former were the fruit of human invention, the latter were essentially empirical and historical in nature and required both detailed analysis and creative imagination ('divination').[38] Taking a similar line to Reill, Jörn Garber has argued that, around 1750, anthropology assumed the role of a lead discipline for various strands of historical studies. The most obvious manifestation of this was the thriving, if short-lived, genre of 'history of humanity', which construed history as the evolution of humanity in the double sense of the word: as the development of humankind in space and time, on the one hand, and the gradual realization of the potential quality of being humane, on the other. Johann Gottfried Herder's *Ideen zur Philosophie der Geschichte der Menschheit* (1782–91) is one of the most prominent examples of this. The link forged between historical writing and anthropological discourses, Garber suggests, not only facilitated the formation of a distinctive subject area (the history of 'man'), it also equipped historical practitioners with a set of strategies and methods, such as comparative analysis, analogical reasoning and intellectual intuition, that made it feasible for historical writing to acquire a scientific identity without recourse to an overall philosophical framework.[39] The fact that in this context the notions of active matter, self-generating motion and purposive development regained some of their former currency – with 'organ', 'organism' and 'organization' replacing 'machine', 'mechanism' and 'mechanization' as lead metaphors – shows that the shift from Aristotelian to experiential practices of knowledge-making was neither a clear-cut process nor one that was ever complete.

Despite this, the Aristotelian theory of knowledge had lost its intellectual predominance for good in the course of the 18th century. While empirical forms of discourse had superseded deductive theories as paradigms of scientific inquiry, the Aristotelian concept of *scientia* had slowly but surely been supplanted by a new concept of scientific rationality that emphasized probability rather than certainty. Conceding that absolute certainty was beyond human grasp in all but a few areas, many advocates of the new scientificity took their bearing on John Locke's *Essay Concerning Human Understanding* (1689), which distinguished between different 'degrees of ascent'.[40] In sharp contrast to the demonstrative certainty demanded by the Aristotelians – and, for that matter, the Cartesians (the followers of René Descartes) – the truth-claims of this empirical concept of scientificity rested on the purely pragmatic criterion of critically tested probability. Not unlike evidence in legal practices, historical evidence was treated as a matter of relative degrees of certainty ('beyond reasonable doubt'). In his article 'Histoire' (1764), Voltaire, one of the century's leading historical thinkers, declared with laconic brevity, 'All certainty which does not consist in mathematical demonstration is nothing more than the highest probability; there is no other historical certainty.'[41] But then again, as the French mathematician and physicist Pierre Simon Laplace argued in his *Essai philosophique sur les probabilités* (1814): 'How few things are demonstrated? Proofs convince only the mind; custom makes our strongest proofs. Who has demonstrated that a new day will dawn tomorrow or that we die? And what is more universally believed?'[42] The passage from Laplace is indicative of probabilistic attitudes to knowledge and the intellectual confidence that went along with them.[43]

The 'probabilistic turn' is in many respects the keystone of the developments discussed in this chapter. As the 18th century drew to a close, it had become possible, on epistemological grounds, to construe historiography as a science. It was around 1800 that – in the German setting – *historia* departed from the edifice of the fine arts under which it had been subsumed along with poetry, rhetoric, painting and music.[44] While a growing number of textbooks, such as Johann Joachim Eschenburg's introduction to the system of knowledge of 1792, came to count history among the sciences,[45] historians themselves now referred with increasing frequency to historiography as a 'truly rational science'[46] that 'justly deserved the name of science'.[47] One of the luminaries of historical scholarship in late 18th-century Germany, August Ludwig Schlözer wanted history even to 'be lectured scientifically' (*'scientifisch vorgetragen werden'*).[48] The idea of history being a science was, however, heterogeneous, fragile and by no means universally shared. After all, the underlying notion of scientificity was a mixed bag of differing concepts and beliefs, reflecting a fast-changing constellation in the turn-of-the-century politics of knowledge.

1.6 Some conclusions

1. The scientificity claimed, discussed and practised in historical writing around 1800 was new in two respects. First, the very linking of the historical and the scientific was novel in empirical historical writing. Second, the new scientificity differed fundamentally from the Aristotelian concept of scientia that had been prevalent in large parts of Europe until far into the 18th century.
2. It was not in opposition to the natural sciences that history developed into a human science. The dichotomy between the humanities on the one hand, and the natural sciences on the other, is essentially a progeny of the 19th century and its particular map of knowledge.
3. There is no reason to assume that at a particular historical juncture historiography successfully crossed the threshold of scientificity by developing certain methods that were, at long last, adequate to the study of history. As Irmline Veit-Brause has put it, 'the scientification of history' was not 'a linear process towards a fixed goal of "proper" scientific practice'.[49] Scientificity is a moving target and so is the very nature of what is considered reliable knowledge.

4 The notion of scientificity not only changed over time; it was also contested, with different people drawing their distinctions in different places. This, in turn, had different consequences for the practical outlook of historical writing. Just as the category of history (as object of inquiry) was understood in radically different ways by different historical practitioners, so too was the concept of scientificity.
5 The idea of scientificity did not float freely in conceptual space. As a code of conduct, way of knowing and set of methodological maxims, it was inextricably linked to social institutions, discourses and practices. (For more about this, see Peter Lambert's chapter in this volume.)
6 Finally, scientific rationality should not be confused with reason. There is no substitute for thinking, not even scientificity.

Guide to further reading

Hannah Arendt, *The Human Condition* (Chicago, 1958).

Peter Burke, *A Social History of Knowledge: from Gutenberg to Diderot* (Cambridge, 2000).

William Clark, Jan Golinski and Simon Schaffer (eds), *The Sciences in Enlightened Europe* (Chicago, 1999).

Lorraine Daston, *Classical Probability in the Enlightenment* (Princeton, NJ, 1988).

Christopher Fox, Roy Porter and Robert Wokler (eds), *Inventing Human Science: 18th-Century Domains* (Berkeley, 1995).

Anthony Grafton, *The Footnote: A Curious History* (London, 1997).

Bruce Haddock, *An Introduction to Historical Thought* (London, 1980).

Reinhart Koselleck, *Future's Past* (1979), trans. K. Tribe (Cambridge, 1985).

George H. Nadel, 'Philosophy of History before Historicism', *History and Theory 3* (1964), pp. 291–315.

Steven Shapin, *A Social History of Truth: Civility and Science in 17th-Century England* (Chicago, 1994).

Rolf Torstendahl and Irmline Veit-Brause (eds), *History-Making: The Intellectual and Social Formation of a Discipline* (Stockholm, 1996).

Björn Wittrock, Johan Heilbron and Lars Magnusson (eds), *The Rise of the Social Sciences and the Formation of Modernity* (Dordrecht, 1998).

Notes

I would like to express my gratitude to Ute Feldner, Graeme Garrard and David Jackson whose stimulating ideas and critical comments I appreciate more than ever.

1 *Times Literary Supplement*, 30 July 1999.

2 For an introduction, see Mary Fulbrook's *Historical Theory* (London, 2002).

3 For a good overview, see Irmline Veit-Brause, 'Eine Disziplin rekonstruiert ihre Geschichte: Geschichte der Geschichtswissenschaft in den 90er Jahren', *Neue Politische Literatur* 46 (2001), pp. 67–78 and 43 (1998), pp. 36–65.

4 Hobbes, *Leviathan* (London, 1651); Wolff, *Vernünfftige Gedancken von den Kräfften des menschlichen Verstandes* (Halle, 1712); Jean le Rond d'Alembert, *Preliminary Discourse to the Encyclopedia of Diderot* (1751), ed. Richard N. Schwab (Chicago, 1995), which also includes Diderot's *Prospectus* (1750); Droysen, *Historik* (1857), ed. Peter Leyh (Stuttgart-Bad Cannstatt, 1977); Droysen, 'Die Erhebung der Geschichte zum Range einer Wissenschaft', *Historische Zeitschrift* 9 (1863), pp. 1–22.

5 Hobbes, *Leviathan*, ch. ix.

6 See John Harvey chapter in this volume (Chapter 5).

7 I draw here heavily on Lorraine Daston's 'Objectivity and the Escape from Perspective', *Social Studies of Science* 22 (1992), pp. 597–618, esp. pp. 597–9.

8 Here and in the following, Arno Seifert, *Cognitio historica: Die Geschichte als Namengeberin frühneuzeitlicher Empirie* (Berlin, 1976) and Horst Dreitzel, 'Die Entwicklung der Historie zur Wissenschaft', *Zeitschrift für historische Forschung* 8 (1981), pp. 257–84.

9 See Björn Wittrock, Johan Heilbron, Lars Magnusson (eds), *The Rise of the Social Sciences and the Formation of Modernity* (Dordrecht, 1998).

10 For these debates and their contexts, see Christoper Fox, Roy Porter and Robert Wokler (eds), *Inventing Human Science* (Berkeley, 1995) and Daniel Fulda, *Wissenschaft aus Kunst: Die Entstehung der modernen deutschen Geschichtsschreibung 1760–1860* (Berlin, 1996).

11 Hannah Arendt, *The Human Condition* (Chicago, 1958), pp. 290, 292.

12 Max Weber, *Economy and Society* (1920), ed. G. Roth and C. Wittich, 3 vols (New York, 1968), 1, p. 339.

13 Peter Burke, *A Social History of Knowledge* (Cambridge, 2000), pp. 81–148, esp. pp. 110ff.; Thomas Ellwein, *Die deutsche Universität* (Wiesbaden, 1997), pp. 38–224, esp. pp. 42ff. and 47ff.; Robin Briggs, 'The Académie Royale des Sciences and the Pursuit of Utility', *Past and Present* 131 (1991), pp. 38–88, p. 40.

14 Burke, *History*, pp. 91f. and pp. 99ff.; Notker Hammerstein, *Jus und Historie* (Göttingen, 1972) esp. pp. 216ff.; Jürgen Voss, *Universität, Geschichtswissenschaft und Diplomatie im Zeitalter der Aufklärung* (Munich, 1979).

15 Burke, *History*, pp. 110, 115, and M. Malherbe, 'Bacon, Diderot et l'ordre encyclopédique', *Revue de Synthèse* 115 (1994), pp. 13–38.

16 The classical account on this is E.J. Dijksterhuis's *The Mechanisation of the World Picture* (1950; Princeton, 1986); more recently, Peter Dear, *Revolutionizing the Sciences* (London, 2001), esp. pp. 80–101.

17 Hobbes, 'Six lessons to the Savillian Professors of the Mathematics', in *The English Works of Thomas Hobbes*, ed. William Molesworth, 11 vols (London, 1839–45), 7, p. 184.

18 Vico, *Scienza Nuova* (final edn, Naples, 1744), esp. Section 331.

19 Wolff, *Gedancken*, ch. I, section 48 and ch. X, section 6.

20 Wolff, *Gedancken*, ch. I, section 48.

21 Chladenius, *Allgemeine Geschichtswissenschaft* (Leipzig, 1752), p. 64.

22 Kant, *Universal Natural History and Theory of the Heavens* (1755), trans. W. Hastie, ed. W. Ley (New York, 1968), p. 17.

23 See esp. Steven Shapin, *The Scientific Revolution* (Chicago, 1996), pp. 65–117; Steven Shapin and Simon Schaffer, *Leviathan and the Air-Pump: Hobbes, Boyle and the Experimental Life* (Princeton, 1985); Lorraine Daston (ed.), *Biographies of Scientific Objects* (Chicago, 2000), p. 4; Burke, *History*, pp. 16f., 204ff.; Bacon, *New Organon* (1620), Aphorisms II, XVI, XIX, XXII, XCV.

24 Here and in the following, esp. Shapin, *Scientific Revolution*, pp. 72–80.

25 Anthony Grafton, *The Footnote* (London, 1997), p. 60.

26 See Kant's 'Prolegomena to Any Future Metaphysics that will be able to come forward as a Science' (1783), in *Immanuel Kant: Philosophy of Material Nature*, trans. J.W. Ellington (Indianapolis, 1985) and 'Conjectures on the Beginning of Human History' (1786), in *Kant: Political Writings*, ed. Hans Reiss (Cambridge, 1991), pp. 221–34.

27 For the institutionalization and professionalization of history in the nineteenth and twentieth centuries, see Peter Lambert's chapter in this volume (Chapter 3).

28 On Ranke and the Rankean tradition, see John Warren's chapter in this volume (Chapter 2).

29 Karl Dietrich Hüllmann, *Entwurf einer bessern Behandlung der Europäischen Staatengeschichte in akademischen Vorlesungen* (Warsaw, 1796), pp. 26f. On Hüllmann, see Heiko Feldner, *Karl Dietrich Hüllmann, 1765–1846* (Frankfurt on Main, forthcoming).

30 Peter Dear, 'From Truth to Disinterestedness in the17th Century', *Social Studies of Sciences* 22 (1992), pp. 619–31.

31 Adam Smith, *The Theory of Moral Sentiments* (1759), eds D.D. Raphael and A.L. Macfie (Oxford, 1976), p. 135.

32 Daston, 'Objectivity'.
33 Chladenius' concept of *Sehepunckt* (theory of viewpoint) is an early example of this; see Chladenius, *Geschichtswissenschaft.*
34 Chladenius, *Geschichtswissenschaft*, p. xiv.
35 Grafton, *Footnote*.
36 Burke, *History*, pp. 208f.
37 Foucault, *The Order of Things* (1966), (London, 1970).
38 See esp. Reill's 'Science and the Science of History in the Spätaufklärung', in Hans Erich Bödecker *et al.* (eds), *Aufklärung und Geschichte* (Göttingen, 1986), pp. 430–52 and 'History and the Life Sciences in the Early 19th Century', in Georg G. Iggers and James M. Powell (eds), *Leopold Ranke and the Shaping of the Historical Discipline* (Syracuse, 1990), pp. 21–35. On Buffon and his reception, see Frank W.P. Dougherty, *Collected Essays on Themes from the Classical Period of Natural Philosophy* (Göttingen, 1996), pp. 59–70, 70–89.
39 Jörn Garber, 'Selbstreferenz und Objektivität: Organisationsmodelle von Menschheits- und Weltgeschichte in der deutschen Spätaufklärung', in Hans Erich Bödecker *et al.* (eds), *Wissenschaft als kulturelle Praxis* (Göttingen, 1999), pp. 137–87.
40 Locke, *An Essay Concerning Human Understanding* (London, 1689), Chapter xvi.
41 Voltaire, 'Histoire', in *Dictionnaire philosophique* (1764), in *Oeuvres completes de Voltaire*, 70 vols (Paris, 1785–9) 52, p. 266.
42 Quoted in Lorraine Daston, *Classical Probability in the Enlightenment* (Princeton, NJ, 1988), p. 221.
43 See esp. Daston, *Probability*; Barbara Shapiro, *Probability and Certainty in 17th-Century England* (Princeton, NJ, 1983); Shapiro, *Beyond Reasonable Doubt* (Berkeley, 1991); Ian Hacking, *The Emergence of Probability* (Cambridge, 1975).
44 See Werner Strube, 'Die Geschichte des Begriffs "Schöne Wissenschaften" ', *Archiv für Begriffsgeschichte* 33 (1990), pp. 136–216.
45 Eschenburg, *Lehrbuch der Wissenschaftskunde* (Berlin, 1792), pp. 3–11, 39–88.
46 Jacob Dominikus, *Über Weltgeschichte und ihr Prinzip* (Erfurt, 1790), p. 29.
47 Augustin Schelle, *Abriß der Universalhistorie*, 2 vols (Salzburg, 1780–1), 1, p. 10.
48 August Ludwig Schlözer, *Vorstellung seiner Universalhistorie* (1772–3), ed. H.W. Blanke, 2 vols (Hagen, 1990) 2, p. 235.
49 Irmline Veit-Brause, 'The Disciplining of History', in Rolf Torstendahl and Irmline Veit-Brause (eds), *History-Making* (Stockholm, 1996), p. 19.

2

The Rankean tradition in British historiography, 1840 to 1950

John Warren

2.1 The Lipstadt/Irving libel case

On 11 January 2000, at the High Court in London, a libel case came to trial. The defendants were the American academic Professor Deborah Lipstadt and Penguin Books, the publishers of her 1993 book *Denying the Holocaust: The Growing Assault on Truth and Memory*. The plaintiff was the British writer David Irving. The author of many books on the period of the Second World War, Irving claimed that Lipstadt had defamed him through alleging that he was a 'holocaust-denier' and a deliberate falsifier of historical truth. Not so, said Irving: he did not, in his view, deny the Holocaust and, although he was as liable as anyone to make mistakes, he was a genuine scholar whose work on the documentary evidence in particular was painstaking and had led to the discovery of vital, untapped sources on the Hitler era.

On the face of it, then, the trial was about a writer's reputation as a historian and the alleged damage done to his publishing career. In practice, it became a sounding-board for any number of academic and pseudo-academic positions on a startling range of issues: freedom of speech, the absolute right to challenge received opinions, the relationship between scholarly and political activity, the historicity of the Holocaust, the writing of history and the nature of history – all served up in a media-friendly adversarial format under the baleful gaze of Mr Justice Charles Gray, who had clearly hoped that any analogies between historical and legal evidence would serve to restrict, rather than fuel, the arguments. Such hopes were indeed illusory. Commentators are clear on the broader implications of the case. The journalist D. D. Guttenplan offered his account of the case under the title *The Holocaust on Trial*, and, in *Telling Lies About Hitler: The Holocaust, History and the David Irving Trial*, Richard Evans – an expert witness for the defence – chose 'History on Trial' as the title for his first chapter.

One reason why the judge's hope was illusory is that the writing of history cannot be divorced from assumptions about the nature and purpose of historiography any more than historians can be divorced from the context in which they write. Both Lipstadt and Irving voice a common view of the obligations, duties and methodology of the historian that is ultimately the product of what can be called the Rankean tradition, and Mr Justice Gray in effect decided against Irving on the basis that he had neither honoured those obligations and duties nor upheld the methodology of the historian as judged by the Rankean model of scholarship.

The purpose of this chapter is to discuss in context the nature of that tradition associated with Leopold von Ranke (1795–1886) and, in particular, to analyse its impact on the world of English-speaking historiography. Richard Evans, in attacking the calibre of Irving as a historian, defended the centrality of the Rankean legacy to the practice of history. It was fitting that he should do so, since his 1997 book *In Defence of History* amounts to a pungent critique of the various philosophical, linguistic and occasionally hermeneutic attacks on the fundamental tenets of Rankeanism. And what, then, are those fundamental tenets? Here is Irving on the subject: 'Real history is what we find in the archives, and it frightens my opponents because it takes the planks out from beneath their feet.'[1]

This emphasis on rigorous study of historical documents, with its implication that such study should be fair-minded and as objective as possible, was precisely the rod with which the defendants sought to beat Irving. Evans was commissioned by the defence to assess Irving's claims to objective scholarship, and found them wanting. According to Evans, Irving certainly employed the appropriate scholarly apparatus of referencing and evaluation of sources uncovered by research, but did so to deceive.

> The footnotes and sometimes the text cited innumerable archival sources, documents, interviews and other material that seemed at first glance to conform to the normal canons of historical scholarship ... It was only when I subjected all of this to detailed scrutiny, when I followed Irving's claims and statements about Hitler back to the original documents on which they purported to rest, that Irving's work in this respect was revealed as a house of cards, a vast apparatus of deception and deceit.[2]

In short, Irving is not a historian wrestling with the demands and inherent difficulties of objectivity and allowing his hypotheses to be amended where necessary by the historical sources: he is a writer with a far-right agenda who is prepared to prostitute what he himself accepts as the credo of the historian in the service of that agenda. Mr Justice Gray concluded in judgement:

> It appears to me that the correct and inevitable inference must be that for the most part the falsification of the historical record was deliberate and that Irving was motivated by a desire to present events in a manner consistent with his own ideological beliefs even if that involved distortion and manipulation of historical evidence.[3]

It is fortunate, perhaps, that the Rankean model lends itself to courtroom practice and fortunate also that, as we have seen, all the participants in the Lipstadt case were agreed on the definition of what constitutes the discipline called history. Such agreement is, of course, by no means universal. The tenets of Rankeanism – the (albeit partial) reality of objectivity, the possibility of meaningful interpretation of documentary evidence in an equally meaningful attempt to understand the past on its own terms, a rejection of the distortion of that evidence with personal and present needs in mind – have been subjected to challenges both noisome and bruising. The further sections of this chapter will discuss Ranke's own historical writings, as well as the use to which his legacy has been put, with reference to such challenges. This does not imply, of course, that Ranke was fully understood by those who felt his influence. Nor does it imply that those who felt his influence did so irrespective of their personal, academic, professional or political milieu. In fact, it will become clear that the tradition of historical scholarship associated with Ranke provided, and continues to provide, a defence against contemporary political and/or philosophical trends that opponents see as fraudulent or dangerous, and deserving of the fate of the Midianites and Amalekites under the sword of Gideon.

2.2 The historical writings of Leopold von Ranke

Ranke's output, over a long life, was simply enormous. He wrote the multi-volume histories of peoples who had, in his rather Eurocentric terms, an impact on the history of the world: hence his *Histories of the Latin and Germanic Peoples* (1824); *The Ottomans and the Spanish Monarchy* (1827); *German History in the Age of the Reformation* (1839–47). His *History of the Popes* (1834) complemented his history of nations as the power of the supranational institution of the Roman Catholic Church inevitably made it a great player throughout Europe and beyond. Towards the end of his life, Ranke expressed his discontent with the narrowness of his subject matter (which he felt did not allow him fully to explore connections and sequences of events). And so, in 1880, he wrote his *Universal History*.

Lord Acton can be used as a convenient starting point for a discussion of Ranke's work and its reception by British historians in the 19th century. His admiration for Ranke was not restricted to his energy or his industry: nor was it unmixed with criticism. Even so, Acton made Ranke the foremost representative

> of the age which instituted the modern study of History. He taught it to be critical, to be colourless . . . he has done more for us than any other man . . . He decided effectually to repress the poet, the patriot, the religious or political partisan, to sustain no cause, to banish himself from his books . . .[4]

Acton judged that Ranke's historical works have been superseded, but through the activities of his own disciples in the newly opened archives of Europe: in short, Ranke was the originator of the 'heroic study of records'[5] on which historical scholarship must be based. Acton's account of Ranke's fundamental position is a seductive one, and certainly has an echo in some of Ranke's comments. In his first published work, *Histories of the Latin and Teutonic Peoples*, Ranke wrote:

> To history has been given the function of judging the past, of instructing men for the profit of future years. The present attempt does not aspire to such a lofty undertaking. It merely wants to show how, essentially, things happened (*wie es eigentlich gewesen*).[6]

He added: 'Strict presentation of facts, no matter how conditional and unattractive they might be, is undoubtedly the supreme law.'[7] Writing about his *English History, Principally in the 17th Century* (1859–68), he said that he had tried to 'extinguish my own self, as it were, to let the past speak'.[8]

This is not the place to discuss in any detail the issue of whether Ranke was indeed a Rankean in Acton's terms. But there is the danger of converting Ranke's thought into a simplistic programme with a set of slogans – 'Tell it as it happened!' 'Let the past speak for itself!' 'Each age is unique: history must not be judged by the standards of the present!' – or of turning him into a crude empiricist or even a positivist, bowing before the twin altars of the facticity of the past and the glory of inductive reasoning. Ranke the out-and-out empiricist sits very uncomfortably with Ranke the Lutheran, or with Ranke the Romantic idealist, who thought that the historian had a sanctified role in uncovering, albeit in a limited way, the 'divine idea' or hand of God behind the unfolding of human history, which Ranke felt was revealed (*pace* Herder) least opaquely in the flowering of national cultures (hence his interest in writing the histories of peoples). Similarly, Ranke's *dictum* 'wie es eigentlich gewesen' needs careful handling: 'eigentlich' has less the sense of 'actually' and more the sense of 'in essence' or 'characteristically'[9] and so need not be taken as a straightforward endorsement of history as a trawling through documents for facts but as a comment pregnant with idealism. One might suggest, with Krieger, that Ranke came to draw a distinction between the method of acquiring historical knowledge and the search for the universal, God-given truths which would emerge from the scholar's methodology. There is a tension between his writing about the history of peoples (seen in a thoroughly Romantic way as an aggregation of individuals) and the moving on from this particular to the general. Unsurprisingly, Ranke's description of the process is bathed in a tone of religious longing:

> A lofty ideal does exist: to grasp the event itself in its human comprehensiveness, its unity, and its fullness . . . I know how far I am from having achieved it . . . Only let no one become impatient about this failure . . . our subject is mankind as it is, explicable or inexplicable, the life of the individual, of the generations, of the peoples, and at times the hand of God over them.[10]

2.3 The writing of history in 19th-century Britain

What matters for our present purposes, of course, is not so much what Ranke's main tenets actually – or in essence – were, but how they were interpreted and responded to by those involved in the writing of history in Britain in the time of Ranke. I have deliberately eschewed the phrase 'British historical establishment', as there was little that could be dignified with such a title. There were indeed Regius professors of History at the universities of Oxford and Cambridge, but their posts were sinecures without teaching, let alone research, commitments. It was 1853 before a School of Jurisprudence and Modern History was set up in Oxford – history being the junior partner in the law-training firm – and 1872 until it had its own School. The process was even more leisurely in Cambridge: the Historical Tripos was set up in 1875. History had previously been examined only as one of five subjects within the Moral Sciences (from 1851). The poverty of formal historical scholarship did not reflect a lack of interest in British history, at least, among the reading public. It was largely met by a motley collection of gentleman-scholars and autodidacts, whose more messianic fringes were gifted with a whole panoply of bolt-on eccentricities. The celebration of national progress, of what he called 'physical, of moral, and of intellectual improvement',[11] was served up hot by Thomas Babington Macaulay (1800–59) with his cast of historical goodies and baddies, his caricatures, his dramatic contrasts and his tendency to assume that his 17th-century heroes on the side of progress had the thought processes of liberal Victorian gentlemen.

For those rocked by assaults on Protestant biblicism from the direction of Tractarianism or German biblical criticism, there was always the splenetic apocalypse that was Thomas Carlyle: son of a Dumfries stonemason and moral prophet of the Dickens generation. James Anthony Froude, for example, trying to salvage something from the wreck of his Christian faith, found an anchor of a sort in Carlyle's *The French Revolution* (1833–42), where the Terror and its aftermath were the visible revenge of God against human wickedness. Carlyle himself commented – as well he might – that it was a work written by a '*wild man*, a man disunited from the fellowship of the world he lives in'.[12] This was no narrative history. It was the French Revolution thrust into the spitting, bile-filled cauldron of Carlyle's mind, stuffed full of German idealist philosophy, despair and dyspepsia and erupting into astonishingly vivid and downright alarming prose (written in the present tense) where Carlyle allowed his imagination to lacerate the reader with his outlandish vocabulary. Towards the end of the book, he yelled:

> IMPOSTURE is in flames, Imposture is burnt up: one red sea of Fire, wild-billowing, enwraps the World; with its fire-tongue licks at the very Stars. Thrones are hurled into it, … and – ha! what see I? – all the *Gigs* of Creation: all, all! Wo is me! … A King, a Queen (ah me!) were hurled in; did rustle once; flew aloft, crackling like paper-scroll.[13]

So much for the death throes of the French Revolution. Carlyle, in idealist vein, was attempting to mediate the Ideal through symbol: in this case, the 'Gigs of Creation' refer to the respectable bourgeoisie (who could afford to own a one-horse carriage) and the reference to paper builds upon Book II – 'The Paper Age' – in which paper is taken as representative of the flimsiness of French society. The croaking frenzy in which the book appears to have been written is explained (more or less) by Carlyle's desperate need to communicate his message: that the poor of 18th-century neo-feudal France had their parallel in the poor of 19th-century industrialized Britain, and that the ruling classes had to learn from the fate of their French counterparts before it was too late.

What Carlyle was doing, of course, was to use his interpretation of history to bewail the evils of his present. Carlyle saw the writing of history as the highest form of poetic expression, by which he meant the fullest exercise of the human imagination. In so doing, he was not cautiously and reverentially hoping that the footsteps of God might be glimpsed through a careful study of the past on its own terms: he was proclaiming where the trampling wrath of God had descended in the past and would descend in the future. In short, as a historian, his business was to interpret the workings of providence in a way that would force itself onto his readers. Clearly, the dispassionate evaluation of original documents and the careful suppression of the authorial voice were utterly foreign to the role of historian-seer. When, in 1845, he published his collection of Oliver Cromwell's letters and speeches, it was riddled with errors of fact, transcription and attribution. It is not likely that he was unduly concerned. The title of the first chapter of his introduction is 'Anti-Dryasdust', and he savaged those who, publishing and using records, failed to give them the shape to make them relevant to the present.

At its best (and particularly in *The French Revolution*), Carlyle's approach has the virtue of engaging the reader's imagination in the most vigorous way. Even so, he was too peremptory and dictatorial to engage in any sense in a *dialogue* with the reader's imagination, let alone with the intellect. By the later 1840s, as Carlyle's increasingly rabid denunciations of his society drew him into sympathy for real and would-be despots and his humanity became obscured under an increasingly illiberal and authoritarian world-view, he lost touch with those who were his erstwhile disciples. Many of those former followers saw the world slowly improving: history written to teach the present day must at least offer a recognizable vision of the present as well as the past, and history written as prophecy had to show some signs of coming true.

No picture of the history written by 'men of letters' would be complete without a discussion of the work of Henry Thomas Buckle (1821–62). A gentleman-scholar relying on his own enormous library, Buckle wished to establish laws of history akin to those applied to 'mechanics, hydrostatics, acoustics and the like'.[14] In so doing, he reflected the contemporary interest in the philosophical positivism of Auguste Comte, whose *Cours de philosophie positive* was translated by Harriet Martineau in 1853 and influenced, to varying degrees, such seminal figures as George Eliot, John Stuart Mill and Frederic Harrison. Comte's approach was relentlessly empirical and inductive, claiming to derive historical laws from accumulated fact. He further claimed to have identified a three-stage development in history (corresponding to a development of mind) that also identified the shape of the future. Comte identified his present with the scientific-industrial, positivist epoch, which would in time culminate in a harmonious and prosperous world where women acted as the priestesses of humanity. Comte's theories were likely to appeal to those with an optimistic attitude towards the impact of scientific discoveries, who had lost a conventional religious faith and who nevertheless felt the need for an alternative moral basis to society. Comte did not provide a historiographical link with his philosophy, but Buckle did. The first volume of his *History of Civilization in England* appeared in 1857, and he died just after completing the second of what was clearly burgeoning into a multi-volume project. His scheme was markedly deterministic and scornful of any form of religion, which he regarded as a hindrance to the development of civilization. His book was the literary sensation of 1857, but its influence on British historiography was limited to the closer followers of Comte: those Comtists who wrote history, such as Frederic Harrison, or Edward Beesly (subsequently Professor of History at University College London), are marginal figures in historiographical terms. Unsurprisingly, the reception in more mainstream historical circles was antagonistic and the pages of the periodicals – those great educators of the aspirant intelligentsia – were replete with complaints about Buckle's materialism, determinism and arrogance. The liberal Catholics Simpson and Acton, in their journal *The Rambler*, objected on a soteriological level to the inductive process of establishing so-called historical laws, which, in denying free will, sabotaged the righteous judgement of God over the soul.[15] The Regius professors at Oxford and Cambridge, Goldwin Smith and Charles Kingsley, similarly objected to the attempt to ground a science of history on natural, rather than moral, laws. These are not what might be called fundamentally methodological objections rooted in a view of the nature of the discipline called history. Given the background of the objectors, this is no real surprise. Kingsley, of course, was best known as a polemical popular novelist, Christian socialist and clergyman, while Goldwin Smith was, to put it charitably, a man with wide-ranging intellectual and political interests (including a quarrel in print with Disraeli with distastefully anti-Semitic overtones).[16]

2.4 Acton, Stubbs and Rankeanism

In 1866, Goldwin Smith resigned, and was succeeded in the Regius chair by William Stubbs (1829–1901). It is under Stubbs that Rankean principles were first employed at the universities in a systematic manner, with the aim to professionalize the teaching and study of history. It is important to recognize and to summarize why those principles should be so appropriate and efficacious in this context. First of all, Ranke offered a methodology based on the critical use of archival material that established history as an autonomous discipline, and one which that could be communicated (as Ranke did at the University of Berlin) to generations of future historians. The historicist insistence on the uniqueness of each age countered the objectionable distortion of the discipline into a mere mechanism for collecting facts from which positivists might horribly and anachronistically derive 'natural laws' of human behaviour. Indeed, the demand for objectivity and the refusal to countenance the exploitation of history for present-day purposes would give it stability and integrity. The Rankean paradigm offered, in short, a defence against Carlylean prophets, positivists, social Darwinists and other, equally objectionable, belles-lettrists who could claim the right to pronounce on history because there was no standard by which to judge their pronouncements. There was a price to pay, of course, that the theologically inclined had to live with if they were to be entirely consistent: history could neither be exploited as a theological weapon, nor as a moral weapon with or without the theology. The most famous victim of tension between the acceptance of the need for scholarly and objective erudition and the call of moral duty was Lord Acton.

John Emerich Edward Dalberg Acton (1834–1902), a Roman Catholic born in Naples, was fluent in English, French, Italian and German. His mentor was the pre-eminent German theologian Johann von Döllinger. Hugh Tulloch[17] ably discusses the conversion of Acton the doctrinaire Catholic to Acton the Liberal Catholic, but we should note in particular one of the most important agents of that transformation: Acton's sojourn with Döllinger in the Vatican archives. Significantly, it was Ranke who had come to Döllinger's University of Munich in 1854 to teach his techniques of source evaluation: as Altholz puts it, 'Döllinger had to train himself in the new methods and to revise his historical outlook in the light of his new studies'.[18] It was through his archival researches with Döllinger that it became clear to Acton that Church historians had compromised with the truth in the service of orthodoxy. Acton came to consider it axiomatic that the truth could never disadvantage the Church and, therefore, that historical truth should serve it. His opposition to the ultramontanes – the enthusiasts for papal monarchy and declaration of infallibility – was therefore buttressed by his conviction that history offered no justification for such claims. This made it all the more important – indeed, a sacred duty – for one's research to be the last word in thoroughness. Rigorous analysis of documents had to be extended to the writings of historians themselves, and there is a sense in which Acton was outranking Ranke (if I may) by relying less heavily on official documents and attempting to expose, without prejudice, the inner lives of his historical characters: as he put it, 'stripping off the borrowed shell, and exposing scientifically and indifferently the soul of a Vestal, a Crusader, an Anabaptist, an Inquisitor'.[19] However, once the historical truth had been ascertained by the humble, devoted, detached historian – then he had the right, the need and the obligation to apply what Acton would have thought of as God's moral judgement on the actors on the stage of history. At this point, Acton appears, not only to have jumped the Rankean ship, but to have torpedoed it. In a bitter controversy with Mandell Creighton over the latter's unwillingness to make moral judgements on the renaissance popes, Acton commented: 'it is the office of historical science to maintain morality as the sole impartial criterion of men and things, and the only one on which honest minds can be made to agree'.[20]

To put it another way, Acton was afraid that the Rankean method was a form of relativism: the unwillingness to judge and the constant demand for context, for understanding, would lead to an debilitating acceptance of base – often political – motives. The problem with this approach is clear, and explains why Acton can justly be accused of lapsing into the anachronistic ways of the so-called Whig historians: assuming that human nature was constant through time, that moral absolutes were similarly unchanging and, in essence, simple, and that, as Providence acted through history, then history was essentially progressive as human beings gradually attained a more complete understanding of individual liberty and conscience.

Notoriously, Acton found it immensely difficult to put his precepts into practice. To make moral judgements without presumption would mean a depth of knowledge of frightening profundity. The result was that Acton never published a single historical work. His projected 'History of Liberty' was never written, submerged as it was under a Byzantine system of index cards and weight of reading. His influence on historical writing, and on the development of the profession of history, is correspondingly limited. He is likely to have done little to discourage the increasing influence of the scholar in the Rankean mould over history at the universities. His inaugural lecture as Regius Professor of Modern History at Cambridge in 1895 was generally supportive of Ranke, as we have seen, and he played a significant part in the founding of the *English Historical Review* in 1886 (which took some time to echo its scholarly German counterparts and eschew the veneer of the literary review). What Acton illustrates best is the strength and limitations of the appeal of Rankean methodology. For those convinced of the value of history, it offered a way of distancing the discipline from dilettantism and mere partisanship. But that was not always enough. Should history not have some deeper purpose, for the elucidation of which the Rankean approach was a preparation? Acton felt this, and so, significantly, did his predecessor in the Regius chair, Robert Seeley. Seeley thought of himself as a disciple of Ranke, but also claimed that 'history, while it should be scientific in method, should pursue a practical object'.[21] In this case, the object was political training, arrived at through appreciating (in a manner not dissimilar to Comtean positivism) the generalizations that were possible once historical data had been accumulated.

It was at Oxford, however, that the purest draughts of Rankeanism were to be drunk. William Stubbs (1829–1901), Regius Professor of Modern History from 1866 to 1884, not only aimed to set to build up a School of History at the university on the Rankean model, but demonstrated through his own publications how it was to be done. In 1860, he published the seminal Stubbs' *Charters (Select Charters and Other Documents Illustrative of English History).* His three-volume *Constitutional History of Medieval England in its Origin and Development* (1873–8) was based on an extensive evaluation of the records, and his inaugural lecture made clear his credo and his programme. As for Ranke himself, Stubbs said:

> Leopold von Ranke is not only beyond all comparison the greatest historical scholar alive, but one of the very greatest historians that ever lived. Unrivalled stores of knowledge, depth of research, intimate acquaintance with the most recondite sources ...[22]

With Ranke, Stubbs shared a distaste for the positivist-style inducing of general laws from history: with Ranke, he shared a sense of the progress of history through divine providence; and, with Ranke, he saw what Burrow has called 'the concept of an animating Individuality, or rather of Individualities, as the protagonists of history: unique historical configurations in each of which is embodied an underlying unique Idea'.[23] In other words, both saw the individuality of nations and a national spirit as God's tool for shaping history. And so, constitutional history attracted him, in part because it was intellectually strenuous (given the complexity of the data), in part because it exploited the growing accessibility of state papers, in part because it encouraged a sense of the uniqueness of the English state, in part because it reflected contemporary experience of a growing governmental machine[24] and in part because it was eminently suited to establishing the prestige of the School of Modern History.[25]

2.5 The very partial triumph of Dryasdust (I): Herbert Butterfield (1900–79)

Herbert Butterfield, a scholar at Peterhouse, Cambridge, in 1919, was elected to a chair of modern history at Cambridge in 1944 and became Regius Professor in 1968. It is, frankly, outrageous to label Butterfield as an exponent of Dryasdustism, but his important contributions to the study of historiography essentially crystallized attitudes towards certain types of history and upheld the British version of the Rankean tradition. What is equally important is that Butterfield's stance was an ambivalent one, and at least suggests the extent to which most practitioners upholding the 'professional' or 'craftsman' model of the historian found that model ultimately rather unsatisfying but nevertheless far preferable to alternatives which would, in their view, have consequences that were unacceptable on several levels.

In *The Whig Interpretation of History* (1931), Butterfield famously castigated historians for 'present-mindedness'. The desire to *use* history for the needs of the present day was, in Butterfield's terms, not simply a methodological aberration, but also dangerous, hubristic and fundamentally blasphemous. Whig historians were those whose teleology was horribly secular and correspondingly presumptuous. History, they claimed, had a detectable sense of direction, sometimes striding, sometimes meandering, but ever progressing towards the consummation devoutly to be wished: liberal parliamentary democracy on the British model. The result was that they wrote bad history: often nationalistic, always anachronistic and distressingly optimistic. Butterfield's objections to Whig history in general were both methodological and theological, and are in this way strongly reminiscent of Ranke. The past deserved to be understood for its own sake, and so the historian was to appreciate its complexity, to eschew the generalization in favour of an appreciation of the role played by the individual and to seek to recover the particular and the concrete without regard to the present (other than to make the past comprehensible to one's own time). Butterfield complained that the present-minded invariably wrote 'abridged' history because they sought to select from the past 'proof' of whatever political or moral goal the past was allegedly advancing towards: similarity and pattern were preferred over the dissimilar and the unique. The wide-ranging popular narrative, terminally complacent and egregiously smug, discarded the inconveniences of rigorous scholarship in favour of the simplistic and spuriously analogous.

It could be argued that fulminating against 'present-mindedness' is something of a luxury ill-suited to times of deep anxiety and turmoil where people might look to history for reassurance and a sense of purpose. Butterfield clearly felt that, in the middle of the Second World War, he could afford to reflect on a positive contribution made by Whig historiography. In *The Englishman and his History* (1944), he accepted that the Whig interpretation, however defective it might be, had entered history itself as a positive force for patriotism and unity.

Butterfield was deeply suspicious of attempts to find answers to transcendent questions within academic history. History was in no way a guide: it could not be reduced to deterministic laws or exalted to the role of prophecy. His perspective, like Ranke, was that of the convinced Christian. Where Ranke feared the influence of the Enlightenment and its denial of the sovereignty of God, Butterfield feared the influence of secularist liberal optimism and atheistic Communism, both of which also denied the sovereignty of God. With Ranke, he would not presume to identify God's purposes in history, but he could not accept that God was in any way apart from it. To claim that God was somehow absent was to sabotage personal religion. In the appropriately titled *God in History* (1958), Butterfield commented: 'And if God cannot play a part in life, that is to say, in history, then neither can human beings have very much concern about him or very real relationships with him.'[26]

World war, cold war, Holocaust and Hiroshima: the crises and horrors through which Butterfield had lived confirmed in his mind the essential sinfulness of humankind. Small wonder that he should object to the optimism of his predecessors. In *Christianity and History* (1949), his words appear to echo, of all people, Acton:

> having in his religion the key to his conception of the whole human drama, he (the historian) can safely embark on a detailed study of mundane events, if only to learn through their inter-connections the ways of Providence.[27]

The difference between Acton and Butterfield is that Acton saw progress towards liberty as part of the ways of Providence; Butterfield saw this as unwarranted presumption, and dangerously close to using history to elicit the meaning to life itself. Such hubris was the besetting sin of the academic. Those who studied history had the absolute obligation to recover it as it really was, because only then could one glimpse those connections between events which reflected God-in-history.

Butterfield's influence over subsequent historiography was profound, but owed little to his overt Christianity *per se*. He confirmed the realist, empiricist and historicist tradition by discarding determinism and emphasizing the role of the individual. His wariness of wide-ranging narrative encouraged the narrow monograph of 'technical' history, which in turn was a mark of the 'professionalism' necessary to 'real history'. In short, Butterfield was misinterpreted. As R. H. C. Davies comments:

> Butterfield himself had never intended that his work should cause historians to stop trying to explain history. But because he had demonstrated that the Whig historians had read their own ideas into historical events, lesser historians have felt timid of expressing any ideas at all.[28]

The clear similarities between Ranke and Butterfield are reflected in the nature of their appeal to their successors. For those who hated the determinism of Marxist historiography, Rankeanism and Butterfieldery was the antidote. For those suspicious of multi-disciplinary approaches to history, they were the guards of the temple within whose Holy of Holies lay the purity of a discipline unsullied by the presumptuous neophytes of social psychology, anthropology, economics and sociology.

2.6 The very partial triumph of Dryasdust (II): Namier and Namierization

The impact of Louis Bernstein Namier (1888–1960) on the historical profession in Britain in the 1950s and 1960s was unrivalled, and not just in his chosen field of 18th-century English political life. To the *Oxford English Dictionary* he gave the word 'Namierization'; and, through the exact and detailed scholarship to which the term refers, he gave to his colleagues and students an example to follow or to eschew, but not to ignore. Namier's capacity for minute documentary research, which clearly complemented and reflected Rankean professionalism, was focused on an approach to parliamentary politics which emphasized individual motivation and local circumstance above ideological/party affiliation. In so doing, Namier rejected teleological approaches of any kind, and offered, not only a striking confirmation of the status of the historian and of the discipline of history, but also a safe passage between the Scylla of Marxism and the Charybdis of multi-disciplinary approaches.

Like Butterfield, Namier distrusted doctrines of progress because he distrusted human reason and its potential; but, if Butterfield's distrust was theological and stemmed from his Methodist beliefs, Namier's distrust was psychological and stemmed from his sense of being an outsider. Born Ludwik Bernsztajn vel Niemirowski in eastern Poland, his parents were of the landowning class – an unusually patrician status for Jews, albeit non-practising ones. Namier was disinherited by his father and emerged from Balliol College, Oxford, in 1915 with his conservative mind-set intact and a first-class degree in Modern History. His outstanding abilities were self-evident and should have led him to an Oxbridge chair, but he was also combative, arrogant and self-obsessed – not a man, in short, to wear his learning lightly in the manner appropriate to the English gentleman whose social éclat he admired and could not emulate. His research interests reflected his admiration and his conservatism. In 1929, he published *The Structure of Politics at the Accession of George III* and, in 1930, *England in the Age of the American Revolution.* In so doing, he undermined the orthodox Whiggish interpretation whereby the King's alleged attempts to restore absolutist rule were thwarted by the opposition of American rebels and the Whigs under Rockingham who sympathized with the colonists' principled stand against tyranny. Namier denied that the King had any such intention; that the Rockingham Whigs represented a party with any ideals beyond those of self-serving factionalism and, for good measure, that to write of MPs' adherence to party at all was to misunderstand their fundamentally personal motivations. Namier's so-called 'structural analysis' therefore rested upon an 'underview' rather than an overview and prosopography rather than narrative exegesis. His detailed reconstruction of the lives and motives of individual MPs demanded a tireless quest for, and evaluation of, family papers. Analysis of MPs' letters led Namier to argue that they saw politics not in terms of ideals, party loyalties or principles, but as an extension of local and personal affairs. His rehabilitation of George III rested on the King's papers held at Windsor Castle. Analysis of his correspondence purportedly revealed that George III was an insecure and rather conventional man with no intention of reviving autocracy.

Namier had succeeded in restoring personalities to politics, but he had also removed political ideas from personality – the likely result, indeed, of using private correspondence and largely ignoring parliamentary debates. His corrective to the traditional Whig approach was timely, but too narrowly focused. To support the contention that party allegiance and party ideology were relatively unimportant to 18th-century politics required a broader time-scale than that provided by Namier. Nor did he provide the necessary evaluation of the functioning of the House of Lords. In short, Namier was entranced by the House of Commons or, rather, by its members. On a professional level, collective biography appealed to Namier as a technique that guarded against overarching narratives resting on the activities of a 'great man', or analyses resting on ideologies (such as Marxism) that eschewed individual motivation in favour of impersonal determinism. On a personal level, Namier found it easy to empathize with self-obsessed landowners. And collective biography gave him the opportunity to exploit the one form of determinism of which he whole-heartedly approved (because it was personal) – Freudian analysis. No stranger himself to the analyst's couch, Namier invited his historical characters to lie back and explain themselves. Predictably, as Namier crossed the no-man's-land between genuine insight and a historian's self-obsession, he sometimes thrust home his attack and sometimes stood on a mine. Reflecting on his own troubled relationship with his father, he was able to take seriously and to discuss the political impact of the fraught relationships between Hanoverian kings and their male heirs, and to explain something of the erratic career of Charles Townshend by reference to his problematic relationship with both parents. On the other hand, was it really best to explain in such terms, say, Townshend's actions as Chancellor of the Exchequer responsible for the bitterly resented American Import Duties Act of 1767? As Linda Colley has pointed out, we are 'left with the impression that perhaps the American Revolution broke out because Britain in the 1760s was governed by an oligarchy of neurotics'.[29]

Namier was far too astute not to make a virtue out of psychological necessity. He commented:

> Really intense research and analysis requires some correlation between the student's emotional life and experience and his subject ... As for accuracy, it is a conception that I would associate with statements rather than with views.[30]

It certainly required more than assiduity to devote, as Namier did, the last decade of his life to a project that provides at once a testimony and an epitaph to his obsessions, abilities and, perhaps, his limitations. In 1951, the History of Parliament Trust gave the go-ahead to Namier to write the appropriate institutional history. What the members of trust got was nothing of the sort. In the three volumes of *The House of Commons 1754–1790*, published four years after Namier's death in 1960, Namier avoided the 'great men' but wrote any number of biographies of MPs – the more obscure, the better – with, it seems, the aim of providing the raw material, not indeed for a political history charting the actual workings of both Houses, but for a social history charting the changing class and economic structure of the Commons. In place of a valediction, there was an introduction and a work that, in its inevitable incompleteness, reflected the frustrations of a quintessential outsider.[31]

2.7 Conclusion

Namier's fate, like that of many of the historians discussed in this chapter, was to be labelled a champion of a type of history that he did not actually write and with which he had an ambiguous relationship. As a product of his time and his own troubled psyche, he wrote a history that was suspicious of ideology, effectively conservative, cynical about human nature and, it appeared, appropriately empirical and objective in the Rankean manner. That this was neither his nor the Rankean manner was not the issue. Peter Novick charts the similar impact of a misunderstood Ranke on the American historical profession.[32] In Britain, Namier's impact, like that of Butterfield, was to confirm a particular version of the Rankean tradition as the right and professional way to write history.

In the later twentieth and early 21st century, the Rankean tradition has been used as a weapon against encroachments on the discipline of history both methodological and epistemological. G. R. Elton disposed of the rival claims of cliometricians (to his own satisfaction) in *Which Road to the Past?* and, in *Return to Essentials*, he tackled (also to his own satisfaction) postmodernists who ventured to argue that there was no road to the past anyway.[33] Richard Evans, whose *Telling Lies About Hitler* was discussed at the start of this chapter, offered in his *In Defence of History* 'the basic Rankean spadework' as the tools of a trade which – postmodernist critiques notwithstanding – continues to deliver an interpretation of the past which reflects, albeit imperfectly, how it really happened.

> History is an empirical discipline, and it is concerned with the content of knowledge rather than its nature. Through the sources we use, and the methods with which we handle them, we can, if we are very careful and thorough, approach a reconstruction of past reality that may be partial and provisional, and certainly will not be objective, but is nevertheless true.[34]

This is not to say that opponents of the bastardized Rankean tradition in British historiography do not have several valid points to make. Of course it frequently rests on an unfortunate reluctance to consider history as an epistemology. Of course there are writers of history, like Carlyle, who have the capacity to engage the reader (for good or ill) in an imaginative pummelling which may spasmodically strike home by conveying the truth through the resources of fiction. And, of course, few avowed or unavowed followers of Ranke were content with history as methodology. Nevertheless, the tradition remains as yardstick or target: it cannot be ignored.

Guide to further reading

The most convenient collection of Ranke's writings is G. G. Iggers and K. von Moltke (eds), The Theory and Practice of History: Leopold von Ranke (Indianapolis, 1973). The authors' introduction offers an excellent brief analysis of Ranke's background, work and historiographical impact. These issues are further developed in G. G. Iggers and J. M. Powell (eds), Leopold von Ranke and the Shaping of the Historical Discipline (Syracuse, 1990). There are valuable chapters on transfers between the German and British historiographical traditions in

Benedikt Stuchtey and Peter Wende (eds), British and German Historiography 1750–1950 (Oxford, 2000).

The professionalization of history is tackled effectively by Philippa Levine, *The Amateur and the Professional: Antiquarians, Historians and Archaeologists in Victorian England, 1838–1886* (Cambridge, 1986), Peter Slee, *Learning and a Liberal Education: The Study of Modern History in the Universities of Oxford, Cambridge and Manchester 1800–1914* (Manchester, 1986) and by Doris Goldstein, 'History at Oxford and Cambridge: Professionalization and the Influence of Ranke', in Iggers and Powell. John Kenyon's *The History Men: The Historical Profession in England since the Renaissance* (London, 1993) offers a characteristically bracing critique. Rather more sympathetic in tone are the valuable books in the Weidenfeld & Nicolson series *Historians on Historians*: Hugh Tulloch's *Acton* (1988), Owen Dudley Edwards' *Macaulay* (1988) and Linda Colley's *Namier* (1989) are particularly good at contextualizing their subjects.

The continued relevance of the Rankean tradition as such is beyond the scope of this chapter, but Richard Evans' *In Defence of History* (London, 1997) makes the case. By way of contrast, Alun Munslow's *The Routledge Companion to Historical Studies* proclaims the death of Rankean empiricism at the hands of postmodernism. Some of Munslow's readers may feel that pallbearers make odd companions.

Notes

1 R. J. Evans, *Telling Lies About Hitler* (London, 2002), p. 27.
2 Evans, *Telling Lies*, p. 110.
3 Mr Justice Charles Gray, quoted in D. D. Guttenplan, *The Holocaust on Trial* (London, 2001), p. 283.
4 J. E. E. D. Acton, *Lectures on Modern History* (London, 1960), pp. 32–3.
5 Acton, *Lectures*, p. 22.
6 Ranke, 'Preface' to the 1st ed. of *Histories of the Latin and Teutonic Peoples* in G. G. Iggers and K. von Moltke (eds), *The Theory and Practice of History* (Indianapolis, 1973), p. 137.
7 Ranke, 'Preface', p. 137.
8 Ranke, quoted in Leonard Krieger, *Ranke: The Meaning of History* (Chicago, 1977), p. 5.
9 Iggers and Moltke, *Theory and Practice*, pp. xix–xx.
10 Ranke, 'Preface', p. 138.
11 T. B. Macaulay, *The History of England from the Accession of James II* (Harmondsworth, 1979), p. 52.
12 J. A. Froude, *Thomas Carlyle: A History of his Life in London* (London, 1884), 1, p. 96.
13 Thomas Carlyle, *The French Revolution* (London, 1889), 3, pp. 273–4.

14 Buckle, quoted in John Kenyon, *The History Men* (London, 1993), p. 113.
15 Richard Simpson, 'Mr Buckle's Thesis and Method', *Rambler* 2nd ser., X (1858), pp. 27–42 and J. E. E. D. Acton, 'Mr Buckle's Philosophy of History', ibid., pp. 88–104.
16 Colin Holmes, *Anti-Semitism in Britain 1876–1939* (London, 1979), pp. 11–12.
17 Hugh Tulloch, *Acton* (London, 1988).
18 Josef L. Altholz, *The Liberal Catholic Movement in England* (London, 1962), p. 55.
19 Tulloch, *Acton*, p. 99.
20 Kenyon, *History Men*, p. 139.
21 J. R. Seeley, quoted in Doris Goldstein, 'History at Oxford and Cambridge: Professionalization and the Influence of Ranke', in G. G. Iggers and J. M. Powell (eds), *Leopold von Ranke and the Shaping of the Historical Discipline* (Syracuse, 1990), p. 146.
22 Stubbs, *Seventeen Lectures and Addresses on the Study of Mediaeval and Modern History* (Oxford, 1900), p. 65.
23 John Burrow, 'Historicism and Social Evolution', in B. Stuchtey and P. Wende (eds), *British and German Historiography 1750–1950* (Oxford, 2000), p. 252.
24 The link between constitutional history and the contemporary experience of burgeoning bureaucracy is explored in P. B. M. Blaas, *Continuity and Anachronism* (The Hague, 1978).
25 P. R. H. Slee, *Learning and a Liberal Education: The Study of Modern History in the Universities of Oxford, Cambridge and Manchester 1800–1914* (Manchester, 1986).
26 Butterfield, 'God in History', in C. T. McIntyre (ed.), *God, History and Historians: An Anthology of Modern Christian Views of History* (New York, 1977), p. 193.
27 Butterfield, *Christianity and History* (London, 1957), p. 87.
28 R. H. C. Davies, 'The Content of History', *History* LXVI (1981), p. 364.
29 Linda Colley, *Namier* (London, 1989), p. 33.
30 Namier, in John Brooke, 'Namier and Namierism', *History and Theory* 3 (1964), p. 343.
31 For a discussion of Namier as outsider, see John Warren, *The Past and its Presenters* (London, 1998), pp. 121–3. In his *Anti-Semitism in British Society 1876-1939* (London, 1979), Colin Holmes reflects on the discrimination faced by Namier and other Jews in terms of scholastic appointments. See in particular pp. 110–11.
32 Peter Novick, *That Noble Dream: The 'Objectivity Question' and the American Historical Profession* (Cambridge, 1988), pp. 21–31.
33 R. W. Fogel and G. R. Elton, *Which Road to the Past? Two Views of History* (New Haven and London, 1983), and Elton, *Return to Essentials: Some Reflections on the Present State of Historical Study* (Cambridge, 1991).
34 Richard J. Evans, *In Defence of History* (London, 1997), p. 249.

3

The professionalization and institutionalization of history

Peter Lambert

The quest for professional status was an endeavour to secure an authoritative status for 'the' historian's work. Unlike practitioners of other professions, historians never achieved a monopoly over their field: the matter of imparting knowledge of the past. But wherever the professionalization project succeeded, it entailed a shift in the balance of the power to interpret the past. Authority was inextricably linked to historians' claims to objectivity. Objectivity, in turn, was secured by the rigorous application of skills in the critical use of evidence. Palaeographic, philological and contextual, the skills and methodologies historians employed were their common property: they were taught, tested and communicated by and to one another.[1] Institutionalization furnished the settings in which this could happen, and provided career structures and mechanisms of what might be called 'quality' control.

Constituting themselves as an imagined community, historians themselves set the standards of their profession, and sought to ensure that conformity to them was an entry requirement. However, even where they achieved autonomy, national historical professions scarcely ever came close to becoming the independent, entirely self-regulating bodies that sociological models of professionalization predict.

This chapter explores the creation of standards of professionalism in the pursuit of history. What conditions were necessary for the discipline to flourish, and what motivated its advocates, are the questions addressed in the first section. In a sequence of 'snapshots', the chapter then discusses key moments in the foundation of history as an academic discipline in 'first-' and 'second-world' countries in the course of a 'long' 19th century. Finally, the chapter broaches the expansion of the discipline into the 'third world' in the second half of the 20th century.

3.1 Conditions and motives

Institutionalization was predicated on demand; the professionalization of research and writing largely presupposed the existence of career structures. Both were contingent on the broadly overlapping existences of adequate literacy rates and of a sufficiently developed middle class in a given society. They were dependent also on the presence of a university system and, crucially, on its public or private paymasters' readiness to see history established within the universities. More than any other, it was the presence or absence of a will to invest in history at a given time that constituted the variable determining the divergent chronologies of the professionalization of history.

Although historians continue to argue about the extent of its influence on later developers, nobody has disputed the fact that Germany was precocious. By the middle of the 19th century, many of the 'classical' features of a fully professionalized discipline were in place. First France, then an (at first sight bewildering) array of countries followed suit – the USA, Japan and Belgium foremost among them. Even in western Europe, however, the progress of the discipline was uneven. Professional Dutch historians remained few in number and woefully under-resourced until after the Second World War. In Johan Huizinga, Holland boasted an historian with a towering international reputation. But Huizinga felt isolated in his own nation, alienated by a national intellectual culture that showed disdain for academic history. In 1907, he sardonically proposed that Holland sell its entire national archival holdings to the highest bidder since – beyond Dutch borders – there might be someone with the time and inclination to work on them. It was a suggestion Holland's paltry dozen professors of history in post three decades later might reasonably have repeated.[2] Britain's experience of the professionalization of history began relatively early. From the 1860s onward, historians battled to inaugurate degree schemes and sometimes to introduce training in research. But the reformers encountered obstacles, and in any case lacked a cohesive vision. Their successes were patchy and sometimes also transitory. Seminars made only fleeting appearances, remaining entirely individual initiatives that ended when their initiators moved on. Frederick York Powell, Regius Professor of History at Oxford, exemplified an attitude wholly antipathetic to any professional ethos. Late in arriving for his own inaugural lecture, he then contrived to get the show itself over within 20 minutes.[3]

Powell's was not an instance of anachronism in late Victorian Britain, nor was it confined to that period. In 1922, Charles Kingsley Webster thought it 'greatly to be regretted' that attempts to establish graduate schools of history at Oxford and Cambridge had been 'so very inadequate', and argued for radical rectification: both universities' effective destruction as undergraduate teaching institutions, and their forced transformation into postgraduate training and research centres.[4] On the eve of the Second World War, Eric Hobsbawm found that Cambridge did next to nothing to supply would-be professional historians with appropriate training: the history faculty presented an overwhelmingly 'discouraging spectacle: self-satisfied, insular, culturally provincial, deeply prejudiced … even against too much professionalism. … [I]n my day, what Marc Bloch called the "trade of the historian" was not taught in Britain'.[5] York Powell, then, was certainly not the last of a dying breed of British historians whose behaviour and approach to teaching and research was distinctly *un*professional.

Patterns of professionalization of history, Eckhardt Fuchs suggests, formed one part of a triad, whose other two aspects were industrialization and modernization.[6] In view of the fact that the professionalization of history was far more advanced in late 19th-century Belgium than in Holland, for instance, Fuchs' remark appears to require some modification. Where a literate, educated public existed at all, prospects for the development of the historical profession stood in inverse proportion to the 'modernity' (and sometimes also the degree of industrialization) experienced by a given country. The educated Dutch public and Dutch governments, confident in the power of their nation-state and in their identity, were prone to look down their noses at the Belgians in general and their historical profession in particular. That Belgium should have required an historical profession in the first place was seen by the Dutch as an index of Belgian backwardness. In such cases, the yardstick by which 'backwardness' was measured was neither economic nor even cultural. Rather, it was the level of attainment in nation-building and state-formation.

That Germany should have housed the first laboratories for experiments in the creation of modern historiography is intimately connected with Germany's want of modernity in other respects. A new ethos of *Wissenschaftlichkeit*[7] served partly as substitute for missing ingredients of modernity, partly as corrective for defects, both exposed in the Napoleonic Wars. Humboldt's reform of the Prussian universities provided at least a measure of academic liberty within the universities, whose subsequent expansion afforded market-driven openings for academic entrepreneurs.[8] These were favourable conditions for the emergence of new disciplines. Competition for students provided the motor. Young, ambitious and innovative professors, distinguished from mid-century by their propensity to move rapidly from one university to another, fuelled it. Some made a generous endowment of their discipline a condition of acceptance of posts offered them, and held the whip-hand in relation to their putative employers.[9] History enjoyed one key advantage over rival disciplines. States that had survived Napoleon's redrawing of the map of Europe – and often grown as a direct consequence – were obliged to seek out new strategies of legitimation after Napoleon's fall. They began to encourage the development of history in universities in pursuit of that quest. But relations between historians and the states that were their ultimate paymasters were frequently strained. Historians' intellectual ambitions were always inherently likely to take them beyond the narrow geographical confines of polities whose provenance was so recent. Petty principalities could be associated with the local imposition of censorship. Thus, in common with other educated bourgeois, historians forged connections with one another across state boundaries, especially through journals and through their correspondence. Long before its culmination in annual German historians' congresses (from 1892 onward), and before the creation of the German Empire in 1871, a 'guild' (*Zunft*) of historians had taken shape, and done so along national lines. At its heart lay the steadily increasing number of holders of established chairs in history – some 28 of them in 1850, rising to 185 over the next six decades.

Research on primary sources lodged in archives, their critical interpretation (*Quellenkritik*) and finally their threading into published narratives were hallmarks of the new species of engagement with history. Leopold von Ranke[10] was – as is now generally recognized – not the originator of this three-step method, but he was certainly its most effective publicist. Remembered as *the* advocate-practitioner of archival research, Ranke in fact much more heavily dependent than he insinuated on secondary sources. He was – certainly at first – reluctant and scandalously inefficient about accurately acknowledging them, and a messy taker of notes throughout his career.[11] But then – for the simple reason that he belonged to a founder-generation of professionalising historians, Ranke had had no training as a historian himself. As in the matter of method, in relation to training, Ranke long, and on the whole undeservedly, enjoyed a reputation for fundamental innovation. Equally, the pervasiveness and durability of Ranke's myth testifies to his abilities as a propagandist of the vital importance of training for apprentice historians.

What Ranke *did* have a training in was philology, and the skills he attained had been developed through philological seminars, which were themselves an 18th-century German invention. In the 1820s, historians simply applied the techniques of philological seminars to history: discursive and critical interaction between teachers and students and among the students themselves. 'Historical exercises' in which select handfuls of students would gather informally in their professors' houses were already being held in the 1820s. As private gatherings, they belong more immediately to the history of the development of civil society in Germany than to that of the institutionalization of history. But in 1833, Ranke held a series of these 'exercises' at the University of Berlin. Thereafter, they were increasingly frequently to be found across the German universities. Gradually, universities began to advertise their existence to students, then even to make attendance at them obligatory. In 1865, when Heinrich Sybel attached a single bookcase and its contents to the 'exercises' he held at Bonn, he not only began another trend – toward the creation of seminar libraries – but implied another. Seminars began to

A sympathetic observer of German nationalism, he was never to tire of holding up German universities as a 'model' and of proclaiming that 'as a rule, good books are in German',[22] and chose a German subject for his first major publication project in his new discipline. Thus, he travelled to Germany in 1873. There, shocked to discover that ministers and not faculties had the final say in determining appointments to Chairs in Germany, he found German historians to be tainted by their governmental associations:

> The Prussian throne appears as surrounded by a kind of priesthood, whose creed is the deity of Caesar. He is their Constantine. And these men are regarded all over the world as oracles, as men whose knowledge is profound and whose collective judgment is almost final, as men especially whose opinions are not, as in other countries, hampered by subscriptions or influenced by any kind of bribe, but are inviolably free![23]

This revelation was confined to Seeley's diary, which was not designed for publication. At no point did he betray to the British public a hint of his concerns. Perhaps British historians had done their work of erecting Germany's as the standard for academic achievement too well. To deny German scholarship now was to risk ruining British plans to professionalize history.

Although 'Germanizers' succeeded in establishing history as a degree subject at Oxford and Cambridge, the founding generation of historians there did not evince the kind of interest in training that had been a hallmark of German, French and US professionalizers. In any case, collegiate structures and traditions of tutorial teaching militated against the introduction of the seminar at these 'old' universities. Seminars took hold in Britain only around the turn of the century, and then only in a handful of universities new enough to be unencumbered by the weight of tradition, but also sufficiently well endowed to be able to hire more than one or two historians. At Manchester, in the course of its liberation from the requirements of the London University degree, Thomas Frederick Tout made seminars a cornerstone of history teaching. Germany was still his chief point of reference when, in a lecture first delivered to a Cambridge audience in 1906, he sought to promulgate the seminar beyond Manchester, but he could now allude also to French and American exemplars.[24] Within London, it was again to be an institution of recent provenance, namely the London School of Economics, that was to prove the most innovative both in training students and in its understanding of the historian's craft itself. Here, in the course of the 1920s and 1930s, economic and social history made its most significant early breakthrough in Britain. But nothing better illustrates the paradoxical nature of history's development than the fact of the LSE's deserved reputation for experimentation in history. Maxine Berg has persuasively argued that it was precisely its pervasive *amateurishness* in the early 1920s that facilitated change. There were no disciplinary boundaries; all the academic staff concerned themselves with history; scarcely anyone taught the subjects they had themselves studied.[25]

3.3 A global discipline? Expansion and crisis after 1945

By the middle of the 20th century, the modern discipline of history had established itself securely in most of Europe, in North America, and in such odd outposts as Japan. The remaining holes in continental Europe were rapidly plugged after 1945: in Holland, for instance, where the discipline now 'caught up' with that of other western European countries, but also in a number of eastern bloc countries, where still recognizably German structures were imported together with their Stalinist deformations. But if history could, at any time after the middle of the 20th century, claim to have become *global* in either its vision or in the distribution of its practitioners, that claim rested – and still rests – on its institution in the 'third world'.

Here, there were intellectual barriers of European provenance to be overcome. Hugh Trevor Roper, addressing a television audience in 1963, found the 'unrewarding gyrations of barbarous tribes in picturesque but irrelevant corners of the globe'[26] unworthy of the historian's attention. Africa, for example, could thus have no precolonial history worthy of the name. Trevor Roper stood four-square in a tradition carried by scholars ranging from Hegel to James Mill. An array of 'Orientalists' working throughout the first half of the 20th century certainly did not share the British historian's contempt for the exploration of tribal customs and everyday life. But they added the blinkers of their disciplines to the rest of Trevor Roper's bundle of prejudices. Thus, anthropologists may have contributed to 'first-world' knowledge of African societies, but their practice added also to a de facto denial of those societies' historicity. Thus, unless university history departments teaching colonial history in postcolonial countries may be imagined, establishing new routes toward an African history was a necessary concomitant of planting the roots of the discipline in Africa.

By the time of Trevor Roper's disparaging remarks, there was a growing community of historians prepared to answer him. History *in* and *of* Africa emerged, like both the colonization and decolonization of the continent, through the interaction of Europeans and Africans. Three impulses may be distinguished here. First, even while propagandists of Empire at home were complacently denying that tribal peoples had histories, missionaries and colonial authorities in India as in Africa were discovering that, if only in the interests of governmental efficiency, the history of the governed was indispensable. In the course of the

19th century, administrators of Empire had grown used to hiring literate Indians and Africans to write down the oral traditions of their societies. Second, the phase of 'developmental colonialism' ushered in by Great Britain in the wake of the Second World War sought to recast colonialism as a service to the colonized. The latter were to be brought up to standards commensurate with their eventual independence, and the provision of an on-the-spot university education was conceived as integral to the strategy. This pattern was replicated across many of those parts of the British Empire with principally non-white populations.[27] At London University's School of Oriental and African Studies, Roland Oliver was appointed in 1948 as the world's first university lecturer in 'the history of the tribal peoples of East Africa'; around the same time, under the tutelage and control of SOAS, a string of University Colleges – in Ghana, Nigeria and Uganda – were established, and history departments were created within them virtually immediately. Third, the experience of the war had promoted nationalism within both colonized and colonial societies, while enthusing a generation of young scholars in Europe and the USA for explicitly anti-racist and anti-imperialist intellectual agendas.

Under these influences, professional historical communities were born in much of tropical Africa. A founder generation of black African academic historians was trained by Europeans. The Europeans' remit upon appointment to posts in African universities was precisely to work their way out of their jobs. Once Africans were ready, they took over teaching in and running departments. But European historians learned as much as they taught. Most often by design, but sometimes by accident, they arrived to undertake research in Africa as well as to train historians. As one veteran British historian of Africa has put it, 'it is axiomatic that African History did not so much emerge in Britain as evolve from – often by the hands of the very same teachers – the needs and experience of university colleges in tropical Africa in the 1950s'.[28]

Trained as a medievalist at the Catholic University in Leuven, the young Belgian scholar Jan Vansina had re-tooled in the techniques of 'participant observation' at University College London in preparation to work as an anthropologist in Africa, researching Kuba society in the Congo. He imagined that he had quit the intellectual world of his MA thesis – an exploration of medieval funerary praise songs, made to be sung at the gravesides of just deceased rulers. Evidently essentially oral compositions, these were nevertheless partly accessible to historical research because, at least occasionally, they had been 'written down as *probatio pennae*' – exercises in trying out new pens. What Vansina was to go on to do once in Africa, however, was not so much anthropology as *history* in the field. Within half a year of his arrival in the Congo in early 1953, he stumbled over his European and anthropologist's prejudices and his mental world underwent a second conversion, this time of Damascene proportions. The householder of a compound with whom Vansina had been conversing suddenly

> interrupted the leisurely pace of his speech and exclaimed rhetorically ... 'We too we know the past, because we carry our newspapers in our heads.' Full of enthusiasm, he recited as proof, a number of short poems ... In a burst of insight, half-forgotten dirges such as *Laxis febris*, 'With loosening strings' ... surged through my mind. Those Bushong poems were just like these medieval dirges. They were texts, and hence just as amenable to the canons of historical method. Once one could assess the value of a tradition, it could be used as a source like any other.[29]

Other historians arrived at similar conclusions. In a meeting of anthropology and history, oral traditions could open up vistas onto precolonial pasts. Of course, historians did not place their sole reliance on one source for one tradition, any more than they concentrated on that generic species of source to the exclusion of others. Written sources were scrupulously drawn on, where available, and archaeology provided historians with further raw materials. Where they had been written down in the 19th century, some versions of oral traditions had already acquired a kind of respectability as sources, even for technically conservative historians. Henceforth, the latter had to be persuaded to take the direct consultation of oral tradition through the conduct of oral history as seriously. As un-Rankean as early professional historians of Africa were in the mere fact of their use of oral sources, they were therefore all the more determinedly Rankean in their critical and comparativist approaches to those sources.

The uses to which they put their sources also echoed the practices of 19th-century European historians, and did so for comparable reasons. On gaining independence, African states found their own motives for continuing the investment in history begun by Britain. The shared nationalist commitments of politicians and historians encouraged the search for evidence of state-formation in precolonial societies. Their fixation on the state, then, confirms that the first academic historians in and of black Africa were Rankeans in most things other than their use of oral sources.

Tropical Africa's version of a statist paradigm enjoyed a brief golden age. Its first base was in the history department at the University of Ibadan in Nigeria. The influence of its approach – researching and writing political histories which concentrated on precolonial periods, and doing so in ways which would be acceptable to international standards of historical scholarship – radiated outward. The Ibadan School set historians' agendas in university departments at Ife, Lagos, Port Harcourt, Nsukka, Jos, Benin, Iloria and Calabar.[30] From the 1950s onward, archive management flourished; historical associations developed; journals were established. In short, tropical Africa had, with remarkable rapidity, acquired all the characteristic institutions of modern historical professions.

The African historians' intellectual efforts dovetailed neatly, Roland Oliver proclaimed, with the work being done by an increasingly numerous body of historians of Africa in Britain. The USA was a latecomer to the field; but there, where Vansina found a long-term institutional home at Wisconsin, a burgeoning student interest in African history, matched by initially generous research funding, also shared many of the preoccupations of historians writing in tropical Africa, and from an African perspective. History, it seemed, was being decolonized. Historians who, like Vansina, were keenly aware that the health of African history in the rest of the world was finally dependent on its strength in Africa, could fleetingly allow themselves to hope that Africans would now take the lead in making their own histories, in their own institutions.

The first challenge to the singularly international paradigm of tropical African history rather added a dimension of vibrant debate, and opened new questions, than damaging the young sub-discipline. Terence Ranger contended that the Ibadan School's nationalism was complacent and elitist, and that it had adopted European concepts uncritically. In turning to the history of ordinary people, African historians would become more really African. By 1968, Ranger had inspired the emergence of a more socially aware nationalist historiography at the University of Dar es Salaam in Tanzania. The new school advocated 'African initiative' in both the writing and the subject of its version of history, and sought to provide 'useful history' for more than just the state.

From the mid-1970s, however, neither the Ibadan School nor its rival at Dar could look ahead with confidence. The further expansion of the discipline was proving patchy, and already there were signs of contraction. In Nigeria, home to several of the earliest university history departments, and to the first historical society as well as the first and most impressive of Africa's crop of historical journals, there was a sense of crisis by the close of the decade. E. A. Ayandele lambasted Nigerian governmental policy for having turned its back on history in its 'irrational, unhealthy and culturally homicidal' pursuit of economic, scientific and technological success. While history remained the most popular discipline among humanities undergraduates, a 'primrose path' leading to well-paid jobs in public administration was seducing potential postgraduates and so militating against the ability of the historical profession to reproduce itself. Harsh as his criticisms of the record of governments were, he reserved his most damning indictments for 'the glaring failure' of Nigerian historians themselves. They had overlooked the poverty of the teaching of Nigerian history in the schools, allowing themselves to be ruled by 'the arrogant feeling that it is academically pedestrian … to descend to the level of secondary school students!' Nor had the professionals compensated by producing enough research, so that white historiography continued to occupy vast territories of Nigerian history. Yet Nigerian historians had been selling themselves into 'academic slavery' since they were 'primarily concerned with impressing the white man', persuading him to accept that African 'is a legitimate branch of History Universal'. Ayandele's recipe for all these ills was a redoubled emphasis on historians' 'patriotic duties': they must write explicitly 'nationalist history'. The international historical community could have no cause for complaint. 'For where are our colleagues', Ayandele asked, 'in the so-called developed parts of the world who are not writers of nationalist history?[31]

Ayandele's worst fears for the future of his profession in tropical Africa were by no means unfounded. In the mid-1980s, as the IMF called in its loans to African states, funding for history and other humanities disciplines dried up. Neither the Ibadan nor the Dar School survived. The *Journal of the Historical Society of Nigeria* ceased publication, as did virtually all the other historical periodicals of tropical Africa. Dictatorships added to the woes of academia.[32] In Zaire, for instance, history teaching 'turned into the telling of tattered tales, buildings into ruins, programs and academic calendars into fiction, and morale into elegiac despair. Mobutu forced historians into exile and, throughout the 1970s and '80s, periodically terrorized campuses until, after the murder of at least twenty students at Lubumbashi and the plunder of the university by elite troops one night in 1990, the universities 'practically ceased to exist'.[33]

As its material base fell apart, new kinds of intellectual trauma threatened to undermine the legitimacy of institutionalized history in and beyond Africa. Ayandele's position had been perched uncomfortably between rejection and emulation of European and US historiography. For historians like Abdullahi Smith, the central problem was just that: the Ibadan and Dar Schools remained trapped within professional and institutional categories that were mere manifestations of 'the terrible corruption of Western society'. Their nationalisms were consequently self-contradictory and threadbare. In 1975, Smith proposed a comprehensive refashioning of history in the universities on Islamic lines. At Zaria, in the Islamic north of Nigeria, Smith's ideas resulted in still another African school of history, this time challenging not only the intellectual and political, but also the institutional precepts of Ibadan.[34]

That challenge, albeit mounted largely in terms very different from those of Islam, was echoed well beyond tropical Africa. The cluster of historians who gathered around the *Subaltern Studies* series of occasional volumes appeared, on the face of it, to have put Indian historiography firmly on the mental map of 'western' historians. They did so by producing a species of 'history from below', and combining that with an anti-imperialism that was not nationalist. Increasingly, however, their originally Marxist-influenced perspectives gave way to an espousal of 'postcolonial', postmodern ones. And with these came a heightened consciousness of the ambiguities of their own position as professional historians. Thus, Dipesh Chakrabarty, a member of the *Subaltern Studies* collective, rejected as 'gratifying but premature' Ronald Inden's congratulatory words to Indian historians who were 'showing signs of reappropriating the capacity to represent themselves' within an international scholarly community. Chakrabarty advanced the 'perverse proposition' that 'all histories' – including those made by *Subaltern Studies* practitioners – 'tend to become variations on a master narrative that could be called "the history of Europe." In this sense, "Indian" history itself is in a position of subalternity; one can only articulate subaltern subject positions in the name of this history.' Europe is invariably 'a silent referent in historical knowledge itself ... Third-world historians feel a need to refer to works in European history', which is not reciprocated. It follows that working 'within the discipline of "history" produced at the institutional site of the university' entails 'deep collusion' with European narratives of modernization. '"History" as a knowledge system is firmly embedded in institutional practices that invoke the nation-state at every step – witness the organization and politics of teaching, recruitment, promotions, and publication in history departments.' The global presence of history within education systems serves only to underscore the point: historians owe that presence to 'what European imperialism and third-world nationalism have achieved together: the universalization of the nation-state'. Even to seek to challenge that version of universalism is 'impossible within the knowledge protocols of academic history'. From secular chronologies to the rules of evidence employed by historians, Chakrabarty leaves no aspect of his discipline unchallenged.[35] Ashis Nandy has gone still further, rejecting the imposition of 'the category of history on all constructions of the past'. Historical consciousness, welcomed by Indian intellectuals on the occasion of its mid-19th century arrival on the subcontinent 'as a powerful adjunct to the kit-bag of Indian civilization', now stands revealed as irredeemably European, and its 'domination' as 'a cultural and political liability'. Instead, Nandy champions strategies of forgetting.[36]

3.4 Conclusions

Nandy unconsciously rehearses a strategy of Stalinism: airbrushing out of history whatever may be inconvenient. Besides, his own denunciations of imperialism depend, as Frederick Cooper has pointed out, on historical knowledge imparted by academic historians. Furthermore, his rejection of academic history relies on a hard-and-fast line between that and other understandings of the past.[37] Though they have done so to varying degrees and with uneven success, modern professional historians have always drawn on and eclectically assimilated ideas emanating from beyond the academy. Nor are they prepared to see amateur historians, or the bearers of oral traditions, only as sources. Though he admits it took him years to do so, Jan Vansina came clearly to see that 'informants' like Mbop Louis were also his 'confreres, historians just as I was, only community historians, not academics like me'.[38] Academic historians may (undeniably) stand too much on their professional dignity at times. They do abuse the 'scholarly apparatus' to confuse readers and to intimidate them, and sometimes in more or less paranoid endeavours to cover their own backs against potential critics among their fellow-professionals. But, probably for the most part, they are also keenly aware of being engaged in a process that is essentially collective, and dependent on debate and criticism both within and beyond the discipline. Pluralism is its necessary condition.

Guide to further reading

Pim den Boer, *History as a Profession. The Study of History in France, 1818–1914* (Princeton, 1998).

Eckhardt Fuchs and Benedikt Stuchtey (eds), *Across Cultural Borders: Historiography in Global Perspective* (Lanham, 2002).

Effi Gazi, *Scientific National History. The Greek Case in Comparative Perspective (1850–1920)* (Frankfurt am Main, 2000).

Doris S. Goldstein, 'The Organisational Development of the British Historical Profession, 1884–1921', *Bulletin of the Institute of Historical Research* 55 (1982), pp.180–93.

Matthias Middell, Gabriele Lingelbach and Frank Hader (eds), *Historische Institute im Internationalen Vergleich* (Leipzig, 2001).

Peter Novick, *That Noble Dream. The 'Objectivity' Question and the American Historical Profession* (Cambridge, 1988).

Bonnie G. Smith, *The Gender of History: Men, Women, and Historical Practice* (Cambridge, MA, 1998).

Jan Vansina, *Living with Africa* (Madison, 1994).

Notes

1 The classic account of these relationships is Peter Novick, *That Noble Dream. The 'Objectivity' Question and the American Historical Profession* (Cambridge, 1988), esp. pp. 51–3. See also Matthias Middell, Gabriele Lingelbach and Frank Hader (eds), *Historische Institute im Internationalen*

Vergleich (Leipzig, 2001) and Eckhardt Fuchs and Benedikt Stuchtey (eds), *Across Cultural Borders: Historiography in Global Perspective* (Lanham, 2002).

2 Christoph Strupp, 'Die Organisation historischer Lehre und Forschung in den Niederlanden bis 1940', in Middell, Lingelbach and Hader, *Historische Institute*, pp. 199–220, 215.

3 Peter H. Slee, *Learning and a Liberal Education: The Study of Modern History in the Universities of Oxford, Cambridge and Manchester 1800–1914* (Manchester, 1986), p. 142.

4 British Library of Political and Economic Science, Webster Papers no. 1/5, 105–9: Webster's 'Memorandum on the Relations of Modern and Ancient Universities'.

5 Eric Hobsbawm, 'Old Marxist Still Sorting Out Global Fact From Fiction', *The Times Higher*, 12 July 2002, p. 18.

6 Eckhardt Fuchs, 'Introduction: Provincialising Europe: Historiography as a Transcultural Concept', in Fuchs and Stuchtey, *Cultural Borders*, pp. 1–26, 9.

7 See Heiko Feldner's contribution to this volume (Chapter 1).

8 R. Steven Turner, 'German Science, German Universities: Historiographical Perspectives from the 1980s', in Gert Schubring, (ed.), *'Einsamkeit und Freiheit' neu besichtigt: Uiversitätsreformen und Disziplinenbildung in Preußen als Modell für Wissenschaftspolitik im Europa des 19. Jahrhunderts* (Stuttgart, 1989), pp. 24–36.

9 Sylvia Palatschek, 'Duplizität der Ereignisse: Die Gründung des Historischen Seminars 1875 an der Universität Tübingen und seine Entwicklung bis 1914', in Werner Freitag (ed.), *Halle und die deutsche Geschichtswissenschaft um 1900* (Halle, 2002), pp. 37–64.

10 See John Warren's contribution to this volume (Chapter 2).

11 Anthony Grafton, *The Footnote. A Curious History* (Cambridge, MA, 1997), esp. pp. 61 and 65–6.

12 See Markus Huttner, 'Historische Gesellschaften und die Entstehung historischer Seminare – zu den Anfängen institutionalisierter Geschichtsstudien an den deutschen Universitäten des 19. Jahrhunderts', in Middell, Lingelbach and Hader, *Historische Institute*, pp. 39–83; Hans-Jürgen Pandel, 'Die Entwicklung der historischen Seminare in Deutschland', in Freitag (ed.), *Halle*, pp. 25–37.

13 Heinrich von Sybel, 'Die deutschen Universitäten und die auswärtigen Universitäten. Akademische Festrede, Bonn, 22. März 1868', in von Sybel, *Vorträge und Aufsätze* (Berlin, 1874), pp. 38–55 (quotations on pp. 53 and 41).

14 Q. Edward Wang, 'German Historicism and Scientific History in China, 1900–1940', in Fuchs and Stuchtey, *Cultural Borders*, pp. 141–61, 142.

15 For further instances, see Stefan Tanaka, *Japan's Orient: Rendering Pasts into History* (Berkely, 1993); Effi Gazi, *Scientific National History. The Greek Case in Comparative Perspective, 1850–1920* (Frankfurt am Main,

2000); Paul Guérin, 'La condition de l'historien et l'histoire nationale en Belgique du 19e et au début du 20e siècle', *Storia della Storiografia* 11 (1987), pp. 64–103.

16 Thomas Saunders, 'Introduction: "A Most Narrow Present"', in Saunders (ed.), *Historiography of Imperial Russia. The Profession and Writing of History in a Multinational State* (New York, 1999), pp. 3–13 (here pp. 8–9).

17 Bonnie G. Smith, 'Gender and the Practices of Scientific History: The Seminar and Archival Research in the 19th century', *American Historical Review* 100 (4) (1995), pp. 1150–76 (here pp. 1158–61).

18 Pim den Boer, *History as a Profession. The Study of History in France, 1818–1914* (Princeton, 1998), pp. 224–308.

19 Pim den Boer, *History*, p. 223.

20 Gabriele Lingelbach, 'Erträge und Grenzen zweier Ansätze: Kulturtransfer und Vergleich am Beispiel der französischen und amerikanischen Geschichtswissenschaft während des 19. Jahrhunderts', in Christoph Conrad and Sebastian Conrad (eds), *Die Nation schreiben. Geschichtswissenschaft im internationalen Vergleich* (Göttingen, 2002), pp. 333–59; Lingelbach, 'The Historical Discipline in the United States: Following the German Model?', in Fuchs and Stuchtey, *Cultural Borders*, pp. 183–204.

21 Senate House, London, Sir John Seeley Papers, MS903/4/3: Notebook: 'Tour of 1873' diary entry for 22 June 1873.

22 Deborah Wormell, *Sir John Seeley and the Uses of History* (Cambridge, 1980), p. 67.

23 Seeley Papers, diary entry for 21 July 1873.

24 Thomas Frederick Tout, 'Schools of History', in Tout, *Collected Papers* (Manchester, 1932), pp. 93–109.

25 Maxine Berg, *A Woman in History. Eileen Power, 1889–1940* (Cambridge, 1996), pp. 144ff.

26 Cit. after J. D. Fage, *On the Nature of African History* (Birmingham, 1965), pp. 1–2.

27 See Robin W. Winks (ed.), *The Oxford History of the British Empire,* Vol. 5, *Historiography* (Oxford, 1999), esp. B. W. Higman, 'The British West Indies', pp. 134–45 and K. M. de Silva, 'Ceylon (Sri Lanka)', pp. 243–52.

28 Anthony H. M. Greene, 'Introductory Remarks', in Greene (ed.), *The Emergence of African History at British Universities. An Autobiographical Approach* (Oxford, 1995), pp. 1–11, 1.

29 Jan Vansina, Living with Africa (Madison, 1994). Quotations on pp. 7, 16, 17.

30 Paul E. Lovejoy, 'The Ibadan School of Historiography and its Critics', in Toyin Falola (ed.), African Historiography. Essays in Honour of Jacob Ade Ajahi (Harlow and Ikeja, 1993), pp. 195–202, 199.

31 E. A. Ayandele, 'The Task Before Nigerian Historians Today', Journal of the Historical Society of Nigeria 9(4) (1979), pp. 1–13. Quotations on pp. 3, 5, 6, 7.

32 See Vansina, Living, p. 201; Andreas Eckert, 'Dekolonisierung der Geschichte? Die Institutionalisierung der Geschichtswissenschaft in Afrika nach dem Zweiten Weltkrieg', in Middell, Lingelbach and Hader, Historische Institute, pp. 451–76, esp. pp. 472ff.

33 Vansina, Living, pp. 175ff. for the Libyan experience and pp. 201 and 166–7 for Zaire.

34 Lovejoy, 'Ibadan School', pp. 198–9.

35 Dipesh Chakrabarty, 'Postcoloniality and the Artifice of History. Who Speaks for "Indian" Pasts?', Representations 37 (1992), pp. 1–26. Quotations on pp. 1, 2, 19, 22.

36 Ashis Nandy, 'History's Forgotten Doubles', History and Theory, Theme Issue, 34 (1995), pp. 44–66. Quotations on pp. 45, 65, 66.

37 Frederick Cooper, 'Africa's Pasts and Africa's Historians', Canadian Journal of African Studies 34 (2000), pp. 298–336, 300.

38 Vansina, Living, p. 17.

Part Two

4

Marxist historiography

Geoff Eley

Until the mid-20th century, Marxist approaches to history could be encountered mainly outside the academic world in the alternative intellectual and pedagogical environments of labour movements. Commitment to the 'materialist conception of history' was associated almost entirely with an oppositional culture of dissent, intellectual polemic and working-class autodidacticism. Marxist historiography only established its presence in the universities as part of the general turning to social history that captured the imagination of the profession in the 1960s. During the long pre-history of that development, the Marxist contribution is best seen as part of a much larger effort at developing the theories and methods that a comparative 'history of society' presupposed. Between the 1930s and the 1970s, a new generation of British Marxists became a principal source of innovation in that respect, joining the comparable influence of the *Annales* school in France, with whom they also entered into dialogue. Varying country by country, this convergence of interest around 'social history' or 'the history of society' grew ultimately from the late nineteenth- and early 20th-century efforts – in politics and social thought – to master the meanings of capitalist industrialization.

4.1 Classical Marxism: The materialist conception of history

For the distinctive thinking of Marx and Engels about history, the sovereignty of the economy was fundamental. Their approach began as a general axiom of understanding: 'The mode of production of material life conditions the general process of social, political, and intellectual life. It is not the consciousness of men that determines their existence, but their social existence that determines their consciousness.' Or, in what became an equally famous statement: 'According to the materialist conception of history, the ultimately determining element in history is the production and reproduction of real life.'[1] Dating from their early collaborations of the 1840s, this robust philosophical materialism graduated during the next decade into a general theory of economics – of the capitalist mode of production and its 'laws of motion' – which was meant to be fully explicated in the serial volumes of *Capital.*

Explicitly linked to a political project of socialism, that general theory sought to bring the European revolutionary crises of 1848–9 into historical perspective, to capture the main logic of social development during a period of capitalist industrialization, and to explain the possibilities of a future capitalist collapse. That theory also bequeathed Marx's most important legacy for the pre-1914 social democratic tradition, whose constituent parties were formed, country by country, during the last quarter of the 19th century. It became what contemporaries mainly understood by 'Marxism' – namely, the role of the 'economic factor' in history, the determining effects of material forces on human achievement, and the linking of the possibilities of political change to the underlying movements of the economy. As a general principle, it made the 'forces of production' and their dominant forms of development into the main motor of history: it made the most important political changes contingent upon the economic crises and associated social forces needed to sustain them.

Marx himself left behind few formal works of history *per se*, although his 'economics', the major work of theory published in the three volumes of *Capital* between 1867 and 1894, contained a high density of historical learning and a variety of sustained historical analysis around particular questions, most famously perhaps in the accounts of 'primitive accumulation' and the transition from manufacture to modern industry, or in the empirically rich discussions of the struggles over the length of the working day.[2] Similarly, if his journalism of the 1850s and 1860s always reflected dense historical investigations, including his intensive contemporaneous analyses of the political events in France, these were not treated historiographically in any sustained way until quite recently. In fact, it was Engels who produced the more extensive catalogue of formally historical writings. These began with his classic account of the development of modern industry and its social consequences, *The Condition of the Working Class in England* (1844–5); continued with *The Peasant War in Germany* (1850); and culminated in his writings of the 1870s and 1880s, the most conventionally historical of which was *The Origin of the Family, Private Property, and the State* (1884).

For Engels this was mainly about properly formalizing Marx's legacy, popularizing his thinking, and converting it into an all-purpose philosophy. A similar ambition inspired the earliest generations of Marx's followers in the new socialist parties, including above all Karl Kautsky, who quickly emerged by the 1890s as the senior disciple. In common with other pioneers like Eduard Bernstein in Germany, Victor Adler in Austria, Georgi Plekhanov in Russia, and Antonio Labriola in Italy, Kautsky sought

> to systematize historical materialism as a comprehensive theory of man and nature, capable of replacing rival bourgeois disciplines and providing the workers' movement with a broad and coherent vision of the world that could be easily grasped by its militants'.[3]

Such an effort often encompassed broad historical themes, including Kautsky's own *The Agrarian Question* (1899) and *Foundations of Christianity* (1923), or sought to analyse the conditions of capitalist development inside their own society, as in Vladimir Ilyich Lenin's *The Development of Capitalism in Russia* (1899) or Rosa Luxemburg's *The Industrial Development of Poland* (1898). Other works include Ernest Belfort Bax's *The Peasant War in Germany* (1899), Jean Jaurès's *Histoire socialiste de la Révolution française* (1900–9), and Prosper Olivier Lissagaray's *History of the Commune of 1871* (1886). The new socialist parties also generated growing numbers of histories of their own emergence, of which Eduard Bernstein's three-volume history of the labour movement in Berlin (1907–10) remains an imposing example.

How might we summarize this 'classical' period in the life of Marxism as a body of thought relevant to historians, extending from the output of Marx and Engels themselves to the writings of their followers at the end of the 19th century? Beyond its underlying philosophical standpoint, four major commitments mainly characterized this approach to history: its progressivist theory of history based on ascending stages of development; its 'base and superstructure' model of social causality; its ascription of meaningful historical change to the conflicting interests and collective agency of social classes; and its sense of itself as a 'science of society'.

In the grand Marxist scheme of history, human society advanced from lower to higher stages of development, demonstrating ever-greater complexity in the forms of organization of economic life and making possible the eventual replacement of material scarcity by material abundance. The primary context for this thinking was the urban-industrial transformation of European society directly observed by Marx and Engels, which they conceptualized as the transition from feudalism to capitalism. In contrast, the social formations preceding feudalism were indistinctly defined, sometimes appearing as the 'Asiatic' and 'ancient' modes of production, at others broken down further into 'oriental', 'ancient', 'Germanic' and perhaps 'Slavonic' patterns of property holding, which grew in turn from the earliest forms of 'primitive communalism'. The engine behind this forward-moving developmental schema was the forces of production, whose dynamism would always eventually outgrow society's given framework of social relations and institutions, thereby requiring violent socio-political upheavals for any further advance to occur. Beyond the exhaustion of capitalism's own developmental capacities, socialism was conceived as the highest level of social development of all. This theory of stages gave Marxists their criteria for periodization. It delivered a template for judging the developmental status of any particular society.

Second, Marx and the earliest generations of Marxists classically reserved a first-order priority – ontologically, epistemologically, analytically – for the underlying economic structure of society in conditioning everything else, including the possible forms of politics and the law, of institutional development and of social consciousness and belief. The commonest expression for this determining relationship was the architectural language of 'base and superstructure', in which the spatial metaphor of ascending and sequential levels also implied the end point in a logical chain of reasoning. This could be very flexibly understood, leaving room for much unevenness and autonomy, including the separate effectivity of the superstructure and its reciprocal action on the base, especially in the context of any detailed political, ideological or aesthetic analysis. But such analyses were ultimately still held accountable.

Third, for Marxists the main motor of change under capitalism was class conflict. Such conflict was considered to be structural and endemic, a permanent and irreducible feature of social life under capitalism, based in the unavoidable antagonisms of mutually incompatible, collectively organized class interests. In this understanding, social identity derived in the first instance from the unequal contest between those who owned and controlled the means of production and those who were dispossessed. This structural antagonism led to struggles over the social distribution of the economic value produced in the economy, which assigned people 'into two great hostile camps, into two great classes directly facing each other: bourgeoisie and proletariat'.[4] Workers were a class of direct producers who no longer owned the independent means of subsistence or even their own tools. Forced back for their livelihood onto the sale of labour power to a capitalist in return for a wage, workers had no resources beyond their own collectively organized strength, mobilized through trade unions and socialist parties. Under deteriorating conditions of capitalist accumulation and profitability, workers' collective mobilizations relayed pressures to the political system that created openings for change. The most extreme form of such a breakthrough, in a crisis of particular and escalating severity, was revolution.

Finally, Marxism was scientific. In his formative intellectual indebtedness to the new natural sciences, for example, Kautsky was entirely typical. The impact of Charles Darwin and the works of Ludwig Büchner and Ernst Haeckel permeated his pre-Marxist thinking. His monthly review *Neue Zeit*, the European movement's most prestigious theoretical organ, effectively carried this dual affiliation with Marx and Darwin on its masthead. For Kautsky, the class struggle – 'the struggle of man as a social animal in the social community' – mirrored the biological struggle for existence. For August Bebel, the leader of the German Social Democratic Party (SPD), Marxism was 'science, applied with full understanding to all fields of human activity'. Engels had established this tone in his funeral oration for Marx – 'Just as Darwin discovered the law of development of organic nature, so Marx discovered the law of development of human history' – and indeed spent much of the 1870s and 1880s seeking to ground this claim, particularly in the posthumously published *Dialectics of Nature.* For most conscious followers of Marx at the end of the 19th century, this equivalence between 'science' and 'society' was axiomatic. It bespoke a certitude in the directionality of history, an objectivist confidence in the knowledge Marxism was expected to deliver.

Fashioned into a unified approach during the several decades before 1914, this powerful combination of standpoints – a theory of societal development permitting the periodizing of history, a model of social determination proceeding upwards from material life, a theory of social change based on class struggles and their effects, and an objectivist approach to social understanding – served Marxists well for the best part of a century. Across that period, Marxist writings on history varied greatly in subtlety, evidentiary groundedness, and general scholarly integrity, fluctuating partly with the climate of socialist and Communist political life, partly with the degree of acceptance Marxists found within the academic world and other arenas of intellectual exchange. Periods of critical ferment within Marxist theory also complicated the straightforwardness of this general description. If the 1940s and early 1950s was a time of rather little creativity in all these respects, for example, then the early 1920s saw tremendous experimentation, as did the 1960s and 1970s.

4.2 Convergences and openings

After 1918, under the radicalizing impact of the war and accompanying revolutionary crises, Marxist ideas achieved markedly wider circulation across much of Europe, acquiring further impetus from the success of the Bolshevik Revolution and the strengthening of civil freedoms in the West. One consequence was the growth of a modest Marxist intellectual presence beyond the organized confines of the Socialist and Communist parties themselves, enjoying greater legitimacy in the marketplace of ideas and establishing some foothold in the universities.

Indeed, a notable convergence of interest occurred in the early 20th century around new forms of historical inquiry – namely, 'social' history in the terms now familiar since the 1960s – for which Marxism, as the 'materialist conception of history', offered the strongest programme. But given the sway exercised over university history departments by statecraft and diplomacy, warfare and high politics, and administration and the law, the earliest social histories developed beyond the walls of academia altogether, either in the labours of private individuals or in the alternative institutional settings of labour movements. The more propitious political climate after 1918 then allowed stronger potentials for social history to emerge, usually abetted from outside the discipline *per se*. If in Germany the main impetus was a flowering of sociology, and in France the ecumenical conception of social science crystallizing around Henri Berr's *Revue de synthèse historique* (launched in 1900) and leading to the founding of *Annales d'histoire économique et sociale* in 1929, in Britain the key was the creation of the Economic History Society and its journal, *Economic History Review*, in 1926–7.

The resulting historiography was certainly not 'Marxist' by conscious affiliation. In France, for example, the foundations of the new history were laid during the first three decades of the century by an exceptionally fertile encounter between historians and social science, occurring partly at the Ecole Pratique des Hautes Etudes in Paris under the influence of the economist François Simiand and Berr's *Revue*, partly among a remarkable grouping at the University of Strasbourg, including Maurice Halbwachs, Georges Lefebvre, and the founders of *Annales*, Marc Bloch and Lucien Febvre.[5] Between the 1930s and the 1960s, the dispositions of *Annales* paralleled those of Marxists: a strongly objectivist idea of history as social science; quantitative methodology; long-run analysis of economic fluctuations through prices, trade flows, and population; 'structural' history; and a materialist model of causation.

Across the Channel in Britain, social history was inspired partly by the grand narratives of the Industrial Revolution and the rise of national economies, partly by left-wing empathy for the social causalities of industrialization. The leading pioneers were each moved by strong political commitments. The early modern economic historian R. H. Tawney, who taught at the LSE, was a Christian Socialist, Labour Party parliamentary candidate, advocate of the Workers' Educational Association (WEA) and prominent public intellectual; G. D. H. Cole, who taught in Oxford from the 1920s and held the Chair of Social and Political Theory from 1945, was a Guild Socialist and leading non-affiliated socialist intellectual; the radical journalists John and Barbara Hammond published an epic account of the human costs of industrialization in a trilogy of works on the labouring poor; and Beatrice and Sidney Webb, who laid the foundations for a fully professionalized social history with an immense corpus of scholarship on trade unionism, local government, the Poor Law and social administration, heavily identified with the advance of the parliamentary Labour Party. In all of these cases, the distance from Marxism as such was clear. But the commitment to studying material life, animated by various kinds of left-wing politics and identification with the 'common people', however paternalist or patronizing, adumbrated the shared ground. The work of Cole in labour history or Tawney on the sixteenth and seventeenth centuries bridged directly to social history after 1945 in its concern with ordinary people, with the broader impact of socio-economic forces like industrialization, and with the ethics of political engagement.[6]

Of course, these early works were also written against something else. In the British case that meant not just the nationalist paradigm of statecraft, constitutional evolution and the law, but also the earlier efforts at a 'popular' or 'democratic' alternative. Thus the precursor to the Hammonds had been the radical parliamentarian and Oxford economic historian Thorold Rogers, who countered the constitutional history of his day with a seven-volume *History of Agriculture and Prices in England* published between 1866 and 1902, which assembled rich materials from which the social history of the labouring poor might be written. Likewise, in his *Short History of the English People* published in 1874, Rogers' younger Oxford contemporary John Richard Green countered the Victorian celebration of a limited English constitutionalism with a popular counter-story of democratic self-government.[7] It helped establish a line of popular history outside the universities, running through the Hammonds and Green's widow Alice Stopford Green's Irish histories to the Communist Leslie Morton's *People's History of England*, published in 1938, which drew its inspiration from the anti-fascist campaigning for a Popular Front.[8]

The rise of a self-consciously Marxist grouping of historians inside the British universities was inseparable from this deeper-running history of political pedagogy. But until new generations of university students were radicalized by the threat of fascism in the 1930s, Marxist historical work remained a subcultural current outside the professional academic world, mainly confined to the political education practised through the Communist Party, the Independent Labour Party, the Plebs League, the National Council of Labour Colleges (NCLC), Ruskin College, parts of the WEA and other areas of the labour movement, often in highly localized ways. There the appeal of Marxism broadly replicated the pattern of thinking summarized in this chapter's previous section, held together by a passionate commitment to the concept of totality as an integrated or holistic approach to knowledge and the interconnectedness of the different spheres of life.[9] This was joined to a populist or democratic belief that history's proper subject should be 'society as a whole'. History should be less about 'the rise and fall of empires' than the 'steady progress of humanity and the succeeding social systems', less about 'battles' than 'the wonderful story of human control over nature', and 'less about kings . . . [than] the peoples'. Moreover, if history was a science, there was room neither for personalities nor for the banal details of ordinary life. As one ex-miner and NCLC student remembered, 'We weren't interested in whether so-and-so had sugar in his coffee or not. What interested us was how and why societies change.'[10]

Also inseparable from this holistic or totalizing approach to history was the firm conviction in history's forward movement or direction, which for both the popular milieu and the most prestigious Marxist theoreticians was borne by a self-confirming teleological optimism. As Peter Beilharz observes of Leon Trotsky's historical works on the course of the Russian Revolution written in this same period, that teleological understanding rested upon the familiar schema of historical stages, where the 'relation between feudalism, capitalism and socialism as successive modes of production remains strictly necessary and evolutionist in conception'. Regardless of any 'sensitivity to specificity and unevenness' characterizing their particular analyses, accordingly, Marxists held fast to their belief in historical materialism as 'a positive philosophy of history, where downward fluctuations or spirals modify but never overpower the dominant and upward tendency of evolution'.[11]

The necessary openings for a more creative Marxist historiography, where the hold exercised by these established rules of thinking (teleology, base-and-superstructure determinism, the idea of a cohesively interconnected totality) might all be relaxed, came mainly outside the official discourse of the Socialist and Communist parties. They occurred in the practical contexts where new generations of social historians began doing their work, whether inside the universities or out. In fact, most genealogies of Marxist, feminist and other forms of radical history presume too much importance for university history departments. For instance, while most of the British Marxist historians claimed as a distinctive cohort by the 1970s had a university education in the 1930s and eventually secured academic appointments, many either occupied a fairly marginal place until later in their careers or worked outside the historical profession altogether. The pioneer oral historian, ex-schoolteacher and writer George Ewart Evans (1909–87), likewise university-educated and then radicalized into the Communist Party during the 1930s, produced his works entirely beyond academia.[12]

These were the settings in which common recognition of the value of materialist forms of analysis energized the intellectual and political imaginations of younger scholars who baulked at the discipline's established protocols and routines of work. This was where the appeal of social and economic history, and the excitement of entering a common project of societal understanding, could allow both Marxists and the followers of *Annales* to converge, as the experience of Labrousse and Lefebvre in France itself implied.[13] Indeed, the motivating commitments for Marxist historians of this first academic generation are to be found not just in the guiding philosophical perspectives, which might seem rather prosaically orthodox when explicated, but far more in the detailed works of scholarship they produced, which might have a great deal in common with those of their non-Marxist colleagues. For this reason, arguably, strict demarcations between the British Marxist historians and the historians of *Annales* in this period really make little sense.[14]

4.3 The British Marxist historians: Shaping an intellectual culture

By the 1960s, British social history had seen the gradual accrual of a scholarly tradition, for which the prestige of Tawney and Cole delivered valuable support and protection. Various strands were important in this respect, including the longer-term institutional strength of economic history, the impact of individual pioneers like Asa Briggs, the nexus of progressive social science at the LSE, the respective influence of J. H. Plumb and George Kitson Clark in Cambridge, significant regional centres in Leeds, Manchester and elsewhere, and the labour history networks solidifying around the Society for the Study of Labour History and its *Bulletin* launched in 1960.[15] But amidst this activity, the Communist Party (CPGB) Historians' Group, whose regular discussions began in 1946, came to exercise disproportionate influence on social history's subsequent expansion. Its members mostly composed a distinct generation, having come to the CPGB via the anti-fascist campaigning of the later 1930s. Most also left during Communism's crisis in 1956–7 when the Group disbanded.

The collective discussions of these British Marxist historians shaped the contours of social history in Britain, with a longer-term significance whose international resonance was comparable to that of *Annales*. They included Christopher Hill (1912–2003), George Rudé (1910–93), Victor Kiernan (1913–2009), Rodney Hilton (1916–2002), John Saville (1916–2009), Eric Hobsbawm (born 1917), Dorothy Thompson (born 1923), Edward Thompson (1924–93), Royden Harrison (1927–2002) and the younger Raphael Samuel (1938–96). Not many taught at the centre of British university life in Oxbridge or London. Some were not historians by discipline, such as the older Maurice Dobb (1900–76), the Cambridge economist, whose *Studies in the Development of Capitalism*, published in 1946, focused a large part of the Group's discussions. Others held positions in adult education. Rudé and Thompson secured academic appointments only in the 1960s, Rudé by travelling to Australia. Their main impulse came from politics, a powerful sense of history's pedagogy, and broader identification with democratic values and popular history. A leading mentor was the non-academic CPGB intellectual, journalist and Marx scholar, Dona Torr (1883–1957), to whom the Group paid tribute with a volume called *Democracy and the Labour Movement* in 1954.[16]

Inspired by A. L. Morton's *People's History of England*, published in 1938 at the height of the Popular Front campaign, the Group's ambition was to produce a social history of Britain capable of contesting established or official accounts. Some members specialized in British history *per se* – notably, Hilton on the English peasantry of the Middle Ages, Hill on the 17th-century English Revolution, Saville on industrialization and labour history, Dorothy Thompson on Chartism. Others displayed extraordinary international range. Hobsbawm's interests embraced British labour history, European popular movements and Latin American peasantries, plus the study of nationalism and a series of unparalleled general histories, which by their conclusion had covered the modern era from the late 18th century to the present in four superb volumes. Kiernan was a true polymath, publishing widely on aspects of imperialism, early modern state formation and the history of the aristocratic duel, as well as British relations with China and the Spanish Revolution of 1854, with an imposing wider bibliography of essays on an eclectic range of subjects. Rudé was a leading historian of the French Revolution and popular protest. Two other members of the Group were British specialists who over the longer term came to enjoy massive international influence – Raphael Samuel as the moving genius behind the History Workshop movement and its journal, and Edward Thompson through his great works, *The Making of the English Working Class* published in 1963, *Whigs and Hunters* a decade later, and *Customs in Common*, which incorporated agenda-setting essays and lectures originally written in the 1960s and 1970s.

This British Marxist historiography was embedded in specifically British concerns. Several voices spoke the language of English history exclusively – Hill, Hilton, Saville, the Thompsons. The broader tradition was intensely focused on national themes, most famously perhaps in Edward Thompson's vigorous general essay, 'The Peculiarities of the English', published in 1965 as a counterblast against a general interpretation of British history advanced by two younger Marxists, Tom Nairn and Perry Anderson.[17] Thompson's writing in the aftermath of leaving the Communist Party also converged with the cognate works of the literary critic Raymond Williams, whose *Culture and Society* and *The Long Revolution*, published in 1958 and 1961, proposed their own general interpretation of modern British history. Both Thompson and Williams sought to recuperate the national past in self-consciously oppositional and democratic fashion, wresting control of the national story from conservative opinion-makers of all kinds and rewriting it around the struggles of ordinary people in a still unfinished democratic project.[18]

During the 1950s, these British concerns were centered most strongly on two areas. On the one hand, the Group decisively shaped the emergent phase of labour history, most obviously through Hobsbawm's foundational essays collected in 1964 in *Labouring Men*, but also via the influence of John Saville and Royden

Harrison, and in the collective setting established by the founding of the Labour History Society in 1960. This rapidly burgeoning context of new scholarship became broadly organized around a chronology of specific questions about the presumed failure of the labour movement to realize the trajectory of radicalization projected by Marx's developmental model, laying out an enduring problematic whose dominance stretched well into the 1980s. Connected with this, on the other hand, the CP Historians' Group also shaped the history of capitalist industrialization in Britain, most notably through the standard of living controversy between Hobsbawm and Max Hartwell during 1957–63 over whether industrialism had improved or degraded the living standards of the working population.[19] At the same time, neither of these momentous contributions – to labour history and to the critique of capitalist industrialization – was thinkable without the prior labours of the Webbs, Cole, Tawney and the Hammonds.

But the vision of these Marxist historians was the opposite of parochial. While doing his pathbreaking research in Paris, Rudé worked with Georges Lefebvre and Albert Soboul; Kiernan practised an eclectic version of global history long before 'world history' became a recognized part of the profession's organization and teaching; Hobsbawm enjoyed incomparably diverse connections across Europe and Latin America; and another Communist, not a member of the Historians' Group, Thomas Hodgkin (1910–82), vitally influenced African history in its nascent years, again from the margins in adult education.[20] Hobsbawm's work developed in dialogue with Braudel and his colleagues and with Labrousse, Lefebvre and Soboul. Internationally, Hobsbawm and Rudé transformed the study of popular protest in pre-industrial societies. Rudé meticulously deconstructed older stereotypes of 'the mob', using the French Revolution and 18th-century riots in England and France to analyse the rhythms, organization and motives behind collective action, in the process specifying a pioneering sociology of the 'faces in the crowd'. Hobsbawm analysed the transformations in popular consciousness accompanying capitalist industrialization – in studies of Luddism and pre-trade union labour protest; in his excitingly original commentaries on social banditry, millenarianism and mafia; and in essays on peasants and peasant movements in Latin America. He pioneered the conversations of history and anthropology. He helped redefine what politics could mean in societies that lacked democratic constitutions, the rule of law or a developed parliamentary system.

The biggest step the CP Historians' Group undertook was the new journal, *Past and Present* (symptomatically subtitled a 'Journal of Scientific History'), launched in 1952 in order to preserve dialogue with non-Marxist historians at a time when the Cold War was rapidly closing this down.[21] In the guiding vision brought by the Marxist historians to the intellectual project of *Past and Present*, 'social history' meant trying to understand the dynamics of whole societies. It was the ambition to connect political events to underlying social forces. During 1947–50, the CP Historians' Group had focused on the transition from feudalism to capitalism and a complex of associated questions – the rise of absolutism, the nature of bourgeois revolutions, agrarian dimensions of the rise of capitalism and the social dynamics of the Reformation. Hobsbawm's two-part article on 'The General Crisis of the 17th Century' in 1954 then prompted the salient discussion of *Past and Present*'s first decade, the various contributions to which were subsequently collected under Trevor Aston's editorship as *Crisis in Europe, 1560–1660* in 1965. That debate energized historians of France, Spain, Sweden, Germany, Bohemia, Russia, Ireland and the early modern era more generally, as well as historians of Britain. It connected the 17th-century political upheavals to forms of economic crisis graspable in Europe-wide terms, in what Aston called 'the last phase of the general transition from a feudal to a capitalist economy'.[22] It built a case for studying religious conflict in social terms, a more general project which also carried through a number of other early debates in the journal, including especially that on science and religion. It grasped the nettle of trying to conceptualize the histories of societies as a whole, with profound implications for their respective later historiographies, exemplified most powerfully perhaps in J. H. Elliott's far-reaching contribution on 'The Decline of Spain'. It re-emphasized the convergence between *Past and Present* and *Annales*, for Hobsbawm's initial intervention had relied extensively on scholarly work sponsored under Braudel. Above all, the debate featured the exciting and constructive possibilities of the 'comparative method'.[23]

It is impossible to exaggerate the enduring contributions to the rise of social history made by *Past and Present* during its early years. While directly sustained by the particular Marxist formation grounded in the CP Historians' Group, the Editorial Board's outlook translated into a series of commitments that shaped the most ambitious historical discussions of the succeeding decades. One of those commitments was internationalism, for the journal brought new and exciting access to European work into the English-speaking world, aided by the editors' political networks, direct exchanges with France, and the impetus provided by the 1950 International Historical Congress in Paris and its new Social History Section.

Secondly, like *Annales*, Hobsbawm and his comrades urged the comparative study of societies within an overall framework of arguments about historical change, posed explicitly at the level of European or global movements and systems. This commitment grew directly from the classical Marxist perspectives learned during the 1930s and 1940s: it crystallized from the working agenda of the CP Historians' Group, and recurred in the annual *Past and Present* conference themes from 1957.

Thirdly, Past and Present pioneered the interdisciplinary exchange with sociologists and anthropologists, encouraged by the axiomatic Marxist recognition of the indivisibility of knowledge, and again paralleling the trajectory of Annales. The model of open-minded and eclectic materialism in this respect, explicitly grounded in a self-consciously cross-disciplinary (or perhaps 'adisciplinary') synthesis of 'historical sociology', was provided by Philip Abrams (1933–81), who joined Hobsbawm as an assistant editor in 1957. Educated during the 1950s in the intellectual-political universe of the first British New Left, rather than the popular-front Communism of the 1930s, Abrams brought a very different generational formation to the journal, one shaped far more by the critical sociologies of postwar Britain.24 On the other hand, Peter Worsley (born 1924), who displayed the most free-ranging and eclectic of cross-disciplinary dispositions, and whose historical sensibility accompanied a training in anthropology, field research in the Pacific and South-East Asia, and an appointment in sociology, had also been in the Communist Party until 1956 and those formative years continued to mould his many varied publications.25

Fourthly, for the Marxist architects of *Past and Present*, social history went together with economics – whether via the *Annaliste* master category of structures, or via Marxism and the materialist conception of history. Within history as an academic discipline, where social history became disengaged from the 'manners and morals' mode of popularizing or from projects of 'people's history', it invariably became coupled with economic history, as in the new departments of economic and social history created in some British universities in the 1960s.

Finally, the Marxist historians' commitment to dialogue and debate, to bringing Marxist approaches not only into the centre of discussions among historians in Britain, but also into a much broader intellectual circulation, as an essential bridge for both international exchange and generous cross-disciplinary explorations, profoundly enriched the intellectual culture of the discipline just at the point of the great higher education expansion of the 1960s, which produced such a notable leap forward in the volume, range and sophistication of scholarly historical research. In that sense, the conditions of take-off for the late 20th-century growth of historical studies were not simply assembled by the creation of national research bodies, the founding of new universities and the growth of funding for research. Those conditions were also to be found in the hard and imaginative labours of the grouping around *Past and Present* and in the politics of knowledge they pursued.

4.4 Maturity and diffusion

Although shortly to join the Board in the late 1960s, one alumnus of the CP Historians' Group not involved in *Past and Present*'s initial phase was Edward Thompson. Known first for his sprawling and energetic study of William Morris and then for his leading role in the British New Left, Thompson came to inspire several generations of social historians with his *Making of the English Working Class* published in 1963, which appeared in its Pelican edition in 1968. His work advanced an eloquent counter-narrative to gradualist versions of British history as the triumphant march of parliamentary evolution, grounding the latter in violence, inequality and exploitation instead: 'I am seeking to rescue the poor stockinger, the Luddite cropper, the "obsolete" handloom weaver, the "utopian" artisan, and even the deluded follower of Joanna Southcott, from the enormous condescension of posterity', he declared in one of the most quoted lines by a historian in the late 20th century. His book was also an anti-reductionist manifesto – attacking narrowly based economic history, over-deterministic Marxism and static theories of class. For Thompson, class was dynamic, eventuating through history – a relationship and a process, a common consciousness of capitalist exploitation and state repression, graspable through culture. Through *The Making*, the move from labour's institutional study to social histories of working people gained palpable momentum, embracing work, housing, nutrition, leisure and sport, drinking, crime, religion, magic and superstition, education, song, literature, childhood, courtship, sexuality, death and more.

Thompson wrote his great work outside the academy, working in adult education in Leeds, as a Communist (until 1956), New Left activist and public polemicist. He created the Centre for the Study of Social History at Warwick University in 1965, directing it until 1970, when he resigned. Beyond the networks of labour history and *Past and Present*, Thompson's *Making* was loudly attacked. But it energized younger generations. It also inspired the newly emergent and differently formed Marxisms that became so central to the developing social history wave.

Thompson's impact helped two initiatives on the margins to form, whose longer-term effects both mirrored the earlier dynamics of the Communist Historians' Group's influence and crucially surpassed its substantive range, organized forms and political intent. One of these was the Social History Group in Oxford, which convened on a weekly basis between 1965 and 1974. This seminar's organizers were a younger generation of graduate student Leftists, who included the Marxist author of *Outcast London*, Gareth Stedman Jones (born in 1942), a specialist on Spanish anarchism, Joaquin Romero Maura (born 1940), and the historian of Nazism, Tim Mason (1940–1990), who for a time was an assistant editor of *Past and Present*. They were inspired by a fourth member, the somewhat older Raphael Samuel (1934–96), who had been a schoolboy recruit to the CP Historians' Group, left the party in 1956 to become a key energizer of the New Left, and then took an appointment at Ruskin, the trade union college based in Oxford but not part of the university, from 1961. Linked to the ambitions of the Social History Group and conceived initially to bring Ruskin students into wider contact with other historians, Samuel's annual History Workshops became a vital engine of social history during the coming period, starting modestly but soon mushrooming into an international event. The first 13 Workshops met at Ruskin itself between 1967 and 1979, before migrating around Britain. They inspired a series of pamphlets – 12 altogether between 1970 and 1974 – and an imprint of more than 30 books between 1975 and 1990. Most impressively of all, Samuel and his group crystallized a much wider movement, grounded in diverse local university and community settings, and linked to public interventions of various kinds, most substantially during the debate over the national curriculum in the 1980s. Its flagship was *History Workshop Journal*, launched in 1976. In common with *Social History*, another new journal founded in the same year, *History Workshop Journal* sought to re-energize the commitments inaugurated through *Past and Present*.[26]

The second movement was women's history. Originally via tense and often angry contention with History Workshop and older mentors like Hobsbawm and Thompson, pioneers like Sheila Rowbotham (born 1943) drew important support and inspiration from both. Future leaders of women's history emerged from History Workshop's milieu, including Anna Davin (born 1940), Sally Alexander (born 1943) and Catherine Hall (born 1945). Rowbotham's early works became markers of the future field.[27] The first National Women's Liberation Conference, which met at Ruskin in 1970, originated as a women's history meeting, and the Seventh History Workshop in 1973 took 'Women in History' as its theme. Social history's emergence, like the earlier 20th-century moments and the Communist Party Historians' Group, was inconceivable outside these new political contexts.

Thompson's influence was international. *The Making* shaped North American, African and South Asian agendas, no less than studies of class formation in Britain and Europe. His 18th-century essays had perhaps even greater resonance, especially 'The Moral Economy', which influenced scholars working across national histories in diverse regions of the world and became the object of a retrospective international conference in Birmingham in 1992. The 1970s internationalized social history in the full sense envisaged by the British Marxist historians who founded *Past and Present*, through a growing proliferation of conferences, new journals and active processes of translation. In one network of particular importance, Thompson and Hobsbawm became central participants in a series of Round Tables on Social History organized by Braudel's Maison des Sciences de l'Homme, which brought together scholars from France, Italy, West Germany and elsewhere.

But by the 1980s, the energizing centre of innovative thinking among historians had moved elsewhere. Internationally, these dynamics varied. In Germany, for example, the challenge of *Alltagsgeschichte* (the history of everyday life) eventually compelled an opening of the discipline's mainstream toward forms of cultural history, partially shaped by an emergent dialogue with anthropology, where gender history also made significant inroads.[28] In Britain, an unexpected questioning of social history's materialist standpoints by Stedman Jones and others initiated a series of long-running debates, whose consequences converged with a variety of other powerful intellectual tendencies, feminist historical work, and the diffusion of cultural studies most notable among them, to dislodge social history from its earlier anticipated primacy.[29]

By the end of the century, a marked diversification was the result, encompassing not only the range of social histories that continued to be practised much as before, but also various redeployed and more sophisticated versions of political history and the history of ideas, distinct and self-consciously demarcated forms of the 'new cultural history', and a small but vociferous avant-garde of self-avowed 'postmodernists'. But the more partisan or self-isolating exponents of these tendencies notwithstanding, the most notable characteristic of this new period was the intermixing of standpoints: it was patently possible now to be both a social historian and a cultural historian, to combine the history of ideas with careful forms of contextualization, and to take the measure of contemporary culturalist critiques without entirely vacating the ground of structural or materialist investigation. Some proponents of a 'non-materialist' or 'linguistic' history might insist on the exclusivity of their approach, but such advocacy neither possessed some undisputed or universally acknowledged epistemological authority nor adequately described the continuing diversity of historiographical practices in and beyond the discipline.

Once this diversity is recognized, the continuing relevance of the Marxist historiography of the 1950s and 1960s should be secure. To make this point, it is worth returning to one of the programmatic statements of that period, which came in 1971 at the end of the forging time described above and at the cusp of the great social history wave by that time already under way. In a much-cited benchmark essay entitled 'From Social History to the History of Society', Hobsbawm argued that the real importance of the emergent approaches was less the advocacy of previously unrecognized subjects than the new possibilities for writing the history of society as a whole. This entailed partly the commitment to generalization and theory, to ways of keeping the overall picture in view, and partly analytical approaches aimed at situating all problems in their societal context. Certainly, for Hobsbawm social causes possessed primacy. But taking seriously the tasks of social significance entails no necessary commitment to materialism of such a foundational kind.[30]

At the same time, the earlier totalizing ambition – the goal of writing the history of whole societies in some integral or articulated way – has gone definitely into recession. That macro-historical understanding of whole societies changing across time evinced by the founders of *Past and Present*, guided by a confident knowledge of developmental or structural models drawn from the social sciences, has become much harder to sustain. 'Society', as a confident materialist projection of social totality in that way, has become much harder to find, because the anti-reductionist pressure of contemporary social and cultural theory since the 1980s has radically de-authorized it. Originally, that anti-reductionist logic was very empowering. As the hold of the economy became loosened during the 1980s, and with it the determinative power of the social structure and its causal claims, the imaginative and epistemological space for other kinds of analysis grew. The rich multiplication of new cultural histories became the invaluable pay-off.[31] Now that much of the heat and noise surrounding the new cultural history has started to die down, and the more extreme anxieties accompanying the so-called 'linguistic turn' seem to have been allayed, it may be easier to reclaim social history in the main sense advocated by Hobsbawm and his contemporaries, which involves always trying to relate our particular subjects, complexly and subtly, to the bigger picture of society in general. Once that happens, the Marxist historiography discussed in this chapter will remain an invaluable resource.

Guide to further reading

Gerald Allan Cohen, *Karl Marx's Theory of History: A Defence* (Oxford, 1978).

Dennis Dworkin, *Cultural Marxism in Postwar Britain: History, the New Left, and the Origins of Cultural Studies* (Durham, NC, 1997).

Dick Geary, 'Karl Kautsky and "Scientific Marxism"', *Radical Science Journal*, 11 (1981), pp. 130–5.

Eric J. Hobsbawm (ed.), *The History of Marxism*, Vol. 1, *Marxism in Marx's Day* (Bloomington, 1982).

Gregor McLennan, *Marxism and the Methodologies of History* (London, 1981).

S. H. Rigby, *Marxism and History. A Critical Introduction*, 2nd edition (Manchester, 1998).

Raphael Samuel, 'British Marxist Historians, 1880–1980: Part One', *New Left Review*, 120 (March–April 1980), pp. 21–96.

John Seed, 'Marxist Interpretation of History', in Kelly Boyd (ed.), *Encyclopedia of Historians and Historical Writing*, 2 (London, 1999), pp. 772–8.

Notes

1 Karl Marx, 'Preface' to *A Contribution to the Critique of Political Economy* (1859), in Marx, *Early Writings*, ed. Lucio Colletti (Harmondsworth, 1975), p. 425; Friedrich Engels to Joseph Bloch, 21–22 September 1890, in Marx and Engels, *Selected Correspondence* (Moscow, 1965), p. 417.

2 Karl Marx, *Capital: A Critique of Political Economy*, Vol. 1, ed. David Fernbach (Harmondsworth, 1974). The discussion of primitive accumulation can be found in Chapters 26–33; the transition from manufacture to industry in Chapters 14–15; the struggle over the working day in Chapter 10.

3 Perry Anderson, *Considerations on Western Marxism* (London, 1976), p. 6.

4 Karl Marx and Friedrich Engels, *The Communist Manifesto. A Modern Edition*, with an introduction by Eric Hobsbawm (London, 1998), p. 35.

5 For the *Annales* school, see the chapter by Matthias Middell (Chapter 6).

6 See esp. G. D. H. Cole and Raymond Postgate, *The Common People, 1746–1938* (London, 1938); see generally David Sutton, 'Radical Liberalism, Fabianism, and Social History', in Richard Johnson, Gregor McLennan, Bill Schwarz and David Sutton (eds), *Making Histories: Studies in History-Writing and Politics* (London, 1982), pp. 15–43.

7 Anthony Brundage, *The People's Historian: John Richard Green and the Writing of History in Victorian England* (Westport, CT, 1994).

8 Sandra Holton, 'Gender Difference, National Identity and Professing History: The Case of Alice Stopford Green', *History Workshop Journal* 53 (2002), pp. 118–27; Harvey J. Kaye, 'Our Island Story Retold: A. L. Morton and "The People" in History', in *The Education of Desire: Marxists and the Writing of History* (New York, 1992), pp. 116–24

9 Stuart Macintyre, *A Proletarian Science. Marxism in Britain 1917–1933* (Cambridge, 1980), pp. 129–32.

10 The first quotation is from an article by Mark Starr on 'The History of History and its Uses' in the April 1926 issue of *Plebs*; the second is from an interview with an 80-year-old ex-miner named Dai Davies. See Ruskin History Workshop Students Collective, 'Worker-Historians in the 1920s', in Raphael Samuel (ed.), *People's History and Socialist Theory* (London, 1981), pp. 17, 16; John S. Clarke, *Marxism and History* (London, 1927). Clarke was a Scottish autodidact Marxist active in the NCLC movement.

11 Peter Beilharz, 'Trotsky as Historian', *History Workshop Journal* 20 (1985), p. 50.

12 Gareth Williams, *Writers of Wales: George Ewart Evans* (Cardiff, 1991).

13 See especially the testimony of Eric Hobsbawm, 'British History and the *Annales*: A Note', in *On History* (New York, 1997), pp. 178–85, and 'Marx and History', ibid, p. 187.

14 See here the reflections of a Marxist member of the *Annales* school, Pierre Vilar, 'Marxist History, a History in the Making: Towards a Dialogue with Althusser', *New Left Review* 80 (1973), pp. 65–106.

15 See Adrian Wilson, 'A Critical Portrait of Social History', in Wilson (ed.), *Rethinking Social History: English Society 1570–1920 and its Interpretation* (Manchester, 1993), pp. 1–24, and Miles Taylor, 'The Beginnings of Modern British Social History?', *History Workshop Journal* 43 (1997), pp. 155–76.

16 Eric Hobsbawm, 'The Historians' Group of the Communist Party', in Maurice Cornforth (ed.), *Rebels and Their Causes: Essays in Honour of A. L. Morton* (London, 1979), pp. 21–47; Bill Schwarz, '"The People" in History: The Communist Party Historians' Group, 1946–56', in Johnson et al. (eds), *Making Histories*, pp. 44–95; David Parker, 'The Communist Party and its Historians 1946–89', *Socialist History*, 12 (1997), pp. 33–58; Harvey J. Kaye, *The British Marxist Historians: An Introductory Analysis* (Cambridge, 1984). For Dona Torr, see David Renton, 'Opening the Books: The Personal Papers of Dona Torr', *History Workshop Journal*, 52 (Autumn 2001), pp. 236–45.

17 Edward Thompson, 'The Peculiarities of the English', in *The Poverty of Theory and Other Essays* (London, 1978), pp. 35–91; Perry Anderson, 'Origins of the Present Crisis', *New Left Review* 23 (1964), pp. 26–54; Tom Nairn, 'The English Working Class', *New Left Review* 24 (1964), pp. 45–57; Tom Nairn, 'The Anatomy of the Labour Party', *New Left Review* 27 (1964), pp. 38–65, and 28 (1964), pp. 33–62; Perry Anderson, 'The Myths of Edward Thompson, or Socialism and Pseudo-Empiricism', *New Left Review* 35 (1966), pp. 2–42.

18 The best introduction is through Raymond Williams, *Politics and Letters: Interviews with New Left Review* (London, 1979).

19 Arthur J. Taylor (ed.), *The Standard of Living in Britain in the Industrial Revolution* (London, 1975).

20 Anne Summers, 'Thomas Hodgkin (1910–1982)', *History Workshop Journal* 14 (1982), pp. 180–2.

21 See Christopher Hill, Rodney Hilton and Eric Hobsbawm, 'Past and Present: Origins and Early Years', *Past and Present*, 100 (1983), pp. 3–14.

22 Trevor Aston (ed.), *Crisis in Europe, 1560–1660* (London, 1965), p. 5.

23 See John H. Elliott, 'The Decline of Spain', *Past and Present* 20 (1961), pp. 52–75. For the subsequent course of the general debate, see Geoffrey Parker and Lesley M. Smith (eds), *The General Crisis of the 17th Century* (London, 1978).

24 See esp. Philip Abrams, *Historical Sociology* (Ithaca, 1982).

25 Worsley's first book was *The Trumpet Shall Sound: A Study of 'Cargo' Cults in Melanesia* (London, 1957), in some ways a parallel text to Hobsbawm's *Primitive Rebels.* He then published *The Third World* (London, 1964), followed two decades later by *The Three Worlds: Culture*

and *Development* (London, 1984), together with a wide variety of other publications, including *Marx and Marxism* (London, 1982). He held the Chair of Sociology at Manchester since 1964 and was President of the British Sociological Association in 1971–4.

26 Stuart Hall, 'Raphael Samuel 1934–96', *New Left Review*, 221 (1997), pp. 119–27, and Sheila Rowbotham, 'Some Memories of Raphael', ibid., pp. 128–32.

27 See Sheila Rowbotham, *Resistance and Revolution* (Harmondsworth, 1972), *Hidden from History: 300 Years of Women's Oppression and the Fight Against It* (London, 1973), and *Women's Consciousness, Man's World* (Harmondsworth, 1973).

28 Geoff Eley, 'Labor History, Social History, *Alltagsgeschichte*: Experience, Culture, and the Politics of the Everyday – A New Direction for German Social History?', *Journal of Modern History* 61 (1989), pp. 297–343; Alf Lüdtke (ed.), *The History of Everyday Life: Reconstructing Historical Experiences and Ways of Life* (Princeton, 1995).

29 Gareth Stedman Jones, 'Introduction' and 'Rethinking Chartism', in *Languages of Class: Studies in English Working-Class History, 1832–1982* (Cambridge, 1983), pp. 1–24 and 90–178.

30 Eric J. Hobsbawm, 'From Social History to the History of Society', *Daedalus*, 100 (1971), pp. 20–45.

31 For these intellectual histories, see Geoff Eley, 'Is All the World a Text? From Social History to the History of Society Two Decades Later', in Terrence J. McDonald (ed.), *The Historic Turn in the Human Sciences* (Ann Arbor, 1996), pp. 193–243, and 'Between Social History and Cultural Studies: Interdisciplinarity and the Practice of the Historian at the End of the 20th century', in Joep Leerssen and Ann Rigney (eds), *Historians and Social Values* (Amsterdam, 2000), pp. 93–109.

5

History and the social sciences

John Harvey

The writing of history can be frustratingly difficult to define within coherent boundaries. By encompassing the past activity of all mankind, the relationship of historiography to its neighboring social sciences, even if limited only to modern academic research in Europe and North America, is a topic of intimidating complexity and scope. With this caveat, the contours of the impact of the social sciences on modern historiography may be revealed with a focus on the development of basic paradigms of social thought, and how formal professional historians interpreted them since the 19th century. As the academic social sciences first developed, historians were challenged to open avenues of intellectual exchange with a vast array of economists, political theorists, human geographers, as well as leaders in anthropology, psychology, sociology and related ethnographic fields. In considerations of limitations of space, this survey will treat professional historical writing with an emphasis on the four national cases of Britain, France, Germany and the United States. With acknowledgement to nuances and cross-currents of development, each case can be considered emblematic of problems that defined the overall integration of social theory with historiography in specific sites of debate.

The parameters of these four national cases, in concert with complementary chapters of this volume, will suggest two threads that have reappeared throughout discussion about the Western legacy of interdisciplinarity. Because the social sciences considered themselves to be objective fields of knowledge with practical, if not predictive, application to the present, the health of interdisciplinarity became wedded to a faith in scientific objectivity and the validation of empirical proof. Since this foundation was questioned under postmodernism, the achievements between Clio and the classic social sciences over much of the 20th century have met with increasing skepticism. To be sure, many new alternatives have been broached. But as opposed to the height of interdisciplinary research in the 1970s, there is far less confidence now in the promise of social theory to enlighten the public about the past and its relationship to the present through a unified body of research. A second theme asks to what extent historians have been influenced by the methodologies or subject matter of social scientists, rather than their actual ideas about the behavior of people, either in communities or as an individual psyche. Research agendas and questions of method are not to be dismissed in any discussion of historiography. Still, it is important to ask to what extent historians divided the issue of methods artificially from the theories of scholars that violated their conceptual intent.

5.1 Enlightenment, science, and historicism

What exactly should we label as "social science," as opposed to "history"? The modern social sciences basically developed from the middle of the 19th century as a conceptual response to the challenges of urbanization, industrialization, and a maturing international capitalist economy. Their institutionalization into disciplines, however, was also the product of the modern university. States supported these permanent centers of thought for the training of expertise that was needed for the burgeoning responsibilities of modern bureaucracies. But if the social sciences had a common intellectual spinal cord, it grew from the heritage of the Enlightenment. With recognition of their inconsistencies, the *philosophes* sought to establish the investigation of the natural and social world through reason and the persuasion of factual evidence rather than explanatory traditions of theology or hierarchical orders of authority.[1] "Theories" of deductive logic were required to frame new questions about how society operated, and the results of inductive research were expected to verify the most authentic patterns of behavior. Once established, these "laws" were considered universal to all types of people, meaning they could be applied to resolve current conflicts. While each social theorist did not fit an exact template, either in comparison to their contemporary scholars or to the Enlightenment project, many of the most important future theorists accepted these postulates. The Enlightenment thus bequeathed a faith in the universality of reason and in the compatibility of theory with empirical proof. And its advocates expected that the cumulative application of knowledge would enable mankind to progress towards a better, beloved community once it was aware of the inner nature of its behavior.

Historical research as a professional activity, however, did not emerge solely from this inheritance. Academic history developed under the guise of a unique method of researching the past. As practiced by critical readers of theology and law, and as perfected by Leopold von Ranke, academic history accepted the imperative for empirical research as evidence of expertise.[2] It adopted a related belief in the open communication of results through a discourse that rested on reason. But professional historians also distanced themselves from the classic social sciences through the ideal of "historicism" and the cohabitation of professional historiography with amateur literature. Interdisciplinary learning from the social sciences has sought to address these factors, but it never overcame them.

Briefly summarized, historicism developed from the late 18th century as a wide-ranging interpretation that the past, or even present-day phenomena, could only be understood through the context of specific historical conditions of time, place, and circumstance as they unfolded in a chronological manner.[3] Scholars trained in the critical reading of texts contended that the exact evidence of primary sources, found chiefly though public documents, were the principal traces of what individuals had accomplished, intended, or thought about in the past. As such, unmistakable evidence would demonstrate the individuality of the research topic in question, as conditions would constantly change for each subject according to place and time. Ideals of "natural Law" as predictable social behavior were invalidated, either as mere philosophy or unhistorical reductionist dogma. Because historicism emphasized the rigorous method of documented research, historians could still consider themselves enlightened scientists. But because this methodology was deeply resistant to social theory, its practitioners tended to marginalize the writing of social history. They approached the field as the study of individuals who rarely became more than the sum of their parts. In return, social theorists were mutually hostile to historicism, because its focus on the unique avoided questions of comparison, or of any wider significance for research about the past beyond the specific case under study. It had little practical utility to the present, and the reliance on public documents inevitably placed academic historians – who were after all employed by the state – beholden to the political agenda of the government that guarded the archives.[4] It was not surprising then that historians of the 19th century who opposed "reductionist" social theory in fact elided their own nationalist ideology that celebrated their respective states and the relative conservatism of government leaders.

The second main tension was with amateur historians who were independent of any institutional training or support of national research centers. Their challenge for both historicism and the social sciences rested with their freedom of authorship and the undeniable popularity of their works. Popular history often wrote with a romantic, or nostalgic, view of the past. The narrative was the primary format for an engaging story that met public expectations about historical knowledge through the simplification of issues and an often obsequious delineation of "heroes" or "villains" who were personal or social.[5] If they were deaf to social theory or the rigors of historicist method, their power seemed to reside in a creative imagination of the past, which emplotted social experience through a narrative considered holistic and tasteful to the public.[6] Whether professional historians either remained wedded to Rankean method or were tempted to the promise of social science theory, over time there remained a continued lack of confidence that formal academic research could in fact compete with the influence of amateur popular history. The popularity of amateur history struck at the very heart of the social role that historians and social scientists had claimed as inheritors of Enlightenment expertise.[7]

5.2 Positivism

What, then, did the social sciences have to offer a historical discipline that was constructing its own "scientific" identity by the middle of the 19th century? The closest "cornerstone" to modern social science is the "positivist" theories of the French philosopher Auguste Comte.[8] Comte's importance among historians was in his promotion of historical knowledge as the product of a systematic science and an evolutionary process, rather than in the reception of specific ideas of his social philosophy. Reduced to a sketch, Comte proposed that civilizations were evolving towards a more intelligent, prosperous, and peaceful future based on the application of rational knowledge. European communities passed from a theological phase in which Christian doctrine explained the natural and social worlds. The Enlightenment liberated intelligent minds to replace dogmatic theology with a new metaphysics of rationalism and universal rights. By his own era of the 1840s, Europe was entering a final stage of "positive knowledge." Comte believed that exact science and reason would enable humanity to resolve all social challenges through empirical research, and thus bestow greater individual freedom to the learned public. Comte was never precise about how people would rationally accept proper knowledge.

As wars have since shown, his expectation that discoveries in the natural and behavioral sciences would be used for the universal betterment of mankind was naïve. But scholars were far more interested in the methodological linkage of positivist validity with a grand evolutionary perspective on social development. On the one level, such a meta-narrative could reveal the wider universal meaning that Rankean method lacked, particularly if embedded in a track of western progress. Predictive law drawn from empirical study could make historians more useful to agents beyond the monarchical status quo. And its allegiance to evolutionary progress, empiricism, and synthetic reason offered the promise of a better society through the application of objective science that was executed "above the masses." It offered an implicitly powerful alternative to the "utopian socialists" or Marxist science that threatened to overthrow the beneficent care of scientific-bourgeois leadership to achieve a paradise of material equality.

5.3 Social theory and history: British limitations

Positivism would have a varied impact on different national traditions across Europe and the United States. But a review of the social sciences and historical writing in Britain offers the best example of how its theoretical framework could have limited influence during the century after its declaration. If "positive knowledge" about society could indicate proscriptive regularities, then historians searching for comparable social relevance would need to adopt positivist laws into grand evolutionary history. This was exactly the program of Henry Buckle, an "amateur" historian who published his *History of Civilization in England* in 1857, soon after the appearance of Comte's volumes. Buckle posed that the English people had developed through a set of basic laws of civilization that were determined by the concrete environment of climate, foodstuffs, and the fertility of soil.[9] These "regularities" could be both measured and used to estimate the relative advancement of a civilization in comparison with others societies. By using modern science to study people, and not political elites, informed leaders could best promote national welfare within these general laws. He was hardly the sole historian to pose social progress driven by objective science and liberal values of individual merit, as François Guizot offered a comparable history of France.[10] Edward A. Freeman, Hippolyte Taine in France, and Karl Lamprecht in Germany would also attempt to establish the character of their national communities through laws of environment and nature. Even John Bagnell Bury at Cambridge would later interpret Buckle's vision through his "scientific" history of the Roman Empire, the papacy, and his cherished ideal of "progress."[11] Well into the 20th century, the philosopher Carl Hempel continued to espouse the existence of historical laws.[12]

The real importance of Buckle's project was perhaps the implications of its rejection by British historians. His countryman Lord Acton immediately published an essay that questioned the capacity of historical generalizations to be proven without a selective use of superficial evidence. More tellingly for his liberal audience, he implied that deductive laws seemed to impose limitations on the free will of any individual, thus calling into the question an emancipatory claim to Buckle's schemata of English development.[13] From Prussia, the liberal historian Johann Gustav Droysen contended that Buckle's survey was a direct assault on the methodological claims of historicism that demarcated professional historians as the qualified guardians of research on the past. Droysen emphasized that the search for universal laws would subvert the actual content of primary sources to the present-day terms of one's pre-established theories. He demanded instead that historians must discipline themselves to adopt an empathetic understanding (*Verstehen*) of the past in its own context, without judgment, and to avoid a fruitless search for causal explanations.[14] As the historical theorist Robin Collingwood proposed, one could encounter the past by reenacting it in one's own mind, as informed by evidence and the author's imagination.[15]

The debate in Britain played out on several levels. Until well into the 20th century, historians at the principal universities of Oxford and Cambridge believed that their institutional responsibility was to train the young English elite for national duty. Sentiments of honor and masculine confidence were deemed more important than either the minutiae of bureaucratic expertise or a synthetic design of social history. The function of historical training was merely to imbibe the student with a sense, rather than any type of critical comparison about the nature or evolution of their social position. In an atmosphere of patrician education and the demands of imperial service, historians considered engaging style and evidence of wide readership, as the best demonstration of scholarship and values of teaching. Professors who were interested in social history turned to write on the level of the "amateur" scholars by proclaiming the history of the British people to be a triumph of their national exceptionalism and the soundness of liberal social achievement.[16] Conservative historians renounced any need for social theory by presenting an image of pre-industrial England as a happy community unsoiled by the pains of modern industrialization.[17]

Under such circumstances, the challenge to narrow historicism only arose with the belated push for the "professionalization" of historical research in competition with foreign universities, and in the more critical demands to direct historical research in response to the growing social problems of modern industrialization. Yet university historians continued to neglect social theory until after the Second World War, and the status of social science research remained uneven. From the 19th century, academic scholars outside of the historicist community interpreted the study of constitutional law and political economy to be the basis of national interest. They confined interpretative theory top the expertise of jurists and the eventual introduction of more formal political science that still centered on the evolution of state policy.[18] Social theory in the realm of economics became divided into two camps. Liberal professors who held the principal chairs in political economy such as William Ashley or John Clapham emulated the historicist method pioneered by the German economic historian Gustav von Schmoller. Inductive research would reveal the development of economic policy or its impact on the market under certain circumstances. Elsewhere, the economic theories of David Ricardo were widely used to defend the autonomy of capitalism from dramatic social reform, and to promote the benefits of a "neomercantilist" imperial policy.[19] The response to social history thus fell to historians outside of the main educational system, such as the Hammonds and Webbs, who studied the industrial revolution as a reformist warning for the introduction of social welfare program and poverty relief. Although their histories centered on actual people rather than state policy, there was in fact practically no utilization of social theory to explain the nexus of urbanization and society in any abstract sense. The sympathies of the Fabian Society altered the focus of historicism, but the method remained intact.[20]

The marginalization of positivism and social theory in Britain until the 20th century brought three basic results. First, sociology was unable to establish itself as a university discipline until the interwar era, and it only gained real academic influence after the Second World War. Liberal academicians embraced empiricism and a moral idealism. But they resisted positivist or Marxist theory out of a fear either of its support of dramatic social upheaval, or because "theoretical structures" were considered incompatible with the complexities that rapid urbanization was imprinting on social values and material life. Lacking institutional support, social theory extended only to vague hopes of transcendent progress and a promise that practical results could be culled inevitably from empirical data.[21]

That conceptual vacuum was filled by the explosion of research on evolution following its promulgation under Charles Darwin in 1859. Darwinian thought seemed a greater promise than positivism to many in Britain. As with Comte, evolution proposed a grand theory of progress, which defined the advancement of organisms from the most simple to the more complex. Its scientific pretenses were more imposing than those of previous philosophies, as physical evidence was rapidly emerging from across the world. But most importantly for historians, Darwinian evolution addressed the issue of change and time across the ages, through the theory of natural selection and the impact of inherited mutation. For theorists at the height of the Victorian empire, the logic of Darwinian evolution seemed to validate claims of ethno-racial inequality into hard biological fact. Even if never intended by Darwin himself, evolutionary theory found a widening audience among historians and social scientists because it seemed to legitimize the claims of "natural" leadership on the path to modernity by many Europeans and (white) Americans.

Herbert Spencer's organic theory of sociology was particularly influential, less for his oft-quoted "survival of the fittest", than his evolutionary model of organic growth, followed by differentiation, a period of disequilibrium or adaptation, and finally disintegration.[22] Spencer's organic theory suggested that communities would encounter daunting pressures from rapid growth, as industrialization seemed to indicate, which would necessitate social selection or adaptation under de-centralized authority. Rather than adopting social theory to explain categories of communal conflict in urban areas, theorists like Leonard Hobhouse were content with evolutionary assumptions of progress led by individual efforts to adapt, or to the collective cooperation of independent citizens.[23] In practice, strands of evolutionary biological were integrated by scholars such as E. A. Freeman into comparative studies that emphasized the racial inequality of societies, or organic theory was deployed in the popular works of J. R. Green to explain the ancient "germ" of Germanic ethnic achievement that was rooted in English self-identity.[24] When social theory finally achieved its conceptual breakthrough from the 1950s, its basis became Marxist interpretations of class consciousness, as treated elsewhere in this volume.

5.4 *Staatswissenschaften* and Max Weber

The intellectual atmosphere in German-speaking central Europe was comparable to the British experience in several notable ways. In both cases professional history developed through a rather rigid adherence to historicism, in part out of sensitivity to competition from popular history or the grand evolutionary designs of philosophical thought, whether it was Hegelian or liberal. The dominance of historicism tended to make German academic historiography methodologically rigid. Historians generally rejected methods of comparison, abstract models, and a focus on collective society, all of which were the central tenets of the emerging social sciences. Concentration on the formal state was reified into an almost mystical faith, to be reinforced by the ministries that funded research in the expectation that writing and teaching would reinforce political loyalty to the monarchical authorities.[25] In the face of social unrest from the 1830s to the First World War, historians nestled themselves in state archives as the legitimizing site for a past conceived through the state, individual elites, or of Christian denominational thought (which would support either Protestant or Catholic state authority.)[26]

The unification of the German Empire in 1871 imposed a new national role onto German historicism. Scholars employed history to justify the inevitability of a common national identity loyal to the federation crafted under Bismarck, despite the wake of lingering Catholic-Protestant tension.[27] And the anti-revolutionary stance of historical writing need to be intensified against a growing socialist presence, even as it began to promote a greater ethnic intolerance against "non-Germanic" people who inhabited the empire's greater European or global expanse. As with the case of Buckle, central European historians encountered a quixotic attempt by their colleague Karl Lamprecht to create a vast evolutionary synthesis of German history, grounded in a cumbersome application of regional geography, Comtean positivism, and nostalgic appeal to an organic "national soul" (*Volksseele*).[28]

Lamprecht's failure to secure a professional following revealed the depth of fear in the German historical guild for a redirection of research from the state or elites to society, particularly if synthesis was to be guided by abstract historical laws and a quasi-romantic collective psychology. But it also revealed how the discipline's refusal to embrace forms of social history with moderate interdisciplinary experimentation could lead to the exploitation of intolerant nationalist sentiment as a blanket mechanism for producing general syntheses that the public and governing authorities clearly desired. As with the case of elements of British historiography, Germans increasingly began to interweave ethno-biological nationalism into their studies. After the disaster of the First World War, conservatives began to embrace a chauvinistic form of *Volksgeschichte* (history of the national people) that was deeply imbricated with a racial characterization of societies and a justification of conquest or even genocide as the destiny of a "strongest" national Volk. Such thinking lent eventual support for the agencies of population control and foreign policy under the National Socialist state.[29]

As with the example of Britain, German universities were compelled to address "the social question" once industrialization inevitably increased the intensity of class conflict and brought new political pressures to bear on the monarchical administration. The response was to expand research within the "sciences of the state" (*Staatswissenschaften*) from its 17th-century origins of state cameralism to include geography, political economy, anthropology and varied forms of early sociology.[30] Though he was denied a professor's chair until just before 1914, Georg Simmel was a leader of social thought who authored influential studies on the modern city, the mentality of money as a means-ends relationship, and the nature of sociability as a pattern of free association adopted for participation in symbolic affiliation.[31] The nature of capitalism captured a great deal of attention, both as a response to Marxism and as means to inform public or commercial policy. Its ambivalence was personified in the form of the economist Werner Sombart, who pleaded for historians to appreciate the value of abstract theory, even as his own history of capitalism identified its origins with a distinctive characterization of European Jews.[32]

By the 20th century, a group of social scientists formed an Association for Social Politics (*Verein für Sozialpolitik*) that would use interdisciplinary research to promote public policy intended to empower limited government reforms for the working class. Some of these *Kathedersozialisten* (socialists of the academic chair) employed abstract economic models in their studies or recommendations. But the influence of historicism remained pronounced under its leadership of Lujo Bretano and Gustav von Schmoller. Schmoller especially posed the research of economics and society through the historical details of his heavily empirical research, especially as his work gave heavy support to nationalist claims for imperial expansion (*Weltpolitik*).[33] Scholars from the historical discipline embraced the results and method of Schmoller's school, because it did not threaten the guild with the abstract models of Simmel, the narrow expertise of the individual social sciences, or the reformist overtones of the center-left.

The German social theorist of greatest influence certainly was the historian and sociologist Max Weber. His importance would merit a chapter itself. But historians were most influenced by his methodological concept for studying society through an emphasis on ideal types. Weber believed that analytical categories, such as "Protestantism" or "capitalism," needed to be studied as abstract concepts in order to sharpen theoretical questions for later testing by historical research. The construction of "ideal types" could be pursued across disciplinary and national boundaries as a near science, as long as researchers adopted Weber's conception of objectivity. Scholars would admit their subjective viewpoints, but make every conscious effort to foreclose the insertion of these sentiments in their analysis.[34] These methodological propositions resonated in the American historical and social science communities after the Second World War, as scholars were searching for a "middle ground" between absolute relativity and obsolescent claims of pure scientific empiricism.[35] The focus on ideal types and a "history of concepts" (*Begriffsgeschichte*) also seemed a more promising path to invigorate the interdisciplinary study of topics, because the crux of Weber's method sought to limit sociological questions around specific concepts, rather than a presumption of scientific laws or totalitizing evolutionary mechanisms.[36] During his own lifetime, Weber's concepts were taken up by the Berlin historian Otto Hintze to expand the range of German historiography (in moderation) by promulgating transnational comparison and the adoption of analytical categories as a means of understanding the development of government types across regions and time.[37]

The degree to which historians adopted actual social theories purported by Weber was more uneven. Weber's early history of the rise of capitalism through the Calvinist mindset, allegedly freed from Catholic economic structures, met with significant interest in Protestant countries that were sympathetic to equating their denominational heritage with a positive idea of modernity.[38] His concepts of "charismatic leadership" and the "patrimonial state" remain vibrant concepts for the writing of biography and political history.[39] But although Weber shared the historicist dislike for positivist laws and evolutionary schemes, his own analysis of capitalism led to a predictive, developmental idealization of modern society. Weber believed that capitalism propelled an "instrumental rationality" of all industrializing communities and government. The nature of the free market engendered processes of efficiency that would permeate all aspects of everyday contractual relationships. The state would follow, as capitalism demanded the bureaucratic regulation of law. This would lead in the end to the secularization of life, and the steady equalization of social status under a rationalized, technocratic society and state.[40] Weber believed that the "disenchantment" of society would bring about greater material wealth or even political-legal freedoms. He feared the splintering of society into autonomous individuals, adrift from common values that he considered essential to the meaningful health of communities.[41] His pessimistic view of a torpid, rationalized modernity reflected the degree to which most of the 19th-century social theorists considered "mass society" as an alarming threat to liberal identity.

5. 5 Durkheim and structural sociology

The relationship between the social sciences and formal historical research was perhaps the most contentious in France, where a very centralized and hierarchical educational system heightened the potential stakes for disciplinary competition.

From 1900 until well into the 1970s, academic advocates of quantitative studies (such as price history) or the history of society based on conceptual structures proposed normative standards of "proper" modern research against traditions of historicism. Within this contest of historiography, the discipline of sociology was especially influential due to its positivist goals and its ideal of theory that explained the totality of human behavior. French theory in sociology perceived development though long-term patterns of communal interaction and holistic value systems, which all would be manifested in empirical evidence beyond the conventional documentation of historicism. Intellectual cooperation, however, was limited to a certain extent by the institutional competition between disciplines or schools of research that pursued limited state funding and official recognition within the national curriculum.[42] When Emile Durkheim propounded his vision of sociology in programmatic statements and his review *Année Sociologique* [Sociological Yearbook], he attacked historicism as a fundamentally inadequate means to explain factors that underlay social development. Far more than social scientists in other states, he concluded that historians were too presentist, and thus unscientific, and fixated on individual causes. They studied surface-level events instead of collective attitudes that were represented in symbolic acts. If they dared to compare their research at all, it was done without rigorous analytical categories or classification.[43] The entire discipline of history thus was useful only to supply data for sociologists, so they could test their more conceptual and systematic hypotheses.

Durkheim launched this offensive at the time that French historical writing had developed an identity attached to historicist methodology similar to counterparts in Germany and Britain. The debate found its sharpest expression between François Simiand, an avid student of Durkheim's circle, and the liberal-republican professor for modern history at the University of Paris, Charles Seignobos. Simiand claimed in 1903 that historians in general suffered under their worship of three mythical idols: 1) a commitment to superficial chronology and the origin of events as a yardstick for human development; 2) an exclusive focus on politics to the detriment of society; 3) and a belief that communities comprised autonomous individuals, rather than collective attitudes or common conditioning factors. While the argument was joined by numerous professors over a period of years, Seignobos led the defense by questioning the degree to which the social sciences could in fact be objective and comprehensive in its conclusions about human behavior. Speaking for many of his era, he believed that comparisons, while of some value, were often based more on analogies than verifiable measurements. And he concluded that only direct, consciously-derived statements from an individual source could be accepted as valid evidence to what people had accomplished or considered from the past.[44] Social history thus could well be written without the use of social theory.

In a period of European history marked by anxiety over the pathologies of modern industrialization, interdisciplinary exchange was not a straightforward appropriation of ideas for the benefit of democratic ideals. Durkheim's most influential work, *The Division of Labor in Society*, borrowed from Herbert Spencer by emphasizing that the pressures of adjustment within complex societies would weaken social norms, thereby eroding the confidence of individuals in collective values that guided life. Durkheim called this process *anomie*, or the harmful collapse of communal traditions broken by consumerism, urbanization, secularization, and large-scale capitalism.[45] He believed that associations which had formed networks of meaning, such as religious denominations, extended families, or the ancient guilds all had been worn away by the modern money economy.[46] Although wages might prove more efficient for commercial growth, mere payment failed to confer broader social recognition for one's place in a society. The corrosive effect of "anomie," could only be ameliorated by reviving new, small-scale personalized associations of labor or familial networks to address the confusion of atomized "masses." Modern materialism could not address this collapse in values, whether promised by a workers' state or a capitalist economy.

Durkheim's evolutionist program from simple to complex communities was mirrored by other leading sociological figures both within and outside of France. The esteemed ethnologist Lucien Lévi-Bruhl and the Durkheimian Marcel Mauss both produced major works that defined earlier societies through a "primitive mentality" that was resistant to modern ideas of logic or empirical reasoning. By different routes, each concluded that the values of an affective "ancient" people were incompatible with rational Western modernity, which would by extension be distinct from more "primitive" non-European societies in the 20th century.[47] As noted, in Germany a concern with the effect of industrialization helped to nurture a similar bifurcation of modern mankind into idealized "organic" communities and the unstable centers of urbanized "masses." The sociologist Ferdinand Tönnies became the most recognized German-speaking theorist to claim that European social bonds had degenerated from the tightly-knit organic community (*Gemeinschaft*) of the small village, to the mechanical consumerism of urban life (*Gesellschaft*). In either national case, modern culture was cast as a cacophony of self-interested voices that threatened a tireless conflict between rival interests and economic classes which a contractual-based society could not alleviate.

The overall influence of Durkheimian social theory is more difficult to measure within the historical profession. As with the case of German social science, methodological paradigms could be appropriated without a necessary acceptance of organic and evolutionary theory. As noted in this volume, the founding generation of the *Annales* attempted to copy the scientific direction of Durkheim's "team" by calling for historians to define analytical terms such as "civilization," partly by considering more rigorous conceptual taxonomies, and partly though a somewhat complacent faith in quantitative research.[48] They echoed his call for the study of collective behavior based on the analysis of communal relationships through relationships considered as "social facts." Students of medieval and early-modern history turned to investigate societies as entities that shared common unconscious attitudes, fashioned and reinforced through public symbols or the practices of religion. Marc Bloch famously interpreted some aspects of Durkheim's emphasis on public symbol as a form of "collective representation" in his work *The Royal Touch*. In other works, he sought to determine the stabilizing coherence of the historical peasantry in comparative studies of French rural life. In America, Alan Bogue proposed that communal representation was a myth of individual independence that historians had traditionally used to define "frontier life." Elinor Barbour distilled sociological notions of religious instinct and anomie in the bourgeoisie of 18th-century in France.[49] Others leaders in the discipline, such as Charles Tilly or David Potter, crafted major interpretations to test the evolutionary concepts of Durkheim and its fear of consumerism on social structures.[50] Historians also drew from individuals closely associated with Durkheimian theories of "collective emblems," but who were less concerned with its evolutionist underpinnings. Perhaps the best example was Maurice Halbwachs, who established much of the theoretical framework on memory as a collective construction of socially-constituted symbols, as opposed to individual perception, Freudian dreams, or an independently objective past.[51]

And yet, a closer examination of Durkheim's actual legacy suggests more ambivalence regarding his specific theories of social behavior. The works cited above employed only elements of sociological concepts, with a notable reluctance to embrace theory to interpret the 'totality" of historical subject matter. A scholar dedicated to interdisciplinary exchange such as Henri Berr, who supported the interest of social history and the utility of scientific hypotheses, could still chide his colleagues that such theory was asserted beyond what empirical research had achieved.[52] More importantly, Durkheim's pessimistic regard for the contractual basis of modern society could lend its influence to historians with conservative views about the pluralism of social values in a healthy modern democracy. By the 1930s, legal and historical writers had begun to explore the revival of ancient "communities" and autonomous vocational associations into a new" corporate" order, which would clearly subvert parliamentary forms of democracy, traditions of natural law, and an open, contractual form of commerce. Various European scholars applied Durkheim and Tönnies to their designs in the "revolutions" of a directed economy in Vichy France, fascist Italy, and the Iberian Peninsula.[53]

After 1945, Louis Chevalier applied Durkheimian theory of social degeneration to his study of peasant migration into Paris. Disassociated from more stable communal customs of the small village, they became "dangerous classes," prone to crime and political upheaval during of crisis. Such a view was meant to explain the apparent inability of the French state to stabilize social-political authority after the 18th century.[54] In the United States, the historian Stanley Elkins employed Durkheim's *anomie* in a comparative study to explain an alleged passivity of African-American slaves in the South by stressing the malleability of their collective will under the plantation system.[55] Of course, Durkheim and his French associates were clearly oriented towards the left in contemporary national politics.[56] However, the negative connotation of modernity with a dissonance of social values lent the school's specific concepts to be used by conservative, as well as progressive-minded historians in Europe up to the 1960s. None other than George Lefebvre, the great historian and admirer of the French Revolution, concluded that the dismissal by the "Durkheimians" of individual agency or a people's capacity to overcome the boundaries of collective mentality was similar to the views of political reactionaries since 1789. Social theory could serve as an unintended intellectual barrier to the potential of social emancipation in the present.[57]

5.6 The new history and social theory in America

In contrast to the European experience, before 1914 the American historical profession offered a somewhat more open attitude towards experimentation in academic historiography. The "New Historians" challenged complacent assumptions about the exceptional greatness of their country's past by crafting their historical research to redress the national conflicts born of industrialization. As progressive-minded historians, they shared a commitment with their colleagues in the social sciences to employ research for the promotion of social reform. But the Americans also posed their research through rather undetermined notions of economic interests, along with classic methodologies of historicist empiricism and individuality as seen in England and Germany.[58] Embracing a similar evolutionary belief in liberal progress, they tended to ignore social in their calls for reform. To a "New Historian" such as James Harvey Robinson, the individul agency that was so important to modern citizenship could be threatened by the collectivist-behavioral directions of sociology or anthropology.[59] To be sure, the development of social theory in America was multifaceted and fragmented across the country's scores of research universities. It was further defined by regions and the complexities of American immigration and racial challenges. But broadly speaking, sociologists along with "outsider" specialists such as Lewis Mumford supported research that echoed the British fixation on social organic communities under the threat of the modern masses.[60] Influenced by an eclectic mix of European writings and traditions of rural nostalgia, American theorists (outside of an explicitly Christian academia) tended to emphasize that new democratic practice was the proper response to a cultural drift from the integrative village and familial networks. Voluntary associations within urbanizing areas, combined with an inclusive brand of participatory politics and the creation of some regulatory government, would engender firmer bonds of "social control" to stabilize value systems in urban settings.

Against these directions of disciplinary development, American progressive historians tended to write social history up to the Second World War in a manner comparable to the English Fabians. A progressive who sought a broad national audience such as Charles Beard tended to limit concepts to the description of economic inequality as a motive for reformist policies under the state. Unlike the European social historians, however, the Americans provoked a debate that questioned the viability of scientific objectivity between the world wars. The long discussion spurred deeper research into European methodological theory and epistemology. It promoted a more inclusive openness to contending historical methods. But in the process, progressive historians weakened their case for cooperation with the social sciences, due to the fact that neighboring disciplines were defining their own identities through a positivist commitment to empirical objectivity, the durability of social "patterns" (even if organic), and the authority of authentic scientific expertise.[61] Until the 1950s, more traditionalist historians tapped these inconsistencies to underscore their suspicion against social theory that claimed unachievable neutrality through "superficial analogies," in contrast to the artistic nature of historical interpretation.[62] Social scientists otherwise were little interested in historical relativity.

5.7 Structuralism in the French social sciences and history

By the 1950s, structural theories of society rose to great prominence in European social thought. In France, perhaps the most acclaimed structural theorist was the social anthropologist Claude Lévy-Strauss, who specialized in the study of non-western, pre-industrial peoples.[63] In works such as *The Elementary Structures of Kinship*, *The Savage Mind*, and *Structural Anthropology*, Lévy-Strauss contended that societies maintained communal bonds through the association of wider family groups, as produced through strategies such as contracted marriages. Heavily influenced by the study of linguistic systems under Ferdinand de Saussure, he suggested that the social practices of every individual or family were comparably "structured" by their unbreakable relationship to wider family networks. These values defined by communal existence far above individual actions, even of a nuclear family. Methodologically, these familial-structures were universal enough in their functional purpose so as to allow extensive cross-comparison across cultures nominally separated by geography or time.

In opposition to existentialist philosophy at its heyday in the 1950s, Lévy-Strauss considered that the social objects of historians were "structured" around these rather permanent systems of communicated values. Scholars needed to study the nature of these relationships, rather than the subject itself (a person, a village, an event or idea).[64] Believing that all of society was conditioned according to these operative relationships, structuralists were led to discount individual agency or the impact of material trends such as commerce as historical factors of study.[65] There was little use of asking about the origin of a belief, or the course of its evolution, because the very function of value systems deemed them inherent in society – one had to discover them, and not ask how they came to exist, change, or dissolve. Popular symbolic practices therefore were viewed as more indicative of culture than actions that were enacted with a conscious purpose, such as in the classic intellectual history of elites.

Because these conditioning relationships were unconscious or implicit, especially within non-literate communities, research now had to locate and interpret the nature of these structures through the non-literary "signs." Historical evidence would include ceremonies, public symbols, written or performance media, or oral stories such as myths that persevered across generations and had notably common characteristics across cultures. In the process, structuralists believed that they were offering methods for writing the history of civilizations that historians reliant on formal written evidence had otherwise ignored.

The influence of Lévi-Strauss and anthropological thought on the historiography of pre-industrial societies was substantial. Although Fernand Braudel eschewed a single paradigm of theory in the social sciences, his own concept of geographic time in the "longue durée" drew from similar interdisciplinary work that emphasized the enduring nature of social identities, and the insignificance of personal agency.[66] Anthropological theory especially influenced the study of *mentalités*, or collective attitudes, by the 1960s. As one of many examples, Georges Duby "read" the symbolic or discursive evidence preserved from the Battle of Bouvines to unlock the cultural framework of 13th-century Europe in relation to its material surrounding.[67] In order to suggest how mentalities might change, Mona Ozouf suggested that festivals during the French Revolution orchestrated symbolic language to graft new values of national citizenship onto the subconscious structure of public attitudes under the old regime.[68] Structuralists had an obvious influence in the growing history of private life and families, even if this research was also vulnerable to conservative ambivalence against modern politics and secular lifestyles.[69] But disciplinary boundaries remained. Despite these fruitful exchanges, even Fernand

Braudel feared that ethnological theory, which challenged the primacy of positivist historical epistemology, would warp the historical discipline away from its basic focus on inductive research, the significance of objective data, and attention to the ultimate reality of material life.[70]

5.8 Talcott Parsons and structural-functionalism in America

Although Continental traditions of social theory entailed analytical assumptions shared across the Channel and the Atlantic, the English-speaking academic communities became increasingly preoccupied with a form of behavioralist thought generally termed as "functionalist," or a "structural-functional model." Its nature, origins, and development were quite complex, but basic elements are reflected by the work of the Polish-born ethnographer Bronislaw Malinowski, the sociologist Talcott Parsons, and his younger colleague Robert Merton. As a concept, functionalist theory poses that the behavior of social organizations or communities is the cumulative result of the efforts of individual agents to meet their own interests. Functionalists considered societies to be a collection of heterogeneous but interdependent groups, which can be distinguished according to public responsibilities, individual identities, or their respective needs for survival. They cooperate towards a common goal, based on a consensual code of social rules and regulatory forces such as families, the market, or government, all of which act to stabilize the social system. A society of inter-connected units, which may be hierarchical or equal in status, maintains equilibrium as long as its component parts continue to function. Thus Malinowski departed from French structuralism by emphasizing an individual's capacity to shape wider cultural values according to needs that were consonant with the collective whole.[71] Behavioral systems were not imposed naturally, as Durkheim tended to suggest. They were under constant negotiation and renewal, according to the "functional" demands of individuals at a given context. Like Lévi-Strauss, Malinowski believed that people internalized habits which one could "read" as a common culture, such as a public greeting. But he considered an individual's conscious desires to be indispensible for both shaping and understanding society, and he was cool to the French notion of static cultural systems.

Among historians a much greater impact was to be made by the expansion of functionalist theory under Talcott Parsons. Parsons also believed that societies comprised the ideas and activities of individuals. He accepted that communities and social conditions shaped the choices of people in their everyday lives, based in part on the expectations that individuals might have about the reaction of others to their own behavior. His "theory of social action" accommodated some communal uniformity, because a subject's expectation was conditioned by the values or "roles" that society would legitimize over time.[72] Yet he asserted that individuals conducted themselves according to expectations and roles that depended upon the specific circumstances under question. For Parsons, communal roles were regulated by the institutional function that each person fulfilled in society, which could be either consciously recognized or internalized as a natural phenomenon. These normalizing processes would reduce social friction within modernizing societies by empowering its functional units to operate according to equilibriums of socialization, assimilation, and persuasion. Robert Merton then modified Parsons' theory by advancing that modern societies would often develop competing "sub-structures" with individualized or conflicting needs. These functional sub-structures were often inharmonious in their pursuit of power. But this conflict compelled communities to regenerate themselves through the competitive innovation.[73] Unlike the evolutionary basis of earlier sociology, Merton was less willing to declare that this dynamism amounted to a definitive direction of progress.

American historians found utility in functionalist theory because it seemed to explain how complex organizations such as modern cities continued to develop despite the unmistakable presence of social or institutional conflict. Against the background of American prosperity during the Cold War, historians such as Louis Galambos drew on Parsons to suggest that social regulatory systems were the driving forces behind an "organizational revolution" between government, business, and labor well after the demise of reform alleged through the paradigm of the "Progressive Era."[74] Merton's theory influenced American reinterpretations of bureaucracy and urban studies, especially in classics such as Richard Hofstadter's *Age of Reform* and Oscar Handlin's *The Uprooted*, which helped to shape the historical analysis of "big city politics" for a generation.[75] In each case, Americans selected elements of functionalist theory to demonstrate how conflict-laden social institutions, such as urban political machines or even organized crime, worked to maintain long-term order through their competition of interests.[76] Social systems did not need structural uniformity in order to reamain intact.

5.9 Modernization theory

Although it would be artificial to divide social theory rigidly between English-speaking and Continental scholarship, functionalism did indicate the relatively greater attention to the industrial era among "Anglo-American" historians, when compared to the focus of French or German colleagues on agricultural economic systems and rural society. To simplify somewhat, Americans were more optimistic about the capacity of "modern" people to moderate conflict through regulating associations and individual choice, without falling victim to Durkheimian anomie or the rationalizing numbness of a Weberian secular state. The implicit linking of these regulating associations with the contemporary era in the "West" led to the promotion of "modernization theory," either by American scholars or European historians who were influenced by study in the United States.

As the intellectual inheritors of Enlightenment thought, scholars of modernization theory claimed that contemporary rational-minded societies would sustain progress as a universal trend across the globe, charted along a stable "scale of advancement."[77] This scale would be measured by rates of commercial and urban economic development. Inevitable economic change would steadily result in the diminution of religious or aristocratic influence in the formation of basic national policies.[78] Historians understood that modernization often implied a period of instability, and frequent social conflict, as old orders resisted the complex and uneven changes determined by the market, uncertain government policy, or innate social discord. These tensions however could be overcome, so that the profit of European industrialization would be applied to the non-Western world and deliver social and political harmony to all. By inverting Weber's pessimistic regard for economic "rationalization," scholars such as Walter Rostow and Neil Smelser posed theories of industrial "takeoff" and social modernization as a common staging process for those seeking to join successful "Western" states. As conceived by Americans, modernization theory also suggested a progressive ideal of historical stages that was freed from the specter of Marxist revolution – a necessity for many during the height of the Cold War.[79]

Its potential benefits were evident to a range of scholars. Modernization theory seemed to facilitate objective empirical results while offering stable comparative measurement for applied research.[80] It promoted teamwork and interdisciplinary experimentation; it was strongly transnational both in conception and its promotion of cosmopolitan contact among researchers who sought to interpret the improvement of socio-economic systems.[81] Scientific pretenses seemed to ensure the useful application to societies that sought to learn from the conflicts of Western nations that had claimed to have passed through the rapids of "modernity." Among intellectual historians, specialists debated the degree to which the French *philosophes* represented the intellectual progenitors of a Western "open society" in contrast to forms of absolutist, despotic, or "totalitarian" rule.[82] Historians suggested an "organizational synthesis" that showed how competing interest groups had stabilized modern societies in the wake of rapid socio-economic change or political crises.[83] When applied by social historians such as Robert Wiebe, the theory tended to suggest that industrialized societies established "a smoothly running, integrated bureaucratic order of a kind theorists imagined to exist in the postwar United States."[84]

Despite its impressive appeal, by the 1970s modernization theory fell under greater critical scrutiny.[85] As noted in this volume's discussion on social history, the use of a vaguely Anglo-American historical template raised doubts about the role of reactionary elites to curtail progress, as well as the degree to which these models of politics and industrialization actually represented the truest path to modernity.[86] It was considered by some scholars to be an ethnocentric extrapolation of European, if not "Western," social norms onto countries that were becoming emancipated from white imperial authority. Indeed, historians and social commentators from beyond European or American shores frequently claimed that ideals of a "Western" template of modernity, such as capitalist markets or traditions of secular natural law, could in fact justify foreign intervention through the realm of markets and cultural values. Other critics contended that the model of technocracy and secularism was too abstract. It was selective in its evidence and seemed uncoupled from specific historical contexts that were often more differentiated than theorists had allowed.[87]

5.10 Conclusion

The great impulse to unite historiography with the social sciences occurred after the Second World War. The extraordinary disasters of the previous four decades all demanded a new effort among informed experts to address crises that ran across the social, economic, political, and cultural-oriented disciplines. Setting aside the communist states, the relative prosperity and democratization of European and American societies enabled a new generation of historians from far more diverse backgrounds to expand the profession's emphasis on social history. A sense of optimism that prevailed seemed to establish more confidence in the nature of modern society. This also fed into a relatively greater willingness to execute historical research as an interdisciplinary empirical science, informed by social theory. Thus the *Annales* and the *International Institute of Social History* resumed their places as transnational centers of exchange soon after 1945. New networks emerged through interdisciplinary reviews including *Past & Present* (1952), *Geschichte und Gesellschaft* [History and Society] (1975), and the institutional expansion of the *Annales* through the creation of the *École des hautes études en sciences sociales* (School of Advanced Studies in the Social Sciences). Americans built upon their publication breadth with new general sites of methodological cross-fertilization such as *Comparative Studies in Society and History* (1958); *The Journal of Interdisciplinary History* (1970); and *Social Science History* (1976). Social history came into its own fully in a decade that saw the appearance of *The Journal of Social History* in 1967; *History Workshop Journal* in 1976, and *Social History* in 1974. Jacques Le Goff seemed to express the prevailing confidence of the time that "economics, society, and culture seem to have monopolized historians' attention for the last half-century."[88]

These unmistakable triumphs should not mask certain problematic tensions that were perhaps inherent in the development of interdisciplinary thought. Doubts remained from historicist-minded scholars about the intellectual and methodological utility of social science theory. With the exception of clinical psychology as framed by Freud or Jung, the emphasis on collective identities in the social sciences threatened to marginalize authors of biography, legal history, or state policy. Academic historians who worked in biography suspected that a sociological history which focused "proper research" on collective material or cultural phenomena seemed to denigrate their genre to the very amateur tradition that they had first sought to supplant.[89] More resistance to interdisciplinary experimentation also grew from a broader dislike for social-cultural history itself, especially from conservatives such as the German nationalist scholar Gerhard Ritter. These historians considered a turn to social theory as either a back-door to Marxist philosophy, or as part of a general re-orientation towards more democratically-minded social history.[90] More mild critics such as Theodore Hamerow joined a number of scholars who feared that grand theories of social causality had led to calcified erudition that was unappealing to the public, intolerant of other forms of history, and overly confident about the definitive nature of its empirical-scientific results.[91] In other cases, historians remained skeptical about the explanatory capacity of quantitative research. Others worried that professional knowledge was not easily understood outside of the field in which its methods or problems were generated.[92]

But perhaps the greater threat to interdisciplinary exchange with the classic social sciences grew from the political left and more innovative movements associated with postmodernism. As suggested in this volume's chapter on poststructualism, the positivist roots of academic social theory were based on a belief that facts existed apart from the mind of the scholar as interpreter. When this scientific paradigm became questioned by the 1980s, the persuasiveness of behavioralist theory met with a severe epistemological and conceptual crisis. Scholars influenced by postmodernism have since disavowed grand theories of universal values or the capacity of an autonomous self to interpret knowledge without some level of subjectivity. At the same time, a greater awareness arose that sociological or ethnographic research could be interpreted to dissuade readers from a faith in the reasoned capacity of people, freed from authoritarian guidance, to resolve the challenges of a modern world. Progressive historians, particularly in the United States and Germany, claim that despite its doubts, a rationalization of society and the potential for democratic means of social order remain quite active in the world. If this process is not defended, and if historians cannot utilize social theory or empirical evidence to demonstrate its achievement in the past, then what would replace such goals as a guide for national identities or international cooperation?

Notes

1 Excellent short surveys include Dorinda Outram, *The Enlightenment* (Cambridge, 1995) and Margaret Jacob, *The Enlightenment: A Brief History with Documents* (New York, 2001), pp. 1–72.
2 For the influence of Ranke, see the preceding chapter by John Warren on historical method and the professionalization of history.
3 The best introductions are Thomas Nipperdey, 'Historismus und Historismuskritik heute,"' *Gesellschaft, Kultur, Theorie* (Göttingen, 1976), pp. 59–73 and Georg Iggers, 'Historicism: The History and Meaning of the Term,' *The Journal of the History of Ideas* 56 (1995), 129–144.
4 On historicism and the archives, see the essays in *Archive Stories: Facts, Fictions, and the Writing of History*, (ed.) A. Burton (Durham, 2005).
5 Romantic era history could celebrate a national "people" either historically as in Jules Michelet, *Histoire de France*, 19 vols., new ed. (Paris, 1976–1977) and *Histoire de la Révolution française*, new ed. (Paris, 1979), or as novelized culture, as with Sir Walter Scott in *The Antiquary* (Oxford, 2002).
6 The relationship of film and professional history has continued, if not intensified, this tension. See as an introduction Robert A. Rosenstone, *History on Film/Film on History* (Harlow, 2006) and Marc Carnes, (ed.) *Past Imperfect: History according to the Movies* (New York, 1995).
7 For this tension, compare Ian Tyrrell, *Historians in Public: The Practice of American History 1890–1970* (Chicago, 2005) to Olivier Dumoulin, *Le rôle social de l'historien: De la chaire au prétoire* (Paris, 2003).
8 Encapsulated in *The Positivist Philosophy of Auguste Comte*, trans. by Harriet Martineau (Bristol, 2001).
9 Eckhardt Fuchs, *Henry Thomas Buckle, Geschichtsschreibung und Positivismus in England und Deutschland* (Leipzig, 1994).
10 Guizot, *A Popular History of France*, 8 vols., trans. R. Black (Ann Arbor, 2005).
11 On Bury, see Doris Goldstein, 'J. B. Bury's Philosophy of History: A Reappraisal,' *American Historical Review* 82 (1977), pp. 896–919.
12 See *The Philosophy of Carl G. Hempel: Studies in Science, Explanation, and Rationality*, (ed.) J. H. Fetzer (Oxford, 2001), pp. 297–310
13 G. A Wells, 'The Critics of Buckle,' *Past and Present* 9 (1956), pp. 75–78.
14 On his concept of *Verstehen*, see Droysen, *Outline of the Principles of History* (Boston, 1893), pp. 61–90. For context, see Robert Southard, *Droysen and the Prussian School of History* (Lexington, 1994).
15 For Collingwood's critique of Bury from this position, see his *The Idea of History* (Oxford, 1994), pp. 147–155.
16 Joseph M. Hernon, Jr., 'The Last Whig Historian and Consensus History: George Macaulay Trevelyan, 1876–1962,' *American Historical Review* 81 (1976), pp. 66–97; Rosemary Jann, 'From Amateur to Professional: the Case of the Oxbridge Historians,' *Journal of British Studies* 22 (1983), pp. 122–147.

17 William Stafford, 'This Once Happy Country': Nostalgia for Pre-Modern Society,' in *The Imagined Past: History and Nostalgia* (Manchester, 1989), pp. 33–46

18 Robert Wokler, 'The Professoriate of Political Thought in England since 1914: A Tale of Three Chairs,' *The History of Political Thought in National Context*, (eds.) D. Costiglione and I. Hampsher-Monk (Cambridge, 2003), pp. 134–157 and Michael Bentley, *Modernizing England's Past: English Historiography in the Age of Modernism 1870–1970* (Cambridge, 2005), pp. 34–44.

19 Gerard M. Koot, *English Historical Economics, 1870–1926* (Cambridge, 1987) and Michael Bentley, *Modernizing England's Past: English Historiography in the Age of Modernism 1870–1970* (Cambridge, 2005), pp. 34–44.

20 David Cannadine, 'The Present and the Past in the English Industrial Revolution 1880–1980,' *Past and Present* 103 (1984), pp. 131–142.

21 Reba Soffer, 'The Revolution in English Social Thought,' *American Historical Review* 75 1970), pp. 1938–1964.

22 Herbert Spencer, *The Evolution of Society; Selections from Herbert Spencer's Principles of Sociology* (Chicago, 1974).

23 Reba Soffer, 'Why do Disciplines Fail? The Strange Case of British Sociology," *English Historical Review* 97 (1982), 787–797.

24 Doris Goldstein, 'Confronting Time: The Oxford School of History and the non-Darwinian Revolution,' *Storia della Storiografia* 45 (2004), pp. 3–27.

25 Best explained through Georg Iggers, *The German Conception of History*, rev. edition (Hanover, 1983).

26 Kasper Eskildsen, 'Leopold von Ranke's Archival Turn: Location and Evidence in Modern Historiography,' *Modern Intellectual History* 5 (2008), pp. 425–453.

27 Kevin Charles Kramer, The Lamentations of Germany : The Historiography of the Thirty Years' War, 1790–1890 (Ph.D. thesis, Harvard, 1998).

28 The best study is Roger Chickering, *Karl Lamprecht: A German Academic Life* (Atlantic Highlands, 1993).

29 See the contributions in *German Scholars and Ethnic Cleansing, 1920–1945*, (eds.) I Haar and M. Fahlbusch (New York, 2005).

30 David Lindenfeld, *The Practical Imagination: The German Sciences of State in the 19th century* (Chicago, 1997).

31 See *Georg Simmel on Individuality and Social Forms*, (ed.) D. Levine (Chicago, 1971), pp. 127–140.

32 On Simmel and Sombart, see Jerry Z. Muller, *The Mind and the Market: Capitalism in Western Thought* (New York, 2002), pp. 242–257.

33 Yuichi Shionoya, *The Soul of the German Historical School: Essays on Schmoller, Weber, and Schumpeter* (New York, 2005), 13–30. His influence is detailed in Nicholas Balabkins, *Not by theory alone. . .: The Economics of Gustav von Schmoller and Its Legacy to America* (Berlin, 1988).

34 *Max Weber's 'Science as a Vocation,'* (eds.) Peter Lassman and I. Velody (London, 1989), pp. 3–31.
35 Guenther Roth, 'Max Weber's Empirical Sociology in Germany and the United States: Tensions between Partisanship and Scholarship,' *Central European History* 2 (1969), pp. 210–211.
36 As an example, James Sheehan, 'Begriffsgeschichte: Theory and Practice,' *History and Theory* 50 (1978), 312–319.
37 On Weber and Hintze, see Iggers, *The German Conception*, pp. 232–234 and Felix Gilbert's introduction to *The Historical Essays of Otto Hintze* (Oxford, 1975), pp. 23–25.
38 Sam Whimster, 'R.H. Tawney, Ernst Troeltsch and Max Weber on Puritanism and Capitalism,' *Max Weber Studies* 5 (2005), pp. 297–316 and the contribution by G. Roth in *Weber's Protestant Ethic: Origins, Evidence, Contexts*, (eds.) H. Lehmann and G. Roth (Cambridge, 1993), pp. 83–122.
39 See Reinhard Bendix, *Max Weber: An Intellectual Portrait* (Berkeley, 1978), pp. 309–314, 334–359.
40 Peter Burke, *Sociology and History* (London, 1980), pp. 70–71.
41 This of course was not the limit of his theory on politics, the state, or society. For context, see Wolfgang Mommsen, 'Max Weber's Political Sociology and his Philosophy of World History,' *International Social Science Journal* 17 (1965), pp. 23–45.
42 Victor Karady, 'Stratégies de réussite et modes de faire-valoir de la sociologie chez les durkheimiens,' *Revue française de sociologie* 20 (1979), pp. 49–82; Terry N. Clark, 'Émile Durkheim and the Institutionalization of Sociology in the French University System,' *Archives Européenes de sociologie* 9 (1968), pp. 37–71.
43 Robert N. Bellah, 'Durkheim and History,' *American Sociological Review* 24 (1959): 447–453.
44 Best treated in Susan Friedman, *Marc Bloch, Sociology and Geography: Encountering Changing Disciplines* (Cambridge, 1996), pp. 39–54 and Philippe Besnard, 'The Epistemological Polemic: François Simiand,' *The Sociological Domain* (Cambridge, 1983), pp. 248–262.
45 Emile Durkheim, *The Division of Labor in Society*, intro. Lewis Coser (New York, 1984), pp. 31–87, and Robert A. Jones, *Emile Durkheim: An Introduction to Four Major Works* (London, 1986), pp. 24–57.
46 Durkheim, *Suicide. A Study in Sociology*, ed. G. Simpson (New York, 1951), pp. 297–325.
47 Christina Chimisso, 'The Mind and the Faculties: The Controversy over 'Primitive Mentality' and the Struggle for Disciplinary Space at the inter-war Sorbonne,' *History of the Human Sciences* 13 (2000), 47–68 and Marcel Fournier, *Marcel Mauss* (Paris, 1994).
48 Lucien Febvre, '*Civilisation*: Evolution of a Word and a Group of Ideas,' *A New Kind of History and Other Essays*, (ed.) P. Burke (1973): 219–257 and Marc Bloch, *The Historian's Craft*, intro. J. Strayer (New York, 1953), pp. 185–190.

49 Alan Bogue, "Social Theory and the Pioneer," *Agricultural History* 34 (1960): 21–34; Elinor Barber, *The Bourgeoisie of 18th Century France* (Princeton, 1955); Marc Bloch, *French Rural History*, trans. J. Sondheimer (Berkeley, 1966).

50 See David Potter, *People of Plenty* (Chicago, 1954); Tilly's own discussion in *From Mobilization to Revolution* (Reading, 1978) and the note of Victoria Bonnell, "The Uses of Theory, Concepts and Comparison in Historical Sociology," *Comparative Studies of Society and History* 22 (1980), p. 161.

51 Halbwachs, *On Collective Memory*, trans. L. Coser (New York, 1982). For his influence, see Paul Ricoeur, *Memory, History, Forgetting*, trans. K. Blamey & D. Pellauer (Chicago, 2006), pp. 120–124.

52 Henri Berr, *En marge de l'histoire universelle* (Paris, 1934), pp. 100–102.

53 For French conservative histories on corporatism, see Henri Denis, *La Corporation* (Paris, 1941); Gaetan Pirou, *Essais sur le corporatisme* (Paris, 1938); François Olivier-Martin *L'organisation corporative de la France sous l'Ancien Regime* (Paris, 1938) and the observations of Emile Coornaert, *Les Corporations en France avant 1789* (Paris, 1941), pp. 286–287.

54 Louis Chevalier, *Laboring Classes and Dangerous Classes: In Paris During the First Half of the 19th century* (London, 2000).

55 S. Elkins, *Slavery: A Problem in American Institutional and Intellectual Life* (Chicago, 1959) and the ensuing controversy in Ann J. Lane, (ed.,) *The Debate Over "Slavery": Stanley Elkins and His Critics* (Urbana, 1971).

56 On the support of sociology by the Third Republic, see George Weisz, 'The Republican Ideology and the Social Sciences; The Durkheimians and the History of Social Economy at the Sorbonne,' *The Sociological Domain*, pp. 106–115.

57 See Georges Lefebvre, *La naissance de l'historiographie moderne* (Paris, 1971): 300–301.

58 Dorothy Ross, *The Origins of American Social Science* (Cambridge, 1991), pp. 299–300, 345–346; Ian Tyrrell, *The Absent Marx: Class Analysis and Liberal History in 20th-Century America* (Westport, 1986).

59 Ernst Breisach, *American Progressive History: An Experiment in Modernization* (Chicago, 1993), pp. 66–77;130–139.

60 Overviews include Thomas Bender, *Community and Social Change in America* (New Brunswick, 1978); Dorothy Ross, *op. cit.*, 234–249 and Robert Casillo, "Lewis Mumford and the Organicist Concept of Social Thought," *Journal of the History of Ideas* 53 (1992), 91–116

61 Peter Novick, *That Noble Dream. The "Objectivity Question" and the American Historical Profession* (Cambridge, 1988), pp. 111–280.

62 William B. Munro, 'Clio and Her Cousins: Some Reflections upon the Place of History among the Social Sciences,' *The Pacific Historical Review* 10 (1941), pp. 404–405, 408 Allan Nevins, 'Recent Progress in American Social History,' *Journal of Economic and Business History* 1 (1929), pp. 365–383.

63 Christopher Johnson, *Claude Lévi-Strauss: The Formative Years* (Cambridge, 1985); Nelson E. and Tanya Hayes, (eds.,) *Claude Levi-Strauss: The Anthropologist as Hero* (Cambridge, Mass., 1970).

64 Albert Doja, 'The Advent of Heroic Anthropology in the History of Ideas,' *Journal of the History of Ideas* 66 (2005), pp. 635–638.

65 James Boon, "Claude Lévi-Strauss" in *The Return of Grand Theory in the Human Sciences*, (ed.) Quentin Skinner, (Cambridge, 1985), pp. 159–176.

66 See the discussion of Braudel in this volume's chapter by Mitthias Middell.

67 Georges Duby, *The Legend of Bouvines* (Cambridge, 1990).

68 Mona Ozouf, *Festivals in the French Revolution* (Cambridge, Mass., 1988).

69 Led by the renowned historian Philippe Ariès, as in Patrick Hutton, *Philippe Ariès and the Politics of French Cultural History* (Amherst, 2004), pp. 37–8, 132.

70 See the "new alliance" discussed in François Dosse's chapter in *Les courants historiques en France 19e–20e siècle* (Paris, 1999), pp. 170–174 and its perceived threat in Werner Conze, "Social History," The *Journal* of *Social History* 1 (1967), p. 7.

71 Especially his posthumous works, *The Scientific Theory of Culture and Other Essays* (Chapel Hill, 1944) and *The Dynamics of Cultural Change: An Inquiry into Race Relations in Africa* (New Haven, 1945).

72 Talcott Parsons and E. A. Shils, *Toward a General Theory of Action: Theoretical Foundations for the Social Sciences* (Cambridge, Mass., 1951) and R. Münch's two-part essay, 'Talcott Parsons and the Theory of Action,' *The American Journal of Sociology* 86 & 87 (1981–1982), pp. 709–739, 771–826.

73 Robert K. Merton, *Social Theory and Social Structure* (Glencoe, Ill., 1957).

74 Louis Galambos, 'Parsonian Sociology and Post-Progressive History,' *Social Science Quarterly* 50 (1969), pp. 25–45.

75 David Rothman, 'The Uprooted: Thirty Years Later,' *Reviews in American History* 10 (1982), pp. 311–319 and David S. Brown, *Richard Hofstadter: An Intellectual Biography* (Chicago, 2006), pp. 73–85.

76 Terrence McDonald, 'A Reassessment of the Urban Political Boss: An Exchange of Views,' *The History Teacher* 21 (1988), pp. 301–303.

77 Charles Tilly, *Big Structures, Large Processes, Huge Comparisons* (New York, 1984), p. 46.

78 Dean C. Tipps, "Modernization Theory and the Comparative Study of Societies: A Critical Perspective," *Comparative Studies in Society and History* 16 (1973), pp. 213–214.

79 Walter Rostow, *The Stages of Economic Growth: A non-Communist Manifesto* (Cambridge, 1960) and Niel Smelser, *Social Change in the Industrial Revolution* (Chicago, 1959). On the context, see Joel Isaac, "The Human Sciences in Cold War America," *The Historical Journal* 50 (2007), pp. 740–741.

80 See especially Cyril Black, *The Stages of Modernization: A Study in Comparative History* (New York, 1966), pp. 170–190.

81 Georg Iggers, *Historiography in the 20th century. From Scientific Objectivity to the Postmodern Challenge* (Hanover, 1997), p. 4.

82 Compare Arthur M. Wilson, 'The *Philosophes* in the Light of Present-Day Theories of Modernization,' *Studies on Voltaire and the 18th Century* 58 (1967), pp. 1893–1913 to Harriet B. Applewhite & Darline G. Levy, 'The Concept of Modernization and the French Enlightenment,' *Studies on Voltaire and the 18th Century* 84 (1971), pp. 53–98.

83 Dorothy Ross, "The New and Newer Histories: Social Theory and Historiography in an American Key," *Imagined Histories: American Historians Interpret the Past*, eds. A. Mohlo and G. Wood (Princeton, 1998), pp. 93–94.

84 Kenneth Cmiel, 'Destiny and Amnesia: The Vision of Modernity in Robert Wiebe's *The Search for Order,' Reviews in American History* 21 (1993), pp. 352–368.

85 For this discussion, see Joyce Appleby, Lynn Hunt, and Margaret Jacob, *Telling the Truth about History* (New York, 1994), pp. 84–88.

86 See Thomas Welskopp in this volume; Randall Collins, "German-Bashing and the Theory of Modernization," in *Macrohistory: Essays in Sociology of the Long Run* (Stanford, 1993), 52–176 and Chris Lorenz, "'Won't You Tell Me, Where Have All the Good Times Gone'? On the Advantages and Disadvantages of Modernization Theory for History," *Radical History Review* 10 (2006): 171–200.

87 Charles Tilly, *Big Structures,* 44–46.

88 Jacques Le Goff, "Is Politics Still the Backbone of History?" in *Historical Studies Today*, (eds.) F. Gilbert and S. Graubard (New York, 1972): 338.

89 For fears of biography as passé during the height of structural history, see Hagen Schulze, "Die Biographie in der 'Krise der Geschichtswissenschaft," *Geschichte in Wissenschaft und Unterricht* 29 (1978), pp. 508–51 and Barrie Ratcliffe, "The Decline of Biography in French Historiography: The Ambivalent Legacy of the 'Annales' Tradition," *Proceedings of the Annual Meeting of the Western Society for French History* 8 (1980), pp. 556–567.

90 Gordon Craig, "Political History," *Daedalus* 100 (1971), p. 324 and Oscar Halecki, "The Moral Laws of History," *The Catholic Historical Review* 42 (1957), p. 422. For Ritter's critique, see Karl D. Erdmann, *Toward a Global Community of Historians* (New York, 2005), pp. 223–224.

91 Most avidly expressed by Theodore Hamerow, *Reflections on History and Historians* (Madison, 1987), pp. 33–37, 170–175, 200–203; Gertrude Himmelfarb, *The New History and the Old* (Cambridge, 1987), pp. 33–69. Setting aside the political undertones, aspects were accepted to some measure by the target of the attack, as in François Furet, "Beyond the Annales," *The Journal of Modern History* 55 (1983), pp. 389–410.

92 Especially Richard Cobb, "Nous les Annales," in *A Second Identity: Essays on France and French History* (London, 1979), pp. 76–83.

6

The *Annales*

Matthias Middell

The *Annales* school is prominent in most surveys of 20th-century historiography. The bibliography of works dealing with the *Annales*, with books written by *Annalistes*, with the stages of the school's development, with its authors and theoretical ideas, is virtually boundless. The *Annales*' far-reaching international influence, as well as the originality of its solutions to the fundamental problems of modern historiography, is repeatedly pointed out. There are also discussions of issues such as the controversies such as that between Lucien Febvre and Marc Bloch on the continuation of the journal during the German occupation of France, the separation of the so-called third generation of the *Annales* from Fernand Braudel at the end of the 1960s, and whether the 'tournant critique' of the late 1980s and early 1990s meant that the *Annales* still existed as a homogenous school, and perhaps whether it had ever been one. There is no agreement either as to what should be included under the *Annales* heading, apart from Bloch and Febvre, the founders of the journal, and Fernand Braudel, the patriarch of the VIe Section en Sciences Sociales in Paris. And although the journal has been hugely important for the identity of the *Annales* and for the reputation of individual members, no content analysis of the journal's output during the last eight decades has ever been attempted.

These remarks are sufficient to show that for all the talk of the 'école des *Annales*', several approaches can be distinguished within it, and we must ask rather how the history of the *Annales* is being construed in individual cases. First there is the notion of the *Annales* as a scientific heritage that must be maintained, yet criticized to displace the older generation. From this latter perspective, the *Annales* is like a family legend (a sort of saga), which is a permanently unfinished project, and yet which culminates teleologically in its current proponents. Secondly, processes of institutionalization may be emphasized. In this perspective the *Annales* journeys from its beginnings in the province of Strasbourg to the French and international academic establishment. This itinerary can be cast either as a story of unstoppable success, or as a critique of the concentration of power within the French system of arts and sciences. Thirdly, a cyclical view may be presented in which the *Annales* displaced German historiographical model at the turn of the nineteenth and twentieth centuries, went on to established hegemony (or supremacy) within the international discipline of history, and in turn gave way to a pluralist historical field in which many of the centres were located in the US. Finally, the history of the *Annales* can be seen as the reflection of the globalization in the 20th century. Globalization has itself been an important topic for the *Annales*. Bloch and Braudel proposed theoretical means – for example, comparative history – to accommodate the challenges posed by globalization to the historical discipline.

The first approach prevailed for a long time and, with its polemic undertones and its intentions of legitimization, has contributed to obscuring the history of the *Annales*. The latter two approaches boomed at the end of the 20th century when a retrospective view (fired by the millennium effect) became possible and a new generation of *Annalistes* encouraged self-criticisms. They were keen to overcome the crisis that characterized the development of the journal and of their institutional stronghold, the Ecole des Hautes Etudes.

Following the defeat of 1870 and the foundation of the Bismarckian Empire in the Palace of Versailles, French elites sought explanations for Prussian superiority. The answer seemed to lie in the German universities and the training facilities for German elites more generally. In the Third Republic, French politicians sought to reform their own schools in the light of what they observed on the other side of the Rhine. They sent younger academics to assess the strengths and weakness of the various German universities, departments and disciplines. The positive features were to be integrated into, and combined with traditions of, the French academic infrastructure. The latter can be traced back to the innovations of the period of absolutism (e.g. the Collège de France) or to the Napoleonic era (divided into the Grandes Ecoles and one single university for the whole of France and its faculties in dozens of cities).[1] This strategy helped promote both an atmosphere international competition and an ongoing transnational cooperation with a growing sense of interdependent intellectual work transcending national boundaries.[2]

Among the young academics recruited by the French ministry of higher education was a historian, born in 1886, the son of an Alsatian historian of the ancient world. He attended the elite Lycée Louis le Grand in Paris in 1896 and in 1904 entered the Ecole Normale Supérieure in Rue d'Ulm. There he became familiar both with French historiography and with German academic production (especially of Karl Bücher, Karl Lamprecht, Theodor Mommsen, Leopold von Ranke and Gustav Schmoller).[3] Having passed the aggregation in 1908, he spent two semesters in Germany, visiting Berlin in 1908 and Leipzig in 1909. Together with Lucien Febvre,[4] who was born in 1878 in the Franche-Comté, studied in

Paris and taught at the faculty of Dijon before 1914, Marc Bloch would become a founder of the *Annales d'histoire économique et sociale*.

Between Bloch's years as a student in the conference rooms of German universities and his subsequent career as a director of the *Annales*, the First World War changed many things. Franco-German hostility was intensified by four years of trench warfare on French territory and by intransigent nationalist rivalry that mobilized masses of people in both countries. German intellectuals were massively involved in legitimizing war objectives and in fabricating propaganda against the declared enemies, and more directly, they were personally involved in mapping the culture of occupied territories for military purposes. Patriotic feelings deepened on the other side as well, as Bloch's account of his experience in the Great War testifies.[5] Henri Pirenne, an outstanding Belgian historian, had been working with his German colleagues on a project of a comprehensive comparative socio-cultural history of European Nations before 1914. After the war he refused to participate in any further discussion with people who had pleaded for the expansionist 'ideas of 1914' and who were plotting vengeance after the German capitulation and the Treaty of Versailles.

At well-equipped Strasbourg University, Bloch and Febvre met and formulated their innovative approach to writing history. Febvre's proposed European review for economic history, with Pirenne as the leading figure failed.[6] It was only in 1928 that Bloch (then more active in the project than Febvre) took the idea up again. However, Pirenne again refused to take the post of director, and so Bloch and Febvre decided to make the *Annales* their own. The first issue appeared in January 1929. In the preface, the two editors first emphasized the multi-disciplinary and international approach, with a strong focus on economic history.[7] They promised to overcome the gap between specialists on the past and scholars of current social tendencies. Thirdly, they aimed to pull down the walls between historians researching the ancient, medieval, early modern and contemporary societies, and between experts in European history and that of so-called primitive or exotic cultures. The ending of pointless disciplinary schisms was expected to lead to methodological innovation.[8]

This project was intended to displace Germany as leader in the historical sciences at a time when German historians had isolated themselves from the international community by their reactionary politics and their methodological shift to 'Volksgeschichte'. The latter was an ethnocentric interpretation of the people's history, which demanded congruence between national boundaries and the settlements of a particular ethnic group – like the Germans. Volksgeschichte was not only a plea for expansion of Germany to territories where German-speaking people allegedly of the Nordic race had settled, but a call for historical and political explanations of the modern world based upon racial theories.[9]

Bloch and Febvre also attacked more traditional Rankean approaches, embraced at the Sorbonne above all by Charles Seignobos and Charles-Victor

Langlois. Both used Ranke's 'critical method' and like him were principally concerned with political history, great men and a teleology of national communities.

Thanks to the support of Henri Pirenne, the two provincial historians – still in the 1920s far from the heart of academic influence in France – won renown in the international arena. Bloch published his pathbreaking *Les Rois thaumaturges* in 1924. The book examined the public attribution of the capacity of salvation to the kings of France at the moment of their coronation in the cathedral of Reims. Bloch developed an early psycho-history of myth, mass mentalities and the political use of representations. A stay at the newly founded Institute for Comparative Research in Human Culture in Oslo in October 1929 gave him an opportunity to resume comparative research on French agrarian history from the thirteenth to the 18th century. This was published a few years later in a 200-page essay on 'Les caractères originaux de l'histoire rurale française'. It is now wellknown as first example of Bloch's 'regressive method'. This involved working back from recent to more distant periods, in the belief that, since we know more about the present, it should be easier to start there than from speculations about historical origins. Later, in his *Apologie d'histoire ou le metier de l'historien*, Bloch systematized this method and argued openly against the 'mystification of origins'.

After his essay on agrarian history, Bloch wrote his masterpiece on *La société féodale*, an ambitious work framing the culture of feudalism. Having analysed the distribution of property, social hierarchy, and the form and functions of the state, he turned to mechanisms of personal dependence, social cohesion, collective memory and consciousness, and 'forms of feeling and thinking'. In *Feudal Society*, Bloch also refined his method. He combined the social history of property and power with that of the legal forms of social relationships, and with the history of cultural representations. The book's two volumes do not stand alone, but link Bloch's interest in the relation between the kings and lords of the manor and their bondsmen. Bloch began his interpretation of the feudal society with a detailed description of representative gestures which both expressed vassal status and creating subordinate position. He tried to explain the 'rhythm' of a given society through description of its customs and habits, its cultural practices and its rites. Such a rhythm, said to be typical of a particular stage of social development, is a sort of 'collective comprehension of time', which oscillates between routine and innovation.[10]

In his work on the forms used by medieval people to express social relationships, Bloch sought the history of modern social gestures. In his *Rois thaumaturges*, Bloch had already underlined the great differences between the medieval period and the period of absolutism and still more the modern state. In the first period there was a direct relationship between the healing king and the people, without any religious or secular institution between them. From the 14th century onwards, direct forms of social relationships were replaced with more indirect forms.

Feudal Society was a large-scale picture of medieval times from the ninth to the 13th century in which Bloch concentrated on analysing micro-politics and the aesthetics of its cultural representations. He endeavoured particularly to understand the importance of liberty and serfdom in medieval society and their social and economic histories. He advanced precise reasons for the failure of slavery at the end of the Roman Empire in Europe and looked for differences between slaves and serfs. Bloch pointed out that in the 9th century, under the rule of the Carolingian dynasty, the *servi* were not members of the community and not accepted as members of the people, for the latter was composed only of free men. In the 13th century the status of bondsmen developed in such a way that under the Capetian kingship serfs obtained a special juridical status of their own. Even if they were citizens of secondary rank, they were nevertheless members of the community called *populus Francorum*. Bloch returned to the question of serfdom and freedom in his 'Caractères originaux', and demonstrated that in the fourteenth and fifteenth centuries the authority of the landlords continued to diminish. Bloch's political ideal shines through. French history was the slow march towards an association of politically free citizens. The two volumes of *Feudal Society* consolidated Bloch's reputation as a specialist in comparative social history.

Bloch's search for structural explanations, which had been inspired to a considerable extent by Durkheim's sociology, was criticized by Febvre. The latter's book on Luther had explored the relationship between the individual and the community, and had focused on the history of mentalities in the period of the German Reformation.[11] In this biography Febvre left behind his earlier interest in the role of geography in history, and turned to the history of early modern mentalities.[12] This field was simultaneously developed by his Strasbourg colleague Georges Lefebvre, the famous expert on the French Revolution.

At the Oslo International Congress of Historical Sciences in 1928, Bloch read a paper on methods of comparative history.[13] His choice was a calculated and symbolic act. He laid claim to Karl Lamprecht's heritage.[14] He discussed Max Weber's approach to historical sociology, and shared Weber's interest in explaining Europe's advantages in worldwide competition through comparison with the East.[15] Internationalism became a hallmark of the *Annales*, and the circle of contributors to the *Annales* was not restricted to the French historical community. Very quickly, contacts with an international group of like-minded historians provided the review with articles from north, south and central Europe.

This founding period was marked by a special *Annales* style. But there was no elaborate paradigm or even an *Annales* school. Nevertheless, correspondence between Bloch and Febvre[16] demonstrates their commitment to the quality of their journal, understood as a common enterprise. They displayed a strategic interest in arranging the historiographical field into an opposition between 'our way of writing history' and representatives of another way. They sought allies, and refused collaboration with people with whom they disagreed. This produced a potentially strong identification with the historiographical project represented by the *Annales*. Bloch and Febvre looked with displeasure upon the efforts of competing journals to develop international cooperation – especially when such rivals appeared in Germany.

In 1933 Febvre was the first of the founders to win a higher academic position when he was elected to the Collège de France after a long and painful campaign. Bloch followed only in 1936, taking over Henri Hauser's chair in economic history at the Sorbonne. Febvre 'translated' his institutional gains into the occupation of a series of powerful and prestigious positions which allowed him to oversee a range of new projects. Thus, for example, he became president of the editorial board organizing the *Encyclopédie française,* published from 1935.

The Second World War interrupted the success story of the *Annales*. Bloch participated in the defence of France in 1940, and described in 'L'étrange défaite' his frustrating experiences in the French army. He had returned to Paris only briefly when, as a Jew, he was forced to retire. He became an active member of the Résistance. At this time he wrote an incomplete introduction to historical methods and theories, which became his scientific testimony. Febvre, who stayed in Paris, edited the *Annales* alone during this difficult time, and disagreed with Bloch on the question of how to deal with the restrictive conditions of occupation. Bloch never returned to work – he was killed in 1944 by the Gestapo. Febvre took sole responsibility for the review.

After liberation, Febvre arrived at the top of the French academic system. He was charged with drawing up proposals for reform of the École Pratique des Hautes Études (ÉPHÉ), founded in 1884. In 1947 he was elected President of its newly founded VIe Section of the University of Paris, which later incorporated the social sciences into the ÉPHÉ. Here, Febvre institutionalized the old idea he had developed together with Bloch in the 1920s. At that time the powerful Centre des Recherches Historiques (which Febvre directed for several years) had been embedded into an institute of social sciences, which concentrated on research. After 1945 Febvre, also French representative on the UNESCO commission for a conceptualization of a History of Mankind, became the key person in the institutionalization of the *Annales* paradigm. He was supported by Fernand Braudel (who had been in close contact with Bloch and Febvre since 1937) in the administration of the Historical Research Centre. Charles Morazé (an expert on 19th-century history) and Robert Mandrou (historian of the pre-modern era and the absolutist state in Europe) supported him in the administration of the review.

The period between 1945 and Febvre's death in 1956 was a time of recovery and consolidation. The formerly heretic historiographical movement was transformed by Febvre into an established institution. This cannot be explained only by Febvre's personal qualities and interests, or by the supported of a network of young and ambitious historians using the innovative image of the *Annales* to establish their academic careers. Political circumstances after the Second World War were also important.

France compensated for its decreasing political role in a world dominated by the USA and Russia with an ambitious cultural and scientific international offensive. The Fourth Republic and, even more, de Gaulle's Fifth Republic, traded its former global political role for intellectual influence. Paris became a laboratory of social thinking on the competition of two ideological systems and political blocs, on the process of decolonization, and on the rise of an individualized, consumer-oriented civic society. American donors helped financially. For example the Ford foundation financed the beginnings of the Maison des Sciences de l'Homme (MSH). The latter was intelligently administered by Clemens Heller – making it a nimble dinghy at the side of the great tanker of the VIe Section (better known later as the ÉHÉSS –École des Hautes Études en Sciences Sociales). The MSH offered grants to fellows from abroad and organized international conferences, projects and publications when national money was not available for such purposes. Under the same roof, and with a coordinated strategy, the ÉHÉSS and the MSH linked French academics with an international network under the patronage of Fernand Braudel.

Even before Febvre's death in 1956 Braudel became the key person in the *Annales*. After having taken over the leading positions of Febvre in the ÉHÉSS and on the review's board he became the undisputed representative of the *Annales* movement for more than a decade. The *Annales* now developed the appearance of an academic school. Acceptance as an author in the review, and/or serving as a collaborator in the vast enterprises of the ÉHÉSS, was a sort of knighthood which could potentially lead to a splendid academic career in French universities or abroad.

Braudel's worldwide reputation was founded upon his monumental *The Mediterranean and the Mediterranean World in the Age of Philip II* (1949), which was partly written in German prisoner-of-war camps. In this book Braudel developed his notion of three historical levels, each moving at different rhythms. First, he claimed that geohistorical foundations of societies changed only over very long periods. Secondly, he distinguished medium term up- and down-swings in economic life and social relationships, which happened more quickly. On the third level, in which Braudel was hardly interested, was the merely artificial history of political incidents (*histoire événementielle*). Braudel had at first intended to write a dissertation on the foreign policy of Philip II of Spain. But having the period from 1923 to 1933 as a teacher in Algeria, he became sensitive to the reciprocal influences of Europe and Africa the formation of a common Mediterranean region. In 1937, on his return from a two-year stay in Brazil, he met Febvre, who encouraged him to write on the influences of the Mediterranean world on the politics of Philip II and on Spanish society. The 1200-plus pages of *The Mediterranean World* ignored politics almost completely. The Spanish victory at Lepanto and the occupation of Tunis by Don

Juan de Austrias were, in Braudel's perspective, of little importance for historical explanation. By contrast, he emphasized the huge influence of natural conditions upon communication, trade and production. Like Bloch in his analysis of the Middle Ages or Febvre in his interpretation of the Reformation era, Braudel emphasized the role of collective structures like economic systems, states and societies, which moved only in a rhythm of generations.

Braudel does link mid-range movements to the rise and fall of Empires. The economic up-swing of the fifteenth and sixteenth centuries was favourable to the Spanish and the Ottoman Empires. But ultimately the size of these empires became an obstacle to development, because of the cost of communication between the various parts of the territory. The core of the book is nevertheless the slow-moving structures encapsulated in Braudel's notion of geo-history. Braudel distinguishes between people living in coastal regions, who were said more open to innovation, and mountain areas, who reacted in a more conservative way. Braudel was aware that patterns of human mobility changed with industrialization and modern mobility. But in the 16th century high cultural performance was not only encouraged, but determined by geo-historical factors.

While Braudel developed a typology of different historical times which emphasized the geo-historical *longue durée*, Ernest Labrousse and his disciples researched long-run cycles of prices and wages, and sought to calculate the economic conditions for the advance of modernity. Labrousse wrote two major books, one on the development of prices during the 18th century (1933) and the second on the crisis of the French economy at the end of the Ancien Régime and during the revolutionary period (1944). Teaching at the Sorbonne, he was associated, more than Braudel, with the traditional culture of the French historical profession, and so was less willing to condemn political history. One of his disciples, Michel Vovelle, would later endeavour, in his history of mentalities during the French Revolution, to overcome the old conflict between the social and the political. Labrousse and Braudel together edited a social and economic history of France published in six volumes between 1970 and 1982.

In the 1960s social structures and economic cycles became the fundamental categories of the *Annales* movement's historiography. Most of its publications were concerned with the so-called *longue durée* and not with a short-term political conflict. *Annales* historians were convinced that the key to historical explanations could be found in an integrated analysis of structures and developments over decades or centuries. The advent of computers seemed to promise a great future to quantification of data, and to the innovative notion of serialization of quantitative data (*histoire sérielle*). On the one hand, the disciples of Labrousse concentrated on a new cartography of the economic regions of France since the 16th century; on the other, Braudel and his colleagues tried to establish a framework of economic world-regions (*économies-monde*). The latter were characterized by their climate, morphology, population, economic behaviour and cultures. Historians traced the material conditions under which the region participated in a world increasingly connected by trade and technological exchange. Braudel created from the products of these investigations a vast panorama of the emerging capitalist system, in which he underlined the role of the Mediterranean region for European expansion to the Americas, Africa and Asia. His three volumes on the progress of material culture in the world from the sixteenth to the end of the 18th century represented an influential attempt to apply the *Annales*' method to world history. Braudel's successor in this field, Immanuel Wallerstein, established the world-system approach in historical sociology.

Under Braudel's directorship the VIe Section and the *Annales* became more hierarchically organized. For the first time there really was a group of historians working collectively in research projects, and linked to specialized and research-oriented teaching at the ÉHÉSS. The idea of *enquêtes*, proposed by Bloch and Febvre in the 1930s, was implemented in the form of systematic and cumulative analysis of individual regions and through combination of case studies. Individual approaches were integrated into the scheme developed by Braudel at the beginning of this period in the *Annales*' history.

The Braudel era was also that in which *Annales* and Marxist historians interacted most closely. Some *Annalistes* – like the specialist in the history of medieval western France, Guy Bois, or the historian of Catalan capitalism, Pierre Vilar – declared themselves to be Marxists. Braudel himself recognized that he owed something to a (rather incomplete) reading of Marx's writings on early modern capitalist development in Europe and overseas. At the same time Braudel criticized Marxist historiography for its orthodox exaggeration of the economic causes for political conflicts and decisions.

The year 1968 changed a lot in France, not only in society but also, and perhaps above all, in the academic world. Generational conflicts were characteristic of the period. Within the *Annales* school a younger generation was looking for emancipation from the rule of the ubiquitous director. Braudel came under attack and, vexed by these conflicts, he retired from the board of the *Annales*. This moment dates the arrival in power of a third generation of *Annalistes*. Leading figures were Emmanuel Le Roy Ladurie, Jacques Le Goff, Georges Duby and François Furet. Some were former Communists, who now explicitly demonstrated their distance from Marxism.

In 1967 Le Roy Ladurie completed a magisterial thesis on the history of climate in Europe during the last 1000 years, a study based on Braudel's geo-historical assumptions. Le Roy Ladurie subsequently became well known for his story of the *Carnival of Romans* – a precise reconstruction of social and cultural tensions among people in a small French town confronted with the Inquisition.

Le Goff and Duby returned to Marc Bloch's globalizing interpretation of the medieval civilization in Europe, and complemented his social and cultural approach with biographical methods. Thus Le Goff tried to integrate the world of medieval representations into a biography of Louis XI. François Furet, together with Mona Ozouf, arrived on the scene with an impressive analysis of the social history of writing and reading in 18th-century France, and this inspired studies on the history of book production and of the literacy in the country. Furet, who became president of the ÉHÉSS in the 1980s, moved from the history of socio-cultural phenomena to the new political history of the French Revolution, and became well known for his attacks on Albert Soboul's classic Marxist interpretation.

While his lengthy book written together with Denis Richet provided a rather classical account of the French revolution from a liberal point of view – emphasizing the first phase of the transformation until 1791 and condemning the Jacobin rulership in 1793/94 as inappropriate to the smooth transition towards a liberal-capitalist order – Furet contributed during the 1970s and 1980s very much to the cultural turn in revolutionary studies. With his – often polemical – articles, collected for the first time in a volume, *Penser la Révolution française* (1978), he argued in favour of a history of discourses resulting in new political constellations and attempted to demonstrate that what he called the *dérapage* of the revolution was the consequence of a radicalized political discourse starting not only with the Jacobins but even in 1789. At the same time he denied any causality between the revolution and social tensions at the time of the Ancien Régime. Some have therefore criticized his perspective as not very coherent, but rather inspired by political conviction than careful archival work.[17] He then revisited the historiography of the nineteenth and 20th century, and concluded in the late 1980s that the French Revolution introduced a specific path to modernity (far from Anglo-Saxon normality) from which it would have to free itself by overcoming the Jacobin legacy revitalized over and over again by leftist historians since the Third Republic. With the decline of Marxist influence (to which Furet contributed as a former insider – he was a member of the French Parti Communiste from 1947 to 1959 – with his 1996 book *Le passé d'une illusion*, shortly before his premature death), Furet's reading of the French Revolution became more popular all over the world, and even highly prominent in Eastern Europe. Nevertheless, with the cultural turn in Jacobin historiography (represented by the work of Michel Vovelle and his disciples) Furet was less successful among specialized academic historians, as research activities around the bicentenary of 1789 demonstrated.

Vovelle, another representative of the third generation of the *Annales* (even if not related to the ÉHÉSS), started to apply the concept of the *histoire des mentalités* to 18th-century French history in a way that combined the more sophisticated cultural interpretation with the strength of quantitative social history when exploring hundreds of grave decorations from southern France for a new history of representations of death and God. After his move from Aix-en-Provence, where he led the creation of an active research group of historians and anthropologists on mentality in history, to the chair in revolutionary history at the Sorbonne in 1983, he focused on a more nuanced interpretation of the decade between Bastille and Napoleon as cultural break with clearly defined elements of continuity of behavioural patterns in the turmoil of political change.[18]

In the later 1980s, the innovative methodology of the *Annales* school was no longer divorced from, and the most prominent topic in, French national history. Competition between the *Furetistes* and the *Vovelliens* for a new cultural history of the Revolution replaced the violent and sometimes sterile opposition between Furet and Soboul in the 1970s. Studies of the late 18th century gained a new impetus at the moment when the commemoration of 1789 coincided with revolution in Eastern Europe.

Roger Chartier, another author from the third generation of the *Annales*, renewed another domain of French historical writing by investigating the history of printing, reading and collecting books, both in its cultural and social dimension, enriching the empirical work on cultural practices by concrete examples from the world of reading.[19] At the same time, historians like Alain Corbin concentrated on the emotional side of culture when analysing the history of noises, tastes and smelling.[20]

One of the most internationally influential approaches proposed by researchers working at the ÉHÉSS in the 1970s and 1980s became Pierre Nora's history of the *lieux de mémoire*.[21] He and his co-authors of the impressive seven-volume work made operational the distinction between history (all that happened in the past) and memory (what is actively remembered and becomes part of a set of collectively actualized items forming the cultural memory of a society). Nora, to some extent motivated by the fear that republican values and memory in France were declining, saw his descriptions of the most valuable 'memory places' as part of an effort to remobilize French historical consciousness in a more sophisticated manner. At the same time his enterprise became a model for historians of remembrance all over the world; many of them followed Nora in identifying *lieux de mémoire* in their respective countries.

As we can see, the third generation was more concerned with national – that is, French – history than Bloch, Febvre or Braudel had been. The search for the 'world we have lost' and the effort to assimilate this into the national heritage was an essential reason for the public success of this generation in the 1970s. The third generation met the demand for a new national metanarrative based upon the newly found and recognized methods in writing history. Le Roy Ladurie, Furet, Le Goff, Duby and others were not only internationally renowned historians, but became media stars in France, inciting jealousy when historians in other countries came under pressure from the rising social sciences. Le Goff and others proudly described their version of the *Annales*' method as a 'new history' (*nouvelle histoire*), thereby ascribing an old-fashioned appearance to other approaches. They did not doubt their own position at the top of the international historiographical tree, yet comparative history was neglected and international interest in the work of the *Annales* was limited to methodological studies. Furet, and later Roger Chartier and others, looked for new transatlantic cooperation with American universities interested in the history of western civilization. In the heat of the bicentenary of the French Revolution in 1989, the new French–North American axis proved reliable.

It was exactly at the moment of the dramatic international political changes of 1989 that the crisis of the *Annales* movement became obvious, and was recognized even by members of the school itself. A so-called fourth generation had appeared at the end of the 1970s. It transformed the history of mentalities, which was at the centre of methodological debates, and had become an identifier of the 'new history' of the third generation, into a more coherent approach owing much to historical anthropology. At the same time women's history came to the fore, as did the history of extra-European territories, especially francophone Africa. In the 1980s Michelle Perrot inspired multi-volume projects on family history, on women's history and on the history of private life. These followed enormous collective enterprises on rural France and urban history in the 1970s. Roger Chartier, amongst others, continued the work of scholars like Henri-Jean Martin in the field of book history and the history of reading. Bernard Lepetit renewed approach to urban history.

During the 1980s tensions among the historians related to the journal and the ÉHÉSS caused bitter polemics inside the *Annales* movement, but in public Duby, Furet and others presented it in terms of continuity. They feared loss of the *Annales* heritage, and the associated academic prestige and worldwide influence. In contrast, a new generation in 1989 openly expressed their criticisms of the established paradigm. They took on board the call of some marginalized French historians, voiced since the beginning of the 1980s, for an end to the domination of a school they regarded as more and more sterile, triumphalist and unfruitful. In 1989 the editorial board of the *Annales* published a widely discussed manifesto that promised a fresh start, and announced at the same time a return to some of Bloch's and Febvre's fundamental ideas. The outcome of the debate was a programmatic shift to new methods and topics. People and agency would replace structures as major explanatory factors. The significance of cultural representation for historical development was recognized and new interest was expressed in comparative history. The cooperation of historians with social scientists was to be enhanced by cooperation with disciplines like anthropology and area studies. The premature death of Bernard Lepetit, who had been at the heart of the reform movement, was a setback for change. Yet the *Annales* of the 1990s was markedly different from that of the third generation. Openness to research in other disciplines and other countries has once again become a characteristic of what is perhaps the most well-known humanities journal in the world.

New approaches have emerged in the last 15 years, some of them related to the new alliances between historians and anthropologists, and others looking for ways to overcome the compartmentalizations of a historiography too much focused on the history of the nation and the nation-state. In particular, it privileged anew comparisons and the study of cultural transfers. If one looks to the content of the *Annales* in the 1990s and at the beginning of the new millennium, a new interest in the findings of area studies can be found, but French historiography in general remained for long reluctant to enter the field of global history.

The future development of the *Annales* cannot be foreseen. But one might point to three tendencies evident in the last decade. First, the enormous influence of the *Annales* school on international historiography seems to have come to an end, and a multi-polar system of innovative centres is coming into existence, partly as an effect of the rise of postcolonial and poststructuralist approaches. Second, historians unrelated to the *Annales* are engaging in interdisciplinary work, and are thus disputing the *Annales*' monopoly in that area (see especially the review *Genèse*). Third, the methodological and thematic shifts effected by members of a fourth generation of the *Annales* school or movement have given French historians an opportunity to integrate themselves into a more internationalized turn in historiography.

Guide to further reading

Peter Burke, *The French Historical Revolution. The* Annales *School 1919–1989* (Cambridge, 1999).

Stuart Clark (ed.), *The* Annales *School. Critical Assessments*, 4 vols (London, 1999).

John G. Craig, *Scholarship and Nationbuilding. The University of Strasbourg and the Alsatian Society 1870–1939* (Chicago, 1983).

Carole Fink, *Marc Bloch, A Life in History* (Cambridge, 1989).

George Huppert, 'The *Annales* Experiment', in Michael Bentley (ed.), *Companion to Historiography* (London and New York, 1997), pp. 873–88.

S. Kinser, 'Annalist Paradigm? The Geohistorical Structuralism of F. Braudel', *American Historical Review* 86 (1981), pp. 63–105.

Lutz Raphael, 'The Present as a Challenge for the Historian. The Contemporary World of the *Annales* E.S.C. 1929–1949', *Storia della Storiografia* 21 (1992), pp. 25–44.

Paul Ricoeur, *The Contribution of French Historiography to the Theory of History* (Oxford, 1980).

Troian Stoianovich, *French Historical Method. The* Annales *Paradigm* (Ithaca, 1976).

Henk Wesseling, 'Fernand Braudel, Historian of the Longue Durée', *Itinerario* 5 (1981), pp. 16–29.

Notes

1 Victor Karady, 'Les universités de la Troisième République', in Jacques Verger (ed.), *Histoire des Universités en France* (Toulouse, 1986), pp. 323–65.

2 Christophe Charle, *La République des universitaires 1870–1940* (Paris, 1994).

3 See Peter Schöttler's reconstruction of Bloch's interests from the Archives of the Library of the Ecole Normale in his essay on 'Marc Bloch und Deutschland', in Peter Schöttler (ed.), *Marc Bloch. Historiker und Widerstandskämpfer* (Frankfurt am Main and New York, 1999), p. 37.

4 There is no comprehensive biography of Febvre; but see Hans-Dieter Mann, *Lucien Febvre, la pensée vivante d'un historien* (Paris, 1971); Guy Massicotte, *L'histoire problème. La méthode de Lucien Febvre* (Paris, 1981); Bertrand Müller (ed.), *Bibliographie des travaux de Lucien Febvre* (Paris, 1990).

5 Ulrich Raulff, *Ein Historiker im 20. Jahrhundert: Marc Bloch* (Frankfurt am Main, 1995), pp. 66–180; Etienne Bloch and Stéphane Audoin-Rouzeau (eds), *Marc Bloch. Ecrits de guerre 1914–1918* (Paris, 1997).

6 Bryce and Martin Lyon (eds), *The Birth of the Annales History: the Letters of Lucien Febvre and Marc Bloch to Henri Pirenne (1921–1935)* (Brussels, 1991).

7 The editorial board comprised the geographer Albert Demangeon, the archivist Georges Espinas, the sociologist Maurice Halbwachs, the economic historian Henri Hauser, the specialist in Roman history André Piganiol, Henri Pirenne (the only one who did not come from France), Charles Rist, professor of political economy in Paris, and André Siegfried, a disciple of the geographer Vidal de la Blache, who specialized in the analysis of political cultures.

8 Marc Bloch and Lucien Febvre, 'A nos lecteurs', *Annales d'histoire économique et sociale* 1 (1929), No. 1, pp. 1–2.

9 The 'Volksgeschichte' paradigm was not restricted to Germany, but can also be found in the Baltic Provinces or in Czechoslovakia, in Hungary or in Romania; see Matthias Middell and Ulrike Sommer (eds), *Volksgeschichte im Vergleich* (Leipzig, 2003).

10 Raulff, *Marc Bloch*, p. 150.

11 Lucien Febvre, *Un destin. Martin Luther* (Paris, 1928).

12 Lucien Febvre, *La terre et l'evolution humaine* (Paris, 1922).
13 Marc Bloch, 'Pour une histoire comparée des sociétés européennes', *Revue de synthèse historique* (1928). An English version is available in Marc Bloch, *Land and Work in Medieval Europe* (London, 1967), pp. 44–76.
14 Lutz Raphael, 'Historikerkontroversen im Spannungsfeld zwischen Berufshabitus, Fächerkonkurrenz und sozialen Deutungsmustern. Lamprechtstreit und französischer Methodenstreit der Jahrhundertwende in vergleichender Perspektive', *Historische Zeitschrift* 251 (1990), pp. 325–63.
15 Hartmut Atsma, André Burguière (eds), *Marc Bloch aujourd'hui: histoire comparée et Sciences sociales* (Paris, 1990), pp. 255–336.
16 Bertrand Müller (ed.), *Marc Bloch–Lucien Febvre. Correspondance*, vol. 1, *La naissance des Annales 1928–1933* (Paris, 1994).
17 François Dosse, *L'histoire en miettes. Des 'Annales' à la 'nouvelle histoire'* (Paris, 1987).
18 For a collection of his essays, see Michel Vovelle, *Combats pour la Révolution française* (Paris, 1993); and, providing a bibliography of Vovelle's immense work as one of the leading French historians during the time of the *Bicentenaire*, see Jean-Paul Bertaud, Françoise Brunel, Catherine Duprat and François Hincker (eds), *Mélanges Michel Vovelle.sur la Revolution – approches plurielles* (Paris, 1997).
19 Roger Chartier and Henri-Jean Martin (eds), *Histoire de l'édition française*, 4 vols (Paris, 1983–6); ibid., *Lectures et lecteurs dans la France d'Ancien Régime* (Paris, 1987); ibid., Guglielmo Cavallo (eds), *Histoire de la lecture dans le monde occidental* (Paris, 1997) ; ibid., *Au bord de la falaise. L'histoire entre certitudes et inquiétude* (Paris, 1998).
20 Alain Corbin, *Les cloches de la terre. Paysage sonore et culture sensible dans les campagnes au XIXe siècle* (Paris, 1994); ibid., *Historien du sensible, entretiens avec Gilles Heuré* (Paris, 2000).
21 Pierre Nora (ed.), *Les lieux de mémoire* (Paris), 3 parts: t. 1, *La République* (Paris, 1984), t. 2, *La Nation* (3 vols, Paris, 1987), t. 3, *Les France* (3 vols, Paris, 1992). It is more than difficult to translate this French expression into English, as can be seen from the two different attempts to publish an American version of Nora's work: the one under the title of *Realms of Memory*, ed. Lawrence B. Kritzman, 3 vols (New York, London, 1996–98); the other as *Rethinking France*, ed. David P. Jordan, 4 vols (Chicago, London 2001–4).

7

Poststructuralism and history

Kevin Passmore

Nothing enrages poststructuralist historians more than the claim that their relativism – their alleged belief that any one account of the past is as good as another – provides no position from which to refute those who claim that the Holocaust is merely a story.[1] Of course, no one claims that poststructuralists are actually Holocaust deniers, but the charge – to which I shall return – remains the most extreme manifestation of disputes precipitated by what Lawrence Stone called poststructuralism's challenge to 'the subject matter of history – that is events and behaviour – and [its] data – that is contemporary texts – and [its] problem – that is explanation of change over time'. Poststructuralists contended that reality, and by extension the past, were unknowable, and that only language and representations mattered.[2]

Some dismiss poststructuralism as evidence of the corruption of history by literary criticism, for there is a history of suspicion between the two disciplines. When history diverged from literature in the late 19th century, aristocratic practitioners of literary history were as contemptuous of the 'tradesman-historian' grubbing about in public archives as were professional historians of the 'non-scientific' methods of the gentleman-scholars. Even now, some literary critics dismiss history as a 'journeyman' activity dependent on easily mastered techniques.[3] In the 1970s, social historians patronizingly – and reductively – called for the explanation of literature in terms of its historical context. Then, poststructuralists declared historical writing to be a branch of fiction, and claimed possession of the special techniques required to understand it. They effectively constituted historians as an object of study for literary critics, and for a few history became the 'other' that legitimated the rationality of literary criticism.

We must avoid essentializing disciplines, for arguably, disputes within them are more important than those between them. As Laura Lee Downs points out in this volume (Chapter 15), historians were questioning the naturalness of class and gender identities well before poststructuralism arrived in the academy. Some deployed structuralism in their critique, particularly in the form of cultural anthropology[4] and the structuralist Marxism of Louis Althusser, which provided a bridge to poststructuralism in literary criticism too.[5] Without underestimating the novelty of poststructuralism, we should not assume too sharp an opposition between poststructuralism and 'conventional' history.

This chapter will explain, through a discussion of poststructuralist thinkers and historians, the nature of the challenge to 'conventional' historical practice. My intention is not to give a definitive account of poststructuralist theory, for like any body of thought it will support multiple interpretations (but not just any). Rather, the focus will be upon the ways in which poststructuralism has been used by historians and their critics. We shall see that in spite of categorical dismissal of history as a discipline on the part of some poststructuralists, the methods and agendas of poststructuralism have become enormously influential in historical writing. This seeming contradiction owes much to ambiguities within poststructuralist theory, particularly concerning the question of whether analysis should focus on language alone, whether language should be related to 'context', and what context means. In conclusion I suggest that M. M. Bakhtin's view of language incorporates the strengths of poststructuralism, and yet and offers a view of language more fruitful for historical practice.

7.1 Postmodernism and poststructuralism

Often the terms 'postmodernism' and 'poststructuralism' are used interchangeably, but for our purpose it is more useful to see the former as a broad category covering a range of tendencies in contemporary art and intellectual enquiry that focus on 'representation' rather than 'reality'. 'Postmodernism' was first used to describe a form of art which rejected modernism. The latter assumed that the artist, a gifted individual standing outside society, could use the special skills of painting or writing to access hidden truths about the human condition. Impressionist painters, rather than merely reproducing the appearance of landscape, claimed to evoke the feeling aroused by looking it. By extension, 'conventional' history is modernist too, in that expert techniques are used to access truths not visible to the lay person.

Postmodernists do not believe it possible to uncover deep meanings. Art must remain at the surface, and cannot even reproduce that unproblematically. The artist must therefore draw attention to the contrived nature of art. This is why postmodernists mix up styles – they combine high with popular art, and use both paintbrushes and photocopiers. In the 1970s postmodernism became influential in popular music (Malcolm McLaren, architect of the Sex Pistols), cinema (*Blade Runner*, Ridley Scott, 1983) and youth journalism (*The Face*, 1982–2004).

Sociologists and philosophers extended the term 'postmodernism' to characterize the condition of contemporary society. Jean-François Lyotard, in *The Postmodern Condition* (1976), argued that the modern phase of history had given way to postmodernity, in which the nature of capitalism was different. Modernist capitalism had produced useful things, like cars and food. Postmodern capitalism produces images. Products are now sold for their cultural meaning. Guinness was once promoted on the doubtful grounds that it did one good. Now it is promised that drinking it will give one a certain image. The French philosopher Jean Baudrillard held that postmodern capitalism 'over-produces images'; reality is inaccessible and our perceptions are shaped by advertisers, television and computer screens.

Poststructuralism is one ramification of postmodernism in that it shares the conviction that we must concern ourselves with representation. Its special contribution is a theory of language, broadly defined as any form of communication, from writing and speech to gestures and computer images.

7.2 Structuralist linguistics

To understand poststructuralism we must begin by looking at structuralism, for poststructuralism was both a critique and a development of structuralism. Loosely defined, the term 'structuralism' is used in many fields. Structural-functionalism, for example, is one of the components of non-Marxist social science and modernization theory. Structuralist linguistics is of a different nature. It originated with the Swiss linguist Ferdinand de Saussure, whose *Cours de linguistique générale* appeared posthumously in 1916.

Saussure questioned the common-sense view that language mirrors or expresses pre-given objects – that words and signs directly reflect things existing in the real world. A tree is self-evidently 'there' and so we must have a concept of it and give it a name. Putting this view more technically, we could say that the 'signifier' (t-r-e-e) reflects the concept of a tree (the 'signified') and this in turn reflects the tree in the real world (the 'referent').

Saussure pointed out that there was no reason why a particular sign should refer to a particular concept or object. We could easily have used the signifiers 'cabbage' or 'frot' to designate the concept of a tree. More problematically still, different languages do not just use different words for the same objects – otherwise, translation would be straightforward. They define their signified and hence their referents differently. The French verb *aimer* can be translated as either 'love' or 'like'. The problem, Saussure said, is that the world is not self-evidently divided into pre-defined objects or concepts to which we can easily apply names. Reality has no intrinsic meaning. We receive a jumble of perceptions, and only language can make them meaningful. Structuralists illustrate this point with the example of the spectrum. We pick out particular points and define them as primary colours, but if we look carefully we find that the colours all merge into each other and we could have picked out other points.[6]

Language, Saussure argued, constructs meaning *relationally*, through a system of binary oppositions. A tree is a tree because it is not cabbage or a king; a man is a man because he is not a woman. Meaning is therefore derived from a system of *difference* within a linguistic system. We should not examine what words *denote* in the 'real' world, but their *connotations* – their relationship with other signs in the system. Saussure called this structure *langue*, and privileged its study over that of more superficial daily speech – *parole*. Indeed, the latter was simply a particular effect of the structures of *langue*. Even the idea of the individual person, the self, is invented linguistically.

Saussure's concepts might seem banal applied to trees and cabbages, but if used to understand ideas about, say masculinity, their significance is potentially immense. Male competitiveness would not be a biological necessity, but a cultural expectation produced in language. The potentially subversive power of structuralism was demonstrated in the 1950s by the cultural anthropologist Claude Lévi-Strauss (1908–2009), who argued that identical cultural-linguistic structures underlay western and allegedly 'primitive' cultures. This implied rejection of the view that societies could be categorized in terms of progress towards 'modernization'. Meanwhile Roland Barthes (1915–80) applied structuralism to literary criticism, and demonstrated how meaning in literary texts depended more on binary opposites than on the authors' intentions – hence his proclamation of the death of the author.

In the 1960s and 1970s structuralism began to influence historical writing, and already there was disagreement as to how far to take the critique of conventional history. In 1966 the literary critic Hayden White argued that historical writings were structured by classic literary forms of plot (or tropes) – comic, tragic, satirical and romantic – and that these shaped historical writing more than evidence did. Historical writing was just like fiction. It had no relationship to the real past.[7] Here already was the sceptical position that history is 'just a story'.

In unwitting defiance of White's pessimism, the historian-philosopher Michel Foucault (1926–84) wrote more conventional historical works. The influence of structuralism lay in his contention that phenomena generally seen as natural were really 'constructed' through language. Thus, in *Madness and Civilization* (1961), Foucault argued that insanity was not a self-evident fact of biology, but was conceived in different ways in different periods. Moreover, no story of improvement gave meaning to the history of psychiatry. On the contrary, the languages of psychiatry constructed mental illness as deviant, silenced it and formed part of an ever more subtle mechanism of social control. This argument was part of Foucault's attack on the notion that western history was a story of progress and reason.[8] It amounts, however, less to a challenge to the foundations of conventional history than to a brilliant reinterpretation of a particular topic using the techniques of structuralism wedded to a conventional, if occasionally lax, historical method. Foucault even attempted to recover the lost history of madness – a project akin to labour historians' restoration of the working class to history, and which assumes that the historian can recover untold true stories.

7.3 Post-structuralism: Textual and worldly

These uncertainties were accentuated by the shift to poststructuralism. Some have described methodological tensions in terms of differences between Foucault and Jacques Derrida (1930–2004). Foucault, we saw, did not entirely abandon the notion of recovering the truth of the past. Derrida saw Foucault's project of writing a history of madness free from the oppression of western rationalism as flawed by its reliance upon the same language of western reason. All thought, Derrida argued, depended on the repression of alternative languages. So simply by writing about madness Foucault marginalized it. The implication of Derrida's view might be that any historical writing is an act of oppression. Foucault retorted that Derrida was concerned with language in isolation, and perceived 'nothing outside the text'. Foucault preferred to analyse language in relation to social and institutional practices and power.[9] Alex Callinicos uses this dispute to distinguish between Derrida's 'textual poststructuralism' and Foucault's 'worldly poststructuralism'.[10] This distinction will help us to understand the way in which poststructuralism has been used by historians. But we must bear in mind that when Foucault spoke of social context he often assumed that social relations were structured like languages as binary oppositions and should therefore be analysed as such. In that view social power had no origin, and the difference with Derrida is not as great as it might seem. At other times Foucault adopted a more Marxist stance, seeing languages as produced in the interests of dominant groups or institutions – notably in his *Order of Discourse* (1971). Rather confusingly, Foucault and Derrida shifted between all three possible relationships between language and context, depending on whom they were addressing. This ambivalence is reproduced in much historical writing.

7.4 Derrida, deconstruction and history

Poststructuralists criticized structuralists for attempting to reduce all languages to an identical binary structure, a move that undermines structuralists' contention that meaning is produced through difference. The term '*post*structuralism' suggests a break with the idea of structure, but this is only half true. In effect, poststructuralists see language as an unstable *system* in which meaning fluctuates. Language (*langue*) remains the object of study, and the mechanisms of language still uniformly undermine meaning through an identical method. Structuralists and poststructuralists both also reject the notion that 'reality' can produce meaning. Not surprisingly, many structuralists embraced poststructuralism without difficulty.

Although Saussure argued that the relationship of language to the real world was problematic, he nevertheless assumed that binary structures established signs in mutual relationship so that the concepts they referred to were equally meaningful. In his *Of Grammatology* (1967), Derrida argued that the connection between words and concepts – signifiers and signifieds – is also uncertain. He advanced several reasons for this. First, each sign differs from an endless number of other signs, so that the 'complete' meaning of a word is never known. We might understand tree in relation to plant, but our understanding of 'tree' changes as we relate it to other words. Second, there is no clear distinction between signifiers and signified. We can only express the meaning (signified) of the signifier t-r-e-e by using other signifiers, such as l-e-a-v-e-s and t-r-u-n-k. Third, meaning changes as we read and listen. Words at the beginning of sentences do not obtain their meaning until we get to the end of the sentence. Even then, the next sentence can change the meaning of the previous, and so on. Fourth, the meanings of signs are altered by the signs around them. 'Tree' means something different when linked to 'family' or 'snake'. Finally, because any sign is defined by things that it is not, its meaning must depend on its opposites. So, while binary oppositions are essential to the operation of language, they are unstable. To express both his debt to and departure from Saussure, Derrida invented the neologism '*différance*', which both reminds us that language operates through difference (between binary opposites) and that meaning is deferred (*différé* in French) – incomplete, or uncertain.

The logic is that all we have is signs, and there is no essential truth. One of Derrida's purposes was to demonstrate, through the technique of 'deconstruction', a sort of close reading of texts for their 'aporias' (blind spots), how writing was based on this futile search for ultimate truth. For him any such assumption is 'metaphysical'. It follows that the past too is inaccessible, and that any attempt to write about it is doomed. What historians do write is a linguistic construction. Some, including Derrida himself, deny that he intended to undermine the category of truth so radically. What Derrida 'really' meant to say concerns us less than the fact that many critics of history have interpreted Derrida thus, and not entirely without reason.

The essentialism of traditional historiography

The logic of Derrida's poststructuralism is that a text or a piece of historical evidence cannot be interpreted in relation to an 'essential' principle lying outside it. Most obviously this implies rejection of Marxist historians' search for reflections in historical documents of class interest. Poststructuralists maintain that classes are not 'essential' objects outside the text, but are linguistically produced by the operation of language. The meaning of class is all the more fluctuating and problematic because, whereas for a structuralist 'worker' might be understood simply in relation to capitalist, for a poststructuralist there is no end to its possible meanings. Thus, poststructuralist historians have shown that ideas of gender, biology, race and many other things have in particular contexts entered into the definition of 'worker'.

If poststructuralism criticized only Marxism of the vulgar variety, it would be of little interest. Marxist historians, notably E. P. Thompson, have long since elaborated a more complex understanding of class, based upon a rejection of economic determinism. Yet it was precisely upon this sophisticated social history, and in particular upon Thompson's *The Making of the English Working Class*, that poststructuralists concentrated their fire.

To begin with, poststructuralists have argued that, in spite of the concern with culture, social history left the primacy of class as an objective reality untouched. Although Thompson replaced determinism with the notion that economic conditions 'set limits', he still assumed that real changes in class relations were inevitably 'experienced' by workers and necessarily translated, albeit using pre-existing ideas about the rights of 'free-born Englishmen', into class consciousness. The idea of 'limits' begs the question of what those limits are, and implicitly restores a looser economic determinism.[11] Thompson insisted that, whatever historical variations might be found, 'a generic mode of production has found roughly analogous expression within different societies and state institutions'.[12] Patrick Joyce argued that Thompson, typically of social historians, assumed that class and politics were rooted materially and that 'society' was a sort of 'explanatory sub-tissue', relating the economic to the cultural. As a poststructuralist, Joyce contends that 'social history does not innocently name the world, but creates it in its own image'.[13]

According to the feminist historian Joan Wallach Scott, Thompson's 'naming' of the working class relied on prejudices about gender roles. Thompson, says Scott, writes about the male world of demonstrations, politics and trade unions. Women, although numerous in the labour force, figure in *The Making* largely as domestic creatures. They leave the home only to listen to the millenarian preaching of Joanna Southcott. Scott's critique is classic poststructuralism: the political rationality of class-conscious men is contrasted with, and defined by, the 'feminine irrationality' of religion. Class is constructed through cultural assumptions.[14]

From a different perspective again, Hayden White argued that each of the four parts of *The Making* is structured by different narrative tropes – metaphorical, metonymic, synecdochic and ironic. The nature of these tropes matters less than White's contention that they, rather than anything 'discovered' in the evidence, and by extension the past, give meaning to Thompson's narrative.[15] Meaning is a product of linguistic structures.

Other scholars extended the poststructuralist critique to embrace any attempt to write meaningful history. Robert Berkhofer, for whom 'contemporary literary theory defies the very intellectual foundations of current professional historical practice', is exemplary. He recognizes that historians are aware of their bias, and that they usually assume a two-way relationship between facts and interpretation. So provisional hypotheses are modified by evidence, and new evidence is sought out in the light of modified hypotheses. Nevertheless, Berkhofer argues, the historian's synthesis still rests on the fantasy of a *reconstructed* past. Historians accept that their monographs represent partial views of history, but nevertheless see them as part of a real past, reconstructed through the interconnections of the whole body of historical writing. Historians falsely believe that the past is inherently structured like a narrative, just as the historian's own writing is organized as a narrative.

For Berkhofer, all historical writing is based on the mirage of metanarrative – not just that which explicitly posits a metanarrative. The methods historians use to guarantee that their accounts 'represent' the past are useless. Historians resolve disputes between competing interpretations by appealing to evidence. Yet, says Berkhofer, facts can arbitrate disagreement only if we assume that they derive from an intrinsically coherent, narratively structured, past. In fact the past has no such meaning. Worse, the past is absent: one cannot point to it as one does a tree. We might have leftovers from the past in the form of evidence, but the past about which historians write is much larger than the evidence will allow. Historians have no idea about how the evidence fitted together. They merely refer to the equally problematic works of other historians.[16]

History as postmodern art

Perhaps surprisingly, Berkhofer does not abandon the possibility of writing history. He echoes Hayden White's calls for 'the historian to tell many different kinds of "stories" from various viewpoints, with many voices, emplotted diversely'. Such histories, like postmodern art, would frankly admit their constructed nature. Such histories would no longer use the 'meta-story' to legitimate their own discourse and disqualify others.[17]

Many of the contributions to the journal *Re-Thinking History*, established in 1997, challenge 'modernist' history. A typical sample is Robin Bisha's article on Russian noblewomen in the time of Peter the Great. The nature of the sources, Bisha argues, means that it is impossible to know much about what Russian noblewomen thought or felt, and she criticizes other historians for basing their interpretations on present-day prejudices. So Bisha resorts to literature. She writes a pseudo-autobiography of the noblewoman in question – the first-person authorial voice calls attention to the article as a story.[18] Simon Schama's compelling *Dead Certainties (Unwarranted Speculations)* (1997) also adopts a postmodern manner, mixing the genres of historical writing, art history and detective fiction.

It is hard to see the novelty of this way of doing history. If we accept, as many 'orthodox' historians do, that art and literature can tell equally valid but different truths about the past from those offered by history, then recasting history in the form of art merely gives us more of what we have already. Sadly, most historians are not blessed with Schama's literary gifts. All we get is moderate art.

In any case, the idea of 'multiple perspectives' concedes too much to the authority of a past that has supposedly been demolished. Simply by claiming that a given story is one angle on a particular event, or that an event may be emplotted in different ways, an event is invested with properties that disqualify some accounts as being perspectives upon it. Some postmodern histories will be perspectives on the Russian Revolution and others on the French. This re-establishes the right of the real past (not evidence, ironically) to distinguish between interpretations.

The logic of textual poststructuralism really is that *nothing* of any value can be written about the past; when poststructuralists deny this, they unwittingly abandon elements of their theory. No standard exists by which any perspective can be ruled out, so all are equally interesting (or uninteresting). Keith Jenkins might be thought to be in tune with relativism when he declares that postmodern society can do without the 'knackered old horse that answers to the name of history'. But he relies on the essentialist assumption that a given historical period is (or, more sinisterly, should be) characterized by the dominance of a particular philosophy.[19]

7.5 Worldly poststructuralism and historical writing

These difficulties might explain why poststructuralist historians generally confine their use of textualism to deconstructing the work of other historians whilst using a more Foucauldian worldly poststructuralism in their own writing. Their histories are poststructuralist in the sense that they examine the ways in which the past has been constructed, and the emplotments that may already exist within the past. They write about the ways in which people in the past constructed their worlds, about how historians have constructed the past, and about the concepts used to construct the meaning in the world – class, society, the individual, truth, nation or race. Derrida called for a history of truth, but such histories are largely inspired by Foucault, who wrote brilliantly historical works himself. In the last quarter-century an immense body of imaginative historical work has demonstrated the fertility of this agenda, and we shall see in subsequent chapters that poststructuralism has transformed each of the fields under discussion. However, since it is difficult to write history at all without departing from some of the major tenets of textual poststructuralism, and since the distinction between textual and worldly poststructuralism is not absolute, tensions can be found in this work; notably slippage into an instrumental understanding of power, referential uses of language and the implicit recourse to a metanarrative.

Discipline and punish

Foucault examined language in relation to social and institutional practices and power. He used the term 'discourse' to mean the study of language in context and in relation to power. Thus in *Discipline and Punish* (1975) Foucault described the way in which the intermittent but violent punishment of the early-modern period, exemplified in 'the spectacle of the scaffold', gave way to the regular, systematic punishment of the 19th-century prison. Once again he denied that this change was the fruit of progress. Rather the prison was a more effective use of 'disciplinary' power. Moreover, the prison constituted a model for surveillance in schools, factories and hospitals. Through discourses of education, medicine and criminality, these institutions assigned people to particular positions – pupil, worker and patient – and deprived them of power. Language, particularly professional knowledge, is intrinsically related to power.

Often Foucault's method is close to Derridean textual deconstruction, in that social relations are assumed to be structured like the languages, the focus is on the equivalent of Saussure's *langue*, and society is examined independently of the intentions of historical actors. Foucault analyses social relations like languages, as binary oppositions in which one term is dominant (doctor/patient, for example). His work is 'poststructuralist' in the sense that he problematizes these binaries, drawing links between armies, prisons and schools, and showing, for instance, the importance of 'bio power', the power to mark and train bodies to all of them. He also emphasizes the relationship between language and power. For Foucault disciplinary power is not localized in a particular institution, state, or ideology. It is 'not', he said, 'the "privilege" acquired or preserved, of the dominant class, but the overall effect of its strategic positions'. Power is 'diffuse' and intrinsic to all social relations.[20] It is independent of the activities, or 'agency' of human beings, and must be examined as a system.

Alongside this view of language and power, Foucault endorses implicitly the more familiar contention that languages are used intentionally by particular social categories, or they somehow arise from the 'needs of the system' (a functionalist argument, which in theory is incompatible with poststructuralism). Either way, for Foucault the shift towards punishment in prisons was a consequence of the needs of developing capitalism. Prison and army became models for the disciplined workforce and society required by capitalism. One may recognize the Marxist idea that institutions and ideas serve the interests of capitalism, even if they are not directly controlled by capitalists. Here Foucault's conclusions could be seen as essentialist, for the economic purposes of capitalists give meaning to the texts he studies.

Patrick Joyce's *Democratic Subjects*

In *Democratic Subjects* (1995), Patrick Joyce explains how working-class and bourgeois radicals made sense of the world through language. This fascinating book inevitably irritated social historians, for it argued for the constructed nature of class consciousness, and contended that the autonomous, self-knowing, agent – another of the sacred cows of social history – was a linguistic construction, too.

In the first part of the book Joyce discusses the self-conceptions of the artisan-autodidact Edwin Waugh. Work figures in Waugh's self-identity only as the myth of the golden age of the morally dignified handloom weaver. Real work he found bothersome. His ideal was less a product of class than of a Protestant and bourgeois discourse of self-improvement transferred from organized religion to 'humanity'. Waugh dreamed of concord amongst men rather than social reform, let alone class conflict. Joyce then shows that John Bright, from a completely different class background, shared this religion of humanity. He details the mix of a Quaker myth of persecution, evangelical Christianity, paternalism and romanticism out of which Bright constructed his persona. Waugh and Bright both depicted themselves as romantic heroes able to transcend the world of experience, and triumph over evil – an example of the romantic narrative as defined by White.

In some of the most interesting passages Joyce shows how music-hall motifs constructed radicalism. Melodramas depicted the poor as victims – usually female and passive – of evil capitalists. The victim was conventionally saved by a high-minded upper-class hero. Virtue triumphed over vice, and the socially low became morally high. The outcome is a cross-class alliance between enlightened workers and bourgeois, rather than class struggle (note the binary oppositions and the interdependence of opposites). Joyce argues melodrama's combination of sensation and moralism was transposed into the reforming press and informed Gladstone's speeches. Thus liberalism was not an expression of bourgeois class interest, but is constructed through language.

In a number of apparently minor turns, Joyce uses a more conventional view of the relationship between language and context. The multiple class positions of those attending the Manchester Athenaeum prove that it was a non-class institution (*Democratic Subjects*, p. 173). The degree of bitterness of political conflict in France, Britain and America is read off from the degree of consensus around the constitution (*Democratic Subjects*, p. 195). Other examples could be given. In all cases something external to the text – an intrinsic property of social relations – explains the nature of the languages used by historical actors. In both *Discipline and Punish* and *Democratic Subjects*, two views of language and its relationship to context vie for supremacy. Ironically, both sometimes unwittingly reproduce an essentialism that is justifiably criticized in 'conventional' historiography.

Postmodernism and modernization

Likewise, poststructuralist historians have found it difficult to free themselves entirely from reliance upon metanarratives. It is often remarked that Foucault's vision of a tendency in the history of punishment towards rationalization, surveillance, efficiency and control recalls the macro-historical teleology of modernization theory. The only difference is that Foucault viewed this teleology pessimistically. Joyce does not explicitly use metatheories, but the same assumption that history moves in a particular direction is present more subtly in *Democratic Subjects*, which is framed by the idea that the 19th century saw a shift from individual to social modes of thinking. Waugh and Bright are positioned (as so often in modernization-based accounts) in the 'transition'. Joyce is evidently uncomfortable, for he comments that this periodization 'can distort the picture by presenting change as a linear process of stages'. Nonetheless, he says 'this very rough sketch has its uses' (*Democratic Subjects*, p. 15).

The disadvantages of teleologies are well known. Particularly relevant is that poststructuralists share the modernization theorist's tendency to characterize historical periods in terms of a 'spirit of the age' (more likely they call it 'the deep structure of the episteme'), be it traditional, modern, postmodern or transitional, and to interpret their particular objects of study in the light of this spirit. Hayden White bases his account of the 'burden of history' on the alleged 'strangeness' of the present, by which he means that rapid change has a disorientating effect. Again we are reminded of modernization theory, which often explained revolutions as a product of the 'disorientation' supposedly caused by 'rapid change'. In situating his subject in a period of 'transition' White is typical. New Historicist literary critics prefer to study the Renaissance because it is supposedly a transition, a 'gap in history', which gave rise to the same feelings of exhilaration and fearfulness.[21] Such generalizations detract from the complexity of views in any given period, and underestimate the extent to which allegedly general characteristics were actually contested. In any case, no law dictates that people living in a period of transition – even if such a blanket term could really be applied to a period – should feel disorientated.

This recourse to metanarrative and essentialism derives largely from discomfort with the idea of causes. Poststructuralist denial of the knowability of the past implies that causes are merely narrative structures gratuitously imposed on an inaccessible past. Yet the assumption that language is a system in itself, independent of human agency, raises the question of why one language should give way to another. The same problem is evident in Foucault's assumption that social relations are structured like languages. Therefore to explain the rise of the prison he resorts to the notion that a mysterious force outside history produces changes – i.e. the rise of capitalism, or the 'need' for a more efficient form of punishment. Large-scale inhuman forces drive history on, just as they give meaning to particular periods.

Agency

It should follow from this predilection for blind forces, and from the contention that language is a system independent of human will, that the agency and choices of individual human beings or social groups mean little. No individual or group should be able to modify the system – albeit shifting and uncertain – which defines them. For poststructuralists the idea of the 'self' is merely a product of language.

Yet in *Discipline and Punish* Foucault argues that resistance to the strategies of power is possible – at least before the emergence of modern systems of surveillance. He uses two kinds of argument, each hard to reconcile with poststructuralist theory. Sometimes he claims that there is a spontaneous and unruly agency of the people, which dominant discourses endeavour to control though prisons, hospitals and schools. This implies that popular agency exists independently of language. Elsewhere Foucault suggests that because social relations are constantly in tension (an essentialist assumption, which is not necessarily true), each exercise of power carries a risk of inversion of power relations. Thus public execution fell out of favour because it brought people together in crowds and enabled them to mock the authorities.[22] This idea is familiar. Marx argued that by concentrating workers in large factories capitalists sowed the seeds of their own downfall. Foucault's idea of resistance poses conceptual difficulties from a poststructuralist perspective, however, for if agency is constructed through language, how can it take on a life of its own outside the linguistic system? This is an odd kind of alchemy.

Similar uncertainties can be found in *Democratic Subjects.* Joyce argues that in the late 19th century new political narratives necessarily created 'new political subjectivities [i.e. conceptions of the self as a person able to act in the world] which *created* agency and legitimacy' (my emphasis). Identities were created *for* leaders and led which ensured the former's *control* over politics (*Democratic Subjects*, p. 192, my emphasis). Sometimes this idea that language creates individual identities is reinforced by recourse to the notion of social control, in which beliefs are inculcated in the masses from above. Thus Bright's oratory is said to operate on the 'political unconscious', giving the people the sense – the illusion – of being active agents in the story of progress (*Democratic Subjects*, p. 201).

Joyce is too good a historian to rely upon generalizations of this sort in his practical analysis. He argues that Bright's self-conception was not just 'given to him' but actively created by him out of his religion. His Quakerism was 'a resource that might be used in different ways to create different kinds of self' (p. 105). All this is convincing, but it sits uneasily with the Joyce's use of Derrida's vocabulary. It represents a break with poststructuralism, in that, rather than being created by language, agency and language are inseparable. Joyce implicitly accepts that language cannot exist without people to speak and write it. From this it would follow that groups and individuals *could* adapt and use language, within limits, for their own purposes.

Method

Both *Discipline and Punish* and *Democratic Subjects* belong to the genre of narrative historical writing. Not for them the experimentation of postmodern histories. Both advance hypotheses designed to improve upon earlier interpretations of the past. Both cite evidence in support of their contentions and use footnotes. Both see their own interpretations as superior – more powerful? – than those of rival historians. Joyce regrets that one of his secondary sources fails to footnote adequately (*Democratic Subjects*, p. 38); the invented nature of Bright's view of the democratic impulses in Quakerism is demonstrated by showing the 'real' nature of mid-century Quakerism (*Democratic Subjects*, p. 107). Many more examples could be given. Suffice it to add that the idea of recovery of the lost past is at the heart of *Democratic Subjects* just as Foucault once sought to recover the voices of the insane. Joyce shows how historical protagonists *really* made sense of the world. He berates social historians for imposing their conception of class on the past, when 19th-century contemporaries *really* understood class in moral terms (*Democratic Subjects*, p. 17). We are at the heart of the difficulty of writing poststructuralist history. Poststructuralists write histories of how meaning was constructed in the past. But it is not clear how such histories can be differentiated methodologically from 'conventional' histories, since both involve the construction of hypotheses about the meaning of evidence.

It would, however, be unfair to charge Joyce, any more than any 'conventional historian', with advocating 'naïve' reconstructionism – the notion that the historian's narrative actually 'reconstructs' the past. In fact, the method used in *Democratic Subjects*, and by many other historians, cannot easily be pigeonholed as either reconstructionist or relativist. Joyce explains that, while there is no position from which we can assess the 'correspondence or non-correspondence between our discourse and the real' (i.e. between historical writing and the past), this does not mean that we are unable to discriminate between true and false data or tenable and untenable arguments (p. 9). The historians' usual protocols for deciding these issues can be used so long as we remember that these protocols are 'the product of history'. Joyce leaves it at that, perhaps because further elucidation would be difficult to reconcile with poststructuralist theory. This cryptic formula must be unpacked.

7.6 Objectivity from a point of view

The great contribution of poststructuralism to historical writing is the demonstration that nothing can be known independently of language, and that the past has no 'essential' meaning. No longer is it possible to regard men as naturally aggressive, women as naturally maternal, workers as naturally socialist, or Celts as naturally wild. No longer can historians assume that people living through periods of rapid change naturally felt disorientated, or that the massive increase in the availablity of information discrients people. Earlier philosophers of history such as Karl Popper (1902–94) criticized essentialism from a different starting point, and in many respects their critique was sounder. But their arguments were generally misconceived by historians. Essentialism, insofar as it has been weakened, has been weakened by poststructuralism.

As poststructuralists argue, the external world impinges upon humans in the form of sensory perceptions which have no inherent meaning. Only through language can we make sense of these perceptions, and the meanings so created could vary infinitely, especially in the case of human constructions such as classes, markets or states. The real question, as Berkhofer rightly argues, is whether the meanings historians purport to find in, or attribute to, the past are all equally valid.

Berkhofer's critique rests on two contentions. The first, that historical knowledge is unverifiable because we cannot 'point to the past', is a red herring. The problem of knowing the past is no greater than that of knowing the present, and rests on the naïve reconstructionist view that only direct confrontation of an object can guarantee truth. Indeed, we cannot be certain that our favourite pub has been destroyed by fire since we last nipped in for a drink. But there is a strong probability that it has not, and so we probably won't ring the pub and check that it's still there before setting off for our evening pint. We could, one might object, go at any moment to check the pub's existence. But even then we would need to be certain that our eyes were not playing tricks upon us, and we could not continually travel around the world to verify the existence of various places. Generally, we rely on the *strong probability* and on *indirect confirmation* that something exists. The same is true of history. We cannot go to the past to confirm that the First World War took place. But we do have plenty of evidence, ranging from memoirs to the presence of the debris of war in the soil of the battlefields. It is theoretically possible that this evidence could have been fabricated, but more *probably* it was not. Berkhofer assumes that only that which can directly be seen is verifiable; but, like people in daily life, historians deal in *probabilities*, not truths.[23]

Second, Berkhofer argues that historians' claim to 'reconstruct' the past rests on the false assumption that the past is already structured like a narrative. In fact, conventional historiography needs neither to assume an intrinsically meaningful past nor attempt to reconstruct it. True, it is sometimes claimed that historians do reconstruct the past – Richard Evans writes that 'the truth about patterns and linkages of facts in history is in the end discovered not invented, found, not made'.[24] Poststructuralist critics have generally concentrated their fire upon 'constructionists' because they present an easier target. Reconstruction of the past genuinely is impossible. Yet the method of hypothesis formulation and testing – the hypothetic-deductive method – favoured by many equally conventional historians actually combines acceptance of the unlimited interpretative possibilities open to historians with the recognition that all interpretations are not equally valid. Interestingly, one of the foremost proponents of this method was Popper (especially as modified by Imre Lakatos), whose critique of positivistic model building and use of probablist method was recommended to historians by no less than Hayden White.[25]

The historian begins with an initial hypothesis or question derived from his/her own interests, in turn dependent upon the existing state of historiography and the contemporary cultural milieu. The historian starts with bias. Dependence on questions means that the resulting account will only be one possible perspective on a problem that is itself constituted by the enquirer, since others might have asked different questions. Furthermore, since we cannot know what viewpoints historians will have in the future, we cannot know what questions they will ask, and what results they will produce. We cannot say how much, or how little, of the past we have made sense of, or whether our knowledge will be superseded.

Questions also determine the relevance of evidence. In effect a hypothesis is a prediction concerning the type of evidence we should find. If we hypothesize that notions of medieval kingship were influenced by contemporary ideas about masculinity, then we predict that certain gendered metaphors will be found in texts concerning kingship. The evidence is itself debatable. But it is treated according to accepted rules of evidence, which determine what is admissible (hearsay, for example, would be treated as a lower form of evidence than direct testimony). Some questions might be deemed unanswerable because of lack of evidence.

If a hypothesis appears to match the evidence, we do not claim to have told the 'truth' about medieval kingship – meaning, we can agree with Derrida, is always deferred. We have simply suggested a provisional answer to a precise question and established one possible way in which what is available to us of the past – the evidence – *might* be conceptualized. Our answer might be modified not only by further research and reassessment of the evidence but by redefinition of the question. Historians attempt to answer properly formulated questions in accordance with rules of evidence, just as a court of law seeks to establish whether a particular law has been broken, not the entire history of an event 'in itself'.[26] The past of the historians is the product of the historians' own protocols for making sense of part of what is reasonably believed to derive from the past – the evidence.

Historians' answers are usually presented in the form of narratives. Poststructuralist critics, perhaps fooled by the everyday language favoured by many historians, attribute to them the view that narratives are 'neutral containers for facts' and that they permit reconstruction of past reality.[27] Many historians know very well that narratives are not innocent, and it is not unknown for them to debate the implication of narrative structures in interpretations. More explicit exploration of the problems raised by White would certainly help make historians more aware of the constructed nature of their accounts, and there is no reason why the use of genre in historical writing should not itself be a subject of research – so long as other perspectives are not disallowed.

Berkhofer is right that historians assume that their particular accounts are compatible with the wider body of historical knowledge. More precisely, the historian assumes compatibility with those accounts that s/he sees as valid, for the method of hypothesis testing entails a critical approach to the work of others. This dependence of a single work upon a wide body of knowledge is not, however, peculiar to history. Presumably Berkhofer himself assumes compatibility of his own work with a corpus of critical knowledge about the writing of history. He does not – I think – claim to have reconstructed the reality of the historical discipline, only to have improved upon previous understandings of it.

The use of narratives is one of several *useful* ways of making sense of evidence – including artistic ones – each with its own rules of representation. The fact that historical writing has a narrative structure does not imply belief that the past itself has a like structure. On the contrary, the historian's account represents one possible way of making sense of a past which has no pre-given meaning, and of which there is an unknowable range of interpretations.[28] Any narrative has advantages and disadvantages; it shows some things and hides others. The historians' account is not a 'reflection' of the past, but, as Perez Zagorin puts it, 'reflective of process selection based on relevance to the problems and questions that the historian poses with respect to his or her subject'.[29]

Historians, poststructuralism and the Holocaust

The controversy over the relationship between poststructuralism and the question of the Holocaust draws together the points made above. There is no space here to enter into the details of the dispute. Suffice it to say that there are two strands to the debate that impinge upon the application of poststructuralism to history.

First, Richard Evans, amongst others, argues that poststructuralism provides no position from which Holocaust denial literature can be refuted, for all interpretations are held to be equally valid. Evans' charge has *prima facie* substance, at least for textual poststructuralists. Why should the Holocaust be exempt from Berkhofer's rule that historians have no way of distinguishing between the truth claims of different accounts of the past? But we must note that, while deniers sometimes profit from the vaguely postmodern notion that all views must be granted a hearing, they are just as likely to resort to a hyperbolic constructionism in which nothing is proved without absolute verification: since the Holocaust cannot be proven beyond *all* doubt – because there are *some* discrepancies in the evidence – it cannot be proven at all. Deniers exploit both relativism and reconstructionism.[30]

Interestingly, in defending themselves against the charge of unwittingly aiding the deniers, poststructuralists abandon the strongest elements of their own position, and resort to reconstructionism. They accept the provability of 'individual facts', while maintaining the possibility of multiple emplotments and interpretations.[31] The same Hayden White, who claims that 'no other discipline is more informed by the illusion that "facts" are found in research rather than constructed by modes of representation and techniques of discoursivization than is history', argues that the Holocaust can be considered as a 'factual statement', which he describes as a 'singular existential proposition'.[32]

This concedes too much to the notion of a reconstructable past, and indeed to the positivist notion that fact and interpretation can be separated. Interpretation and indeed emplotment are already involved in the contention that the Holocaust is a fact. As poststructuralists insist, we have used language to make sense of the world, for the term 'Holocaust' makes sense only in language. Indeed, without in any way denying mass murder, some perfectly respectable historians doubt that the term is the best way of making sense of the evidence. Some historians prefer the term 'Judeocide', on the grounds that it defines the event differently, and thus makes better sense of the evidence. Furthermore, establishment of the fact of the Holocaust is not simple. The question of when the Holocaust began has produced much complex debate among historians. And the 'simple' fact of the Holocaust actually consists of many other facts: the remains of gas chambers, memories of torture, memoirs, court records, administrative documents, political programmes, murders, anti-Semitic tracts, intentions and so on, all of which are themselves subject to debate, but which have been arranged in accordance with historians' hypotheses about the past. If it is legitimate to use the concept of the Holocaust to organize these phenomena, why is it illegitimate to relate the 'fact' of the Holocaust to other 'facts', from the rise of Nazism to the development of the war in the east? The result, of course, would be a historical narrative.

It does not follow that *any* interpretation is acceptable. Revisionist and 'conventional' views of the Holocaust are indeed both stories. Both attempt to make sense of a past that can be construed in infinite ways. Revisionism is illegitimate, however, because its historical method is a sham. Historians' questions predict that if a hypothesis is true, then certain types of evidence will be found. In effect revisionists predict that *no* evidence of the systematic murder of the Jews can be found. When such evidence *is* found – in plenty – they resort to the classic response of the conspiracy theorist: the evidence has been planted. Or they claim that because there are some inconsistencies in the narrative, then the Holocaust did not happen. In other words, the deniers' case cannot be falsified; nothing could contradict their hypothesis.

In fact, evidence *can* be fabricated. But here another of the rules of historical method comes into play: probability. The evidence for the Holocaust is so overwhelming that the possibility that it has been manufactured is quite simply improbable. It is so unlikely that the deniers' narrative can only be maintained in ignorance or bad faith. In sum, we can never reconstruct the past, still less the Holocaust, in some transcendent sense. There is always, as postmodernists put it, an 'excess'. Neither can it be denied that literature and film can tell different kinds of truths. But historians can decide between two answers to a specific question. Returning to court, the denier is convicted not just on the 'balance of probabilities', but 'beyond reasonable doubt'.

Historians cannot usually be so categorical. There is a continuum from facts established as fully as possible, in the sense that all reasonable historians agree upon them, including the Holocaust, world wars, Crusades and so on, to more debatable issues such as peasant mentalities in the early medieval period, where there is some agreement and much debate. In any event historians do not reconstruct the event, but advance more or less probable ways of making sense of what is left over from the past. The question of objectivity cannot be resolved by recourse to the binary opposites of relativism and reconstruction – just because truth claims cannot be established absolutely, does not mean that they cannot be established at all.

The second question can disposed of more briefly. Once it is accepted that the Holocaust is a fact, do historians and others have a free choice of how to represent it? Wulf Kansteiner feels that factually correct histories can be turned to almost any political purpose. One could have racist, Fascist, Stalinist or democratic views of any given event, each of which would be factually correct. One could distinguish between them only on moral or political grounds, not on the basis of their truth claims.[33] In a sense Kansteiner is right. The statement that the Nazis systematically murdered six million Jews cannot be refuted historically, but it can be interpreted either as a tragedy or, sadly, by anti-Semites as rightful vengeance. The historian has little control over the moral conclusions that will be drawn from her/his work – even if a historian begins with a question prompted by a particular moral concern, there is no guarantee that the reader will interpret his/her findings in the manner expected.

Yet it remains possible to distinguish analytically between historical and moral statements. The very fact that we are able to show that the meaning of historical writing varies according to context depends on our ability to distinguish these two kinds of statements. Historians, as citizens, have the right, perhaps even a duty, to discuss moral implications of their work, but they cannot claim special expertise in morality. Morality is a question for society as a whole. It does not derive automatically from historical work, but is *ascribed* to it by a cultural context. Even though moral lessons will inevitably be drawn, they are not, in analytical terms, the same as interpretative issues, such as why and how the Holocaust happened and who or what was responsible. Here the historian can claim some special skill.

7.7 Agency and language

Binary oppositions, such as that between objectivity and relativism, are no more helpful in understanding the problem of structure and agency. We saw in our discussion of *Democratic Subjects* that the idea that human agency is constructed through language is problematic. Languages cannot *do* anything. Only people and natural forces (such as earthquakes) can act upon the world and change it. Without people and their physical capabilities, there would be no language. Yet it is equally true that without language human action would be random and meaningless. Human activity is more effective and meaningful when it is organized intellectually, institutionally and socially. Language and agency are actually inseparable. Joyce recognized this in depicting Bright as simultaneously shaped by linguistic and cultural conditions, and as using these conditions to modify his world. Joyce restores the mutuality of language and agency, but at the cost of abandoning the tenet that the binary structures of language give the world all the meaning it has.

Some historians – including Joyce in later work – see the linguistic theory of the Russian M. M. Bakhtin (1895–1975) as a more convincing alternative to poststructuralism (although it must be borne in mind that he wrote as a critic of structuralism, and that poststructuralism was unknown to him). Whereas the followers of Saussure argued that the formal structures of language produced meaning, Bakhtin argued that language should be analysed as a dynamic system in which the writer, the reader and the context all work together to produce meaning. In other words, meaning arises from *dialogue* between people – it is *dialogic*. Language is dialogic in the double sense that the writer draws upon and modifies, consciously and unconsciously, all sorts of pre-existing ideas (just as Bright did). The speaker also tries to anticipate the reactions of the listener, as s/he understands them, and thereby incorporates something of their views into the work. Any given text is *multi-vocal* or *heteroglossic* in that it contains, alongside the voices of the author, those of his/her sources and unconscious influences, and the voices of the audience, all cast in terms of narrative structures.

Thus John Arnold argues that records of interrogations by the Inquisition should be treated as heteroglossic. They contain the voices of interrogator and interrogated as well as competing discourses of heresy, confession, crime and sexuality. In these texts there is no voice, only *voices*, which cannot be completely separated from each other.*

The Bakhtinian approach also allows the listener to use modify these ideas in their own writing and speech, and not necessarily in ways foreseen by the speaker. And the text can be used by other speakers in unpredictable ways. Bakhtin regarded *parole* and *langue* as inseparable. Thus the historian Evelyn Brookes Higginbotham argued that racism in the southern states of America was a 'metalanguage', in that it ascribed negative characteristics to African-American people and legitimated discrimination against them. But the idea of race was also taken over by black nationalists, invested with positive characteristics, and used as a force for liberation.[34]

Bakhtin's approach retains the advantages of poststructuralism: the close analysis of texts, the rejection of the idea that a primary category, such as class or biology enables us to explain the nature of our sources or of the course of history (essentialism). But it also is stronger than poststructuralism in that it allows both for human agency *and* for social and linguistic structure, without claiming that one is primary, or even that they are separable.[35]

7.8 Conclusion

History has survived poststructuralism. Many historians continue to write as if poststructuralism – indeed, theory of any kind – did not exist. Yet the subtle influence of poststructuralism has spread through the profession, shifting the object of historians' attention towards culture. Historians have become somewhat more wary of essentialist simplifications, and are somewhat less inclined to claim that they can reconstruct the past. Many poststructuralists meanwhile have largely retreated from the radical scepticism espoused by Berkhofer and others. An example is Miguel Cabrera, who in *Postsocial History* (2005) has the great merit among advocates of the cultural turn of discussing

* John Arnold, 'The historian as inquisitor' *Rethinking History* (1998), pp. 379–86.

actual works of history. He does not deny that social structures condition and constrain practice, only that 'a given social situation involves, in any way, in and of itself, a specific course of action'.[36] He means, for instance, that that rapid social change does not necessarily provoke a retreat into old certainties. He argues that the work of Pat Joyce, among others, epitomizes postsocial history, in that it deals with the ways that language articulates experience and generates consciousness. Cabrera's position earned criticism both as 'idealist' and as 'realist',[37] a fact that underlines the difficulty of attempts to synthesize cultural and social history, and the theoretical uncertainty of much historical writing that purports to be poststructuralist. In principle, both sides are now less likely to think in polarized terms of objectivity versus relativism or structure versus agency. Meanwhile, history has settled back into a routine. New research tells us more of what we already know. Poststructuralism was productive as much, if not more, because it provoked new questions than because of its methodological innovation. The time may be ripe for new questions.

Guide to further reading

Catherine Belsey, *Poststructuralism: A Very Short Introduction* (Oxford, 2002).

Miguel A. Cabrera, *Postsocial History: An Introduction*, intro. Patrick Joyce, trans. Marie MacMahon (Oxford, 2005).

Richard Evans, *In Defence of History* (London, 1997).

Mary Fulbrook, *Historical Theory* (London, 2002).

Michael Holquist (ed.), M. M Bakhtin, *The Dialogic Imagination*, trans. Caryl Emerson and Michael Holquist (Austin, Texas, 1981).

Keith Jenkins, *On 'What is History'* (London, 1995).

Keith Jenkins (ed.), *The Postmodern History Reader* (London, 1997).

Alan Munslow, *Deconstructing History* (2nd ed., London, 2006).

S. H. Rigby, 'History, discourse, and the postsocial paradigm: a revolution in historiography?', *History and Theory* 45(1) (2006), pp. 110–23.

Notes

1 See the exchange between Richard Evans, *In Defence of History* (London, 1997), p. 252 and Diane Purkiss, IHR Website, http://www.ihrinfo.ac.uk/reviews/discourse/dianne1.html, 2002.

2 Lawrence Stone, 'History and postmodernism' *Past and Present*, 131 (1991), pp. 217–18.
3 Hayden V. White, 'The burden of history', *History and Theory*, 5(2) (1966), pp. 111–34: 124.
4 Natalie Zemon Davis, 'The reasons of misrule: youth groups and Charivaris in 16th-century France', *Past and Present* 50 (1971), pp. 41–75 and 'The rites of violence: religious riot in 16th-century France', *Past and Present*, 59 (1973), pp. 51–91; Alan MacFarlane, *Witchcraft in Tudor and Stuart England: A Regional and Comparative Study* (London, 1970).
5 Richard Johnson, 'Edward Thompson, Eugene Genovese, and Socialist-Humanist History, *History Workshop Journal*, 6 (1978), pp. 79–100.
6 Note, however, that other analogies work less well. Colours might merge, but do the sensations of a blow on the head and reading Barthes?
7 White, 'The burden of history'.
8 Michel Foucault, *Madness and Civilization: A History of Insanity in the Age of Reason* (London, 1967).
9 Jacques Derrida, 'Cogito and the History of Madness', in *Writing and Difference* (London, 1978, first published 1967), pp. 31–63; Michel Foucault, 'My Body, This Paper, This Fire', *Oxford Literary Review*, 4 (1) (1979, first published 1972), pp. 9–28.
10 Alex Callinicos, *Against Postmodernism: A Marxist Critique* (Cambridge, 1989).
11 Patrick Joyce, *Democratic Subjects: The Self and the Social in 19th-Century England* (Cambridge, 1994), pp. 3–4.
12 E. P. Thompson, *The Poverty of Theory and Other Essays* (London, 1978), pp. 289, 350–1.
13 Patrick Joyce, 'The End of Social History', *Social History*, 20 (1) (1995), pp. 73–91.
14 Joan Wallach Scott, 'Women in *The Making of the English Working Class*', in Joan Wallach Scott, *Gender and the Politics of History* (New York, 1988), pp. 68–90.
15 Hayden White, *The Tropics of Discourse: Essays in Cultural Criticism* (Baltimore, 1978), pp. 15–17.
16 Robert Berkhofer, 'The Challenge of Poetics to (Normal) Historical Practice', *Poetics Today* (1988).
17 Berkhofer, 'The Challenge of Poetics'.
18 Robin Bisha, 'Reconstructing the Voice of a Noblewoman of the Time of Peter the Great: Daria Mikhailovna Menshikova', *Re-thinking History*, 2 (1998), pp. 51–63.
19 Jenkins, *The Postmodern History Reader*, p. 28; Keith Jenkins, 'A Postmodern Reply to Perez Zagorin', *History and Theory*, 39 (2) (2000), pp. 199–200.

20 Michel Foucault, *Discipline and Punish: The Birth of the Prison* (London, 1977, first published 1975), pp. 26–8.
21 H. Aram Veseer, 'The New Historicism', in H. Aram Veseer (ed.), *The New Historicism Reader* (London, 1994), p. 13.
22 Foucault, *Discipline and Punish*, pp. 27, 52.
23 R. F. Atkinson, *Knowledge and Explanation in History: An Introduction to the Philosophy of History* (London, 1978), pp. 45–51.
24 Evans, *In Defence*, p. 252; Perez Zagorin's 'History, the Referent, and Narrative: Reflections on Postmodernism Now', *History and Theory*, 38 (1) (1999), pp. 1–21 also leans towards reconstructionism.
25 White, 'The Burden of History', pp. 129–30.
26 Tony Bennet, *Outside Literature* (London, 1990).
27 Hayden White, 'Historical Emplotment and the Problem of Truth', in Saul Friedlander (ed.), *Probing the Limits of Representation: Nazism and the Final Solution* (Cambridge, MA, London, 1992), p. 37.
28 Karl Popper, *The Open Society and its Enemies*, 2 vols (London and Chicago, 1943), Vol. 2, Chapter 25.
29 Zagorin, 'History, the Referent, and Narrative', p. 21.
30 Dominick LaCapra, *History and Memory after Auschwitz* (London and New York, 1999), p. 12.
31 Hayden White, *The Content of the Form*, pp. 78–80.
32 Hayden White, 'Afterword', in Victoria E. Bonnel and Lynn Hunt (eds), *Beyond the Cultural Turn: New Directions in the Study of Society and Culture* (Berkeley, Los Angeles, and London, 1999), pp. 315–24, esp. 322; 'Historical Emplotment and the Problem of Truth', in Friedlander, *Probing the Limits*, pp. 37–8.
33 Wulf Kansteiner, 'Mad History Disease Contained: Postmodern Excess Management Advice from the UK', *History and Theory*, 39 (2) (1999), pp. 218–29, esp. 225–6.
34 Evelyn Brookes Higginbotham, 'African-American Women's History and the Metalanguage of Race', *Signs*, 17 (2) (1992), pp. 251–74.
35 For a lucid example of the use of Bakhtin's theory, see S. H. Rigby, Chaucer in Context (Manchester, 1996).
36 Miguel A. Cabrera, Postsocial History: An Introduction, intro. Patrick Joyce, trans. Marie MacMahon (Oxford, 2005), p. 99.
*John H. Arnold, 'The Historian as inquisitor', *Re-thinking History*, 2,3 (1998), pp.379–86.
37 S. H. Rigby, 'History, Discourse, and the Postsocial Paradigm: A Revolution in Historiography?', History and Theory 45 (1) (2006), pp. 110–23; Alan Munslow, 'Review of Postsocial History', Rethinking History 9 (2005), pp. 125–8.

8

Psychoanalysis and history

Garthine Walker

Sigmund Freud (1856–1939) coined the term 'psychoanalysis' in 1896. Freud was one of several thinkers who questioned the idea, popular in some quarters in the 19th century, that human beings were rational creatures who always acted in full knowledge of what they were doing. He suggested that unconscious impulses influenced people's behaviour. Freud's ideas, like those of Darwin and Marx, have profoundly impacted on human beings' idea of themselves. His concept of the unconscious, use of free association and emphasis on the importance of dreams informed movements like Dadaism and Surrealism in the visual arts, and works of fiction such as Virginia Woolf's novel, *The Waves*. His ideas also influenced historical writing. Biographers began to explain personality traits by referring to their subjects' pasts. Historians became more interested in causation. Before Freud, historians were not much concerned with the causes or origins of historical phenomena, being more interested in judging how great certain individuals were. After Freud, historians were more likely to consider that people might have been unconsciously influenced by causes of which they were unaware.

Explicit psychoanalytic theory enjoys a somewhat uncertain intellectual status. Despite many adherents in literary and cultural criticism and in therapeutic practice, it tends to be dismissed by academic psychologists. Its reception by historians has been mixed. In 1958, William L. Langer, then President of the American Historical Association, proclaimed that incorporating 'psychoanalysis and its developments and variations' into historical research was the way forward for the discipline.[1] The decades since then, although witnessing no paradigm shift of the sort envisaged by Langer, have heard several such clarion calls.[2] Psychoanalytic theory has made a particular contribution to the fields of historical biography, early modern witchcraft, and Holocaust studies. It is attractive to biographers because it provides a useful – some would say facile – way of giving unity to a life. In the two latter cases, the behaviour to be studied is seen as 'irrational' or the product of 'trauma' and is thus anchored in the unconscious.[3] Psychoanalytic ideas and vocabulary have also permeated historical writing in the form of popular 'common sense' assumptions about human behaviour. There is, however, no consensus. Whereas some argue that the historian's and the psychoanalyst's tasks are similar,[4] others maintain their distinctiveness and incompatibility.[5] Overall, explicit psychoanalysis has remained on the margins of the historical project.[6]

Various reasons have been given for this state of affairs: 'the overwhelming majority' of historians 'have not been analyzed', so they fail to understand psychoanalysis and their objections 'probably ... spring from deep emotional sources'; they have a 'narrow, empirical outlook, and fail 'to come to grips with theoretical challenges'; they fear that psychoanalysis undermines the humanistic tradition of historical explanation.[7] These may all be valid criticisms in that they may apply to certain individuals. But the historical profession is extremely diverse. Psychoanalytic theory fails to appeal to many historians because it seems to assume historical constants and essentialism. According to Freud, 'unconscious mental processes are ... "timeless"': they 'are not ordered temporally', 'time does not change them in any way', and 'the idea of time cannot be applied to them'.[8] Many historians favour theoretical traditions that stress anti-essentialism. An anti-essentialist position denies that particular responses universally arise from given causes: one cannot interpret ambiguous feelings towards one's child as *inevitably* arising from the condition of childbirth and motherhood, for instance. Even when things have appeared constant, it does not follow that they *must* be constant – *pace* the oppression of women. The apparent essentialism of psychoanalytic theory that seems to render them ahistorical goes some way to explaining its little impact among historians.

However, psychoanalysis has been a far from stagnant field. During the past century, myriad theoretical positions have emerged. Some theorists have challenged the importance of essentialism. Others have explored the relationship between biological drives and culture. Certain scholars have claimed that particular versions of psychoanalysis *are* historical and quite compatible with historical change, arguing that they may investigate the 'varied expression in different times and places' of universal drives and fantasies.[9]

In this chapter, I shall outline some salient points for historians of certain types of psychoanalytic theory, and examine and evaluate examples of their influence in actual historical writing. I have distinguished between three bodies of thought: first, Freudian psychoanalysis and ego psychology; second, object-relations theory as developed by Melanie Klein; and third, Julia Kristeva's modification of Lacanian psychoanalysis. There exist many more variants than this, and I do not attempt to summarize all the main concerns of even these three. Rather, I introduce in brief and therefore simplified terms certain of their characteristics in order to consider their use by historians. Whereas critics of psychoanalytic theory have conventionally focused on the fragility of its truth-claims or have engaged in *ad hominem* attacks on Freud, I examine the mechanics of the arguments of practical historical writing informed by psychoanalytic ideas.[10]

8.1 Some Freudian concepts

Like Marxism and Darwinism, Freud's theory is a structural theory. Although it deals with the individual psyche, it does not privilege individual agency or choice. Freudian psychoanalysis emphasizes the tripartite structure of the personality. First, *id*, the unconscious, where mental activities occur without the individual's awareness but which affect his or her behaviour. The unconscious contains universal human drives and impulses, the primitive biological instincts of sex and aggression. Dreams, free association, slips of the tongue, art and comments made under hypnosis all provide access to the unconscious. Second, *ego*, the conscious mind, involving perception, understanding and decision-making. We experience this part of the personality as 'I', or 'self'. Third, *superego*, the ideals and values derived from the familial and cultural environment, such as social mores and taboos. Of these three, the unconscious is the key concept. Freud did not invent the idea of unconscious motivation – that feelings or impulses of which we are unaware influence our behaviour. In the 17th century, Pascal, for instance, observed, 'The heart has its reasons of which reason knows nothing.'[11] But Freud developed the notion that a mental entity called the unconscious actually exists and contains real truths about ourselves. Hence, the term 'Freudian slip', whereby a person consciously means to say one thing, but their unconscious breaks through with a slip of the tongue to reveal their 'true' feelings. Freud also adapted pre-existing concepts of 'repression' – the idea that painful experiences are kept out of conscious awareness – and 'projection' – that people project feelings of anxiety and guilt onto others and lash out defensively, so that these hostile feelings are experienced as part of the external world rather than internally. These psychological phenomena are recognized both within and beyond psychoanalysis.

Freud stated that all individuals pass through certain stages – oral, anal, phallic and genital – of personality development. A pivotal moment in this journey is termed the Oedipus complex, after the Greek mythical hero who unknowingly killed his father and married his mother. Within Freudian theory, boys experience the Oedipus complex during the phallic stage of development, between the ages of three and five. The little boy has an instinctual sexual desire for his mother. He therefore begins to see his father as a rival for his mother's love, whence arises the desire to remove his father by murdering or castrating him. But the little boy fears reprisals, especially being castrated himself. A conflict emerges between, on the one hand, loving his mother and hating his father and, on the other, self-preservation.

The latter wins and the little boy represses his feelings of sexual love and hate towards his parents. The Oedipal stage ends with the boy entering the genital stage. Having recognized his father's masculine superiority, he identifies with him rather than with his mother. Freud termed a roughly comparable process for girls the Electra complex, after the mythological female who killed her mother to avenge the mother's murder of her father. In Greek myth, Electra lures her mother to her death by appealing to her maternal instincts, and after killing her is overwhelmed with remorse. Freud did not clearly theorize the female complex. Feminist psychoanalytic theorists have since developed versions of the female unconscious.[12]

In addition to emphasizing structure, Freudian psychoanalysis stresses conflict rather than consensus. Conflict occurs between the three parts of the personality. For instance, a little boy's conscious fears of reprisal conflict with his instinctive sexual desire for his mother and so repress that impulse within the unconscious. In turn, repressed sexual urges produce anxiety, along with the fear, guilt and shame associated with sexual and aggressive fantasies. The unconscious conflict arising from these infant experiences determine behaviour in adulthood. Indeed, all variants of human activity are caused by the unconscious interaction of and conflict between the two instinctive drives: sexual urges, which are associated with constructive behaviour, and the death instinct, the source of all destructive urges. This places a question mark over how much room for individual or collective choice there is within the theory. Overall, Freudian psychoanalysis is an essentialist, structural theory based in biology. Where a Marxist would look for the underlying economic interest, a Freudian might try to explain history in terms of the historical subject's unresolved unconscious conflicts.

Ego psychology, pioneered by Anna Freud (Freud's daughter) and developed by Heinz Hartmann and Erik Erikson, follows the parameters of Freudian psychoanalysis, retaining a concern with the significance of biological drives. Personality is seen to develop from the dominance of the unconscious in infanthood to the adult's conscious control over the internal and external world. In Erikson's formulation, society and culture (in the form, for instance, of economic opportunities as well as child-rearing methods) influence how adults behave and make sense of their experiences. Individuals absorb and internalize cultural values so that their ego functions appropriately within their particular society. On the surface, there is less biological determinism in ego psychology than there is in classic Freudianism. Yet the theory depends upon the premise that humans are biologically programmed to adapt to their culture as part of the struggle for survival. Ego psychology was developed within a framework of functionalism and shares characteristics with modernization theory. Consensus is seen as positive and conflict negative, for example. A failure to conform is the result of a lack of desirable adaptation to the social environment. Ego psychology assumes a necessary historical direction towards greater ego stability and more successful adaptation to the environment.

Application in historical writing of Freudianism

We find Freudian psychoanalytic theory particularly informing historical biographies, such as Erik Erikson's *Young Man Luther* (1958) and E. Victor Wolfenstein's study of Lenin, *The Revolutionary Personality* (1973).[13] Freud himself published a psychobiography of Leonardo da Vinci (1910). The example I discuss here is an examination of Bismarck by Otto Pflanze.[14] Otto von Bismarck was Prime Minister of Prussia, and is largely held responsible for the unification of Germany in 1871, after which he became the first Chancellor of the German Empire.

Psychoanalytic theory allows Pflanze to reconcile two contradictory statements made by Bismarck. In 1838, aged twenty-three, Bismarck wrote in a letter that he was not motivated to be a great statesman by patriotism but by 'ambition, the wish to command, to be admired, and to become famous'. In 1874, aged fifty-nine, Bismarck contrarily described himself to the Prussian parliament as 'a disciplined statesman who subordinates himself to the total needs and requirements of the state in the interests of peace and the welfare of my country'.[15] Pflanze explains the difference between these two pronouncements not in terms of their different contexts and audiences but in psychoanalytic terms:

> ... the Bismarck of 1874 was still the Bismarck of 1838. What occurred may be understood in terms of a common psychic process ... Instinctual impulses that the conscience cannot tolerate are either repressed (i.e., 'thrust back into the id') or projected (i.e., 'displaced into the outside world'). Bismarck projected his quest for power and renown onto the Prussian state. Goals that would have been intolerable if conceived as personal, could, when conceived as in the interests of the state or public welfare, be sought without a sense of guilt ... [and] therefore acceptable to his conscience.[16]

The reason Bismarck experienced this conflict was that between these two dates he had undergone a religious conversion, and so was compelled to 'protect his ego from the sting of conscience'. Bismarck's ambition of 1838 has been repressed by 1874. This demonstrates how psychoanalytic theory can perpetuate sameness and fails to allow for historical change. Psychoanalysis allows evidence that conflicts to be interpreted as having the same meaning. A theory that allows for evidence and lack of evidence to lead to the same conclusion is obviously highly problematic.

Pflanze also draws on psychoanalysis in arguing that Bismarck was a 'phallic-narcissistic' character, drawing on Wilhelm Riech's 1933 descriptions of Freudian personality types. 'Phallic-narcissistic' types are 'self-confident, often arrogant, elastic, vigorous, and often impressive ...The facial expression usually shows hard, sharp masculine features'; they have an aggressive manner; the 'outspoken types tend to achieve leading positions in life', and so on. Such types have 'an identification of the total ego with the phallus', 'serious disappointments' at the genital stage in the relationship to the mother, and a home in which the mother was the stronger parent. Pflanze superimposes this on to Bismarck's character and past. (He claims that psychoanalytic theory provides 'character suits' in which to dress and tailor to fit historical characters). Pflanze writes that Bismarck 'undoubtedly' displayed 'a rather exaggerated masculinity'. As a student, Bismarck had fought 25 duels in three semesters. He boasted of his ability to drink six bottles of wine without getting drunk or vomiting. He had exhibitionist tendencies, quaffing an entire bottle of wine in one gulp to impress assembled officers.[17]

Pflanze views events from Bismarck's early life in the light of the Oedipal situation associated with the phallic-narcissistic character type. He quotes a letter in which Bismarck remembered his childhood feelings towards his parents: 'it often appeared to me that [my mother] was hard, cold toward me. As a small child I hated her.' In contrast, Bismarck wrote that he 'really loved' his father, but felt remorseful, because at times 'I made a pretence of loving him ... when innerly I felt hard and unloving because of his apparent weaknesses.' The letter seems to conform to Freudian theory only where the father is concerned. Bismarck feels an Oedipal ambivalence towards his father, feeling sometimes loving and sometimes unloving. This ambivalence is caused by a mixture of respect for his father's authority and jealousy over his possession of Bismarck's mother. According to the theory, Bismarck should have felt love for his mother, not hate. But here, Pflanze operates a remarkable shift of perspective typical of psychoanalysis. 'Toward his mother he expressed a sense of guilt, but no ambivalence and no love. Yet appearances deceive, and here too Bismarck conforms to the pattern.' The evidence that conflicts with psychoanalytic theory – that Bismarck hated rather than loved his mother – is made to fit the theory after all. For

> it is a common phenomenon within psychoanalysis that strong negative feelings towards the parent of the opposite sex turn out to be ... concealing the opposite of what they purport to be. Interpreted in this way, Bismarck's attitude toward his mother has to be read as love rather than hatred.[18]

Effectively, the theory is confirmed whether evidence is present or absent. Freudian psychoanalysis would thus seem to be incompatible with the historical method because its self-confirming nature means that it cannot be tested against evidence. Pflanze exemplifies how psychohistorians may come to the past with their explanation already in hand. Psychoanalytic theory is treated as if it constitutes a body of universal laws. The past is applied to the model rather than the model or hypothesis being tested against evidence.

While this sort of psychohistory was produced primarily in the 1960s and 1970s, Freudian assumptions continue to lead historians to treat historical documents as if they allow us to 'reconstruct the mental life of an individual', to identify 'the themes of [that individual's] psychology', and to see into 'the well-springs of . . . personality, motives and emotions'.[19] The problem of reading texts in this way is, of course, a non-problem for Freudian psychoanalysis. It is irrelevant whether the subject describes responses to 'real' external or imagined internal events because what matters is the individual's construction of reality, which is based on the need to contain the expression of the libido and death drive.[20] But psychoanalytic theory also allows for anxiety to arise from external factors, and the historian has no way of determining whether the origins are internal or external in any particular case. Moreover, psychoanalysts have acknowledged that theirs is not a predictive theory and have warned against 'transposing back', reducing human situations to the 'earliest, simplest, and most infantile precursor which is assumed to be its "origin"'.[21] Yet this is precisely what Freudian psychohistories attempt, thereby producing arguments that are essentialist, circular and unfalsifiable.

8.2 Object-relations theory and Melanie Klein

Object-relations theory is a development of Freudian psychoanalysis, so labelled because it focuses on the first year of life when the infant learns to distinguish its self (subject), from 'objects' with which it comes into contact. The objects in question are people (primarily the mother) or parts of people (the mother's breast). The infant initially experiences all 'good' things, such as the mother's breast, as parts of itself, and 'bad' things, such as pain, as external. Although the concept of the unconscious remains central, the experience of individuals is explained in psychosocial terms. Instead of the primary impulse being a biological need to express the sexual and aggressive drives, it is social, a need to form relationships with other humans. The desire for personal relationships explains the sex drive (the need to express intimacy) and aggression (the need to express frustration). In an ideal, romanticized mother–infant relationship, the infant's psyche is not conflicted or split. However, psychological conflict and splits originate in frustrating experiences with the maternal object. By paying particular attention to the early mother–infant relationship in the pre-Oedipal period, object-relations theorists move maternality to the fore, and play down the father-centred Oedipus complex. This has been attractive to some feminists. Problematic from certain feminist perspectives is object-relations theory's naturalization of mothering, which might imply that mothering is biologically determined rather than socially constructed. Feminist object-relations theorists have drawn attention to the way that discourses of motherhood are constructed ideologically. As the individual is interpreted in a social context and social relations are central to the construction of the self, object-relations theory is perhaps more compatible with historical analysis than is Freudian psychoanalysis. However, the defining characteristic of human existence remains biologically rooted in the impulse to form relationships with others.

Unlike later object-relations theorists who posited an idealized pre-Oedipal stage and a rosy picture of mother–infant relations, Melanie Klein, whose works were published between 1919 and 1961, emphasized the aggressive anxieties, frustrations and splitting that the infant experiences in relation to the breast.[22] Klein was the first to argue that babies initially relate to parts, such as the breast, rather than to the mother as such. This mode of identification ('paranoid-schizoid position') is eventually replaced by the infant's ability to relate to whole objects, such as the mother (the 'depressive position'). Klein also believed that the infant psyche is experienced in the inner world of 'phantasy'. Freud's instinctual drives of desire and aggression, and the negative emotions of envy, greed and loss, are dealt with within this phantasy realm. The child experiences in phantasy the mother's breast as split into good (gratifying) and bad (frustrating). The infant aims to incorporate and identify with the good breast, which represents the life instinct, and projects the anxiety provoked by the death instinct onto the bad breast.

Whereas other object-relations theorists came to stress the fundamental unity of the infant psyche, Klein's internal infant world is never unified. Although the infant's ego develops towards integration, it tends to fragment and split into good and bad as a way of dealing with anxiety. The anxiety itself is a defensive action to protect the ego from the death drive's destructiveness. Gradually, a more integrated psyche emerges and the infant begins to fear that his or her own destructive impulses might have destroyed the mother or the breast. This introduces feelings of ambivalence – rage and, afterwards, guilt, and loss for the phantasized destruction of the bad object, as well as love – towards the mother, who now becomes seen as a whole that embodies both bad and good. This 'depressive position' heralds a process of 'reparation', wherein the infant experiences restorative phantasies in which harm done to objects is undone. While the mother is now phantasized as a whole object, the infant still does not fully differentiate the mother from the father. This lack of differentiation is possible because the infant does not identify a whole 'real' mother. For Klein, the mother is a fluid construction of the infant's desires and anxieties.

Klein identified envy as a key emotion imbuing this early stage of infanthood. Envy involves the desire to be as good as the envied object (the good breast), and when this is felt to be impossible, the object is attacked in order to remove the source of envious feelings. But the infant hates and envies the bad breast too. This envy is usually dealt with in the process of resolving Oedipal feelings of rivalry; if it remains powerful, the Oedipal stage is not successfully resolved.

The problem for historians is not that this body of theory is 'wrong', as critics often assert. Rather, object-relations theory, like classical Freudianism, is based on imaginative constructions that cannot be falsified, disproved. We have no means by which to discriminate between interpretations. This makes it incompatible with a historical method that rests upon relative probabilities.

An example of Melanie Klein's object-relations theory informing historical writing

In 'Witchcraft and Fantasy in Early Modern Germany', Lyndal Roper argues that to understand witchcraft we must attend to the 'imaginative themes' of the cases.[23] These themes are maternal. The motifs in witchcraft narratives were suckling, giving birth, food and feeding, childcare. Several accused witches were lying-in maids; their accusers were newly delivered mothers; witnesses were other women for whom the lying-in maids had worked. Roper asks why witchcraft accusations took this form and why some accused lying-in maids confessed to their crimes. She contends that psychic conflicts provide the answers to both questions. Psychoanalytic concepts are central to this conclusion.

With regard to the mothers who accused lying-in maids of witchcraft, Roper stresses the biological significance of childbirth. A baby's first weeks were a period of anxiety for mothers, not only because of high infant mortality, but because this time might invoke memories of the mother's own pre-Oedipal stage, when she 'may have experienced unadmitted, intolerable feelings of hatred as well as love' towards her own mother.[24] If things went wrong – if the child fell ill or died – these pre-Oedipal residues formed a psychic dramatic script that allowed her to project her anxiety and guilt on to the lying-in maid whom she duly accused of witchcraft.[25] Whereas the modern woman might internalize feelings of guilt and experience postnatal depression, the early modern mother used the Kleinian mechanism of 'splitting' to project these feelings onto someone else. Thus, for Roper, the early modern psyche is regulated by the same psychically induced states as the modern one. Lying-in maids were also marked by ambiguous pre-Oedipal feelings, especially envy, for they had no hope of having young families of their own. Drawing again on Klein, Roper states that it is in the pre-Oedipal phase that envy develops. The lying-in maid's admission of envy could lead to a full confession of witchcraft in the context of early modern understandings that associated envy of a woman with a wish to harm her.

There is much brilliant analysis in this. Roper's identification of conflicts between women seems incontrovertible, and her contribution to understanding the nature of these conflicts is very important. The *questions* she asks and the areas she explores owe much to her knowledge of psychoanalysis, and on this score, its use has clearly been productive. But when we look at the mechanics of her argument, psychoanalysis plays a lesser and sometimes redundant role.

Critics of psychohistory are fond of denouncing it for its circular arguments. Following Karl Popper's claim that psychoanalytic propositions are unfalsifiable – that because they are self-affirming no statement can refute them – they have argued that historians cannot legitimately use psychoanalytic ideas.[26] Roper concedes that her argument may seem circular. Indeed, she seems positively to embrace circularity: 'this conceptual difficulty', she says, 'is inherent in the productive use of ideas'.[27] One example of circularity is Roper's explanation for why envy marks witchcraft cases.

Envy, psychoanalytic theory informs us, is pre-Oedipal in origin; therefore the explanation for the presence of this envy is pre-Oedipal conflict. This is a perfect circle, in that the conclusion is contained in the premise. The primary problem with circularity, however, is that it is *un*productive. It reproduces the same knowledge whatever the sources or evidence. Roper is far too good a historian not to see this. She immediately qualifies her apparent commitment to circularity by rejecting reductive readings in which 'everything speaks of phallologocentrism, or betrays the Oedipal complex'. In fact, she offers a means for psychoanalysis to break out of circularity. On the one hand, she argues that 'there are some primary areas of attachment and conflict – between those in maternal positions and children – which are pretty fundamental to human existence'. This is an unfalsifiable statement: it is difficult to conceive of any kind of evidence about motherhood that would not confirm the presence of either attachment or conflict or both. On the other hand, she says, 'the *form* those conflicts may take and the attitudes societies adopt to them may change. This . . . is the territory of the historian.'[28] In other words, historians can investigate the varying forms taken by unvarying emotions. The fact of multiple forms renders any common root academic, or makes it merely one influence among many. Roper has effectively constrained the reach of psychoanalysis in that she has admitted that all aspects of human behaviour cannot be reduced to basic psychic mechanisms. This concession – that psychoanalysis should be used alongside other forms of investigation for it alone cannot provide an explanation – is undoubtedly a theoretical gain.

Nevertheless, the explanatory status of psychoanalysis is reduced more than Roper would seem to realize. Roper's explanation for why early modern women sometimes projected their guilt in witchcraft accusations, whereas modern mothers are more likely to be labelled as depressive, is a range of historically rooted cultural assumptions about childbirth, the body and women. The argument is very convincing. The psychological predisposition towards guilt and envy enters the explanation only at the level of a *potential* – a potential that rules nothing out. Who knows what 'forms' psychic conflict will take in the future? Moreover, the postnatal period often passed without incident, as Roper points out, and presumably, even when things went wrong, a witchcraft accusation did not always follow. In effect, a confluence of historical factors explains the response to a psychological conflict that *might* result from something going wrong in the postpartum period. These are serious qualifications upon the explanatory power of psychoanalysis. The cost of getting around the problem of circularity has been conceptually to remove psychic conflicts from the centre of the analysis.

Underlying this is a logical issue. Roper actually classifies her two types of causation hierarchically. Historical circumstances explain the 'form' taken by psychic conflicts, which implies that the latter is a sort of base. Psychology is primary and history secondary. But this hierarchy is difficult to maintain. Since a given behavioural outcome (the witchcraft accusation) depends on two sets of causation – (a) psychic conflicts rooted in the pre-Oedipal phase and (b) a range of historical circumstances and phenomena,[29] if either (a) or (b) were removed, the accusation of witchcraft would no longer follow. As both (a) and (b) are necessary to the explanation, we cannot say which is the more important.

Psychoanalytic theory pervades Roper's argument. Yet she also operates a form of analysis in which, if I understand it correctly, it was 'the social organization of motherhood' that made possible ambivalent feelings of mother towards child, so that 'a certain kind of psychic dramatic script was available should things go wrong'.[30] The idea of 'available scripts' might imply that other scripts could be used as well or instead and that the women concerned had a degree of agency in terms of their response to adversity.[31] So, here too, although a *claim* is made for the primacy of psychoanalytic explanation, the actual analysis is multi-causal.

In sum, although in theory, and sometimes in practice, Roper applies psychoanalytic theory in a way that suggests biological essentialism, circularity and unfalsifiability, she also integrates it into a more historical and fruitful analysis. It seems entirely possible to answer those who advocate the wholesale rejection of psychoanalytic theory with evidence that, in *practical* historical writing, a belief in psychic causality need not lead to historical determinism.[32]

8.3 Lacanian psychoanalysis and Julia Kristeva

Like Klein, Jacques Lacan denied that the ego is a unified and coherent structure and posited that splitting is the fundamental developmental process. Also like object-relations theory, Lacan's psychoanalysis was based on imaginative constructions that cannot be disproved. However, Lacanian psychoanalysis, heavily influenced by poststructuralist linguistic theory, offers a rigorous critique of object-relations theory. For Lacan, there is no 'true' or 'real' biological self, and no separation between self and society. Rather, like language, the self is produced by binary relationships. Lacan is concerned with how the subject becomes formed in 'otherness'.

The infant is initially a non-subject, having no concept of the self. This changes in two major splits. First is the 'mirror phase', which occurs in the pre-verbal and pre-Oedipal 'Imaginary' realm between six and eighteen months of life. The mirror phase invokes the binary opposites of poststructuralism. The gaze of whomever the infant interacts with provides, as it were, a mirror in which the infant perceives him- or herself as a unified self. This wholeness is illusionary. The second split comes when the child enters the 'Symbolic' realm of language; with the appropriation of language, the child becomes social. The Symbolic is a set of external meanings embedded in language, which structure and define the social and cultural order. These meanings saturate the unconscious. Linguistic determinism has thus replaced Freud's biological determinism. However, the poststructuralist tenets that the meanings of language are never fixed and that words convey multiple meanings have led to some allowing for the theoretical possibility of change. For Lacan, human behaviour cannot be predicted.

Lacan's work appeals to some feminists because it challenges biological explanations of sexual difference: culture imposes meaning on anatomy, nature is mediated through language. Lacan also deals directly with patriarchy. Within the Symbolic realm of language, a specific law, the Law of the Father, structures culture. All interpersonal experiences, including mother–infant interaction, are organized according to this patriarchal law and its symbolism. The Oedipus complex, for instance, is resolved by the acceptance of the Symbolic Law of the Father. For Lacan, the Oedipus complex occurs not literally but as a linguistic transaction. He writes about the phallus rather than the penis as Freud does. The phallus is an attribute of power within the Symbolic realm of language, not the anatomical property of males. The phallus also signifies the desire for wholeness. Desire is thus not a sexual force as it is for Freud but an unconscious compulsion to strive towards (unattainable) wholeness. Because the unconscious is structured like language, unconscious desires reflect not the individual subject but the patriarchal power structure of society. In the patriarchal Symbolic order, the man is self and the woman 'other'. Hence, female existence is given meaning only in relation to the male. Lacan has been criticized for this eternal repression of the feminine and for defining femininity in patriarchal terms of lack. Yet some feminist theorists have developed Lacan's idea of woman as lack or 'other'.

Julia Kristeva (born 1941), like Hélène Cixous and Luce Irigaray, has developed the idea of femininity as marginal and rejected. For Kristeva, femininity's position in the pre-Oedipal, unconscious, Imaginary realm allows it to challenge and refuse dominant meanings imposed by the Symbolic. It thus offers an authentic expression of the self for women (and indeed for men) beyond the Law of the Father's grasp. However, by speaking from the Imaginary, there is a risk of being engulfed by a terrifying infantile realm characterized by abjection.[33] Kristeva's concept of the 'abject' is a shapeless, boundless, damp, monstrous realm outside culture that threatens to bring culture to chaos. Abjection is associated, above all, with the body fluids and bodily processes of the adult female body, which are similarly perceived in terms of the dissolution of boundaries and certainties, and permeability, a blurring between inside and outside, exemplified in menstruation, conception, pregnancy, childbirth, lactation and menopause. Abjection 'is the body's acknowledgement that the boundaries and limits imposed on it are really social projections – effects of desire, not nature'.[34]

It has been argued that Kristeva takes an anti-essentialist view of femininity in which feminine identity is produced culturally rather than biologically.[35] Actually, while eschewing biological determinism, in (for instance) seeing the pre-Oedipal mother encompassing both masculinity and femininity, Kristeva evokes a kind of cultural determinism. For example, the infant experiences the mother as all-powerful and therefore as phallic. This is essentialist. But Kristeva offers more than this. She argues that 'there is no essential womanhood, not even a repressed one' that can be revealed or recovered by cultural critics or historians. Instead, she analyses feminine and masculine modes of language.[36] Moreover, much of her formulation could be rephrased to allow for the availability of potential discourses of femininity and the body that women and men could utilize in various ways. The abject's association with the female body itself may be viewed as a cultural discourse. In an argument compatible with Bakhtin's view of language, Kristeva suggests that the marginality of abjection means that it can be appropriated and used positively by women. Nor does she relegate femininity absolutely to Lacan's pre-Oedipal Imaginary realm. Women can speak from the positions of both the Symbolic and the Imaginary. The former prevents women's identity being subsumed into that of the mother, while the latter allows women to challenge and resist what the Law of the Father presents as rigid patriarchal certainties. It is the job of analysis to say which they do speak in particular circumstances. Crucially, Kristeva also acknowledges the historical and social aspects of how we understand the world and ourselves. Language for Kristeva is productive; it does not merely reflect social relations. Kristeva's theoretical formulation allows for a greater degree of historicization and agency than does Lacan's. Arguably, this too aligns her as much, if not more, with Bakhtin as it does with Lacan or Derrida.[37]

Application in historical writing of Kristeva's modification of Lacanian psychoanalysis

Kristevan psychoanalysis partly informs Diane Purkiss's analysis of English witchcraft. In general, Purkiss owes more to Lacan's critique of biological essentialism than she does to Freud, and to Lacan's emphasis on the social and collective aspects of subjectivity, which dissolve conventional distinctions between the individual and the social. More specifically, Purkiss draws on Kristeva (and others of the French feminist psychoanalytic school). In 'The House, the Body, the Child', Purkiss identifies and explores similar themes – food and feeding, the breast, transformation, the transgression of boundaries – in women's stories of witchcraft to those dealt with by Roper.[38] Purkiss borrows what she terms a 'quasi-psychoanalytic' notion of fantasy: a story in which people express and relieve unconscious and conscious fears, conflicts and anxieties. She argues that the fantasy of the witch as antimother and antihousewife enabled early modern women to 'negotiate the fears and anxieties of housekeeping and motherhood'.[39] For Purkiss, these fears and anxieties are historically and culturally constructed. They do not necessarily exist for all time but in particular contexts. There is nothing essentialist about her analysis.

Purkiss seems to perceive this to be a radical break with the methods of historians. She characterizes historians as torn between explanatory grand narratives and a simple-minded empiricist rejection of theory. She sets herself apart from what she sees as historians' questions, stressing her interest in the *meanings* of witchcraft narratives but expressly not 'in what "natural" events underlay them'.[40] This appears to be a response to historical accounts that have tried to explain away witchcraft by understanding it predominantly in terms of something else. Witchcraft accusations are understood in terms of pre-Oedipal residues in Roper's work, discussed above, for example, and other historians have interpreted witch beliefs in terms of illness, political tools and social categories.[41] However, Purkiss's analysis is much more conventionally historical than she seems prepared to accept.

To start with, Purkiss uses the same binary opposition between psychologically generated constants and historical variability that we find in Roper. In 'No Limit, the Body of the Witch', Purkiss says that the fantasy-image of the boundless maternal body, and its associations with dirt and disorder, is one of the constants of western civilization. Drawing on Kristeva (and Cixous), Purkiss argues that this image is 'intrinsically' threatening and powerful for women. However, like Roper, she immediately qualifies this essentialist idea with the contention that this constant can only be understood 'in relation to specific historical circumstances'. She says that the maternal body does not inevitably represent particular forms of disorder or uncleanliness. Rather, it is culture – in the early modern period, a 'confluence of medical discourses and social factors' – that produces such links. Furthermore, Purkiss's formulation is less open to criticism than Roper's. Purkiss does not attempt to reduce her evidence to psychic conflicts. Whereas Roper states that ambiguous maternal feelings towards the infant are inevitable, Purkiss's formulation of the boundless female body is much more precisely specified, and is therefore perfectly falsifiable. Although it remains arguable whether this fantasy of the body has been a *constant* of western civilization, Purkiss shows convincingly and productively that it is a useful way of understanding the discourses she examines. The claim that this fantasy is a pre-given, in western culture at least, does not really affect the practical analysis.

Purkiss aims to show that women's desires, fears and anxieties about maternity and the household 'reflected and reproduced a very specific fantasy' of the witch. She demonstrates brilliantly that the witch's deeds could be imagined in terms of a 'fantasy-image of the huge, controlling, scattered, polluted, leaky fantasy of the maternal body'. She shows how this was made possible by a range of elite and popular discourses of the body, household, transformation and femininity, and by social practices surrounding women and childcare, the maintenance of household order, the dispersal of dirt and pollution, and more.[42] Therefore, this particular figure of the witch is a social and cultural construct, and not caused by biology at all. Moreover, because Purkiss stresses the cultural construction of subjectivity, she rejects the essentialist idea that a particular effect must 'naturally' follow a particular event. She uses the notion of psychic conflicts non-essentially in that they do not necessarily lead in a particular direction. Thus she argues that it is not inevitable that a woman should feel threatened in any particular way by a woman speaking to her in a certain way, or entering her home. She points instead to a combination of discourses and social practices, which vary greatly.

Purkiss's method is a critical method that would be acceptable to many historians. Despite Purkiss's claim that psychoanalysis 'offers the richest, most rewarding and most serious ways of reading texts concerned with the supernatural',[43] Purkiss's approach is not distinctively psychoanalytic.[44] Does psychoanalysis cease to be psychoanalysis, or even quasi-psychoanalysis, when the primacy of psychic conflicts is sidelined to such an extent?

In sum, although Purkiss seems at first sight to privilege psychoanalytic over other modes of explanation, in practice she employs it alongside other forms of analysis, and produces a non-essentializing historical account of witchcraft. She does evoke the binary opposition between psychoanalysis and historical circumstances in the same way that Roper does, but this primarily appears to be a method of positioning within and between disciplines. As pieces of historical writing, Purkiss's chapters exemplify an excellent historical method.

8.4 Conclusion

What does all this mean for the status of psychoanalysis as an historical theory? To some extent, the debate over whether psychoanalysis can inform historical work is based on misunderstanding. Purkiss characterizes historians as believers in realism, in a correspondence view of truth in which fears of witches must represent 'real' fears. Actually, many historians work within an entirely different method, a critical method that goes beyond the false opposition between reality and relativism, truth and fiction, just as she does. Purkiss's mode of analysis would be perfectly acceptable to certain types of historians. Historians in this tradition – perhaps a conceptually informed empiricism – do not attack psychoanalysis in the name of realism, but ignore it on the grounds that it cannot deal with change, because they see it as an essentializing metanarrative. This, too, is based on a misconception. Historians who dismiss psychoanalysis have missed the extent to which psychoanalytically informed historians *have* grappled with change and essentialism. One reason why historians make this mistake is that psychoanalytically inclined historians tend to make a *claim* for the theoretical primacy of psychoanalysis. However, while this claim sometimes undermines the analysis, it does not always do so – even in problematic work like Roper's, the entire analysis is not characterized by essentialism and circularity – and in Purkiss's case it hardly is at all. In both literary criticism and history there are antitheorists, those who believe in Theory, and those like myself (and, I would guess, Purkiss), who engage with theory in the lower case: in other words, those who favour a conceptually informed history that does not have the answers in advance.

Guide to further reading

Sally Alexander, 'Feminist History and Psychoanalysis', *History Workshop Journal* 32 (1991), pp. 128–33.

Tim Ashplant, 'Psychoanalysis in Historical Writing', *History Workshop Journal* 26 (1988), pp. 102–19.

Stephen Frosh, *The Politics of Psychoanalysis: An Introduction to Freudian and Post-Freudian Theory* (2nd ed., Basingstoke and London, 1999).

Peter Gay, *Freud for Historians* (Oxford, 1985).

Rosalind Minsky (ed.), *Psychoanalysis and Gender: An Introductory Reader* (London and New York, 1996).

Toril Moi (ed.), *The Kristeva Reader* (Oxford, 1986).

Fred Weinstein, 'Psychohistory and the Crisis of the Social Sciences', *History and Theory* 34(4) (1995), pp. 219–319.

Notes

1 William L. Langer, 'The Next Assignment', *American Historical Review* 63 (1958), pp. 284–5.

2 Tim Ashplant, 'Psychoanalysis in Historical Writing', *History Workshop Journal* 26 (1988), pp. 102–19; Tim Ashplant, 'Fantasy, Narrative, Event: Psychoanalysis and History', *History Workshop Journal* 23 (1987), pp. 165–73; Karl Figlio, 'Historical Imagination/Psychoanalytic Imagination', *History Workshop Journal* 45 (1998), pp. 199–221; Peter Loewenberg, 'Why Psychoanalysis Needs the Social Scientist and the Historian', in Geoffrey Cocks and Travis L. Crosby (eds), *Psycho/History: Readings in the Method of Psychology, Psychoanalysis and History* (New Haven and London, 1987), pp. 17–29; Hans Meyerhoff, 'On Psychoanalysis as History', in Cocks and Crosby (eds), *Psycho/History*, pp. 30–44. Two journals dedicated to psychoanalytic history are the *Journal of Psychohistory* (formerly the *History of Childhood Quarterly*) and the *Psychohistory Review*.

3 Works of historical biography and about witchcraft are mentioned below. For an example of psychoanalysis in the field of Holocaust studies, see Dominick LaCapra, *History and Memory after Auschwitz* (Ithaca and London, 1998).

4 Thomas A. Kohut, 'Psychohistory as History', *American Historical Review* 91(2) (1986), p. 337.

5 Fred Weinstein and Gerald M. Platt, 'The Coming Crisis in Psychohistory', *Journal of Modern History* 47(2) (1975), p. 212.

6 Peter Burke, *History and Social Theory* (Oxford, 1992), p. 114.

7 David E. Stannard, *Shrinking History: On Freud and the Failure of Psychohistory* (New York and Oxford, 1980), p. ix; Peter Gay, *Freud for*

Historians (Oxford, 1985), p. 52; Diane Purkiss, *The Witch in History: Early Modern and 20th-Century Representations* (London and New York, 1996), pp. 60, 69; Paul Robinson, *Freud and his Critics* (Berkeley, Los Angeles and Oxford, 1993), p. 10.

8 Cited in Peter Loewenberg, 'Psychohistorical Perspectives on Modern German History', *Journal of Modern History* 47(2) (1975), p. 261.

9 Loewenberg, 'Psychohistorical Perspectives', p. 262.

10 Frederick Crews et al., *The Memory Wars: Freud's Legacy in Dispute* (London, 1997); H. J. Eysenck, 'What is Wrong with Psychoanalysis?', in Cocks and Crosby (eds), *Psycho/History*, pp. 3–16; Adolph Grünbaum, *The Foundations of Psychoanalysis: A Philosophical Critique* (Berkeley, 1984); Stannard, *Shrinking History*; Frank J. Sulloway, 'Reassessing Freud's Case Histories: The Social Construction of Psychoanalysis', *Isis* 82 (1991), pp. 245–75.

11 Cited in Richard Webster, *Why Freud Was Wrong: Sin, Science and Psychoanalysis* (new edn, London, 1996), p. xii. See also George Frankl, *The Social History of the Unconscious* (London, 1989).

12 See the work of Hélène Cixous, Luce Irigaray and Julia Kristeva.

13 See also the case studies in Bruce Mazlish (ed.), *Psychoanalysis and History* (revised edn, New York, 1971).

14 Otto Pflanze, 'Toward a Psychoanalytic Interpretation of Bismarck', *American Historical Review* 77(2) (1972), pp. 419–44.

15 Pflanze, 'Psychoanalytic interpretation of Bismarck', pp. 420–1.

16 Pflanze, 'Psychoanalytic interpretation of Bismarck', p. 423.

17 Pflanze, 'Psychoanalytic interpretation of Bismarck', pp. 426–7, 420.

18 Pflanze, 'Psychoanalytic interpretation of Bismarck', pp. 429–30.

19 Lyndal Roper, 'Oedipus and the Devil', in Roper, *Oedipus and the Devil: Witchcraft, Sexuality and Religion in Early Modern Europe* (London and New York, 1994), pp. 229, 230, 234.

20 Weinstein and Platt, 'Coming Crisis', p. 204.

21 Weinstein and Platt, 'Coming Crisis', pp. 217–18; Kohut, 'Psychohistory', pp. 342–3; Peter Blos, 'The Epigenesis of the Adult Neurosis', *Psychoanalytic Study of the Child* 27 (1972), pp. 107–8; Fred Weinstein, 'Psychohistory and the Crisis of the Social Sciences', *History and Theory* 34(4) (1995), p. 304.

22 Janice Doane and Devon Hodges, *From Klein to Kristeva: Psychoanalytic Feminism and the Search for the 'Good Enough' Mother* (Ann Arbor, 1992), p. 8.

23 Lyndal Roper, 'Witchcraft and Fantasy in Early Modern Germany', *History Workshop Journal* 32 (1991), pp. 19–33; reprinted in Roper, *Oedipus*, pp. 199–225. Further page references are to the latter.

24 Roper, *Oedipus*, p. 211.

25 Roper, *Oedipus*, p. 215.

26 Stannard, *Shrinking History*, pp. 24–5; Karl Popper, *Conjections and Refutations*, p. 37; Robinson, *Freud and His Critics*, p. 208.

27 Roper, *Oedipus*, p. 218.

28 Roper, *Oedipus*, p. 218.

29 For slippage between psychic and historical causation in another of her essays, see Roper, *Oedipus*, p. 240.
30 Roper, *Oedipus*, pp.210, 215
31 See also her comments in the essay 'Oedipus and the Devil', *Oedipus*, pp. 229, 230. She writes, 'The psychic conflicts attendant on the feminine position – whether Oedipal or related to motherhood – provided the substance of the psychic drama of the witchcraft interrogation'; 'most women', however, managed these psychic conflicts 'without falling prey to morbid diabolic temptation . . . nor did all witches produce witch fantasies'; but when they did, it was 'the possibilities present in [the] culture' that 'enabled' the 'combustion of interests to occur' that produced stories of witchcraft.
32 Cf. Edwin R. Wallace IV, *Historiography and Causation in Psychoanalysis* (Hillsdale, New Jersey and London, 1985), p. 177.
33 Feminist object-relations theorists such as Nancy Chodorow have also developed the role of the mother in the pre-Oedipal phase, stressing that the mother, in being both gratifying and frustrating, is experienced by the infant as both all-powerful and all-engulfing. This intense relationship between mother and infant leads to both sexes maintaining a terrifying maternal image in the unconscious, and a rejection of the mother that works to perpetuate patriarchal dominance.
34 Elizabeth Grosz, 'The Body of Signification', in John Fletcher and Andrew Benjamin (eds), *Abjection, Melancholia and Love: The Work of Julia Kristeva* (London and New York, 1990), p. 90.
35 Rosalind Minsky (ed.), *Psychoanalysis and Gender: An Introductory Reader* (London and New York, 1996), pp. 181–2. For an opposing view, see Doane and Hodges, *From Klein to Kristeva*, Chapter 3.
36 Chris Weedon, *Feminist Practice and Poststructuralist Theory* (Oxford, 1987), p. 69.
37 On the relative merits and demerits of alternative views of language, see Chapter 7 in this volume.
38 Purkiss, *Witch in History*, pp. 91–118.
39 Purkiss, *Witch in History*, p. 93.
40 Purkiss, *Witch in History*, pp. 3–4, 93.
41 Purkiss, *Witch in History*, p. 79.
42 Purkiss, *Witch in History*, pp. 119–21.
43 Purkiss, *Witch in History*, p. 76.
44 Similarly, Robin Briggs insists that historians neglect at their peril pre-Oedipal and Oedipal conflicts within the human psyche, yet he argues for a method that incorporates psychoanalytic concepts into a general, multi-factoral interpretation of witchcraft. Robin Briggs, '"Many Reasons Why": Witchcraft and the Problem of Multiple Explanation', p. 63; Robin Briggs, *Witches and Neighbours: The Social and Cultural Context of European Witchcraft* (London: HarperCollins, 1996), esp. Chapter 10.

9

Anthropological approaches

David Gentilcore

The appeal of anthropology to historians is varied: its concern with the everyday, the small-scale, with alien mentalities, with a concept of culture that includes attitudes and values (and is not simply concerned with 'high' culture), the construction of reality.[1] The early modern period, for instance, is different enough from the present day to make the approach insightful, while the records are rich enough to make it viable. Why historians turned to anthropology at a specific point in time has much to do with the trends then being followed within both disciplines and with the kinds of history historians were trying to write. And, while many historians have called their work 'historical anthropology', on closer inspection their approach is generally more modest: not really trying to 'do' anthropology, but borrowing according to perceived usefulness and applicability.[2] My aims here are likewise modest. This is not a survey of the entire range of anthropological approaches, touching on all the subjects which have benefited from anthropology – from kinship to ritual, from gender relations to gift exchange. This would require a volume of its own. Rather, I offer a critical discussion of a few 'classic' studies in which historians of early modern Europe have made use of anthropology. Most of these concern the problem of culture. Indeed, there are many kinds of anthropology, but the social-cultural is the approach that has most influenced historians. Where possible, I have paired the studies with the reactions of anthropologists, as well as other historians. The exchanges serve to highlight the strengths – and some of the limitations – of an anthropological approach. It also suggests some of the evolving concerns of both disciplines over the last four decades and, I hope, why the approach continues to be of value to historians. Some of the issues raised concern the intelligibility of past beliefs, expressions and usages; the apparent otherness or alienness of the past and the people (at least some of them) who inhabited it; the homogeneity or diversity within cultures; and cultural change and how it happens.

In 1961, one of Britain's best-known anthropologists, E. E. Evans-Pritchard (1902–73), published a lecture in which he advocated a rapprochement between the by then very separate disciplines of anthropology and history.[3] The response of one anthropologist was less than enthusiastic. Isaac Schapera's (1905–2003) answer to his own highly charged question of whether anthropologists should be historians was a firm 'no'. At most, the past might be an aid to understanding the social systems of the present, Schapera argued.[4] But at least one historian was quite keen to take the dialogue forward. Keith Thomas (born 1933) argued in 1963 that historians could learn much from anthropologists: their 'discipline and precision of thought', their skill at relating 'their findings to their understanding of the wider social system', their 'experience of matters about which historians have only read in books' (like witchcraft and blood-feud) and their knowledge of 'primitive mentality'. Thomas's 'case for anthropology' rested on two broader points. First, he suggested that it could widen the subject matter of academic history, to include subjects that historians now take for granted but were then little studied: the family, children's education, attitudes to birth, adolescence and death, to name but a few. Second, it could enhance historians' methods of historical explanation, providing them with new techniques. The historian familiar with 'the findings of the anthropologist', Thomas modestly (if somewhat vaguely) proposed, would be better able 'to ask intelligent questions of his material and more likely to come up with intelligent answers'.[5]

9.1 'Functional' or 'structural'? Keith Thomas and Hildred Geertz

In the book that followed a few years later, Thomas practised what he preached. His 1971 *Religion and the Decline of Magic* has justly become a classic, never out of print and the subject of a retrospective study 25 years after its initial publication.[6] It is a seminal work for the study of early modern witchcraft in particular, for it gave an importance to what had previously been dismissed by early modern historians as a marginal phenomenon. The study employed a wide range of sources to explain witchcraft and magic on a variety of levels – intellectual, sociological and psychological – and account for their subsequent decline. The work is generally associated with *functionalist* anthropology, a school that explains phenomena in terms of the function (or purpose, utility) they purportedly serve. Thomas explored witchcraft in terms of social tensions by means of village-level analysis.[7] For Thomas, 'function' meant the way magical beliefs in general, and witchcraft beliefs in particular, provided a meaningful explanation for the apparently inexplicable in individual life. Magic, interconnected with religion, provided a coherent 'system of belief'. To understand this, Thomas urged historians to take early modern magic beliefs as seriously as they had taken religious beliefs of the time. Thomas succeeded in rendering the apparently irrational rational, an aim which owes a great debt to anthropology (and to Evans-Pritchard's study of Azande witchcraft in particular).[8]

For all his advocacy of anthropology, Thomas was actually quite cautious in his own use of it. He cited anthropologists to suggest hypotheses and provide analogies, but never to prove a point or sustain an argument – he preferred to quote contemporary Tudor and Stuart writers for that. His use of anthropology is most evident in his focus on the accused–accuser relation in witchcraft accusations. Thomas suggested that most accusations of witchcraft developed out of social situations where the accused was refused charity by the accuser. The latter would then feel guilt and attribute subsequent malady and misfortune to the ill will of the person refused. Witchcraft was thus a gauge of social tension. Known as the charity-refusal model, this has become common currency among historians of early modern witchcraft. While it is true that discussion of this model occupies only one chapter in his witchcraft section, Thomas can be accused of placing more weight on the model than it could bear. More recent historians have been careful to reconstruct the precise nature of the social relationships of those involved in specific accusations, and to study how the cases themselves were affected by the wider judicial context.[9]

Inevitably, Thomas's use of anthropology now appears dated. Indeed his preference for the language of primitivism and his concentration on African anthropology were outmoded in anthropological circles when the book was published. 'Primitive', as the anthropologist Hildred Geertz pointed out in her critique, was used by Thomas as a synonym for 'magical' (beliefs and practices that were goal-orientated, though ineffective, and incoherent), both of which were quite distinct from 'religious' (seen as less goal-centred, but comprehensive and organized).[10] Besides the obvious artificiality of the magic–religion distinction, Geertz argues, Thomas employs the terms in such a variety of ways that we are not always sure whether we are dealing with contemporary (that is, pre-modern) cultural ideas or the historian's. Thomas stands accused of taking 'part in the very cultural process that he is studying' (anachronism, in other words).[11] In hindsight, this is doubly ironic: first, in view of the fact that Thomas had praised the distancing from one's subject matter as one of the skills that anthropology could offer the historian and, second, since the imposition of the anthropologist's own (western, white, frequently male) world-view on the society under study was one of the main criticisms which would be levelled at anthropology itself from the mid-1980s onwards (on which, more below), though of course Geertz could not have known that. In his reply, Thomas stressed that he had written English history and not cross-cultural analysis. 'Magic' was therefore used as a convenient label, one that was derived from various contemporary usages, rather than as a category awaiting application to 'some more exotic context'. The question of effectiveness did not come into it, he explained. If there was a distinction between magic and religion, it was the one originally formulated by 16th-century Protestant reformers, later exported to other societies by early anthropologists like E. B. Tylor (1832–1917) and James Frazer (1854–1941). Thomas did, however, concede that his study would have benefited from greater attention to vocabulary and classification, in particular a discussion of the shifting boundaries between 'religion', 'magic' and 'science', in terms of the varying outlooks of the different social and religious groups. Thomas put his finger on one of the key issues in the ongoing history–anthropology debate when he wrote that 'from the anthropologist's point of view, much of what historians call social change can be regarded as a process of mental reclassification, of re-drawing conceptual lines and boundaries'.[12]

Thomas was also criticized by Geertz for rejecting *structuralism*, a then dominant theoretical approach most associated with the French anthropologist Claude Lévi-Strauss (1908–2009). This would have meant studying witchcraft as part of a broader system or language of cultural classification. As a theory of anthropology, structuralism seeks to identify cultural codes as a means of exploring important themes in human thought and action. In his book Thomas dismissed structuralism's applicability to complex societies like that of early modern England (relegating it to the analysis of culturally homogeneous societies). His response to Geertz a few years later is more helpful. Here he questioned the model of unitary cultural systems, favouring instead something more pragmatic and practical, and firmly rooted in its social and technological context. Changes in the context helped account for changes in beliefs and practices. If this meant empirical observation and an historical approach to the problem, instead of Lévi-Strauss's advice to examine the 'unconscious foundations' of social life, then so be it.[13]

Thomas viewed culture as a resource, a concept that has stood the test of time, outliving structuralism among cultural anthropologists. It is therefore somewhat surprising that Thomas did not pay more attention to the processes of cultural transmission. We need to know more about social differentiation: how ideas circulated among different levels of society throughout the period. Compare this to the approach taken by French historian Robert Muchembled a few years later. Here witchcraft beliefs are seen as an example of acculturation: how popular culture was reformed by the elites though the imposition of learned notions of magic and associated legal mechanisms, as part of a broader programme of social and ideological control.[14] It is worth noting that if the 'decline of magic' referred to in Thomas's title occurred when it ceased to occupy a central position in educated thought, during the 18th century, then a depiction of popular beliefs during that period in survivalist terms is inadequate. Why, for instance, did educated beliefs change, while village ones did not, despite the modernization that apparently affected both levels? In describing the former, Thomas refers to the role of faith and science and to a new commitment to self-help in marginalizing magic. Geertz found this explanation problematic, since there was no reason to consider recourse to magic any less self-reliant than other responses.[15]

9.2 An authoritative ethnographic document? Emmanuel Le Roy Ladurie and Renato Rosaldo

Thomas regarded his own work as a contribution to what anthropologists refer to as ethnography: the product and process of fieldwork which is one of the building blocks of anthropology but which generally eschews contributions to the theory of anthropology. In this sense, 'ethnographic history' is a much more accurate label of what historians have tried to do. This is how we might categorize another significant contribution to the approach: Emmanuel Le Roy Ladurie's (born 1929) study of the southern French medieval village of Montaillou.[16] His introduction to the original French edition of 1975 is entitled 'de l'Inquisition à l'ethnographie' (from Inquisition to ethnography) and the bishop-inquisitor behind the trial which forms the basis of the book is styled an 'ethnographe et policier' (ethnographer and detective).[17] The implication is that interpreting a historical document could resemble undertaking anthropological fieldwork. Though the chronology was medieval, the book's impact upon early modernists was great. This was due as much to its use of an inquisitorial trial as an ethnographic source for the study of peasant life, as its focus on a single community. The influence of the American anthropologist Robert Redfield (1897–1958), pioneer of village ethnography, on both aspects was clear.[18] As the last village that actively supported the Cathar heresy, or Albigensianism, Montaillou was the subject of an inquisitorial investigation lasting some seven years and carried out by the tireless bishop Jacques Fournier (born around 1280). While Fournier diligently recorded evidence of heresy in this mixed Catholic-Cathar village of some 200 souls, he also inadvertently provided posterity (in the form of Le Roy Ladurie) with an extraordinarily detailed and vivid picture of the villagers' everyday lives.

Historians had hitherto used Inquisition records either to study the institution itself or explore the nature of heresy. Instead, Le Roy Ladurie used what he referred to as 'the direct testimony of the peasants themselves' to explore the villagers and their society. This represented a shift away from historians siding with the producers of documents, towards those whose lives might be tangentially reflected in them. The book's layout reflects the author's place in the French *Annales* school, in its preoccupation with historical geography, and the setting of economy, society and culture. It is divided into two sections. The first, 'ecology', deals with structures that remained unchanged over a long time-span (physical environment, household, transhumant pastoralism); the second, 'archaeology', delineates apparently equally long-lived cultural forms (body language, life cycle, social relationships, religion and magic). The descriptions are lively and detailed, interspersed with direct quotations from the depositions. The effect is to give to the reader the impression of overhearing the peasants' own speech from centuries ago. The peasants themselves seem to come across as reliable informants, articulate and aware, their evidence assembled and collated by the capable (and invisible) hands of the expert and meticulous inquisitor.

What was the role of the book's author in all this? Le Roy Ladurie was aware that the evidence he was using was not an objective ethnographic document. The depositions – peasants under suspicion of heresy interrogated by an inquisitor – were the fruit of what he called, in his introduction, an 'unequal dialogue'. And yet, as the anthropologist Renato Rosaldo (born 1941) pointed out some years later, despite this caveat, it is as if the rest of the book takes the evidence at face value, presenting it as authoritative.[19] Rosaldo used his critique to make wider points about the distorting effects of authority in ethnography, pairing *Montaillou*'s inquisitor with the once-influential voice of Evans-Pritchard, whose *The Nuer* was long regarded as an exemplary ethnographic study.[20] Yet Rosaldo's discussion of *Montaillou* is just as thought-provoking for the historian. Le Loy Ladurie confines his (brief) methodological discussion to the introduction; even the figure of Fournier, the inquisitor-cum-ethnographer, makes no significant appearance in the rest of the book. This gives the false impression that what follows is objective, disinterested and unproblematic. This is much too reminiscent of traditional ethnography for Rosaldo, where the ethnographer appears briefly in the preface only to disappear from the main text. The ethnographer's role in fashioning the text is thus not reflected upon. With regard to *Montaillou*, Rosaldo argues that the reader needs to understand more fully the implications of power relations and cultural differences between judge and accused. Rosaldo's criticism boils down to Le Roy Ladurie's failure to take Fournier's role as mediator into account and to consider the implications this mediation had on the testimony and its use as evidence by the historian. Gaps in the record – as when female witnesses do not go into detail about courtship practices – are more than 'cultural silence'. They stem from the very structure of what were after all inquisitorial proceedings: of women testifying before male judges, unwilling to talk about possibly heretical love magic. In Le Roy Ladurie's defence, however, he was reading the depositions 'against the grain'; that is, to learn, not about the inquisitor's chief concern, heresy, but about everyday life from the peasants' point of view. Le Roy Ladurie's target is thus distinct from the inquisitor's and should be less affected by his perceptions. However, Le Roy

Ladurie fails to go into any detail about another potential problem: the implications of the language of testimony, which would have been the vernacular Occitan, then translated into Latin by scribes (in turn read back to the witnesses in Occitan for corroboration), transcribed into a fair copy, and finally translated into modern French by Le Roy Ladurie. The different usages of terms such as 'family' and 'household', for instance, tend to get blurred as a result. The rather ecclesiastical Latin of the document, and Le Roy Ladurie's not always careful use of it, have been pointed out by another critic, the medievalist Leonard Boyle (+1999).[21] Finally, for a purported ethnographic account, Le Roy Ladurie makes too many undocumented assumptions regarding the nature and behaviour of the villagers, emphasizing their sameness or difference from the modern (French) reader, as he sees fit. At the same time, he follows the practices of much traditional ethnography in ascribing a timelessness to pastoral life, as evinced in the figure of 'the happy shepherd', Pierre Maury.

9.3 Clues, signs and new standards of proof: Carlo Ginzburg and Paola Zambelli

If Le Roy Ladurie can be identified with a particularly French historiographical tradition, Carlo Ginzburg (born 1939) can be identified with intellectual traditions that are particularly Italian. Ginzburg can also be said to have identified somewhat with the subject of his study, the 16th-century Friulian miller Domenico Scandella (1532–99), whom he calls by his familiar name of Menocchio. Moreover, he too is able to tell this story thanks to an inquisitorial trial for heresy. Menocchio is much more contextualized in time, place and circumstance than the shepherd Maury. But, like Le Roy Ladurie, Ginzburg aims to present the reader with 'a story as well as a piece of historical writing'.[22] And, like him, he tells a good one. Ginzburg still dazzles with the virtuosity of his methods and the boldness of his conclusions. From a village focus in *Montaillou*, we move to a single individual, the miller Menocchio. This may not seem particularly 'anthropological': the exploration of the life and thoughts of a single individual certainly was not then an approach favoured by anthropology.[23] But Ginzburg saw Menocchio as a privileged informant, who might serve as a gateway to the wider world of traditional oral culture. The use of the single informant, identified as expert in some aspect of their own culture by the ethnographer conducting fieldwork is one of the key techniques employed to access another society. That said, it is not without its risks. This is especially so for the historian, for whom the problem of ascertaining typicality is ever-present. Menocchio, a literate and widely read miller, free-thinking, eccentric and outspoken, was hardly representative of peasant culture. At the same time, by closely analysing the trials of 1582–6 and 1599 to reconstruct what Menocchio read and how he read it, Ginzburg sought to explore the filter of peasant culture that Menocchio interposed unconsciously between himself and the books he read. This filter was the patrimony of a vast segment of 16th-century society, peasant culture. On the one hand there is Menocchio's philosophical system: pantheist, egalitarian and materialist. On the other hand there is the filter: a matrix of primordial oral culture, partly Asian in origin (we are told), partly independent of (while contributing to) contemporary learned culture. This is where the cheese and worms of the title come in: for Menocchio, life emerged from the sea like worms from cheese. This notion of spontaneous generation out of chaos, Ginzburg explains, was the echo an ancient myth, which had survived by 'oral transmission from generation to generation'.

Ginzburg once described himself as 'halfway between history and anthropology'.[24] In his case it is a very particular anthropology, part cross-cultural, part European (that is, Europeans studying Europeans). In Ginzburg's case there are close links with the Italian anthropological tradition, with its distinct disciplines of ethnology, the history of popular traditions and cultural anthropology, and its concentration on religion, subaltern groups and cultural complexity, emphasis on historical approaches, and tendency to study Italian society.[25] All of these are summed up in the work of Italian anthropologist Ernesto de Martino (1908–65).[26] Consistent with this tradition is Ginzburg's notion of circularity between the culture of the dominant classes and the subordinate classes in pre-industrial Europe. What he hoped Menocchio's case demonstrated was a cultural relationship composed of 'reciprocal influences', where ideas travelled 'from low to high as well as from high to low'.

Ginzburg went to great pains to stress the nature of this relationship in the preface to the English translation of his work. This was in response to a lengthy criticism from Paola Zambelli, a historian of philosophy with a specialization in natural magic.[27] Zambelli brings to the fore some of the difficulties inherent in Ginzburg's approach, the first regarding origins, the second touching the nature of peasant culture. Zambelli pointed out that at the University of Padua, not far from Menocchio's village, there were scholars putting forward ideas on spontaneous generation. Menocchio may simply have had contact with someone who was a student there, rather than come up with such a notion himself based on an ancient myth. Using the well-travelled, office-holding Menocchio as a spokesman for popular culture thus has serious risks. At times the ideas are said to be his own; at other times they are a refraction of peasant culture. This may show the circularity of culture in the period, but it also points out a circularity in Ginzburg's own argument. The only testimony for this peasant culture is Menocchio himself.

For all his stress on cultural transmission – and this remains the most fascinating and ambitious aspect of the book – Ginzburg still has a gut sympathy for the immemorial and collective nature of popular tradition. Zambelli questioned Ginzburg's notion of the 'autonomy and continuity' of peasant culture. Both aspects pose difficulties for historians. How can we believe that such long-term and autonomous, but almost hidden, structures exist, if their existence is not amply and independently ascertained and documented? What is most interesting about Ginzburg's response to Zambelli is his suggestion that what was needed for any investigation of popular culture was a new standard or criterion of proof.[28] In the unequal struggle between dominant and subordinate cultures, the latter – largely oral – was obviously going to be the loser, leaving fewer traces in the records for historians to pick up. In Ginzburg's view, when it comes to determining the origin of ideas, our conventional standard of proof exaggerates the importance of the dominant culture, as against what can only remain the hypothesis of an origin in remote oral tradition. This justification of his approach is somewhat lame, confined as it is to a footnote, but he did expand on it elsewhere.[29] Historians, he suggested, must be like detectives or medical doctors in looking for clues and signs. He called it the 'evidential paradigm': identifying unknown objects through single, seemingly insignificant, signs, rather than through the application of laws derived from repeatable and quantifiable observations. The historian should carefully select exceptional documents and read them to neutralize distortions. Using the atypical to get at the normal meant ascertaining and exploring what another Italian historian, Edoardo Grendi (1939-99), termed the 'normal exception'.[30] In this way the apparently exceptional or the unusual could be turned on its head, to shed light on the experience of the everyday world in the past.

The issue of evidence is crucial: historians of past societies cannot interact with their sources as anthropologists do. This is one of the main sources of difficulty in the dialogue between historians and anthropologists. In another article in his collection, Ginzburg explored the use of inquisitorial records by historians as sources of ethnographic data.[31] To what extent could the inquisitor stand in for the anthropologist, and the defendants for the 'natives'? The records were far from neutral. Nonetheless Ginzburg believed it was possible to get beyond the judges' own convictions, and the psychological and physical pressures they exerted, in order to mine the rich evidence available. He argued that the inquisitorial trial resembles the anthropological approach in the sense of being a permanent confrontation between different cultures. Borrowing from the literary critic Mikhail Bakhtin, he called this a 'dialogic disposition'. Most defendants simply echoed the interrogator's questions, which was easier and safer. This was 'monologic', in that what was expressed seemed to come from a single, unified source, the perspective of the inquisitor. Occasionally, however, we can detect a clash between different, even conflicting voices. (Bakhtin argued that all discourses are multivocal.) This clashing cultural reality could be turned to the historian's advantage, allowing us 'to disentangle the different threads which form the textual fabric of these dialogues'. Ginzburg concluded that a close reading of a relatively small number of texts, related to a possibly circumscribed belief, could be more rewarding than the massive accumulation of repetitive evidence.

9.4 You say 'historical anthropology', I say 'anthropological history'

It is ironic that just when some historians were turning to anthropology for evidence of what was timeless and unchanging, *l'histoire immobile* in the French phrase, some anthropologists were turning to history as a means of escaping the assumptions of a timeless and unchanging native culture. As a sort of intermezzo it might be useful to examine the state of the relationship at this midway point in our survey. A 1981 collection of articles in the *Journal of Interdisciplinary History*, a journal that prided itself on being cutting edge, took stock of 'anthropology and history'.[32] By then it was quite common to refer to a dialogue between history and anthropology. But what sort of dialogue was it? It was also quite common to use 'historical anthropology' as a label. How accurate or useful was it?

It is possible to have a foot in both camps, as in the case of Alan Macfarlane,[33] William Christian[34] and Richard Trexler ,[35] to name but three. This is not the same as saying that historical anthropology is itself a specialized discipline, however. It was, and continues to be, more of an approach. Here history and anthropology overlap and collaborate with one another. However, what we are dealing with is not so much 'historical anthropology' as 'anthropological history'. The latter suggests the pragmatic use of certain of anthropology's themes and methods by historians, who nevertheless never cease to see themselves first and foremost as practising historians. E. P. Thompson (1924–93), commenting on the Thomas–Geertz exchange, suggested it was all well and good to be stimulated by anthropologists, but historians should avoid becoming ensnared in their debates and ulterior assumptions.[36] Natalie Zemon Davis (born 1928), herself one of the pioneers of an anthropologically informed history, affirmed that historians needed to know about the different schools of anthropological interpretation in order to be able to integrate it into their own vision. Yet she asked whether it was necessary 'to import all the special reservations that anthropologists have about each other's work or all their in-fighting'. After all, historians turn to anthropology for suggestions rather than prescriptions, comparisons rather than universal rules. There was 'no substitute for extensive work in the historical sources'.[37] This remains salutary advice. But if historians were to contribute to anthropological theory, rather than simply borrow from it, as Davis hoped, would it not be necessary to pay more attention to what she belittled as 'in-fighting'? To give this disputatious habit a more positive connotation, it is potentially the kind of reflexive exercise that benefits any discipline. Failure to give internal debates a more important place may be one of the reasons why historians have tended to borrow from a few key, established anthropological names – Clifford Geertz (1926–2006) and Victor Turner (1920–83) are the obvious ones – giving the impression that these were the winners and that the debates were settled.[38] By and large, historians have eschewed a deeper engagement with anthropology as a whole. They have 'dabbled', according to the anthropologist John Adams. They have borrowed concepts from anthropology without attempting to make a contribution to anthropology in return.[39]

Historians have made off with the expression 'historical anthropology', he might have added. In Germany, for instance, it was used from the 1960s onwards by historians as a (partly critical) parallel to the then dominant 'historical social science'.[40] It was linked to *Alltagsgeschichte* (the study of everyday life), as well as the study of *mentalités* and popular culture, and eventually spawned its own journal.[41] As this suggests, history as a discipline has a seemingly unique capacity for adding on bits and pieces from other disciplines without ceasing to be 'history'. Debates range round the edges without affecting the core. 'Historical anthropology', though it occupies history's boundary zones, comes closer to the status of a sub-discipline within anthropology.[42] Most of those calling themselves historical anthropologists are to be found in departments of anthropology. In this context it is viewed as one way of doing anthropology. Other historical anthropologists, who have written and taught as anthropologists, include Marshall Sahlins, who writes about Hawaii and Fiji, Bernard Cohn on India, and Eric Wolf. The latter's most famous work, Braudelian in sweep, typifies the aims, dealing as it does with the troubled interactions between Europe and 'the people without a history', an ironic reference to traditional western notions about 'the natives'.[43] Most work in the field is colonial and postcolonial, studying native North America, Africa, Asia, Australia and Oceania. One of the key areas of interest is how local people coped with change.

The historical anthropologists proper raised a range of issues regarding the overlapping efforts of historians. Bernard Cohn praised some historians for being aware that anthropology suggested a certain reading of documents, providing hypotheses rather than clear-cut answers. They sought to build this ambiguity into their narratives. But he took historians in general to task for concentrating on the version of anthropology 'concerned with stability, structure, regularity, the local, the common, the small scale, and the expressive symbolic, and magical'. Even when studying fast-changing, complex societies, historians focused on 'immobile' groups within them – the peasantry, working class, women – and the relevant anthropology, Cohn argued. It is worth noting, however, that this was due not only to a (perhaps misplaced) perception of what anthropologists were good at. These were just the kinds of issues that historians were then keen on exploring in a serious and purposeful way, after being preoccupied with 'mobility' for so long. It turns out that what was once perceived as unchanging and ahistorical, and as such incidental to the historical process, can both be historically significant and possess a complex history during the early modern period. In historiographical terms this importance and complexity is exemplified by the shift from women's history to gender history,[44] and by the lively debate on conceptions of popular culture.[45] Socio-cultural anthropological ways of seeing can shake us from our unilinear historical complacency. Apparently marginal phenomena, like begging, can suggest important new ways of understanding broader developments, like economic changes or attitudes towards the poor.[46] It can bring to the fore new meanings for long-studied subjects, as well as suggest possible contours for new areas, as Davis argued.

9.5 A question of scale: Peter Burke and Rosario Villari

This is just what Peter Burke (born 1937), one of the historians to use the label 'historical anthropology' with most confidence and flair, attempted in a 1987 collection of essays.[47] The collection was praised for its narrative style: a series of detailed cases or vignettes where the theory and analysis is embedded into the story.[48] In one of the essays, a study of an urban revolt which took place in Naples in 1647, Burke illustrates how the smallness of scale can suggest new interpretations of a much-studied event, permitting an alternative reading of the 20 or so contemporary narratives that have survived.[49] In particular, Burke reinterprets the revolt through the lens of ritual. The study of ritual has been one of the most exciting contributions of anthropologically minded historians to the study of early modern Europe.[50] In this case, ritual is seen as a means of communication, providing collective actions with a meaning for those involved. This is particularly applicable to the first phase of the revolt, the second week of July 1647, led by the fisherman Masaniello against the introduction of a tax by the Spanish. Burke uses the notion of 'social drama', developed by the Scottish anthropologist Victor Turner.[51] In a symbolic way, the various events of the riot had three functions: expressive (sending a message to the authorities), legitimating (as popular justice, lynchings became executions) and organizing (exemplified in the coherence of crowd actions). As Burke puts it, 'the rituals both expressed community cohesion and created it', the community in question being located near the city's Piazza del Mercato and the church of the Virgin of the Carmine.

Burke's radical new approach to the insurrection goes beyond earlier interpretations based on social and economic grievances. It is an attempt to add a dimension based on the culture of the crowd to a behavioural approach based on economic determinism. In this respect it is a model of the microhistorical style, which looks at the small scale to ask new questions and suggest hypotheses, with the aim of relating these back to larger questions and trends. However, the article has been criticized for sacrificing historical detail to anthropological structure and hypothesizing. Rosario Villari (born 1925), an authority on the riot and among the scholars cited by Burke, commented on the 'value and deceptiveness of symbols' for the historian in his critique.[52] Villari is less than clear in identifying what he thought the 'value' of Burke's approach to be, or even the 'symbols', but he made the 'deceptions' clear enough: singling out the first ten days of a 'revolution' which lasted nine months and went through several phases (and whose demands were at least partially met); underplaying the revolt's political content and its appeal to the masses (in the process exaggerating the function of the Carmine as a focus, as well as the centrality and personality of Masaniello); all but ignoring the particular social, political and economic context of the city itself (then Europe's largest); and, finally, following the well-worn stereotype of the city as one lacking in urban structure and organization (a distortion which began with literary accounts of the event immediately afterwards).

The anthropological approach, as exemplified by Burke, risks satisfying neither the historian nor the anthropologist. For the anthropologist, it papers over the theoretical cracks between different anthropological theories and interpretations, reducing everything to a kind of diluted functionalism, of the kind generally favoured by early modern historians. For the historian, it downplays the bread and butter of historical research: context and detail. In addition to these cross-disciplinary perils, there are the pitfalls inherent in narrative style historians have often adopted in the presentation of their 'anthropological' material: the in-depth microhistory, as developed in the form of an essay. These can fall short of the mark, however, with densely presented detail masquerading as the 'thick description' advocated by Clifford Geertz, storytelling at the expense of analysis, the problematic relationship between the 'exceptional' and the 'normal' in legal records, the failure to relate the microhistorical to the macrohistorical.[53] There is the risk of 'atomizing' the past, as John Elliott has put it.[54] At the same time, the best microhistory excels in turning the small-scale into an opportunity to shed light on the previously unnoticed or marginalized, delving into unexplored social attitudes, behaviours and structures, by means of a narrative strategy rich in explanatory value.[55] The best microhistorians are actually trying to discover very big things with their microscopes and magnifying glasses.[56] However small the scale, the same criteria of relevance and applicability apply. The 'archives are full of stories of unknown people', Ginzburg has said apropos *The Cheese and the Worms*; 'the problem is why one has to choose that story instead of another story, why that document instead of another'.[57]

Related to this is what is the 'small' in small-scale, the 'micro' in microhistory? And how can we relate the macro (the major processes of the past) to the micro level? Relating local-level responses to the Protestant and Catholic Reformations – in terms of continuities and changes in beliefs, attitudes and practices – would certainly qualify as an exploration of the complex relationship, with each level shedding light on the other. I sought to do this for the Terra d'Otranto in southern Italy and, more recently, Margo Todd has done this for Scotland.[58] Both works are influenced by anthropology, in particular the notion of religion as a cultural system. Neither are examples of microhistory as such, although each is profoundly rooted in their different locales and in individual experiences. In this regard, however, at least two anthropologists have referred to historians' 'analytical sleight of hand' in stressing the 'local' while at the same time picking useful examples from a range of different localities.[59] Historians, especially early modernists, do not have the anthropologists' luxury of laying down roots in a single community; our data are far too scarce and we are forced to roam. Then again, scale reduction should be as much about widening horizons beyond the village, the small group or the individual as a self-contained unit of activity, and therefore of study. The point is that small-scale data must be made to speak to large-scale or abstract and conceptual issues. They will not do so by themselves.[60] Historians often have difficulty accepting a description of past phenomena that does not treat these phenomena as homogeneous. Microhistory, by contrast, takes advantage of the exceptional normal, relating in concrete detail how actual entities, personal experiences or events can relate the micro with the macro. It represents a new way of describing and analysing the micro–macro link.

9.6 Texts and meanings: Robert Darnton and Roger Chartier

If the influence of Clifford Geertz looms large in much microhistory, if only as an obligatory point of reference, in the final exchange his contribution is more significant. It concerns Robert Darnton's 'great cat massacre'.[61] In the study, Darnton (born 1939) uses a 1762 account of gruesome prank to explore the lore of a group of Parisian artisans. It and the book of which it is part are significant in another way: as an attempt to abandon the distinction between elite and popular culture and look at how both coped with the same sort of problems. Darnton is an expert guide to what he calls the 'anthropological mode of history', not least because he has taught a course on history and anthropology together with the anthropologist Clifford Geertz. Indeed, Geertz's influence as ethnographer-essayist is evident throughout the chapter. From Geertz, historians learn to see culture as consisting in systems of often ritualized meaning. Actions are systems of meaning; they are symbolic. They can be read as 'texts', and texts have meaning without reference to anything other than themselves. Geertz was able to 'read' a foreign culture as a 'text': both metaphors drawn from the poststructuralist work of anthropologist Paul Ricoeur because he was there; it is to Darnton's credit that he gives the reader of his essay the illusion of his (Darnton's) having been there, too.

When a group of apprentice printers stage a trial and execution of the neighbourhood cats, including their mistress's favourite, and retell the event to much hilarity on later occasions, we are confronted with an alien culture. Where a culture is at is most opaque the anthropologist seizes the opportunity to unravel a different system of meaning. This is what Geertz did with his analysis of the Balinese cockfight;[62] this is what Darnton attempts to do here. The meaning of the cat massacre revolves around identifying and understanding different parts of the cultural repertory of the time which the workers drew upon: fears of witchcraft and sorcery, the carnival mock trial, the charivari, their code of sexual relations, and so on. To do so means reconstructing the social and cultural world of the apprentice printers, which Darnton does in an effective and lively way. Underlying this is Darnton's working conviction that this meaning, however multivalent, is fully recoverable, through a close reading of the text.

Both meaning and text were called into question by poststructuralist-influenced historian Roger Chartier (born 1945). He worried that certain borrowings from anthropology would create problems 'by destroying the "textuality" of the texts that relate the symbolic practices being analyzed'.[63] On the one hand, there is the text itself, the 1762 account of the event, taken from Nicolas Contat's *Anecdotes typographiques*. Contat was a participant in the event. However, Chartier argues that his *Anecdotes* belong to a literary genre, and yet Darnton treats it as a transparent vehicle for the full recovery of meaning. Then there is the meaning itself. Surely, Chartier suggests, we would be better off seeking out contemporary commentaries on symbols, rather than trying to come up with our own interpretations. For example, we have 'the native's point of view', in the form of Antoine Furetière's dictionary of 1727.

Darnton took the opportunity of a reply to Chartier to elaborate on his own symbolic approach, rather than comment point-for-point on Chartier's remarks.[64] This has been called a non-exchange, a dispute not over facts but over preferred narratives of the past.[65] The dispute highlighted the differences between the two scholars, downplaying the more significant aspects of the history of reading and cultural practices in which they agree.[66] Doubtless, Darnton asks a lot of his text. Indeed his belief in the authority of the text recalls Le Roy Ladurie. Basic questions remain. Was this a typical form of popular ritual? Did it actually happen? Darnton has also been called to task for reducing clashing anthropological definitions of culture to a shared 'general orientation', one that was based on seeing things from the native's point of view and exploring the social dimensions of meaning. He was criticized for using anthropology as a 'quick fix' for certain historiographical difficulties. We have certainly heard this before. Finally, Darnton was criticized for the overall argument in the book; that there was both a significant shift in 'mental worlds' between the ancient regime and the present and a persistence in 'Frenchness' throughout. Seeing culture in terms of shared symbols risks missing the variety of contemporary voices, sometimes in conflict or negotiation, risks painting a picture of uniformity.

9.7 A 'pidgin paradigm'?

The late 1980s was just about the time when interest in socio-cultural anthropology among early modernists showed signs of declining. This was due in part to anthropology's crisis of postmodernism. An increasingly reflexive anthropology began pondering its own claims to authority in a fragmented world. We saw an element of this in Rosaldo's critique of *Montaillou*. Some fields of early modern history actively engaged with anthropology's encounters with postmodernism. Ideas concerning cultural relativism and social construction have been particularly useful in the history of medicine and science. Here, we also see a complementary tendency among anthropologists: the return to detailed, empirical, comparative ethnography in an expanding range of sub-fields, such as medical anthropology.[67] Meanwhile, other areas of history have transposed their version of socio-cultural anthropology into a paradigm with an almost canonical range of authors, methodologies, interpretations and topics. It has become a 'pidgin paradigm', with its implications of simplification and debasement, on the one hand, and fluidity across boundaries and flexibility, on the other.[68] If anthropology does not provide early modern historians with the 'buzz' it once did, that is because some of its basic premises and approaches have entered the historical mainstream (actor's categories, native's point of view, symbolic interpretations). Some of its themes – ritual being the most obvious – are now widespread amongst historians, and have been applied to more traditional historical genres, now revitalized, like the study of elite groups and politics. But there is still much anthropology can teach us. For instance, historical anthropology reminds us not to take our archival sources for granted: that the archive itself (to say nothing of the individual holdings) is the result of a historical process. Rather than worrying solely whether a historical source can stand in for fieldwork, we should also be conducting 'extensive fieldwork on the archive itself'.[69] How did it come into being and with what purpose? How is it structured, used and read today?

Just how much anthropology is good for early modern historians? When does the law of diminishing returns set in? Lawrence Stone (1919–99) argued that anthropology was useful at shedding light on, but not explaining, phenomena in the past.[70] This is certainly true; but it seems more than enough to ask of a related discipline. At least one of anthropology's fervent advocates, Bob Scribner (1942–98), was actually lukewarm when it came to applying it to his own work. This was partly because he was aware of its limitations and pitfalls, partly because he wanted to be free to choose from other interpretations and methodologies as he saw fit. The use of 'theory' for the historian lay in its applications, Scribner believed.[71] Historians are probably wise to stress the practical applications of 'theory', of whatever sort. At the same time, it would do us no harm to be more reflexive about our choice and use of theories from other disciplines. We should aim to reduce the theory–practice dualism that mars much historical research and writing (as if theory did not lie at the root of all practice). Whatever role it assumes in historical theory and practice, socio-cultural anthropology has much to offer. We are still a long way from understanding the belief systems, range of social relationships, change and persistence underpinning early modern cultures. As historians continue to explore how things fit together in the past, we are conscious of acting as mediators, in this case between the past and the present. Whenever we want to investigate people's thought and action we shall benefit from the translation and interpretation skills and experience provided by anthropologists.

Guide to further reading

Brian Axel, 'Introduction: Historical Anthropology and its Vicissitudes', in B. Axel (ed.), *From the Margins: Historical Anthropology and its Futures* (Durham, NC, 2002), pp. 1–44.

Peter Burke, *The Historical Anthropology of Early Modern Italy: Essays on Perception and Communication* (Cambridge, 1987).

Elizabeth Cohen and Thomas Cohen, 'Anthropology and History', in D. R. Woolf (ed.), *A Global Encyclopedia of Historical Writing* (New York and London, 1998), Vol. 1, pp. 33–6.

David Gentilcore, 'The Ethnography of Everyday Life', in John Marino (ed.), *Early Modern Italy, 1550–1796* (Oxford, 2002), pp. 188–205.

Don Kalb, Hans Marks and Herman Tak (eds), *Focaal: European Journal of Anthropology* 26/27 (1996): monograph issue entitled *Historical Anthropology: The Unwaged Debate.*

Matti Peltonen, 'Clues, Margins and Monads: The Micro–Macro Link in Historical Research', *History and Theory* 40 (2001), pp. 347–57.

Renato Rosaldo, 'From the Door of his Tent: The Fieldworker and the Inquisitor', in James Clifford and George Marcus (eds), *Writing Culture: The Poetics and Politics of Ethnography* (Berkeley, 1986), pp. 77–97.

Robert Scribner, 'Historical Anthropology of Early Modern Europe', in R. Po-Chia Hsia and R. W. Scribner (eds), *Problems in the Historical Anthropology of Early Modern Europe* (Wolfenbüttel, 1997), pp. 11–34.

Notes

1 I am indebted to Elizabeth Cohen and Thomas Cohen, who commented on an earlier draft of this chapter. Their entry on 'Anthropology and History', in D. R. Woolf, *A Global Encyclopedia of Historical Writing* (New York and London, 1998), Vol. 1, pp. 33–6, provides a useful starting point.

2 On history and theory, see Ludmilla Jordanova, *History in Practice* (London, 2000), pp. 59–90.

3 E. E. Evans-Pritchard, *Anthropology and History* (Manchester, 1961).

4 Isaac Schapera, 'Should Anthropologists be Historians?', *Journal of the Royal Anthropological Institute of Great Britain and Ireland* 92 (1962), pp. 143–56.

5 Keith Thomas, 'History and Anthropology', *Past & Present* 24 (1963), pp. 3–24.

6 Keith Thomas, *Religion and the Decline of Magic: Studies in Popular Beliefs in Sixteenth- and 17th-Century England* (London, 1971); Jonathan Barry, 'Introduction: Keith Thomas and the Problem of Witchcraft', in Jonathan Barry, Marianne Hester and Gareth Roberts (eds), *Witchcraft in Early Modern Europe: Studies and Culture and Belief* (Cambridge, 1996), pp. 1-45.

7 Thomas's own explanation can be found in his 'The Relevance of Social Anthropology to the Historical Study of English Witchcraft', in Mary Douglas (ed.), *Witchcraft Confessions and Accusations* (London, 1970), pp. 47–80.

8 E. E. Evans-Pritchard, *Witchcraft, Oracles and Magic Among the Azande* (Oxford, 1937).

9 As discussed in Brian Levack, *The Witch-Hunt in Early Modern Europe* (London and New York, 1995).

10 Hildred Geertz, 'An Anthropology of Religion and Magic, I', *Journal of Interdisciplinary History* 6 (1975), pp. 71–89.

11 Geertz, 'An Anthropology', p. 77.

12 Keith Thomas, 'An Anthropology of Religion and Magic, II', *Journal of Interdisciplinary History* 6 (1975), p. 98.

13 Thomas, 'An Anthropology', p. 105, quoting Claude Lévi-Strauss, *Structural Anthropology*, trans. C. Jacobson and B. Grundfest Schoepf (London, 1968), p. 18.

14 Robert Muchembled, *Popular Culture and Elite Culture in France, 1400–1750*, trans. Lynda Cochrane (1978; Baton Rouge, 1985).

15 Geertz, 'An Anthropology', pp. 81–3.

16 Emmanuel Le Roy Ladurie, *Montaillou: Cathars and Catholics in a French Village, 1294–1324*, trans. Barbara Bray (London, 1978). The US edition bears the title *Montaillou: The Promised Land of Error* (New York, 1978).

17 *Montaillou, village Occitan de 1294 à 1324* (Paris, 1975), p. 10. The highly abridged English translation omits these references.

18 Robert Redfield, *The Little Community and Peasant Society and Culture* (Chicago, 1960).

19 Renato Rosaldo, 'From the Door of his Tent: The Fieldworker and the Inquisitor', in James Clifford and George E. Marcus (eds), *Writing Culture: The Poetics and Politics of Ethnography* (Berkeley, 1986), pp. 77–97.

20 E. E. Evans-Pritchard, *The Nuer: A Description of the Modes of Livelihood and Political Institutions of a Nilotic People* (Oxford, 1940).

21 Leonard Boyle, 'Montaillou Revisited: *Mentalité* and Methodology', in J. A. Raftis (ed.), *Pathways to Medieval Peasants* (Toronto, 1981), pp. 119–40.

22 Carlo Ginzburg, *The Cheese and the Worms: The Cosmos of a 16th-Century Miller*, trans. John and Anne Tedeschi (1976; Baltimore and London, 1980), p. xiii.

23 Life histories do, however, play an important part in more recent attempts to reconstruct 'ethnographies of the particular'. See Lila Abu-Lughod, 'Writing against Culture', in Richard Fox (ed.), *Recapturing Anthropology: Working in the Present* (Santa Fe, 1991), pp. 137–62.

24 Anne Jacobson Schutte, 'Carlo Ginzburg', *Journal of Modern History* 48 (1976), p. 315.

25 George Saunders, 'Contemporary Italian Cultural Anthropology', *Annual Review of Anthropology* 13 (1984), pp. 447–66.

26 One of Ginzburg's earliest published works was a review of de Martino's *La terra del rimorso*, in *Centro sociale* 51/52 (1963), unpaginated. De Martino's ethnographic study of Apulian tarantism is a classic interdisciplinary investigation, mixing religious, intellectual, social and cultural history with anthropology, sociology, musicology and psychology. De Martino, *La terra del rimorso: contributo a una storia religiosa del Sud* (Milan, 1961). Eng. trans.: Dorothy Louise Zinn, *The Land of Remorse : a Study of Southern Italian Tarantism* (London, 2005).

27 Paola Zambelli, 'Uno, due, tre, mille Menocchio?', *Archivio storico italiano* 137 (1979), pp. 51–90.

28 Ginzburg, *Cheese and Worms*, pp. 154–5.

29 Carlo Ginzburg, 'Clues: Roots of an Evidential Paradigm', in Carlo Ginzburg, *Clues, Myths and the Historical Method*, trans. John and Anne Tedeschi (Baltimore and London, 1989), pp. 96–125.

30 Edoardo Grendi, 'Microanalisi e storia sociale', *Quaderni storici* 35 (1977), pp. 506–20.

31 Carlo Ginzburg, 'The Inquisitor as Anthropologist', in *Clues*, pp. 156–64.

32 Bernard Cohen, 'Toward a Rapprochement', John Adams, 'Consensus, Community, and Exoticism', and Natalie Zemon Davis, 'The Possibilities of

the Past' – all in *Journal of Interdisciplinary History* 12 (1981), pp. 227–52, 253–65, 267–75 respectively.

33 Alan Macfarlane, *The Family Life of Ralph Josselin: A 17th-Century Clergyman* (Cambridge, 1970); *Resources and Population: A Study of the Gurungs of Nepal* (Cambridge, 1976); *Witchcraft in Tudor and Stuart England: A Regional and Comparative Study* (1970; London, 1999 edn), which has a useful introduction by James Sharpe).

34 William A. Christian, Jr, *Person and God in a Spanish Valley* (New York, 1972), and *Local Religion in 17th-Century Spain* (Princeton, 1981).

35 Richard C. Trexler, *Religion in Social Context in Europe and America* (Tempe, 2001), and 'Making the American Berdache: Choice or Constraint?', *Journal of Social History* 35 (2002), pp. 613–36.

36 E. P. Thompson, 'Folklore, Anthropology and Social History', *Indian Historical Review* 3 (1977), p. 248.

37 Natalie Zemon Davis, 'Possibilities of the Past', p. 273. From *Society and Culture in Early Modern France* (Stanford, 1975) to *The Gift in 16th-Century France* (Oxford and New York, 2000), Davis has been one of anthropological history's most eloquent exponents.

38 Jordan Goodman, 'History and Anthropology', in Michael Bentley (ed.), *Companion to Historiography* (London, 1997), pp. 787–8.

39 Adams, 'Consensus, Community, and Exoticism', p. 265.

40 Hans Medick, '"Missionaries in the Row Boat"? Ethnological Ways of Knowing as a Challenge to Social History', *Comparative Studies of Society and History* 29 (1987), pp. 76–98.

41 *Historische Anthropologie* has been published since 1993. See Michael Mitterauer, 'From Historical Social Science to Historical Anthropology?', in M. Jovanovi?, K. Kaser and S. Naumovi? (eds), *Between the Archives and the Field: A Dialogue on Historical Anthropology of the Balkans* (Belgrade, 1999), www.udi.org.yu/projects/archives/mitterauer.htm.

42 Brian Keith Axel, 'Introduction: Historical Anthropology and its Vicissitudes', in Brian Keith Axel (ed.), *From the Margins: Historical Anthropology and its Futures* (Durham, NC, 2002), pp. 1–44.

43 Eric Wolf, *Europe and the People without History* (Berkeley, 1982).

44 Olwen Hufton, 'Women, Gender and the *fin de siècle*', in Bentley (ed.), *Companion to Historiography*, pp. 929–40.

45 Compare Peter Burke, *Popular Culture in Early Modern Europe* (London, 1978), and the collection of essays in Tim Harris (ed.), *Popular Culture in England, c. 1500–1800* (Basingstoke, 1995), particularly Harris's contribution, 'Problematising Popular Culture', pp. 1–27.

46 For instance, Norbert Schindler, 'The Origins of Heartlessness: The Culture and Way of Life of Beggars in late 17th-Century Salzburg', in Norbert Schindler, *Rebellion, Community and Custom in Early Modern Germany*, trans. Pamela E. Selwyn (1992; Cambridge, 2002), pp. 236–92.

47 Peter Burke, *The Historical Anthropology of Early Modern Italy: Essays on Perception and Communication* (Cambridge, 1987).
48 Review by Randolph Starn, *Journal of Modern History* 62 (1990), pp. 628–30.
49 Peter Burke, 'The Virgin of the Carmine and Revolt of Masaniello', *Past & Present*, 99 (1983), pp. 3–21, reprinted in Burke, *Historical Anthropology*, pp. 191–206.
50 Edward Muir, *Ritual in Early Modern Europe* (Cambridge, 1997).
51 Victor Turner, *Schism and Continuity in African Society* (Manchester, 1957), was the first of several books exploring ritual and symbols.
52 Rosario Villari, 'Masaniello: Contemporary and Recent Interpretations', *Past & Present* 103 (1985), pp. 117–32, reprinted in Villari, *The Revolt of Naples*, trans. J. Newell (Cambridge, 1993), pp. 153–70.
53 'Thick description' refers to how even the smallest detail of human life is embedded in layers of contextual significance. On 'microhistory', see Edward Muir's entry in Woolf's *Global Encyclopedia*, Vol. 2, pp. 615–17. For an exploration of the link between anthropology and microhistory, see David Gentilcore, 'The Ethnography of Everyday Life', in John Marino (ed.), *Early Modern Italy, 1550–1796* (Oxford, 2002), pp. 188–205.
54 John Elliott, *National and Comparative History: An Inaugural Lecture Delivered before the University of Oxford* (Oxford, 1991).
55 In support: Edward Muir, 'Introduction: Observing Trifles', in Edward Muir and Guido Ruggiero (eds), *Microhistory and the Lost Peoples of Europe* (Baltimore and London, 1991), pp. vii–xxviii, and Giovanni Levi, 'On Microhistory', in Peter Burke (ed.), *New Perspectives on Historical Writing* (Cambridge, 1991), pp. 93–113. Against: Thomas Kuehn, 'Reading Microhistory: The Example of *Giovanni and Lusanna*', *Journal of Modern History* 61 (1989), pp. 512–34, and Samuel Cohn, *Women in the Streets: Essays on Sex and Power in Renaissance Italy* (Baltimore and London, 1996), esp. pp. 98–136.
56 Matti Peltonen, 'Clues, Margins and Monads: The Micro–Macro Link in Historical Research', *History and Theory* 40 (2001), p. 350.
57 Maria Lúcia Pallares-Burke, *The New History: Confessions and Conversations* (Cambridge, 2002), p. 197.
58 David Gentilcore, *From Bishop to Witch: The System of the Sacred in Early Modern Terra d'Otranto* (Manchester, 1992); Margo Todd, *The Culture of Protestantism in Early Modern Scotland* (New Haven and London, 2002).
59 Marilyn Silverman and P. H. Gulliver, 'Inside Historical Anthropology: Scale-Reduction and Context', *Focaal: European Journal of Anthropology* 26/27 (1996), pp. 149–58.
60 Don Kalb, Hans Marks and Herman Tak, 'Historical Anthropology and Anthropological History: Two Distinct Programs', *Focaal: European Journal of Anthropology* 26/27 (1996), pp. 5–13.

61 Robert Darnton, *The Great Cat Massacre and Other Episodes in French Cultural History* (New York, 1984), pp. 79–104.

62 Clifford Geertz, 'Deep Play: Notes on the Balinese Cockfight', in Clifford Geertz, *The Interpretation of Cultures: Selected Essays* (New York, 1973), pp. 412–53. But see William Roseberry, 'Balinese Cockfights and the Seduction of Anthropology', *Social Research* 49 (1982), pp. 1013–28.

63 Roger Chartier, 'Texts, Symbols, and Frenchness', *Journal of Modern History* 57 (1985), p. 690.

64 Robert Darnton, 'The Symbolic Element in History', *Journal of Modern History* 58 (1986), pp. 218–34.

65 Dominick LaCapra, 'Chartier, Darnton, and the Great Symbol Massacre', and James Fernandez, 'Historians Tell Tales: of Cartesian Cats and Gallic Cockfights', both in *Journal of Modern History* 60 (1988), pp. 92–112, 113–27 respectively.

66 For Darnton's take on it, see Pallares-Burke, *New History*, pp. 169–70.

67 Michael MacDonald, 'Anthropological Perspectives on the History of Science and Medicine', in Pietro Corsi and Paul Weindling (eds), *Information Sources in the History of Science and Medicine* (London, 1983), pp. 61–80; Jordan Goodman, 'History and Anthropology', in Bentley (ed.), *Companion to Historiography*, pp. 796–8.

68 Mary Fulbrook, *Historical Theory* (London, 2002), esp. pp. 47–8, 86.

69 Nicholas Dirks, 'Annals of the Archive: Ethnographic Notes on the Sources of History', in Axel, *From the Margins*, p. 51. See also Stephen Milner, 'Partial Readings: Addressing a Renaissance Archive', *History of the Human Sciences* 12 (1999), pp. 89–105.

70 Lawrence Stone, 'History and the Social Sciences in the 20th Century', in Lawrence Stone, *The Past and Present Revisited* (London, 1987), p. 30. The article was first published in 1977.

71 Robert Scribner, 'Historical Anthropology of Early Modern Europe', in R. Po-Chia Hsia and R. W. Scribner (eds), *Problems in the Historical Anthropology of Early Modern Europe* (Wolfenbüttel, 1997), pp. 11–34; Thomas Brady, 'Robert W. Scribner, a Historian of the German Reformation', introduction to R. W. Scribner, *Religion and Culture in Germany (1400–1800)*, ed. Lyndal Roper (Leiden, 2001), pp. 9–26.

10

Comparative history

Stefan Berger

Historians compare. They cannot avoid it, unless they restrict themselves to listing dates and events. If history is more than chronology, any attempt to explain and interpret what has been going on in a particular place and time involves comparing it with what has been going on before or later or at other places at the same time. Take, for example, explanations of the rise to power of the National Socialists in Germany. If we say that the weakness of democratic traditions in Germany contributed to the Nazis' success, we also say that the strength of democratic traditions elsewhere, say in Britain, helped prevent the rise of Fascism. Narrative structures depend on comparison but these comparisons are often implicit rather than explicit.

Calls for explicit comparative history are old, and attempts to formulate a specific theory are usually traced back to John Stuart Mill.[1] In the first half of the 20th century, eminent theoreticians and practitioners of the comparative method include Marc Bloch, Max Weber, Otto Hintze, Henri Pirenne and Emile Durkheim. These pioneers were archipelagos in a sea of nationally constituted histories, in which the vast majority of historians found it difficult to transcend the study of the societies in which they had grown up. Yet, over the last 25 years, the practice of comparative history has taken off in many societies and cultures.[2] Scholarly exchange programmes have increased international contacts after 1945, and scholars now work in national contexts different to those in which they were raised. Globalization has also directed the historians' attention to past interlinkages and comparisons between different parts of the world.[3] If comparative history is practised more frequently today than ever before, it is not done to the same extent everywhere. One of its foremost practitioners in Britain, Geoffrey Crossick, argues that comparative history has had relatively little influence on historiographical research in Britain.[4] In the Cannadine debate about

British history, Neil Evans was one of the few contributors to demand more 'rigorous and empirically grounded' comparisons to deconstruct British history into 'the building blocks of regional and national distinctiveness within the British state' and to 'see it within the perspective of Europe and the whole Atlantic world'.[5] In America, by contrast, the comparative method has made a real difference.[6] Yet comparative history courses are also taught in British undergraduate programmes (e.g. on Fascism, revolutions, labour movements and nationalism), and students are encouraged to write comparative essays. This chapter sets out to assist students taking courses in comparative history and to encourage them to work comparatively. For comparative history to succeed, it is essential, as Thomas Welskopp points out, to make it an integral part of a theoretically aware analytical history, rather than a specialist sub-discipline that stands apart from other forms of history writing and is only practised by the initiated few.[7] To widen the appeal of comparative history this article will, first, discuss different kinds of comparisons. Second, it will summarize some of the benefits of comparative history. Third, it will analyse problems and pitfalls of the comparative method. Fourth, it will discuss the relationship between comparative studies and cultural transfer studies, and finally it will introduce an example of comparative history to demonstrate how comparisons work.

10.1 Different kinds of comparisons

Comparisons often involve nation-states. The rise of professional history writing in the 19th century coincided with the rise of the nation-state. Historians looking to legitimate their nation-state[8] did so by comparing it – implicitly rather than explicitly – to other nation-states, identifying allegedly unique characteristics of their own that distinguished them from and made them superior to others. The legacy of transnational comparisons is so strong that we often forget that nations do not have to be our units of comparison. In fact, as economic historians particularly point out, regions might constitute better units of comparison.[9] Since they are less heterogeneous than larger nations, regional comparisons are possibly less vulnerable to reductionism. A micro-comparison can take account of the totality of structures, experiences and values in a way that is impossible for a macro-comparison. Yet total comparisons of social contexts are still rare. The larger the comparison, the more necessary it is to select particular aspects for comparison. In fact, some historians have attempted to compare across whole civilizations and cultures.[10] Some themes can indeed best be discussed in transcultural perspectives, e.g. multi-culturalism or cosmopolitanism. Max Weber famously compared diverse world religions and their impact on the evolution of specific economic orders.[11] As we can see from these brief remarks, comparisons have an important spatial dimension. We need to reflect on which geographical units we wish to compare as it will influence the whole set-up of the comparison.

It is not only geography that matters. We also need to think about the purpose of the comparison. Most comparisons can be divided into two categories: individualizing and universalizing. Individualizing comparisons set out to demonstrate the uniqueness of one particular case by comparing it with others. They tend to be asymmetrical in that they use a variety of cases only to shed light on the one case that the comparison seeks to understand better. If one wants to examine 'American exceptionalism' or the German *Sonderweg*, or ask whether Britain really was 'the first industrial nation', then only comparison can establish what was specific about the particular history. Universalizing comparisons aim to identify similarities between cases. They are usually symmetrical in that they give equal weight to all cases compared. Jack Goody's comparison of family structures in Europe and Asia found similar domestic structures in this vast area.[12] Between these two ideal types of comparison are a range of hybrids. Charles Tilly has usefully distinguished between four types of comparison.[13] Encompassing comparisons are related to individualizing comparisons. They are primarily concerned with explaining differences between cases that share an overarching commonality. Nationalism studies, for example, are often concerned with delineating different ideas and types of nationalism while recognizing at the same time that all nationalisms are connected to one another.[14] Variation-finding comparisons are closer to universalizing comparisons. Here different cases are understood as variations of one particular phenomenon. Comparative Fascism studies often fall into this category. They assume that there is one phenomenon called Fascism and proceed to discuss its variations through place and time. Barrington Moore's classic study on the origins of dictatorship and democracy started from the observation that agricultural societies seemed particularly vulnerable to Fascism and set out to explore variations within this pattern.[15]

Individualizing comparisons and their variants are more common among historians, as they are more concerned with questions of the uniqueness of a particular time and place. Their strong historist, positivist and empiricist assumptions make historians partial towards complex analysis, which allows detailed understanding of particular contexts. They approach the evidence in as unbiased a manner as possible, and seek to reconstruct the past from the evidence that remains. Historical sociologists and geographers, in contrast, are happier with universalizing comparisons and their variants, as they habitually work at greater levels of abstraction. They are more willing to reduce historical complexity in order to answer specific questions for diverse societal contexts. However, as disciplinary barriers have fallen over the past decades, those differences have become less marked. On a basic level, one could say that comparativists are always interested in establishing both differences and similarities between cases.

The intention of the comparative historian is important for other reasons.[16] Historians undertake comparisons because they want to question national explanations, build typologies, stress historical diversity, encourage scepticism vis-à-vis global explanatory models, or contextualize and enrich research traditions of one society by exploring and contrasting them with research traditions of other societies. Many comparisons are concerned with highlighting the constructedness of historical identities. Often they endeavour to relativize notions of exceptionalism by demonstrating that identity is situational. A multiplicity of identities exists at any one given time: which one is foregrounded largely depends on the specific historical context. The emphasis in these cases is on the detachment of scholars from their object of enquiry. Yet other comparativists explicitly seek to teach the lessons of history. They may want to explain what went wrong in one particular society by contrasting its development with that of other societies. Or they may be concerned with highlighting the pioneering and model function of particular societies. This kind of comparative history is often informed by moral judgements. Their practitioners reject the assumption – still widespread among historians – that it is not the task of the historian to act as judge. Instead they point out that moral judgements cannot be avoided in the writing of history, as the nature of all knowledge is perspectival. A fact is only ever a fact within a specific framework of description. This not only allows for a plurality of true statements; it also means that the realm of facts cannot neatly be separated from the realm of values and hence morality. Factual statements already presuppose normative choices. They can be hidden (as is usually the case with historists) or they can be brought out in the open. Whichever is the case, knowledge is only possible within particular moral–normative–ideological 'horizons of expectation'.[17]

10.2 The promises of comparative history

Most historians have been drawn to comparative history, because they want to obtain a better knowledge of their own society through comparison. Even where historians engaged in comparative history in order to understand other societies better, their interest was frequently motivated by a desire to learn from the experiences of others and to encourage adaptation of positive features of other societies. Having studied a problem or theme in different social contexts, they could draw up typologies of how different societies dealt with the same problem. They might also ask whether the same problem was present in different societies to a similar degree. Such an observation might have escaped the attention of historians who focused on one particular society. For example, the focus on national histories in Europe in the nineteenth and twentieth centuries hid from sight the fact that, beyond the boundaries of national states, something like a European experience in economic, social, political and cultural life was developing.[18] The comparative method also allows for the identification of problems not evident from observation of a single societal context. Thus only through comparison with other countries have historians asked why was there no significant Marxism in the USA and Britain.[19]

Many comparativists have argued that there is no better test in history than comparison. As far back as 1895 Emile Durkheim saw comparison as the equivalent to the natural scientist's experiment, in which variables were isolated and causal relationships proven.[20] Even if we are today more sceptical than Durkheim about the 'scientificity' of history,[21] comparison does allow us to differentiate good causal explanations from bad ones. It has, for example, been fashionable to argue that it was, above all, the economic slump of the early 1930s that caused the rise of Nazism in Germany. Yet, the slump was just as severe in the USA, which did not face a serious fascist challenge. But the USA did have a republic established in 1776 with a much revered constitution from 1787/8. Germany, by contrast, was a republic only after 1918/19 and its constitution was at best tolerated. The slump is therefore unlikely to have been the only explanation for why Hitler came to power. Take another example: comparisons allow linkage of the strong reception of Marxism in European working-class parties with the degree of state repression that these parties faced. The more repression they faced, the more likely it was that they would turn to Marxism as an explanatory framework for social and political developments.[22] Comparisons are able to test existing models and explanations, but they are equally capable of developing new models. Miroslav Hroch, for instance, compared the emergence of small-nation nationalism in central Europe and developed a model that can now be tested by further comparison.[23]

Comparisons may draw attention to the fact that similar outcomes, such as strikes, sometimes have different causes and follow different patterns.[24] Inversely, comparisons may account for how similar developments produced different results. Thus, in a classic of the genre, Alexander Gerschenkron explored the impact of industrialization on different societies. He found that late industrializers such as Germany, in which a belated take-off was followed by a sprint, experienced significant social and political problems. Similarly, John Breuilly demonstrated the initial appearance of liberal labour movements in Britain and Germany, and went on to explain why in Britain a liberal labour movement succeeded, whereas in Germany it soon lost out to a rising socialist movement.[25] Overall, developments in one country can be explained better by comparing them with developments in others. No other historical method is so adept at testing, modifying and falsifying historical explanation than comparison. No other method demonstrates so effectively the range of developmental possibilities.

It allows historians to gain a vantage point outside one particular regional or national history and makes history a less provincial undertaking.

10.3 Problems and pitfalls in comparative history

If the promises of comparative history are manifold, so are the problems connected with its practice. Four preconditions need to be fulfilled before successful comparisons can be made. First, the historian needs close familiarity with more than one social context. Second, comparativists need to reflect on spatial and time constraints. Third, they have to consider theoretical and conceptual frameworks for their comparison. Finally, they have to have a feeling for linguistic pitfalls in transnational comparisons involving more than one language. In the following I would like to expand on those four potential stumbling blocks.

The first point might seem obvious, but it is nevertheless important, as it forces us to recognize the immense work involved in gaining knowledge of archival sources and secondary literature in two or more social contexts. There is a particular problem with archival sources: rarely do we find comparable sources that exist in different societal contexts. Even if we deal with secondary literature alone, we must be aware of different research traditions. Historians have asked different questions in different societies. Different questions might produce different views of developments, structures, organizations and mentalities. Therefore a comparison of historiographies must precede any historical comparison. Take, for example, the coalfields of the Ruhr and South Wales, where historians face the problem of a much more diverse and richer historiographical tradition for the former. The impression of greater diversity of experiences in the Ruhr might, after all, be the result of different historiographical traditions rather than of actual lived experience.[26] We also need to keep in mind that familiarity with more than one social context often cannot be achieved by reading about it. It is necessary to experience a different social context first hand, which involves extended stays in other regions or countries. Looking at two social contexts we might find similar events and institutions in one context, but their mere existence might not tell us very much about their functioning, their relevance and their wider meaning in society. We might, for example, find that most nation-states have myths of origin. But that tells us little about their impact or function in different nation-states at different times. Careful contextualization of any phenomenon to be compared is necessary.

Contexts are provided in time and space, which brings us to the second precondition for comparative history: we need to be clear about our geographical and time boundaries. We need to justify our choice of geographical comparisons.

Geographical boundaries are somewhat arbitrary; they have been defined in different contexts for different purposes. Borders must be treated with extreme caution; they do not define 'natural' units of comparison. Look again at the Ruhr and South Wales. The former has been divided into three zones of industrial development that, in several respects, had very different histories. South Wales includes both the coalfield and the coastal strip with the important coal ports of Cardiff and Barry and cities such as Swansea and Newport. Even within the coalfield, the anthracite coalfield in the west differed significantly from the rest of the coalfield.[27] To presume that the geographical boundaries of the Ruhr and South Wales were fixed and self-evident is a dangerous illusion.

If geographical boundaries are rarely straightforward, we also need to attend to why beginning and end points of our comparison are chosen. Time can be particularly tricky, as similar structures, institutions and ideas might develop at different times in different social contexts. Possible time-lags need to be taken into account in comparative studies. We must justify comparison of similar (synchronic comparisons) or different (diachronic comparisons) times for different social contexts. Synchronic comparisons are more usual, but not always the most appropriate. If labour movements, for example, are seen as reactions against rapid industrialization, it follows that since industrialization happens at different times in different social contexts, labour movements must be compared diachronically rather than synchronically.[28] The use of particular time caesuras and geographical boundaries influences the way in which particular events or structures are seen.

The next question to ask is, Which units of comparison do we choose for which end? Theoretically, anything can be compared with something else. Everything depends on which theoretical and conceptual framework we choose for the comparison. This brings us to our third precondition. We must choose the cases that fit the question(s) that we want to ask. The research question(s) might well be modified in the light of our increasing knowledge about the units of comparison, but they form the basis of the theoretical and conceptual framework that structures all comparative work. Concepts are often interrelated. Comparisons that are concerned with establishing causal relationships between particular variables have to be aware of such dependencies. If, for example, we want to explain different degrees of nationalism in different countries, we cannot use notions such as enmity towards foreigners and willingness to defend one's country against foreign invasion as explanations, as they are related forms of nationalism. They can be used to indicate different degrees of nationalism but they do not explain the existence of nationalism.

Historical theories and concepts structure comparisons but are not free from agendas. Many comparative labour historians, for example, have assumed that the emergence and development of labour movements was tightly related to the industrialization process and to working-class formation.[29] In this they borrowed heavily from Marxist and Weberian theories of industrialization and the evolution of capitalism. The usefulness of such grand social theories for historical analyses has been questioned by postmodernism.[30] Postcolonial and subaltern perspectives have been wary of western developmental concepts and their imperialist ambitions.[31] Edward Said's analysis of 'orientalism' has been immensely influential in explicating the West's construction of an image of the other (in his case, the Orient) by defining the terms of the debate through the use of concepts such as development or modernization.[32] For comparative history, these interventions constitute a serious warning: concepts, terminologies and theories must be used self-reflexively. Comparative historians need to consider origins and politics of their concepts. No longer must they pretend that concepts can be used within a value-free scientific paradigm. Yet, comparativists need not be disheartened by postcolonial scepticism about western concepts. As Jürgen Osterhammel has pointed out, many western concepts and terms had already been transferred to non-western contexts before European colonization from the 16th century onwards, and this makes it almost impossible to draw a neat line between western and non-western concepts and terminologies.[33] What is ultimately important is not the origins of concepts and terminologies but their usefulness and appropriateness for the research question(s) we want to pursue comparatively.

Some famous large-scale comparisons have paid inadequate attention to conceptual problems. One example is Samuel P. Huntington's book about the alleged clash of civilizations, which predicts major conflicts between the West and the Islamic world.[34] Both units of comparison are set up in such a way that mutually incompatible cultural entities were confronted and the many differences within each ignored. Huntington's and other similar studies ignore postcolonialism's concern with 'hybridity', 'alterity' and the differences of experiences in different social context at their own peril. Arguably grand comparisons based on universal social theories work best where they first ask about processes of diffusion, communication and exchange that took place between different cultures. Only in a second step can concrete research questions be formulated and specific conceptual and terminological frameworks be developed, which then guide the comparative practice.[35]

Comparative historians should be suspicious about theories and concepts, yet every comparison requires specific research questions in conjunction with larger theoretical and conceptual frameworks.[36] If we do not approach the material with specific questions in mind, we will face the problem of excess information (this problem is obviously more serious the larger the comparison), and will run the risk of merely narrating parallel stories rather than comparing. Furthermore, the method of investigation has to fit the questions that are being asked. For example, a statistical analysis of strikes in a particular industry across various nations does not yet tell us anything about the radicalism of workers employed in that industry. Only a qualitative assessment of motivations for strikes, the workings of different systems of industrial relations and the potential variations in the meanings of strike activity will permit assessment of degrees of radicalism of the workers in question.[37]

All qualitative analysis is based on texts and language. And language is a veritable minefield for comparative historians. There is often little correspondence between the meanings of historical terms in different languages. Words that seem similar may carry different meanings in different languages. The word 'functionary', for example, in English carries with it a whole host of negative connotations involving bureaucracy, pig-headedness and stupid application of the rule book. In German, the very similar *Funktionär* did not carry such negativity – at least before 1933. Even key concepts and terms are difficult to translate and carry different meanings. Jörn Leonhard, for example, has persuasively argued that the genesis of the word 'liberal' in Germany is quite different from that of the word 'liberal' in Britain. In Germany, it was a French conception of the word and its meanings, carrying positive connotations, which was imported. In Britain, the word was conveyed from Spanish and carried markedly negative connotations.[38] Similar difficulties of translation arise with terms such as 'middle class' and 'gentry'. The English university was different in many respects from the German *Universität* in the 19th century, which in turn was something altogether different from the French *Université*. Concepts and terms often do not travel well from one society to another; linguistic and conceptual worlds are often different, and clarity concerning these differences is a very important precondition for any comparison.

Another problem with language concerns the need to find common terminology for related phenomena. Terms such as 'working-class parties', 'socialist parties' and 'labour parties' all carry different meanings even within a single historiographical tradition, let alone multiple ones. One needs to tread carefully in choosing, and comparative historians are usually well advised to start by exploring the meanings of terms and concepts in different social contexts.[39]

10.4 Cultural transfer studies and comparison

Comparative history is a difficult and labour-intensive affair. Despite its potential pitfalls, a growing number of scholars have been convinced of its merits. More recently, French and German scholars have questioned the value of comparative history, and prefer the history of cultural transfer. Since these debates have not been prominent in English-speaking countries, I will introduce the history of cultural transfers. I will then examine its challenge to comparative history.

Michael Werner's and Michel Espagne's studies of Franco-German cultural transfers have been particularly influential in generating interest in cultural transfer studies.[40] They break up the picture of homogenous and internally stable national cultures by demonstrating that national cultures depend on a dialectical process through which indigenous and foreign elements are selectively appropriated. Cultural transfer historians call into question national modes of argumentation, relativize national yardsticks, and problematise national explanatory frameworks. National identity appears as a process of cultural appropriation and mediation, and what is imagined as 'one's own' is bound up with what is conceived of, whether in negative or in positive terms, as 'the Other'. That 'Other' can often appear, at once and in equal measure, attractive and dangerous. As a rule, therefore, appropriation and rejection are two sides of the same coin. Research on cultural transfers thus contributes to exposing the absurdity of notions of the national character and of national cultures composed of national essences. In this way, the process of creation and evolution of plurally constituted national cultures is made visible. National memory comprises innumerable fragments of cultural assets, a goodly proportion of which are imported and adapted.

The reception of imports can take very different forms, ranging from total adoption through selective appropriation to conscious rejection. Cultural transfer research focuses on those groups most suited to the role of mediators – authors, publishers, journalists, cultural tourists, exiles, migrants, spies, translators, artists, musicians, diplomats, academics and teachers of foreign languages. These groups share the opportunity for contact with other national contexts and they settle, as it were, at the crossroads of two or more cultures. They are often able to develop or to exploit new and interconnected spheres of activity. But certain preconditions – such as linguistic competence, opportunities to travel or the availability of translations or of press reports – must be met for a cultural transfer to be rendered possible. Work on cultural transfers typically asks how newspapers and periodicals reported on the other country considered. Which books were imported or exported, and translated? What migratory movements were there? Which authorities, agencies and people knew something of the other country, and from what sources? What problems and misunderstandings arose in conveying terms and concepts from one language into the other? In what discursive and agential connections was the 'Other' used, and in pursuit of what interests? What preconditions had to be fulfilled for transfers to be completed successfully? How do selection, transportation and integration occur in different national contexts? Is an instance of integration effective over the long term, or is it temporary, its success contingent on particular circumstances?

Borders are of particular importance for research on transfers. On the one hand, a border can mean demarcation, putting off limits that which is defined as not belonging. On the other hand, however, borders can indicate preparedness for exchange and appropriation – a transmission belt of 'the other' on the way to its adoption as one's own. Border territories may variously be understood as sites of confrontation, intolerance and the collision of fundamentally incompatible 'national' values and normative horizons.[41] But they can also be terrains of an altogether different kind. Thus, delineations between 'national cultures' are blurred, for there is exchange between the mutually 'Other' and foreign.

Not every transfer is immediately recognizable as such. Once the foreign has been embedded in indigenous discursive and agential contexts, its foreignness tends to disappear. The archaeological capacities of the historian are required to bring the connections to light once more. The transmitters and the means of transmission must first be identified. Transmitters shared a transnational consciousness that permitted them to raise their sights above and beyond the merely national. This kind of international orientation was facilitated by personal contacts, lengthy stays abroad, and by opportunities for institutional cooperation. The cultural transfer approach is, for example, promising for work on the history of scholarship, since scholarly communities evinced particularly pronounced processes of internationalization in the nineteenth and twentieth centuries.[42] However, cultural transfer studies are also being employed fruitfully in a wide range of other areas, e.g. in the history of social reform.[43]

There has been considerable tension between comparative historians and historians of cultural transfer. The former have sometimes drawn strict demarcation lines, arguing that cultural transfer studies are different from comparisons, in that they do not look for similarities and differences between social contexts.[44] The latter have replied that comparativists single out artificial units of comparison, which are then contrasted without any consideration of the transfers taking place between them. Comparisons thus construct homogeneous entities, contrast them with one another, and thereby re-enforce homogeneous identities. Cultural transfer, by contrast, is about hybridity, breaking up constructed entities, and undermining homogeneous identities.[45]

Historians of cultural transfer have indeed identified a potential weakness of comparative history, and comparativists have been unnecessarily exclusionary in their treatment of cultural transfer studies. Comparisons should take account of those mutual dependencies and relations, but there is no necessary methodological reason why they should not do so.[46] In fact the analysis of transfers would sharpen understanding of similarities and differences. Indeed, it was one of the founding fathers of comparative history, Marc Bloch, who pointed out that transfers need to be considered in any comparison.[47] However, it is unlikely that cultural transfer approaches will replace comparative studies.

Even more recently than the arrival of cultural transfer studies, we find references to transnational history. It differs from international history, as it does not want to be mistaken with IR-type studies and aims to transcend the traditional focus on inter-state relations. Transnational history aims to look at relationships that go beyond national borders and take into account non-state actors, cultural and economic dimensions and forms of transfer. It typically looks at the interaction between local and global processes, networks and material things/products, which have been produced, traded, transported and consumed globally.[48]

10.5 The practice of comparative history

Finally, I would like to demonstrate how comparative history works in practice. I have chosen an article written by Eric Hobsbawm and Joan Scott on 'political shoemakers'.[49] Like every good comparison, it starts with a specific question: Why did 19th-century shoemakers have such a reputation for political radicalism and for being worker-intellectuals? In many national historiographies we find the observation that shoemakers were radicals, but rarely do we find any explanation for this phenomenon. In fact it is almost taken for granted. It is only by looking at shoemakers comparatively that, first of all, the universality of their radicalism comes into view. Hence only the comparative method allows the authors to identify the problem they subsequently seek to explain.

The spatial breadth of the argument is truly breathtaking. Although British, French and German shoemakers are arguably at the core of the authors' argument, there are references to at least a dozen other European countries and a range of non-European ones, including Australia, Argentina, Brazil, India and Japan. We are clearly not dealing with a totalizing comparison here. Rather, the article chooses to concentrate on a very specific theme or aspect, i.e. explaining the political radicalism of shoemakers. It comes very close to a universalizing comparison in that it is not concerned with specific national characteristics of shoemakers but looks for evidence from shoemakers around the world to explain what it identifies as a universal phenomenon, i.e. the political radicalization of shoemakers and their prominence among worker-intellectuals.

While the comparison aspires to geographical universality, its chronological framework is specific. Three time zones are evoked. First, a time before the Industrial Revolution – the golden age for the radical shoemaker. In this period they established their credentials as radical spokespersons for the people. Second, the article explores the fortunes of craft radicalism during the Industrial Revolution. Finally, it asks why the once-radical shoemakers were less prominent among the mass socialist movements of the more advanced capitalist age. Although the article includes references to dates for these distinct time periods, they are not too specific, and arguably they cannot be too specific, for the Industrial Revolution happened at different times for different social contexts. The article has to compare diachronically as well as synchronically, and this makes the specific dating of the three time zones impossible.

Hobsbawm's and Scott's theoretical framework is not spelt out, but the reader soon encounters assumptions about the development of capitalism derived from a broadly Marxist understanding of history. Capitalism impacts on the organization of work, which in turn has repercussions for cultural expressions – in this case the artisanal culture of shoemakers. This materialist conception of history assumes that work forms the basis of people's social existence and out of it grows a particular culture. Hobsbawm and Scott carefully avoid the determinist implications of Marxist theory. They argue that the shoemaker radicalism cannot be seen exclusively in terms of a response to early industrial capitalism, for it precedes the Industrial Revolution. Nevertheless, their basic theoretical framework remains historical materialism. Both authors, as theoretically aware Marxists, had also been influenced by Gramscian notions of the development of 'organic intellectuals' – intellectuals who emerge from the working class. Hobsbawm's and Scott's shoemakers are the very epitome of organic intellectuals.

The authors' method of investigation is varied and always fits the questions that are being asked. We have much qualitative analysis of literature, poems, autobiography, social and political commentary, and dictionaries. Where appropriate, they resort to quantitative analysis – for example, to establish that cobblers often could not live by shoemaking and shoe-repairing alone, or to document the vast size of the shoemaking trade in the 19th century, or to demonstrate the numbers of shoemakers among socialist deputies in the German Reichstag.

Hobsbawm's and Scott's comparison is noteworthy for its careful treatment of language and concepts. The key analytical concept of radicalism is not taken for granted, but carefully examined for its contextually varied meanings. The authors demonstrate that words that signify the profession of shoemakers in different languages such as 'cobbler', 'cordonnier' and 'Schuster' actually are comparable and mean the same thing. They point out that the proverb 'Shoemaker stick to your last' exists in a great variety of languages and suggest that this indicates shoemakers' readiness to be involved in intellectual debates more usually perceived as the preserve of the educated classes.

Comparisons are about establishing similarities and differences, and this is clearly what this article does. It compares shoemakers' militancy with that of other artisanal groups. It discusses carpenters, tailors, construction workers, printers, metalworkers and many other craft groups, always delineating what they had in common with shoemakers and what made shoemakers distinctive. What was it about the shoemakers' trade that fostered their strong intellectual interests? The answers, mostly related to the world of work, are complex and varied, but they are laid out before the reader with wonderful clarity and a superb command of the literature on the worlds of artisans in very different social contexts. The intention of the comparison is analytical: the authors analyse the shoemakers' socialization, their values, institutions, work practices and mentalities. The article is an excellent example of how even the most wide-ranging comparison can avoid reductionism and improve our understanding of artisanal culture, which transcended diverse social contexts. If we are specialists on one particular social context, say a particular country such as Britain, we learn about artisans in other countries and through this we learn to rethink our knowledge of British artisans.

By raising the problem of universal artisan cultures, Hobsbawm and Scott make it possible for other authors to follow up their comparison with a more detailed typology of artisan radicalism. Sure enough, their article was the inspiration for a host of articles and monographs that examined artisanal cultures as defences of their independence and expression against an encroaching capitalist system .[50] The article is thus a pioneer and at the same time a model for subsequent comparisons of artisanal cultures from the pre-industrial to the industrial ages.

A masterpiece of comparative historical investigation, this article is also not blind to the importance of cultural transfers. It discusses the English conviction that French shoemakers were instrumental in the French Revolution of 1789. English shoemakers received and appropriated an image of the 'Other' in order to underline their own love of liberty. The authors specifically discuss the importance of travel for the socialization of shoemakers. During their journeymen days, shoemakers would visit different regions and countries and familiarize themselves with diverse experiences in a variety of contexts. As transmitters of different social contexts they were able to transplant their own politicization (as journeymen) wherever they eventually settled. In the context of changes brought about by agricultural capitalism, shoemakers often voiced discontent among the rural population. They could do this only because they had the intellectual means to appropriate, adapt and mediate experiences from different contexts. Few comparative historians can aspire to the heights reached by Hobsbawm and Scott. Yet their article serves as a reminder of the power of comparative history and an enduring inspiration to future generations of comparative historians.

Guide to further reading

A. A. van den *Braembussche, 'Historical Explanation and Comparative Method: Towards a Theory of the History of Society', History and Theory* 28 (1989), pp. 2–24.

John Breuilly, 'Introduction: Making Comparisons in History', in Breuilly, *Labour and Liberalism in 19th-century Europe: Essays in Comparative History* (Manchester, 1992).

Deborah Cohen and Maura O'Connor (eds), *Comparison and History: Europe in Cross-National Perspective* (London, 2004).

George Frederickson, 'From Exceptionalism to Variability: Recent Developments in Cross-National Comparative History', *Journal of American History* 82 (1995), pp. 587–604.

Heinz-Gerhard Haupt, 'Comparative History', in Neil J. Smelser and Paul B. Baltes (eds), *International Encyclopedia of the Social and Behavioural Sciences* (Amsterdam, 2001), pp. 2397–403.

Jürgen Kocka, 'Asymmetrical Historical Comparison: The Case of the German "Sonderweg"', *History and Theory* 38 (1999), pp. 40–50.

Chris Lorenz, 'Comparative Historiography: Problems and Perspectives', *History and Theory* 38 (1999), pp. 25–39.

Charles Ragin, *The Comparative Method: Moving Beyond Quantitative and Qualitative Strategies* (Berkeley, 1987).

Jörn Rüsen, 'Some Theoretical Approaches to Intercultural Comparative Historiography', *History and Theory* 35 (1996), pp. 5–22.

W. H. Sewell, 'Marc Bloch and the Logic of Comparative History', *History and Theory* 6 (1967), pp. 208–18.

Michael Werner and Benedict Zimmermann, 'Beyond Comparison: "Histoire Croisée" and the Challenge of Reflexivity', *History and Theory* 45(1) (2006), pp. 30–50.

Notes

1 John Stuart Mill, *Philosophy of Scientific Method* (New York, 1950), pp.211–33.

2 Hartmut Kaelble, 'Vergleichende Sozialgeschichte im 19. und 20. Jahrhundert. Forschungen europäischer Historiker', *Jahrbuch für Wirtschaftsgeschichte*, Part 1 (1993), pp. 173–200, for an attempt to provide a survey of the rise of comparative history in Europe from around 1980.

3 Roland Axtman, 'Society, Globalization and the Comparative Method', *History of the Human Sciences* 6 (1993), pp. 53-74.

4 Geoffrey Crossick, 'And What Should They Know of England? Die vergleichende Geschichtsschreibung im heutigen Großbritannien', in Heinz-Gerhard Haupt and Jürgen Kocka (eds), *Geschichte und Vergleich. Ansätze und Ergebnisse international-vergleichender Geschichtsschreibung* (Frankfurt/Main, 1996), pp. 61–76.

5 Neil Evans, 'Debate: British History: Past, Present – and Future?', *Past and Present* 119 (1988), pp. 194-203.

6 An early marker was C. Vann Woodward, *The Comparative Approach to American History* (1968; reprinted Oxford, 1997). Studies of slavery, race

relations and the frontier have been transformed by comparisons. See, for example, Carl N. Degler, *Neither Black nor White. Slavery and Race Relations in Brazil and the United States* (New York, 1971). On frontier history, see Howard Lamar and Leonard Thompson (eds), *The Frontier in History: North America and Southern Africa Compared* (New Haven, 1981).

7 Thomas Welskopp, 'Stolpersteine auf dem Königsweg. Methodenkritische Anmerkungen zum internationalen Vergleich in der Gesellschaftsgeschichte', *Archiv für Sozialgeschichte* 35 (1995), pp. 339–67, esp. p. 342f.

8 On the close relationship between nationalism and historiography, see Stefan Berger, Mark Donovan and Kevin Passmore (eds), *Writing National Histories. Western Europe Since 1800* (London, 1999) Stefan Berger (ed.) Writing National History : a Global Perspective (Houndmills, 2007).

9 Sidney Pollard, 'Industrialization and the European Economy', *Economic History Review* 26 (1973), pp. 636–48. See also Pollard, *Peaceful Conquests. The Industrialisation of Europe 1760–1970* (Oxford, 1981). On the long tradition of comparative economic history, see Rondo Cameron, 'Comparative Economic History', *Research in Economic History*, Supplement 1 (1977), pp. 287–305.

10 On the theory and practice of comparative transcultural history, see Jürgen Osterhammel, *Geschichtswissenschaft jenseits des Nationalstaats. Studien zu Beziehungsgeschichte und Zivilisationsvergleich* (Göttingen, 2001).

11 On Weber see Helmut Schmidt-Glintzer, 'The Economic Ethic of World Religions', in Hartmut Lehmann and Günther Roth (eds), *Weber's 'Protestant Ethic': Origins, Evidence, Contexts* (Cambridge, 1993), pp. 347–55.

12 Jack Goody, *The Oriental, the Ancient and the Primitive. Systems of Marriage and the Family in Pre-Industrial Societies of Eurasia* (Cambridge, 1990).

13 Charles Tilly, *Big Structures, Large Processes, Huge Comparisons* (New York, 1985), pp. 81–143.

14 Liah Greenfeld, *Nationalism: Five Roads to Modernity* (Cambridge, MA, 1992).

15 Barrington Moore, Social Origins of Dictatorship and Democracy. Lord and Peasant in the Making of the Modern World (Boston, 1966).

16 Hartmut Kaelble, Der historische Vergleich. Eine Einführung zum 19. und 20. Jahrhundert (Frankfurt am Main, 1999), pp. 48–92.

17 I have not got the space here to explicate the complex relationship between facts/science and values/morals. For a recent up-to-date and succinct introduction to these issues, see Chris Lorenz, Konstruktion der Vergangenheit. Eine Einführung in die Geschichtstheorie (Cologne, 1997), esp. pp. 400–14, 422–36; Lorenz, 'The View from Anywhere (or: On Facts, Fiction, Football and an Indian). Some Reflections on the (Im)Possibility of the Writing of History', in Jan Denolf and Barbara Simons (eds),

(Re)Constructing the Past (Brussels, 2000), pp. 411–41; Lorenz, 'Historical Knowledge and Historical Reality: A Plea for "Internal Realism"', History and Theory 33 (1994), pp. 297–327. An English-language translation of Lorenz's seminal book is currently prepared by Princeton University Press.

18 Hartmut Kaelble, 'Social History of European Integration', in Clemens Wurm (ed.), Western Europe and Germany. The Beginnings of European Integration 1945–1960 (Oxford, 1995), pp. 219–47.

19 Werner Sombart, Why is There No Socialism in the United States? (London, 1976; first published in German in 1906); Ross McKibbin, 'Why was There no Marxism in Great Britain?', English Historical Review 99 (1984), pp. 297–331.

20 Emile Durkheim, The Rules of Sociological Method and Selected Texts on Sociology and its Method (London, 1982, [1895]).

21 See Heiko Feldner's contribution to this volume (Chapter 1).

22 Stefan Berger, 'European Labour Movements and the European Working Class in Comparative Perspective', in Berger and David Broughton (eds), The Force of Labour (Oxford, 1995), pp. 245–62.

23 Miroslav Hroch, Social Preconditions of National Revival in Europe: A Comparative Analysis of the Social Composition of Patriotic Groups among the Smaller European Nations (Cambridge, 1985).

24 Friedrich Boll, 'Changing Forms of Labour Conflict: Secular Development or Strike Waves', in H. L. Haimson and Charles Tilly (eds), Strikes, Wars and Revolutions in an International Perspective (Cambridge, 1989).

25 John Breuilly, Labour and Liberalism in 19th-century Europe: Essays in Comparative History (Manchester, 1992), Chapters 6 and 7.

26 Stefan Berger and Neil Evans, 'The Face of King Coal in the Ruhr and South Wales: Different Historiographical Traditions and their Impact on Comparative History', in Stefan Berger, Andy Croll and Norman LaPorte (eds), Towards a Comparative History of Coalfield Societies (London, 2005), pp. 29–42.

27 Stefan Berger, 'Working-Class Culture and the Labour Movement in the South Wales and the Ruhr Coalfields, 1850–2000: A Comparison', Llafur. Journal of Welsh Labour History 8(2) (2001), pp. 5–40, esp. p. 7.

28 This point was first made by Lujo Brentano, 'Die englische Chartistenbewegung', Preußische Jahrbücher 33 (1874), pp. 431–47, 531–50. On Brentano, see also Christiane Eisenberg, 'The Comparative View in Labour History: Old and New Interpretations of the English and German Labour Movements before 1914', International Review of Social History 34 (1989), p. 411f.

29 One example among many is Ira Katznelson and Aristide R. Zolberg (eds), Working-Class Formation: 19th century Patterns in Western Europe and the United States (Princeton, 1986).

30 See Chapter 7. Compare also Andy Croll, 'The Impact of Postmodernism on Modern British Social History', in Stefan Berger (ed.), Labour and Social

History in the United Kingdom: Historiographical Reviews and Agendas 1990 to the Present, special edition of the Mitteilungsblatt des Instituts für soziale Bewegungen 28 (2002), pp. 137–52.

31 Gregory Castle, Postcolonial Discourses. An Anthology (Oxford, 2001).

32 Edward Said, Orientalism (London, 1978).

33 Osterhammel, Geschichtswissenschaft, p. 72.

34 Samuel P. Huntington, The Clash of Civilisations and the Remaking of World Order (New York, 1996).

35 A prime example of such universal history is the work of William H. McNeill. Among his many publications see, for example, Keeping Together in Time. Dance and Drill in Human History (Cambridge, MA, 1996).

36 Edgar Kiser and Michael Hechter, 'The Role of General Theory in Comparative-Historical Sociology', American Journal of Sociology 97 (1991), pp. 1–30.

37 An excellent example of that type of comparison is provided by Dick Geary, 'The Myth of the Radical Miner', in Berger, Croll and LaPorte (eds), Towards.

38 Jörn Leonhard, '"An Odious but Intelligible Phrase ...". "Liberal" im politischen Diskurs Deutschlands und Englands bis 1830/32', Jahrbuch zur Liberalismus-Forschung 8 (1996), pp. 11–41.

39 Ian Hampsher-Monk, Karin Tilmans and Frank van Vree (eds), History of Concepts: Comparative Perspectives (Amsterdam, 1999); Melvin Richter, '"Begriffsgeschichte" and the History of Ideas', Journal of the History of Ideas 48 (1987), pp. 247–63.

40 Michel Espagne and Michael Werner, Transferts. Les Relations interculturelles dans l'espace franco-allemand (Paris, 1988); Bénédicte Zimmermann, Claude Didry and Peter Wagner (eds), Le Travail et la nation: histoire croisée de la France et de l'Allemagne (Paris, 1999).

41 There are many studies on border territories. See, for example, Peter Schöttler, 'Le Rhin comme enjeu historiographique dans l'Entre-Deux-Guerres. Vers une histoire des mentalités frontalières', Genèses 14 (1994) pp. 63–82, and Sharif Gemie, 'France and the Val d'Aran: Politics and Nationhood on the Pyrenean Border, 1800–25', European History Quarterly 28 (1998), pp. 311–43.

42 On processes of cultural transfer between Britain and Germany in historical scholarship, see Peter Wende and Benedikt Stuchtey (eds), British and German Historiography 1750–1950. Traditions, Perceptions and Transfers (Oxford, 2000); Stefan Berger, Peter Lambert and Peter Schumann (eds), Historikerdialoge. Geschichte, Mythos und Gedächtnis im deutsch-britischen kulturellen Austausch 1750–2000 (Göttingen, 2003).

43 A. Mitchell, The Divided Path. The German Influence on Social Reform in France after 1870 (Chapel Hill, 1991); E. P. Hennock, British Social Reform

and German Precedents. The Case of Social Insurance, 1880–1914 (Oxford, 1987); Daniel T. Rodgers, Atlantic Crossings. Social Politics in a Progressive Age (Cambridge, MA, 1998).

44 Heinz-Gerhard Haupt and Jürgen Kocka, 'Historischer Vergleich: Methoden, Aufgaben, Probleme. Eine Einleitung', in Haupt and Kocka (eds), Geschichte und Vergleich, p. 11.

45 Michel Espagne, 'Sur les limites du comparatisme en histoire culturelle', Genèse 17 (1994), pp. 112–21.

46 Johannes Paulmann, 'Internationaler Vergleich und interkultureller Transfer. Zwei Forschungsansätze zur europäischen Geschichte des 18. bis 20. Jahrhunderts', Historische Zeitschrift 267(3) (1998), pp. 649–85; Matthias Middell, 'Kulturtransfer und historische Komparatistik – Thesen zu ihrem Verhältnis', Comparativ 10(1) (2000), pp. 7–41.

47 Marc Bloch, 'Toward a Comparative History of European Societies', in Jelle C. Riemersma and Frederic C. Lane (eds), Enterprise and Secular Change: Readings in Economic History (London, 1953). Bloch's article was originally published in Revue de synthèse historique in 1928. An attempt to integrate cultural transfer and comparative approaches can be found in Fernand Braudel's masterpiece about the Ottoman and Hapsburg empires: The Mediterranean and the Mediterranean World in the Age of Philip II, 2 vols (London, 1972 [1966]).

48 Christoph Conrad, 'Vergleich und Transnationalität in der Geschichte', in Andreas Wirsching (ed.), Oldenbourg Geschichte Lehrbuch Neueste Zeit (2nd ed., Munich, 2008), pp. 317–32.

49 Eric Hobsbawm and Joan W. Scott, 'Political Shoemakers', in: Past and Present 89 (1980), reprinted in Eric Hobsbawm, Worlds of Labour (London, 1984), pp. 103–30.

50 An impressive attempt to synthesize the vast literature on artisans in Europe can be found in James R. Farr, Artisans in Europe 1300–1914 (Cambridge, 2000).

Part Three

11

Political history

Jon Lawrence

It would be an exaggeration to say that there are as many conceptions of 'political history' as there are political historians – but only just. Certainly, historians of politics disagree not just about the usual issues of theory and method, but also, more fundamentally, about what their basic subject matter should be. For some 'true politics' is a rarefied thing – the preserve of policy-makers and administrators at the heart of government, for others it is the stuff of everyday life – the driving force behind both individual and collective aspirations in a mass society. Moreover, within both traditions there are many conflicting notions of how politics should be studied, and how (or indeed whether) the worlds of state policy and mass politics should be combined.

To understand why 'political history' represents such a fractured field of intellectual enquiry we must first examine its development as a subject during the nineteenth and twentieth centuries. For the most part I will tell this story through the prism of British historiography, partly because this is the field I know best, but also because political history has long enjoyed an unusually privileged position within British academe. At the end of the 19th century few historians in any country would have dissented from Sir John Seeley's famous borrowed aphorism that 'history is past politics, and politics present history' (*The Growth of British Policy*, 1895), and most would have assumed that 'politics' here meant statecraft and its impact on the long-term development of constitutional government. Indeed, throughout the 19th century there had been a strong tendency across Europe to understand present politics through an historical framework, and to assume that history followed a linear and progressive course. Famously true of Marx, following as he did in the Hegelian tradition of seeing history as the necessary unfolding of the inner logic that shapes human destiny, this 'teleological' approach (i.e. one assuming a known ultimate purpose) was also characteristic of 19th-century liberal thinking. Profoundly influenced by the legacy of the Scottish Enlightenment and 18th-century Whig constitutionalism, 19th-century liberals placed the evolution, and gradual perfection, of political institutions at the heart of their understanding of history. Nowhere was the influence of this thinking stronger than in Britain, where the Whig tradition of gradual political reform had its roots, and where political history written in the Whig tradition in consequence assumed an especially triumphalist tone. The model for such work was set by Thomas Macaulay's brilliant multi-volume *History of England* (1848–61), and was continued in the work of men such as W. E. H. Lecky and George Otto Trevelyan.

However, the influence of Whig constitutionalism was already in decline before the First World War. Historians had begun to turn their backs on grand narrative in favour of the meticulous archival work long championed in Germany by historians such as Leopold von Ranke, while political scientists passed increasingly harsh judgements about the ability of political systems to deliver rational government as democratic pressures grew. But if liberal optimism was fading in the Edwardian era, it was all but destroyed by the traumas of war and postwar transition between 1914 and the early 1920s. Even in Britain, 'Whig history' had become an object of ridicule long before the publication of Herbert Butterfield's scathing critique of its English, Protestant prejudices in *The Whig Interpretation of History* (1931). By the time Butterfield had pronounced the death of Whig history, a new school of political history was emerging in Britain – a school that focused not on the evolution of political systems, and the grand ideals they were supposed to embody, but rather on how individuals manoeuvred for advantage within more or less stable political systems. The key figure here was Lewis Namier, whose *Structure of Politics at the Accession of George III* (1929) established a new school of political history that ultimately found institutional expression in the official 'History of Parliament' project. Namier's method focused on reconstructing the motivations, not just of the 'great men' of politics, but of all the political actors who made up the system of their day. This exercise in 'collective biography' (often termed 'prosopography') tended to downplay ideology and belief as motivating factors in politics, and to stress instead the pre-eminent influence of psychological, personal and material factors. Strongly influenced by Freudian psychoanalytic thinking, Namier placed the individual at the centre of his historical analysis, and insisted that historians should explore the hidden, unconscious and often dark forces that frequently determined individual action. In this respect the charge that his method called on historians to 'psychoanalyse the dead' was not misplaced, though it was undoubtedly only one element to the intensive, biographical approach he advocated.[1]

11.1 High politics and the history of ideas

The modern 'high political' approach to political history has its roots in this shift from grand constitutional narratives to the micro-level analysis of political conflict within the state. However, the advocates of the 'high politics' approach, such as Maurice Cowling and Michael Bentley, generally insist that historians should focus only on 'the politicians that mattered', as Cowling described them in his 1971 study *The Impact of Labour*. In this work Cowling explained that he would treat 'back-benchers and party opinion' as off-stage 'malignant or beneficent forces ... with unknown natures and unpredictable wills'.[2] Advocates of the 'high political' approach also show a much greater scepticism towards the virtues of biography as a key to understanding political action. Emphasis is placed less on individual psychology than on 'situational necessity' – on the imperatives generated by mutual suspicion and rivalry within the closed world of a small political elite. According to Cowling, after the First World War '[t]he political system consisted of fifty or sixty politicians in conscious tension with one another whose accepted authority constituted political leadership'.[3] In essence, 'high political' historians argue that politics should be understood as a self-contained game, with its own elaborate and well-understood rules. Politicians play to win, and they adopt policy initiatives and rhetorical strategies as gambits to this end – fully aware that their rivals are playing for the same high stakes. In this sense the 'high political' approach represents one of the most thorough applications of social science 'game theory' in the historical field – though this pedigree is no more trumpeted than is the Namierite legacy.

In its most cynical form the 'high politics' approach assumes that politicians play only to win, and that consequently belief and principle play little part in the policy initiatives and rhetorical strategies they adopt. However, this bastardized version of the method is rarely adopted by those most directly influenced by Cowling and his Cambridge associates. Cowling himself tends to take the agnostic line that one can only penetrate so far into a politician's thought world, and that one can therefore never know whether he or she really *believed* what they said; one can merely reconstruct the interconnections between public utterances and actions. But 'high political' historians have always placed a strong emphasis on ideas, and in recent years many have stressed that politicians are motivated first and foremost by belief. For instance, in *British Politics and the Great War* (1992), John Turner argues that supporters of Lloyd George's wartime Coalition were united by the belief that party rivalries must be suspended in the national interest – calculations of party advantage, he insists, were very definitely secondary. Similarly, in *Stanley Baldwin: Conservative Leadership and National Values* (1999), Philip Williamson explores the underlying values and beliefs that shaped both his subject's approach to politics and the ends he sought to pursue when playing the 'party game'. Michael Bentley does something similar for an earlier Conservative leader in *Lord Salisbury's World: Conservative Environments in Late-Victorian Britain* (2001). Both works deliberately eschew the narrative structure adopted in conventional political biographies in favour of a thematic approach that is much better suited to the exploration of a mind in the context of its times.

All these works appear to reflect a loosening of the narrow, self-limiting ordinances that shaped many early works in the 'high political' tradition. For instance, Turner is happy to explore the impact of constituency politics and intricacies of electoral sociology alongside his blow-by-blow account of intrigues within the political elite, while the studies by Williamson and Bentley are indicative of a growing openness to intellectual history among practitioners of the 'high political' approach (though as the author of *The Liberal Mind, 1914–1929* (1977) it must be acknowledged that Bentley has always been interested in the relationship between thought and political action).[4] Such works retain a central emphasis on 'situation' – on reconstructing the context within which elite politicians operated – but they also register developments in other fields of political history writing, notably the history of ideas and the history of popular politics. It is to these two fields that we must now turn.

There can be little doubt that much of the best political history writing of the last few decades has been informed by an interest in the history of ideas and, in consequence, by a determination to make sense of the intellectual context in which political struggles were played out. Many historians approaching politics in this way have been influenced, more or less explicitly, by the approach to intellectual history championed by J. G. A. Pocock, Quentin Skinner and J. W. Burrow (the so-called 'Cambridge School'), with its emphasis on reconstructing the political discourse of an epoch through the systematic analysis of speech acts (i.e. texts and utterances anchored in their discursive and social context). It is an approach which allows the historical focus to shift away from the world and the actions of elite politicians by focusing on the wider debates that shaped their political world, and defined what politics itself was thought to be about at any given moment. Over the past 20 years, the historiography of 19th-century Britain in particular has been greatly enriched by studies of this kind, many of them emanating from the Cambridge History Faculty. For instance, in *The Age of Atonement* (1988) Boyd Hilton traces the influence of Evangelical Christianity on the understanding of social and economic change in early 19th-century Britain, and demonstrates its crucial role in shaping the politics of liberal Tories from Pitt, through Peel, to Gladstone. Similarly, in *The Decline of British Radicalism* (1995) Miles Taylor charts the growing Radical disillusionment with purely Parliamentary conceptions of sovereignty from the later 1850s, and shows how this helped create the political space for a new, constituency-based popular Liberalism in the 1860s. In *Democracy and Religion: Gladstone and the Liberal*

Party (1986) Jon Parry emphasizes the essentially religious dimension of mid-Victorian political discourse, and demonstrates that religious differences within the Liberal party, both at Westminster and in the country, raised fundamental questions about the meaning of 'Liberalism', as well as culminating in the electoral debacle of 1874. Finally, in *Liberty, Retrenchment and Reform* (1992) and *British Democracy and Irish Nationalism, 1876-1906* (2007), Eugenio Biagini reconstructs the ideas and aspirations that bound plebeian radicals to the Gladstonian Liberal Party, and that ultimately saw Liberalism forge a new politics of altruism based on internationalism and humanitarianism. Each is offering much more than a study in the history of ideas – these are studies acutely aware of the need to understand ideas within their social and political context, especially the shifting context of practical political conflict – but their sophisticated reconstruction of the ideas that informed political practice and defined what was, and was not, 'politics', remains a particular virtue. In effect they are broadening the method of the 'high political' tradition, reconstructing the world of public politics as a whole in order better to understand the forces that help to define the 'situational necessities' confronting 'the politicians who really mattered'.

11.2 Elections and popular politics

We must turn next to forms of political history that place greater emphasis on electoral politics and popular political culture. Again, such histories take many forms and are therefore difficult to categorize. In this analysis I propose to examine two main traditions – the constituency politics tradition and the 'history from below' or social history tradition – mindful that the borderlands between them are not always as clear cut as this typology might suggest. The constituency politics tradition has always been strongly influenced by political science methods, especially between the 1950s and 1970s, when 'electoral sociology' – the sociological analysis of election data – was at the height of its influence among political historians.

During this period modern British political history was largely rewritten through the frame of postwar pluralist/functionalist sociology and political science, with its emphasis on political parties and representative institutions as agencies for channelling and neutralizing social conflict.[5] Histories written under the influence of electoral sociology sought to analyse how political parties responded to the underlying processes of social change and class formation in the nineteenth and early twentieth centuries. For the most part they played down the impact of parties on these processes of change, and assumed that the key to understanding the course of political history lay in politicians' greater or lesser success in *adapting* to the social forces changing their world. Thus Hanham analysed how Liberal and Conservative politicians competed to mould the allegiance of the new urban voters created by the 1867 Reform Act (*Elections and Party Management*, 1959), James Cornford analysed how late 19th-century forces of suburbanization created the social basis for 'villa toryism' ('Transformation of Conservatism', *Victorian Studies*, 1963), while Peter Clarke analysed how Liberals responded to this challenge by constructing a new, non-socialist programme of state 'welfare' that could appeal to working-class electors (*Lancashire and the New Liberalism*, 1971, discussed below). Today the linearity of these arguments – with their emphasis on supposedly inexorable forces of 'modernization' such as the rise of class, the decline of religion and the supposed 'nationalization' of politics – has lost favour, partly thanks to changing intellectual fashions, but also because we now see the political realities of the post-Second World War era as a unique historical moment, rather than as the natural end point of modern, democratic political development. It now seems curious than John Vincent should feel the need to detract from his brilliant analysis of the ideas and aspirations that sustained mid-Victorian popular Liberalism by presenting this as a pre-industrial form of 'class struggle' (according to Vincent, vertically integrated 'operational collectivities' fought over the structure of political and religious authority, but not over the distribution of things – supposedly the hallmark of 'modern', class-based politics).[6]

Since the mid-1970s studies of constituency politics have relied less heavily on the reductionist assumptions of the electoral sociology tradition, but they have continued to insist that historians place the relationship between politicians and the electorate centre stage, and that they pay attention to the local contexts within which national political struggles were so often waged. Champions of this approach such as Stuart Ball and Duncan Tanner are more interested in reconstructing the voices 'off-stage' than conventional 'high political' historians, and they assume that these voices played an important part in determining both the electoral fortune of parties and the freedom of manoeuvre available to elite politicians. Indeed Stuart Ball, whose own *Baldwin and the Conservative Party* (1988) has a strong Westminster focus, explicitly argues that the 'high political' approach is poorly suited to the analysis of 20th-century politics because it exaggerates the extent to which politicians could remain insulated from outside pressures in an age of mass media and mass politics. Ball argues that by the late 1920s politicians were becoming increasingly sceptical of the press as a guide to public opinion, and consequently placed renewed emphasis on political meetings, and especially on internal party mechanisms for judging the mood both of the voters and of the party workers who remained so vital to electoral success.[7] Tanner also stresses the need to recognize 'the *interactive* nature of politics', and argues that combining the techniques of social and political history at constituency level helps us to understand the limited explanatory value of national studies that 'fail to identify the importance of a spatial or contextual perspective to electoral and political change'.[8]

Most historians working within the 'constituency politics' tradition have shown a special interest in questions about party activism and electioneering. Indeed, they have pioneered research into the franchise, electoral law, party organization and campaigning, in order better to understand the context within which politicians sought to court popular support. Perhaps sometimes more could be done here to interrogate the gap between politicians' roles as legislators at Westminster and as candidates in the constituencies, but even when it has focused narrowly on the mechanics of electoral practice, such work has made an invaluable contribution to our understanding of political history. Conversely, the main weakness of the tradition has been its tendency to focus too narrowly on organizational history – so that 'constituency politics' comes to mean the history of constituency parties when it should really be about the relationship between those parties and the wider electorate. Instead, this wider electorate has tended to be studied largely from the perspective of party activists, sometimes reinforced by the insights that can be gleaned from aggregate election data – but that, of course, simply brings us back to the problematic reductionism of electoral sociology.

Since the burgeoning of social history as a discipline in the 1960s, the study of elections and local politics has also been championed by historians whose primary interest is precisely the underlying attitudes and allegiances of voters themselves, rather than the fate of political candidates and their parties. Believing even more than the champions of electoral sociology in the *social bases of politics*, historians who have taken 'popular politics' as their core concern have tended to see politics as a prism through which to analyse social structure and (especially since the 'linguistic turn') popular culture. Consequently studies of 'popular politics' tend to foreground the analysis of social cleavages around class, gender and ethnicity, rather than conventional questions about party organization and techniques of voter mobilization. As part of the 'history from below' movement that flourished during the 1960s and 1970s, this approach (like so much history of the era) often turned its back on questions of policy formation, and even on the impact of state policies within localities. In many respects, as Miles Taylor has pointed out, this reflected the fact that, whilst E. P. Thompson's clarion call 'to rescue the poor stockinger … from the enormous condescension of posterity' may have inspired the move to write political history 'from below', non-Marxist influences which played down questions of ideology and governance exercised a more formative influence on the new social history, and tended to dilute the political imperatives of Thompson's project.[9]

As we shall see, the energies of the 'history from below' movement have mostly been directed into cultural history since the 1980s under the influence of the so-called 'linguistic' or 'cultural' turn, but some political historians have continued to work in a more resolutely social history tradition. In particular, Trevor Griffiths and Marc Brodie explicitly see themselves as offering an empirically rooted corrective to the 'constructivist' fallacies of the linguistic turn. In place of the bold, macro-level generalizations about social class associated with electoral sociology, Griffiths and Brodie advocate an approach that focuses on reconstructing micro-level social and cultural contexts. According to Brodie the aim is to focus on how 'ideas were filtered by localized social and economic structures and processes of communication and popular culture', while Griffiths talks of the need to reframe the debate about political language to recognize how it was 'formulated and interpreted in the light of the structural and ideological forces shaping working-class life'.[10] However, in practice neither spends much time discussing either the ideas that are supposedly being 'filtered', or the activities of the political organizations seeking to promote those ideas at the local level. The distinction between popular culture and party politics (between what some have called 'informal' and 'formal' politics) is lost. The result is that, as with 'electoral sociology,' we are left with a model where popular politics appears somehow to arise naturally from social life. In consequence, whilst we learn a great deal about the structure of working-class life, it is arguable that we learn much less about how mostly 'outsider' politicians sought to mobilize support from those who lived that life.

Case study: Peter Clarke and Ewen Green

Though now almost 40 years old, Peter Clarke's *Lancashire and the New Liberalism* (Cambridge, 1971, revised 1993) still merits close attention as a brilliant synthesis of all the approaches so far discussed. The worlds of political ideas, elite strategies and popular politics are not just present; they are systematically combined throughout the book. Thus we see how new ideas about Liberalism as a movement for social reform coalesced during the 1890s, and how they won adherents among prominent politicians after the Boer War. We see how the growing band of professional politicians made it easier for champions of the new ideology to gain a foothold in constituencies, and how new techniques of communication (posters, mass leafleting, etc.) made it easier for them to proselytize the new politics. In outlining these arguments Clarke offers subtle readings of street politics and the role of the candidate in Edwardian electoral politics which remain unsurpassed. Of course there are problems – the decline of localism is overdrawn, as is the class appeal of New Liberal social legislation, but there remains something compelling about Clarke's argument that politicians played an active part in the shift to a more materialist, class-centred politics in Britain. For this, it should be stressed, is no crudely reductionist analysis – Clarke's new Liberal politicians are not simply passive beneficiaries of class polarization in Edwardian Britain; they are the architects of a political strategy intended to undermine popular Toryism in the towns, and thereby counteract the Liberal Party's damaging loss of support in suburbia. Thus Clarke argues that when old-style politics were 'overthrown in the early 20th century, it was not because of a change in the economic infrastructure. It was a political initiative which precipitated the decisive class polarisation of the electorate.'[11] In his later work Clarke has tended to focus more exclusively on the battle for political ideas, with major studies of Edwardian progressivism (*Liberals and Social Democrats*, 1978), and the genesis of Keynesianism (*The Keynesian Revolution in the Making*, 1988), but he has continued to encourage a broad approach to the study of political history. This can be seen most clearly in *Hope and Glory* (1996, revised 2004), his Penguin history of 20th-century Britain, and in the work of former research students such as Duncan Tanner and Ewen Green, both of whom have consistently sought to integrate the study of ideas, intrigue and popular politics. Tanner's *Political Change and the Labour Party* (1990) challenged ideas about the inevitable rise of Labour through a systematic investigation of the ideological coherence and organizational strength of the party both nationally and region by region. Green also built directly on Clarke's studies of Edwardian Britain by examining Conservative attempts to counter the twin challenges of rapid social change and a revitalized 'New' Liberalism. In *The Crisis of Conservatism: The Politics, Economics and Ideology of the British Conservative Party, 1880–1914* (1995), Green argued that Conservatism faced a potentially terminal crisis in the late Victorian and Edwardian period as it sought to develop a coherent response to rapid social, economic and political change. As its title suggests, Green's book is encyclopaedic in its coverage, and as such represents one of the most sustained attempts so far to integrate the history of ideas with the history of practical party politics at Westminster and in the country. Green demonstrated that, beneath the distractions of Empire and Ireland, the Conservatives' electoral dominance between 1885 and 1905 had been built on sand. Intended as a balm for internal frictions and as an answer to the threat of national decline, the 'Tariff Reform' movement that flourished after 1903 merely opened up new fault lines in the party, whilst simultaneously breathing new life into Liberalism (a story subsequently elaborated by Frank Trentmann in *Free Trade Nation: Consumption, Commerce and Civil Society in Modern Britain* (2008), itself another important example of the trend to take the history of ideas deeper into the world of the everyday). Arguably, Green and Trentmann underestimate both the vitality of Tariff Reform as a popular mass movement in the constituencies, and the likelihood that the Conservatives would have won any 1915 election, but their work is nonetheless pioneering.[12] Green went on to publish two further major studies of 20th-century Conservatism – *Ideologies of Conservatism* (2002) and *Thatcher* (2006) – before his death at the tragically young age of 47. Besides decisively refuting the argument that British Conservatism had been somehow inherently unideological before Thatcher,

Green's work offers original insights into how ideas come to be embedded in the fabric of mass parties and mass societies – a process too often taken for granted by more purist historians of ideas. Like Clarke and Tanner, Green was interested in identifying and understanding ideas with 'purchase'. This could mark him off from more self-consciously postmodern historians concerned with deconstructing public political 'discourse,' but, as will be argued later, this emphasis on questions of *reception* is exactly what histories of discourse too often lack.[13] Green's loss is a profound one for political history, as well as for all who knew him.

11.3 New political histories

From the early 1980s social history was facing a new, *post*-Marxist challenge, which struck less at its neglect of the state and politics than at the reductionist assumptions underpinning its whole conception of 'the social'. Explanations positing simple, unmediated links between social class and political allegiance were the special target of this anti-reductionist critique, which perhaps explains why so many advocates of the 'new political history' thought that they were attacking Marxist heresies, when in truth there was precious little Marxist political history to attack, and even less that was unambiguously reductionist given the strong influence of E. P. Thompson on would-be Marxist social historians, especially in Britain. In many a footnote, my own included, John Foster, Eric Hobsbawm and sometimes the Gramscian-influenced Robert Gray or the Althusserian Gareth Stedman Jones, had to stand in for the imagined army of orthodox Marxist political historians. This critique of reductionism formed part of a broader 'shift to culture' or 'linguistic turn' in social history and hence in the history of popular politics. The origins of this growing emphasis on 'culture' lay in an engagement with cultural anthropology (especially through the work of Clifford Geertz), and with postmodern modes of thought more generally (notably through the work of Michel Foucault and Jacques Derrida[14]), though most political historians probably encountered these influences indirectly, via Gareth Stedman Jones's ground-breaking linguistic analysis of the dynamics of Chartist radicalism and revisionist critiques of the social bases of the French Revolution.[15] At its best such work has encouraged a more nuanced study of popular political culture, broadly defined – i.e. the diverse political ideas and customs within society as a whole, rather than just within the closed world of professional politics. Since the reconstruction of meaning is the defining feature of this school, it has already greatly expanded our understanding of political culture – especially our understanding of what politics meant to contemporaries. In the British case the postmodernist emphasis on 'culture' has generated pioneering studies exploring the centrality of ideas about empire, race and gender to contemporary understandings of citizenship and the political nation.[16]

Whereas political historians interested primarily in ideas focus on reconstructing the intellectual context that defined the terrain and the terms of politics, so those influenced by the 'new political history' tend to focus on reconstructing the broader cultural context (sometimes deterministically suggesting that ideas are merely an artefact of 'culture').[17] But it is not necessary to discount the importance of ideas in politics to believe that cultural norms and expectations may also have played a vital role in influencing both the form and the content of political practice. It is probably in the field of gender studies that the value of this approach has been most clearly demonstrated. Feminist historians' interest in exploring shifting ideas about 'public' and 'private' spheres encouraged important work on the processes of inclusion and exclusion involved in debates about the boundaries of 'citizenship'.[18] It also encouraged political historians to think more deeply about the gendered nature of political appeals under the exclusive 'male polity' that survived until 1918, and how the parties sought to adapt their politics to the altered circumstances of the new mixed-sex polity.[19] More recently, attention has shifted to exploring the gendered roles of politicians themselves; how ideas about 'manly' behaviour may have shaped not just politicians' public personas, but also how they operated within the world of 'high politics'. Here the work of Matthew McCormack and Martin Francis has probably been most ground-breaking. Francis, in particular, has focused on mid-20th-century high politics to 'recover the broader cultural hinterland that lay behind, but also informed and gave meaning to, the discourses of formal politics'. He explores the dilemmas politicians faced seeking to conform to expectations about manly 'control' and 'restraint' against the backdrop of rapid social and cultural change, and the countervailing pressure to appear 'authentic' under the scrutiny of an increasingly intrusive mass media.[20]

In many respects the 'new political history' strongly complements the high political tradition, or at least high political analysis that eschews cynical instrumentalist explanations, since both place a strong premium on the reconstruction of political culture and on the importance of taking political rhetoric and political ideas seriously, rather than treating them merely as codes for more fundamental class or personal interests.[21] However, this is not a point widely acknowledged by practising historians in either tradition, perhaps because each is more anxious to assert the primacy of the political world they find it congenial to study. Historians of 'popular politics' – including the new generation of postmodernists – like to mock 'high political' historians for their obsession with the closed, claustrophobic world of elite politics.[22] They argue that just because Lord Salisbury, or whoever, failed to understand 'villa Toryism', let alone working-class Toryism, we are not absolved from trying to understand why 'villa' or working-class Tories thought that they understood and could trust Lord Salisbury (I know, I've done this myself).[23] Similarly, historians of 'high politics' like to mock popular politics for its naive assumption that the beliefs and aspirations of political nobodies in Blackburn, Wolverhampton, or wherever, should be taken as seriously as the beliefs and aspirations of the political giants who controlled the destiny of a nation and its empire. The result is a fundamental bifurcation of political history into two almost wholly separate sub-disciplines – the one focusing on policy formation and elite intrigue within the state, the other on popular politics as a convenient window through which to study popular culture and the politics of everyday life. The big question, of course, is whether these approaches must *necessarily* be seen as discrete and antagonistic. Are the worlds of 'popular politics' and 'high politics' really separate worlds requiring ring-fenced academic endeavours, or is the distinction between them simply one of personal temperament rather than historical substance? In other words, can political history be reconceptualized so that it embraces questions both about popular mobilization *and* policy formation, popular beliefs *and* elite beliefs?

But before we explore the prospects for developing a reintegrated approach to political history we should perhaps confront the thorny question: What are we trying to do as political historians? Or, to be more precise, what, if anything, are we trying to explain? I say 'if anything' because it must be acknowledged that there has been a dramatic scaling down of the explanatory ambition of political history in recent years, and a headlong flight from ideas of 'causation'. Moreover, this is not simply true of the 'new political history', where indebtedness to postmodernism has led both to an understandable scepticism about the totalizing ambitions of the expert, and to a less helpful scepticism about the ultimate 'knowability' of the past. It is equally true of much 'high political' history written in recent years. Thus in his study of Salisbury's thought-world, Michael Bentley rejects the idea of political change 'as a process whose structural features can be identified and explained', and tells us that he will 'follow his [Salisbury's] mental processes rather than give them a coherence that eluded him'.[24] As with much recent postmodern political history, the result is a fascinating, almost anthropological reconstruction of a political culture, but one that is defiantly indifferent to any broader claims to historical explanation. In this sense both 'new political' and 'high political' history can be indicted for many of the same failings as the old, non-Marxist social history of the 1960s and 1970s. Not, of course, an indifference to politics *per se*, but rather a reluctance to focus directly on questions of policy formation and the structure of state power. Here exponents of 'high political' history come out better, since their focus is at least the seat of power, even if they are generally uninterested in broader questions about the long-term development of state power or the consequences of its deployment. By contrast, those reconstructing the rituals and languages of popular political culture need to demonstrate both the connections between popular culture and organized, formal politics, and the relationship between popular perceptions of authority and the actual mechanisms for wielding authority in any given society.[25]

11.4 Reintegrating political history?

I want to end this chapter by examining how we might transcend the divisions, not just between historians of 'high' and 'popular' politics, but also between advocates of the linguistic turn, and those who insist on the continued relevance of understanding the social context of political practice. I will suggest that any such 'integrated' political history should display four essential characteristics: first, an analytical interest in the reception as well as the construction of political discourse, and hence in the social as well as the cultural dimension of politics; second, an ambition to develop plausible explanations of change over time, rather than simply offering frozen snapshots of the system at any given point; third, an acute awareness of the interconnectedness of politics as a competitive, conflict-driven system where individuals, groups and parties can never be adequately understood if studied in isolation; and fourth, an appreciation of the ability of state policy to shape both the form and the content of popular politics.

Let us turn first to the claim that we should retain a strong interest in the material context of politics. This is most obviously important for those focusing on popular politics since here the potential for individual and group mobilization is likely to be directly related to the distribution of social, economic and cultural capital – that is to say, to issues such as hours of work (and thus of free time), levels of residential stability, the relationship between wages and subsistence, ethnic homogeneity, literacy levels, etc. Such factors will not magically explain the nature of popular politics, that was the old reductionist illusion, but they will tell us a great deal about the scope for popular political mobilization, and also about the everyday lives of the people that politicians sought to address through discourse. The freedom to weave new discourses about the social world, to conceptualize political identity and interest in new ways, may be considerable, but it is not infinite, and material 'reality' is one of the factors circumscribing plausible languages for describing the social world in politics.[26]

But if professional politicians must be mindful of material realities as they polish their rhetorical flourishes, in other respects they are likely to be much less constrained by material circumstances than those they seek to represent. Almost by definition most possess the social, economic and cultural capital necessary to sustain political activism, though perhaps only a few could genuinely be said to have amassed such capital without accruing obligations likely to compromise their freedom of political action. This was, after all, one of the great forces legitimating aristocratic rule in 19th-century Britain – Lord Salisbury and his ilk might be denounced by opponents as 'idle parasites', but they were their *own* idle parasites – they, at least, could plausibly be said to be in no one else's pocket. But of course even the greatest landed aristocrats experienced constraints on their freedom of action; perhaps not the crude constraints of material interest beloved of rational choice theorists (except where the interests of land itself were at stake), but certainly subtler constraints such as the preservation of social and cultural capital amongst their peers.

A second key point is that political history must adopt a diachronic as well as synchronic frame – that is to say it must be concerned with charting and *explaining* change over time, as well as with describing the intricacies of politics at any given moment. We must not lose sight of the need to offer a 'thick description' of political culture – elite and popular alike – but we should ask, not only what were the ideas and assumptions that informed political behaviour at any given moment, but also how did those ideas and assumptions become the orthodoxies of their day, and why did they ultimately lose their power to explain the social world. Of necessity this means that we should focus particular analytical attention on those moments when politics were most in flux – for instance on 1830–46, 1914–31, 1940–51 and 1973–83 in the case of modern Britain, though not to the exclusion of broader studies that can encompass both continuity and change over the *longue durée*.[27]

Thirdly, and perhaps most importantly, we need to take seriously the injunction to focus critical attention upon the interrelationships between the worlds of 'elite' and 'popular' politics, as well as between the strategies and arguments of rival parties. One starting point for such a reintegrated political history would be to foreground specific *sites* where the two worlds are routinely brought together. The political meeting is an obvious example, and one I have studied at length myself, but there are many others, including individual lobbying of MPs, collective petitioning of Parliament, the MP's surgery, constituency correspondence, the internal party gatherings where activists and leaders are brought together, and the myriad forms of indirect, 'mediated' communication through which politicians speak to the people. At the same time we should also focus attention on politicians' contrasting actions and arguments within different political sites – exploring tensions between their private writings and public utterances, but also between their actions in Parliament and in the constituencies.

As James Vernon has argued, in some respects politics became less participatory as they became more democratic. Many of the symbolic rituals of political inclusion associated with eighteenth- and early 19th-century elections, most notably the hustings, were abolished in the name of 'rational reform', although this process was undoubtedly a slow and uneven one (*Politics and the People*, 1993). Even in the early 20th century there were still instances of victorious politicians being 'chaired' through their constituencies by joyous supporters, and it was only with the rise of television in the late 20th century that politicians finally felt able to save themselves from the indignity of facing genuine public meetings during elections (as opposed to showpiece gatherings of the party faithful). Moreover, if in some respects politics became less participatory with democratization, there is little doubt that politicians felt an increasing need to speak to (and for) the people with each successive extension of the franchise, and each advance in the means of communication. The need to shape popular opinion, and to mobilize it for partisan purposes, had become a central factor in political life by the 1870s. Most of the time this could be done at arm's length (much the most congenial method for most politicians): newspapers carried lengthy reports of Parliamentary debates and set-piece platform speeches, while the messy business of street politics could mostly be delegated to constituency party workers and professional party speakers, who toured the country embroiling themselves in the unseemly controversies that most politicians sought to avoid. But at election times, and at other times of great political excitement, the public demanded – and generally got – much more direct contact with their political 'masters'.[28] Moreover, there is considerable evidence that, down to the 1930s at least, politicians continued to tolerate the forced indignities of elections as a test of temperament and character. In 1937 Churchill wrote that

> [n]o part of the education of a politician is more indispensable than the fighting of elections ... Dignity may suffer, the superfine gloss is soon worn away; ... much has to be accepted with a shrug, a sigh or a smile; but any rate of in the end one knows a good deal about what happens and why.

These comments were prompted by recollections of Lord Rosebery's failed attempt to present himself as a man of the people at the turn of the century. According to Churchill, '[h]e would not go through the laborious, vexatious and at times humiliating processes necessary under modern conditions ... He would not stoop; he did not conquer.'[29]

The study of political language should also be about connections. We have gained much from subjecting the language of politics to more systematic analysis, but too often our focus has been only on the construction of discourse, not on its reception – so that the effectiveness of a particular strategy is more often inferred than demonstrated. We certainly need to pay careful attention to how politicians sought to communicate ideas and policies to general public, and also how they sought to counter the efforts of their opponents (even on the platform political argument is always dialogic). But we also need to evaluate the relative 'purchase' of different political discourses, and it is here that the contextually sensitive micro-histories advocated by historians such as Tanner, Griffiths and Brodie come into their own. Only within specific social, economic and cultural contexts can we hope to assess what Peter Mandler has called the 'weight' or 'throw' of different discourses (in this case, different political appeals).[30] Although we also need to recognize, first, that this will always be an inexact science, and second, that it is made even more uncertain by the expansion of national communication media such as radio, cinema and television during the 20th century.

Finally, in taking the 'linguistic turn' in our pursuit of a fuller understanding of the complex relationship between politicians and people, we must not forget that actions often speak louder than words. Political rhetoric may play its part in shaping political identities, but so too can state legislation. Sometimes this is done explicitly, as with the discretionary power to waive school fees under the 1870 Education Act, which codified the distinction between paupers in receipt of Poor Law assistance and a broader population who were nonetheless still recognized as living in 'poverty'. One might also point to the rent control legislation of 1915, which was designated as applying only to 'working-class' housing (although this was defined in monetary terms, not by tenants' occupation), and which created not only a new political interest group, but also a new, more stable pattern of working-class life, since after the war only uninterrupted tenancies continued to enjoy controlled status (and hence below market rents). But even when legislation does not play an active part in defining a new social or political constituency, it frequently transforms the terrain of politics, creating new issues around which politicians can seek to mobilize support. Thus ad hoc legislative responses to the challenge of war between 1914 and 1920, including not only rent control, but also more extensive unemployment benefits (the dole), created material gains for many workers that Labour politicians subsequently felt obliged to defend, even though they bore little resemblance to the party's historic vision of social reform, which had stressed higher wages as the key to workers' 'welfare'.

In short, in our rush to explore the subtle powers of language to constitute meaning and identity, we must not lose sight of that cry from the 1980s to 'bring the state back in'.[31] State power matters, not just as an end in itself (as the spoils of the party game), but as a force for transforming social structures and for redefining perceptions of social identity. In Britain 'revolutions from above' have generally been much more subtle than in, say, Stalinist Russia, but changing practices of taxation and expenditure, and changing official definitions of citizenship and entitlement have done much to shape political expectations and aspirations. Despite the rhetoric of disinterested governance, politicians have frequently sought to wield state power in accordance with their vision of the 'good' society and polity – bolstering or curtailing the state church, extending or reducing entitlements to state benefits, increasing or reducing the burden of taxation on different groups. For sure, their freedom of action has usually been constrained by concerns to preserve 'legitimacy' – rhetoric about 'fairness' and 'disinterestedness' set real constraints on politicians' freedom of action – but the mysteries of state power could still provide significant insulation from popular pressure. While high political histories often exaggerate this isolation from external pressures, pretending that the world of elite politics is all but hermetically sealed from demotic influences, histories of popular politics too often make the opposite mistake – assuming that state power is of no matter, and that the discursive and legislative strategies of 'elite' politicians played little part in shaping plebeian political traditions. Needless to say, both perspectives are inimical to the more integrated approach to political history advocated here.

Guide to further reading

Michael Bentley, 'Party, Doctrine and Thought' in Bentley, *High and Low Politics in Modern Britain: Ten Studies* (Oxford, 1983),,pp. 123–53.

Peter Clarke, 'Electoral Sociology of Modern Britain', *History 57* (1972), pp. 31–55.

Maurice Cowling, *The Impact of Labour: The Beginning of Modern British Politics* (Cambridge, 1971).

Ronald P. Formisano, 'The Concept of Political Culture', *Journal of Interdisciplinary History* 31(3) (2001), pp. 393–426.

Catherine Hall, Keith McClelland and Jane Rendall, *Defining the Victorian Nation: Class, Race and Gender and the Reform Act of 1867* (Cambridge, 2000).

Gareth Stedman Jones, *Languages of Class: Studies in English Working-Class History* (Cambridge, 1983).

Jon Lawrence, *Electing Our Masters: The Hustings in British Politics from Hogarth to Blair* (Oxford, 2009).

Jon Lawrence and Miles Taylor (eds), *Party, State and Society: Electoral Behaviour in Britain Since 1820* (Aldershot, 1997).

Susan Pedersen, 'What is Political History Now?', in David Cannadine (ed.), *What is History Now?* (Basingstoke, 2002), pp. 36–56.

Philip Williamson, *Stanley Baldwin: Conservative Leadership and National Values* (Cambridge, 1999).

Notes

1 See Linda Colley, *Lewis Namier* (London, 1989), esp. pp. 24–31.
2 Maurice Cowling, *The Impact of Labour: the Beginning of Modern British Politics* (Cambridge, 1971), p. 3.
3 Ibid., pp. 3–4.
4 Michael Bentley, 'Party, Doctrine and Thought', in Bentley, *High and Low Politics in Modern Britain: Ten Studies* (Oxford, 1983), pp. 123–53; Maurice Cowling, *Religion and Public Doctrine in Modern England*, 3 vols (Cambridge, 1980–2001).

5 Jon Lawrence and Miles Taylor (eds), *Party, State and Society: Electoral Behaviour in Britain Since 1820* (Aldershot, 1997), pp. 1–27.
6 John Vincent, *Pollbooks: How Victorians Voted* (Cambridge, 1967), pp. 24–8, 31.
7 Stuart Ball, *Baldwin and the Conservative Party: The Crisis of 1929–1931* (New Haven, 1988), pp. xiv–xv.
8 Duncan Tanner, *Political Change and the Labour Party, 1900–1918* (Cambridge, 1990), esp. pp. 12–15.
9 E. P. Thompson, *The Making of the English Working Class* (1963: London, 1980), p. 12; Miles Taylor, 'The Beginnings of Modern British Social History', *History Workshop Journal* 43 (1997), pp. 155–76.
10 Marc Brodie, *The Politics of the Poor: The East End of London, 1885–1914* (Oxford, 2004), p. 12; Trevor Griffiths, *The Lancashire Working Classes, c. 1880–1930* (Oxford, 2001), p. 4.
11 Peter Clarke, *Lancashire and the New Liberalism* (Cambridge, 1971,revised 1993), p. 402.
12 David Thackeray, 'The Crisis of the Tariff Reform League and the Division of "Radical Conservatism", c. 1913–1922,' *History* 91 (2006), pp. 45–61, and Thackeray, 'Radical Right Activism and the Transformation of the Conservative Party, c. 1910–24' (University of Cambridge PhD, forthcoming).
13 E.H.H. Green and D.M. Tanner, *The Strange Survival of Liberal England: Political Leaders, Moral Values and the Reception of Economic Debate* (Cambridge, 2007), introduction.
14 See Kevin Passmore's chapter in this volume (Chapter 7).
15 Gareth Stedman Jones, 'Rethinking Chartism' in Stedman Jones, *Languages of Class: Studies in English Working-class History* (Cambridge, 1983); Lynn Hunt, *Politics, Culture and Class in the French Revolution* (Berkeley, 1984).
16 For instance, Kathleen Wilson, *The Sense of the People: Politics, Culture and Imperialism in England, 1715–1785* (Cambridge, 1995); Catherine Hall, Keith McClelland and Jane Rendall, *Defining the Victorian Nation: Class, Race and Gender and the Reform Act of 1867* (Cambridge, 2000); Catherine Hall, *Civilising Subjects: Metropole and Colony in the English Imagination, 1830–1867* (Cambridge, 2002); James Vernon, *Politics and the People: A Study in English Political Culture, c. 1815–1867* (Cambridge, 1993). See also the special issue of *Journal of British Studies*, 41 (3) (July 2002), 'New Directions in Political History'.
17 Gareth Stedman Jones, 'The Determinist Fix: Some Obstacles to the Further Development of the Linguistic Approach to History in the 1990s' *History Workshop Journal*, 42 (1996), pp. 19–35.
18 See Laura Lee Downs' chapter in this volume (Chapter 15).
19 Jon Lawrence, 'Class and Gender in the Making of Urban Toryism, 1880-1914,' *English Historical Review*, 108 (1993), pp.629-52; David Jarvis,

'Mrs Maggs and Betty: the Conservative Appeal to Women Voters in the 1920s,' *20th Century British History*, 5 (1994), pp. 129–52.

20 Martin Francis, 'Tears, Tantrums and Bared Teeth: the Emotional Economy of Three Conservative Prime Ministers, 1951–1963,' *Journal of British Studies*, 41 (2002), pp.354–87, at 256; also Francis, 'The Labour Party: Modernisation and the Politics of Restraint' in Becky Conekin, Frank Mort and Chris Waters (eds), *Moments of Modernity: Reconstructing Britain, 1945–1964* (London, 1999), and Matthew MacCormack, *The Independent Man: Citizenship and Gender Politics in Georgian England*, (Manchester, 2005).

21 See Susan Pedersen, 'What is Political History Now?', in David Cannadine (ed.), *What is History Now?* (Basingstoke, 2002), pp. 36–56.

22 Vernon, *Politics and the People*, p.8, and his 'Who's Afraid of the "Linguistic Turn"? The Politics of Social History and its Discontents,' *Social History*, 19 (1994), pp. 81–97, at 86–8.

23 Lawrence, 'Class and Gender'; Jon Lawrence and Jane Elliott, 'Parliamentary Election Results Reconsidered: an Analysis of Borough Elections, 1885–1910', *Parliamentary History* 16, 1 (1997), pp.18–29.

24 Michael Bentley, *Lord Salisbury's World: Conservative Environments in Late-Victorian Britain* (Cambridge, 2001), p. 3.

25 For a helpful discussion of these issues see Ronald P. Formisano, 'The Concept of Political Culture', *Journal of Interdisciplinary History* 31, 3 (2001), 393–426.

26 Jon Lawrence, *Speaking for the People: Party, Language and Popular Politics in England, 1867–1914*, (Cambridge, 1998), especially ch. 3.

27 For an example, see Ross McKibbin, 'Classes and Cultures: a Postscript,' *Mitteilungsblatt des Instituts für Soziale Bewegungen*, 27 (2002), 153–66.

28 Jon Lawrence, *Electing Our Masters: the Hustings in British Politics from Hogarth to Blair* (Oxford, 2009).

29 Winston S. Churchill, *Great Contemporaries* (London, 1937), pp.17–19.

30 Peter Mandler, 'The Problem with Cultural History,' *Cultural and Social History* 1 (2004), pp. 94–117, at 96–7.

31 Peter B. Evans, Dietrich Rueschemeyer and Theda Skocpol (eds), *Bringing the State Back In* (Cambridge, 1985).

12

Social history

Thomas Welskopp

For Eric Hobsbawm, 1971 was 'a good moment to be a social historian'. In a triumphant assessment of achievement and in anticipation of things to come, he predicted synthesis of a centrifugal field. In a decade, social history had immensely broadened historians' views of the past. Yet close inspection revealed a fragmented picture. Writing from an unorthodox Marxist perspective, Hobsbawm called for a move from 'social history to the history of society'. This entailed a socio-economic interpretation of societies as structured entities, which would bring together the history of the 'many' with that of the powerful, and provide a more profound understanding of politics, which would be rooted in the material life of the people.[1] This anti-idealistic and anti-individualistic view of politics nevertheless retained the political sphere as the proper site of synthesis. Furthermore, Hobsbawm revived a notion of history as a coherent and continuous process with an inherent meaning that could be traced back to Leopold von Ranke's historism.

Hobsbawm carefully avoided the determinist inclinations of orthodox Marxism. Yet he deemed 'history of society' capable of grasping the totality of a society's past in a coherent narrative intended to describe and explain change over time, and he hoped to produce a 'metanarrative' fusing recognizably Marxian contours with the richness and contingencies of historical experiences. He expected this new metanarrative to challenge – and ultimately displace – the conventional political history of 'great men' privileged by historism and conventional political history.

Eight years later, social history had profoundly reshaped the landscape of the historical profession in the West. Yet in his stocktaking essay of 1979, Tony Judt cunningly opened with the remark that '[t]his [was] a bad time to be a social historian'. He called social history a pretentious 'clown in regal purple'. It was allegedly near to losing 'touch with the study of the past' altogether, had severed its links with chronology, and had ignored the historical importance of ideas.

Despite claims to the contrary, it lacked proper 'theory' – which for Judt meant that it lacked a Marxist perspective. Instead, social history had collapsed theory into method, and method into statistical techniques. Its borrowings from sociology and the political sciences had resulted in self-induced dependency. This in turn permitted uncritical reception of abstract 'models' like 'modernization'. These had produced a metanarrative quite unlike Hobsbawms's vision:

> [R]eceived ideas and stereotyped models too often take the place of theoretical insight or careful research ... Thus a term such as 'modernization' or some 'model' of progress is applied to a historical situation, which in its circular turn becomes source and justification for claims made on behalf of the word or concept in question.

For Judt social history had no story of its own to tell and that which it did tell was no longer history proper.[2]

In 1995 and 1996, Geoff Eley and Keith Nield revisited the debate. The picture they draw of social history is one of existential crisis. They seem engaged in a two-front battle. In one direction they struggle hard to sensitize their structural realist and materialist colleagues to the challenges of postmodernism. In the other, they simultaneously try to fend off Patrick Joyce's proclamation of an 'end of social history' altogether, revoking the latter's indispensable potential to critique capitalism and class structures in an age of globalization. In their attempt to historicize social history, it remains unclear whether they still consider the field more than a politically correct tradition while the future would lie in a Foucauldian and poststructuralist discursive history of 'the social' and 'society', or if they, as Joyce contends, 'look to the past of social history as a way of looking to the future'.[3]

These views tell us much about social history's achievements and shortcomings. They reflect the continuing inability of protagonists and antagonists alike to move beyond the polarized terms of the debate. Social history has indeed opened up the historical discipline to new topics and methods. It has democratized history. It has turned the study of the past into an instrument of social critique.[4] Yet it has not provided a convincing synthesis beyond the Scylla of specialized empiricism and the Charybdis of modernization theory (including its Marxist variant). Paradoxically, therefore, social history has been the junior partner to various lead-disciplines while retaining a surprisingly conventional notion of what history is.

12.1 A genealogy of pendulum swings

Social history originated in the Enlightenment. In the 19th century, social historical approaches developed under the disciplinary umbrellas of the 'historical school' of political economics, nascent sociology (Max Weber and others) and Marxist philosophy – particularly in Germany.[5] In Great Britain and – much more so – in the USA, a pluralist historiographical landscape provided room for positivist studies which today would be seen as social history. In the early 20th century the British 'Fabian' socialists, American 'New Historians' and French *Annalistes* all produced genuine social history.[6] In German historiography, which lacked a positivist tradition and remained bound to the strict disciplinary rule of 'late historism', social historical approaches remained marginalized until well after 1945.

Despite these older traditions, social history experienced its breakthrough only after the Second World War. There was enough common ground between national trajectories of this ascendancy to call it a transnational project. Social historians studied human collectivities and movements in the past, as well as social structure and change. They analysed demographic, economic and social processes and the ways they interacted. World-views, mentalities and 'cultures', standard of living and everyday life, the family, associations and other social groupings became objects of enquiry. Yet to define social history as a discipline devoted to the past of the 'social', the realm between the economy and the state, would not grasp its global aspirations. The interchange between capitalist economy and the 'social' has always figured large in social historical research. Particularly in Germany this combination of 'social and economic history' still marks a double opposition to the history of political ideas and events and an increasingly ahistorical economic science. Furthermore, only in certain specialized sub-fields social history ever resembled Trevelyan's 1942 notion of 'the history of a people with the politics left out'.[7] Social history owed too much to its Marxist roots ever to consider politics irrelevant. Social protest, conflict and revolutions became major fields of interest. Social history initiated the study of classes – especially the working class – as an emancipatory project. At the same time it confronted political history, with its emphasis on ideas and great men, with a potentially deeper and more adequate mode of explaining the political past. Hobsbawm's history of society examined the impact of social structures and processes upon polities, politics and policies.[8]

Social historians everywhere encountered common theoretical problems. The relationship between 'structure' and 'agency' remains a controversial issue. How should the historian capture 'impersonal' socio-economic forces or collectivities like 'social classes'? What was the role of the historical subjects – now conceived as the 'ordinary people' rather than great men – within or against these forces and collectivities? How could one link the different dimensions of analysis in a convincing narrative? What causal weight should be attributed to 'structures' and 'meaningfully acting subjects', or 'social factors' and 'culture', in historical explanation?

Yet these common orientations did not produce a truly *international* social history. The discipline was largely confined by national boundaries. History of society developed no feasible working concept of society, instead retaining the nation-state as its focus. Most 'national' social histories thereby differed markedly from Anglo-American historical sociology, with its universalist modernization model and its preference for macro-sociological comparisons.[9] This 'nationalization' of social histories derived from both the peculiarities of the discipline in each nation, and from the national histories they were part of and helped shape. Social history has never resolved the tensions between a universalist political perspective and a desire to narrate a coherent national history superior to traditional political histories. Universalist concepts – class, capitalism, modernization – were incorporated into individualized national histories. Despite its systematic approach and international ambition, social history merely generated national exceptionalisms. Theory, method, and national metanarratives became difficult to disentangle.

British social history developed in the context of a lively pluralistic – and contentious – Marxism. It set out to explain the Industrial Revolution, the ascent of class society, and the rather British conundrum that these processes produced a highly organized labour movement, but not the class consciousness predicted by Marxist theory. After 1945, Marxist social history fragmented into conflicting wings. One was spearheaded by Hobsbawm, Perry Anderson, Edward P. Thompson, Gareth Stedman Jones, and *History Workshop Journal* (1976–). The latter became a centre for 'history from below' and later for women's history, thus fostering many theoretical and methodological innovations. These British social historians rejected the determinist Marxist orthodoxy associated with Stalinism. New social history set out to overcome the paralysis of the standard-of-living debate of the 1950s by rejecting the debate's economist perspective and its preoccupation with 'nominal' and 'real wages'. Meanwhile, the Soviet invasion of Hungary in 1956 encouraged social historians to revitalize British Marxism. Theoretical issues and political imperatives combined to make a strong anti-structuralist case in favour of 'agency'. 'Experience' and 'hegemony' became buzzwords in labour history, respectively from below or above.[10] In Britain, therefore, social history reaffirmed the old dualism of structure and agency, and pushed the pendulum towards the latter.

US social history emerged in a more diverse landscape. Marxist influence was weaker, and it competed with a strong positivist tradition drawing on Talcott Parsons' structural functionalism and modernization theory. The latter profoundly shaped the national metanarrative generated by the 'new social history'. This relegated Marxism to a variant of the mainstream or an oppositional minority. Diversification spread further because American social history had more than one story to tell. Colonial society, the American Revolution, slavery, the Civil War, the Frontier, and ethnic diversity imposed themselves as topics alongside the history of the Industrial Revolution and class society. Furthermore, non-class social differences, characteristic of a nation of immigrants, often appeared to cross class lines.[11] American social history leaped at the apparently limitless opportunities created by the computer, and quantitative urban history, historical demography and family history, sophisticated sub-fields in Britain, France and Scandinavia, flourished. American 'new social history' was largely quantitative history.

Unlike the British variant, 1960s American social history was markedly *structuralist*. This predilection resulted from methodological preference rather than politics, although 'modernization' concepts added legitimacy. Statistical analysis of demographic data, migration and social mobility became the mediating element between economic, social and political aspects of social history. The discovery of a geographically and socially mobile population in nineteenth- and early 20th-century America was interpreted as evidence of the interaction of structure and agency. Most social history monographs were studies of single cities, and this permitted the combination of demographic, urban, ethnic and working-class history.[12] Analysis of local economic and demographic change was intended to lay the structural groundwork for an account of social mobility patterns, and then to provide the link between economic base (structure) and social and political associations (agency) – with an emphasis on the importance of ethnicity as a part of the political sphere. Agency was virtually collapsed into structure.

Social mobility studies attracted considerable criticism. Monographs were methodologically sophisticated to the point of statistical 'overkill' but seldom conclusive. Social mobility data was just as likely to confirm widening class cleavages as increasing upward mobility due to 'progress'. The explanatory deficit of social mobility studies rested in their inability to decide whether mobility patterns resulted from structural conditions or individual preferences.

American 'new labour history' defined itself against an 'old labour history' that had concentrated on trades union organization and labour leaders and had glorified the American tradition of conformist 'bread-and-butter-unionism'.[13] New labour history originally developed as part of 'new social history' but soon branched off in a Marxist direction. A first cohort of practitioners endeavoured to use quantitative methods to grasp the ordinary workers neglected by the 'old' labour history. They produced local monographs similar to the aforementioned studies, but with a leftist political punch.[14] They sought to recover a labour radicalism hitherto neglected in the historical record. The first radicals were said to have been immigrant workers excluded from white Anglo-Saxon trade unionism. Yet since statistical evidence for this radicalism was elusive, the 'new' labour history increasingly sought confirmation in qualitative material on symbols and rituals. Others pointed to hegemonic 'ruling ideologies' as an explanation for the absence of radicalism.

In this 'cultural turn' of the late 1970s optimistic and pessimistic accounts of American labour history emerged. Optimists stressed the agency displayed in workplace militancy during the 19th century, and tried to link it with later radical manifestations. They wrote an optimistic story of a repeatedly crushed, but ever resurgent, labour activism.[15] The pessimists, adopting neo-Marxism, saw American workers as victims of capitalist 'hegemony'. They too emphasized 19th-century militancy, but incorporated it into a tragedy of long-range defeat. They interpreted the late nineteenth and early 20th century as a period in which managers used Taylorism and Fordism to wrestle technical knowledge from the workers, deskill labour and subordinate it to capitalism. Ethnic diversity played in the hands of management and ensured the lasting fragmentation of the workforce.[16]

Thus, in the late 1970s and early 1980s, American 'new labour history' witnessed a cultural turn towards agency and hegemony, with the concept of experience mediating between the two. Since experience could be linked to identity so easily, American social history was even more open to poststructuralist ideas of difference and symbolic representation than its British counterpart. The swing of the pendulum started with quantitative structuralism, passed grassroots experience, Antonio Gramsci and Clifford Geertz's anthropology on its way and eventually arrived at Foucault and Derrida.

In Germany, social history entered the historical discipline under peculiar circumstances. On the one hand, it had to struggle against a still hegemonic late historism, with its anachronistic emphasis on great men and politics. On the other, it had to avoid identification with Marxist-Leninist historiography in the GDR. Thus it began as a non-Marxist, even anti-Marxist endeavour. Social history was launched by historians like Werner Conze and Theodor Schieder, who had been prominent in the pro-Nazi *Volksgeschichte* of the 1930s. Revoking contaminated *völkisch* jargon after 1945, Conze and Schieder incorporated essential elements of historism into a 'history of structures' (*Strukturgeschichte*). This transformed anti-modernist *Volksgeschichte* into a social history able to face the realities of the 'technical-industrial era'. Conze still avoided the concept of society because of its Marxist connotations.[17] *Strukturgeschichte* was therefore rather elusive, for 'society' was never defined. Rather, structure served as an abstract substitute for politically suspect terms like 'relations of production' and 'class'. Critics argued that, since structures were everywhere, the history of modern society would remain imprecise without a more specific socio-economic vocabulary.

Conze and Schieder replaced the organic community once represented by the *Volk*, with a neo-humanist concept of the 'autonomous subject' derived from 19th-century historism. Drawing on the 'German sociologist' Hans Freyer, they combined a structuralist analysis of contemporary cultures with reassertion of the role of great personalities. *Strukturgeschichte* dug into the histories of industrialization, workers, urban cultures and social vocabulary (*Begriffsgeschichte*) to uncover continuities beyond the ruptures apparently caused by the Industrial Revolution and democratization. *Strukturgeschichte* thus took issue with the Marxist preoccupation with class conflict. It sought to write the epic of the eternal confrontations between structures, and 'great personalities' capable of resisting and shaping them.[18] Conze and Schieder's synthesis aimed to amalgamate these confrontations into a sequence of 'individualities' in which even structural configurations assumed an individual quality.

Because *Strukturgeschichte* never produced this synthesis, and because it separated into a score of loosely linked sub-fields, its influence during the 1960s and 1970s has often been underestimated. Economic, urban, labour, demographic, agricultural and settlement histories have all been inspired by its programme, as has the history of social semantics. *Strukturgeschichte* therefore deserves credit for having established social history on the fortified territory of the German historical profession. It is noteworthy that this social history openly rejected Marxism. It sought to reconcile an outright 'structuralist' notion of the social (originating in Freyer's sociology and Fernand Braudel) with a concept of 'agency' as inherited from historism. This meant that 'agency' was reserved for 'great men' whose intentions the historian tried to 'understand' by a hermeneutic reading of the sources (that is, to uncover the *intentions* of historical actors). *Strukturgeschichte* placed structure and agency side by side, without accounting for the relationship between them.

The sudden emergence of a new generation of social historians in Germany in the late 1960s was responsible for *Strukturgeschichte*'s lack of recognition. Most of the new generation had actually been trained by Conze and Schieder (Gerhard A. Ritter, a student of Ernst Fraenkel, provided another major recruitment centre). Yet the new generation claimed for itself a rather different genealogy in which émigrés and interdisciplinary contacts – especially with sociology – were stressed. Marx was reintroduced, in an unorthodox adaptation indebted to Max Weber, Hans Rosenberg and Eckart Kehr. This self-proclaimed critical social history preached 'history as a social science'. It discarded *Strukturgeschichte* as inconsequential, empiricist or – worse – historicist, and reduced it to a mere staging post on the way to the true paradigm shift of the late 1960s.[19] A relatively coherent group of young historians around Hans-Ulrich Wehler and Jürgen Kocka, the newly founded Bielefeld University and the influential journal *Geschichte und Gesellschaft* (1975–) swiftly surpassed their social history predecessors.

Critical social history developed a radical *structuralism*. It re-established a causal chain between economic, social and political dimensions of historical analysis. A vaguely Marxian materialist conception of 'base' and 'superstructure' re-entered the field. Social history in Germany thus embraced a structuralist paradigm very different to the cultural emphasis found in Britain, and later the USA. German social history took this turn in reaction against historism and *Strukturgeschichte* alike. Epistemologically speaking, *ideological criticism* replaced hermeneutics. First, this meant that critical social historians rejected the notion that the past could be understood by exploring the intentions of historical subjects, for the latter were said to lack full insight into the structural constraints upon their own actions. Instead, these constraints became the focus of enquiry.[20] Second, social historians denounced historiographical approaches – particularly historism – that used hermeneutic methods to understand the past through the intentions of the personalities involved.[21] They discounted these approaches as methodologically naive apologetics for the ruling class. Only structural analysis would free the real past from ideological distortion.

German 'social-science history' explicitly applied theory. In this 'quest for theory' (Reinhart Koselleck) it borrowed 'middle-range concepts' from economics, sociology and political science. The inventor of the 'middle-range concept', the American sociologist Robert K. Merton, saw it as a form of social theory that allowed for close empirical analysis. German social historians converted this into a means to understand limited historical periods. Thus models like 'imperialism', 'organized capitalism' or 'class formation' informed interpretations of very specific periods of history. Ultimately this limited the concepts' theoretical value. Social historians did not worry, however, because they considered theory purely 'instrumental', as if historical narratives were coloured, but not deeply affected, by choice of theory. Kocka, for instance, defined the historical 'story' as the sequence of divergences between the chosen model – the normal path – and past 'reality'.[22] 'Social-science history' openly professed a cheerful eclecticism. Yet all its concepts were firmly embedded in modernization theory.

'Social-science history', despite its proclaimed departure from *Strukturgeschichte*, retained a similar concept of 'structure' for a different purpose. Koselleck's 'theory of historical time' defined a specifically modern type of 'experience'; historical time, he suggested, had accelerated so much in modernity that even 'structural moments' could be experienced as events. Kocka drew from this contention the opposite conclusion that 'structure' was almost entirely beyond the grasp of human understanding. Consequently, a comprehensive explanation required a structural analysis of the conditions of and restraints upon 'agency'. 'Agency' – except as interest and conformity to 'structure' – moved to the margins of the historical account.[23]

'Social-science history' pushed for synthesis more energetically than its predecessor. Wehler developed *Gesellschaftsgeschichte* ('history of society') in pursuit of this ambition. *Gesellschaftsgeschichte* came to mean systematic analysis of the four key dimensions of modern society (the economic, social, political and cultural sphere interlinked by systems of social inequality) in order, ultimately, to explain the political process. This 'political social history' resonated with the concerns of a generation socialized in postwar Germany to expose the origins of Nazism. Whereas *Strukturgeschichte* had stressed long continuities that lessened the significance of this 'crime against civilization', and had transferred its investigation to an isolated sub-field called *Zeitgeschichte* ('contemporary history'), *Gesellschaftsgeschichte* sought long-range causes of Nazism back in the 19th century. Wehler and others designed a 'metanarrative' of a failed German modernization.[24]

Take Wehler's *German Empire* as an example.[25] In his polemical introduction Wehler demanded a 'critical' history of the German Empire of 1871–1918 able to expose its responsibility for Nazism. His history proper starts by portraying the 'constellation of 1871' as a highly explosive coincidence of modernizing and anti-modern forces, foreshadowing the contradictions of the *Reich* up to 1914. The 'agrarian revolution' had commercialized agriculture and buttressed the dominance of the reactionary landed elites, especially in the eastern provinces of Prussia. Compared to the 'West' – Great Britain and America – Germany was a late industrializer. Yet, because it began only in the 1850s, industrialization was all the more rapid, and created severe social strains. Consequently, the German bourgeoisie, especially the leaders of heavy industry, rejected liberalism in favour of a lasting political alliance with the conservative high bureaucracy and aristocracy. The failure of liberalism weakened civil society, while the repressive Bismarck regime stifled democratization and crippled parliamentary government and social reform with a pseudo-populist 'revolution from above'.

Wehler's chapter on industrialization further develops his picture of rapid economic modernization and the consequent pressures on the political system. Ironically, these 20 pages contain the only truly social historical considerations in the book. The remainder – nearly five-sixths – deals with politics. Wehler summarily dismisses the political parties as impotent forces in a political process dominated by traditional elites and the newly organized heavy industrial interest. He sees Bismarck's government as a flexible power broker juggling informal elite coalitions forced together by shared interests, ideological integration and hostility to 'Reich enemies' like the Social Democrats. The regime – even more under Wilhelm II – controlled society by manipulation. Integrating and stereotyping ideologies like anti-Socialism, anti-Semitism and anti-Catholicism were propagated. Wehler presents the family, schools, universities and military as agents of authoritarian socialization. Class justice reinforced the authoritarian mentality in the upper half of German society, and that increased submissiveness to the monarch, the state and the elites.

The politics of manipulation kept the old order in place but did not create stability. On the contrary, it fostered tensions and alienated potential allies. State politics became a reactive crisis management and the regime resorted to an increasingly aggressive nationalism in order to maintain loyalty. German imperialism, for instance, was a strategy designed to divert attention from internal conflict and channel aggression into international relations. German *Weltpolitik* thus was really a manipulative domestic policy. Germany became the driving force in the European arms race, building a fleet intended to contest British naval hegemony. These foreign-policy adventures provoked anti-German coalitions and ultimately international isolation. Militarism in German society made war inevitable. For Wehler, the German invasion of France and Russia in 1914 represented a last-ditch attempt to save the moribund Wilhelmine system. Yet Germany's defeat brought about the very social revolution the war had been supposed to prevent. Elite adversity to the democratic institutions of the Weimar Republic then helped Nazism to power during the Great Depression.

Wehler's strongly argued book has been immensely controversial, not the least because it combines ascetic brevity with pointed judgements and blunt commentary. Each chapter draws on its own theoretical concept, so that theory often appears as a short-cut interpretation of a past 'reality', illustrated by a few historical details. Social history proper enters the picture surprisingly little. It is evident largely in a broadening of the 'political' to include organized interest groups and social institutions. Whereas almost no historical actors figure in the depiction of economic and social structures, the arena of politics is populated with stunningly personal stories of 'great men' and events. 'Manipulation' has to bear the whole burden of Wehler's attempt to bring society and politics together – great men seek to manipulate social processes. This metanarrative of a 'German divergence from the West' (*deutscher Sonderweg*) became influential because it fused modernization theory, structuralism, ideological critique and a morally accentuated interpretation of a crucial period into a 'critical' national history.[26]

12.2 Theoretical cornerstones of 'traditional' social history

In order to reunite national trends for more systematic discussion, I want to discuss some essentials of 'traditional' social history. A field representative of the discipline at large shall serve as an example: the approach to labour history as set forth in the 'working class formation paradigm' of the 1970s and 1980s. For most of the 1960s and 1970s, social history had been almost synonymous with labour history or, more generally, of ordinary men (literally 'men'). The concept of 'working class formation' represented an attempt to combine the history of workers in workplaces, neighbourhoods, families, bars and leisure associations, with *labour movement history* – strikes and class conflict, trade union and party organization, ideology and 'class consciousness'. E. P. Thompson's *Making of the English Working Class* (1963) triggered the development of a series of models of 'working class formation'.[27]

Their common approach was to turn a core concept of an 'economic base' determining an 'ideological superstructure' into a sequence of levels causally linked to each other and representing a progression from the advent of capitalism to the founding of socialist parties. Another commonality was the use of models of singular linear processes in history, against which 'histories proper' would be measured. Such theories promoted an idealized historical path to a morally defined end (liberal democracy or socialism) and were in vogue in contemporary economics (e.g. the 'long waves' approach) and sociology (modernization, Marxism).[28] It is not hard to discern the desire to reconcile theory with the old idea that history is a *unitary process*.

Kocka's essay on 'working class formation' in Germany (1800–75) is a case in point.[29] He starts by outlining a theoretical model distinguishing 'four analytical dimensions'. First, the overarching processes that transformed the Ancien Régime into modern 'class society', most notably the rise of capitalism, state building and the demographic transition. Second, he depicts the concomitant spread of wage work in centralized production facilities as the motor for homogenization of workers' class positions. Third, workers will hypothetically develop – on this basis – a collective identity, expressed in language, family structures, marriage patterns, residual segregation and culture. Finally,

> under certain conditions those who share a common class position and become a social class ... may, on the same basis, act collectively and perhaps organize [in trade unions and socialist parties], in conflict with other classes and perhaps the state.[30]

Kocka then describes in detail the 'lower classes' around 1800. As always, he brilliantly synthesizes a vast literature into a 'class' interpretation. He follows up with a minute account of the legal, economic and demographic changes outlined in level one of his model, drawing on legal decisions and a much statistical data. The next chapter shows that servants, agricultural and casual workers, the largest occupational groups, were largely unaffected by wage work, and remained embedded in older production settings and legal restraints. Workers in 'domestic industries', in contrast, were increasingly dependent on merchant capital, but were not yet employed in a capitalist factory system. Journeymen had largely turned into wage workers, while their masters were on the brink of becoming petty employers. Yet guild traditions still lingered in collective organization along trade lines. Finally, factory workers almost matched Kocka's prototypical 'pure wage worker'. In this chapter Kocka relies largely on 'structural' analysis, but he does speculate on the 'typical experiences' of the groups in question. He does so in order to deal with the rather puzzling observation that some domestic workers and many journeymen 'contributed' to the early German labour movement, while factory workers held aloof.

Kocka's final section covers levels three and four of his model. He first points to unifying tendencies in the language of 'work' and 'class', social mobility and marriage patterns, and social protest – most notably the rapidly growing frequency of strikes in the late 1860s and early 1870s. Kocka then traces the emergence of trade unions and the rise of Social Democratic parties. The former first appeared in certain artisan trades, a fact which does not confirm the prediction in the model that they should be developed first by factory workers. Kocka explains artisan unionism as a belated product of class conflict between masters and journeymen back in the revolution of 1848. Another development rather specific for Germany was the 'premature' appearance of independent labour parties. Kocka attributes this to the receptiveness of many journeymen for socialist ideologies and the inability of German liberalism to maintain political hegemony – in contrast to Britain. Kocka concludes that, whereas a working class was present on levels one and two of his model, 'class formation' remained limited on the higher levels, in spite of progress between 1800 and 1875. 'Class formation' did result from the extension of capitalism and wage work, but it only translated into 'class consciousness' and collective action, where a 'supplementary' 'conflict between tradition and modernization' entered the picture.[31]

It is interesting to note how Kocka deals with 'structure' and 'agency' in the causal architecture of his argument. Levels one and two provide mainly structural analyses. On level two he invokes typical 'experiences' but does not back them up empirically. Instead, the largely structural phenomena on level three sustain his earlier assumptions about 'experiences'. Instead of developing each level out of the preceding one, he implicitly reverses the causal order. Kocka also fails to convincingly explain the timing and the forms of German labour organization, for he actually has recourse to variables *external* to his model (socialist ideologies, weakness of liberalism). Finally, the role of 'traditions' in his argument is unclear. While the model should regard traditions as retarding labour organization, they sneak into the explanation as a 'sufficient cause' for the 'early' organization of artisan trades.

Kocka's model, like all concepts of 'class formation', attributes different qualities of 'structure' and 'agency' to each dimension of 'historical reality.'[32] Whereas all formulations of the model distinguish between demographic/economic, social and political/ideological levels of 'class formation', with Katznelson inserting a fourth, cultural level in between the social and the political, they differ largely in the degree they allow for the historical subjects to be 'meaningful agents'. Zwahr's account of spreading kinship relations among 'born proletarians' is structural and leaves agency out entirely. For Katznelson and Kocka, industrialization and wage work provided homogenizing 'experiences' which workers had *passively* and which were *then* translated into 'agency' at the cultural and political levels. Agency exists only on the higher level, and is constrained by the lower. Thompson's 'reintroduction of the subject into history', by contrast, led him to define 'experience' *as* 'agency'. In Thompson's eyes, 'class' had to be 'experienced' – *actively made* and transformed into cultural and political 'class consciousness'. Yet, on a closer look, Thompson's seemingly totalizing concept of 'experience' is deceiving, since material 'relations of production' ('structures') determine what 'experiences' can be made in the first place. The novelty of Thompson is that he takes account of new forms of 'experience' (like the tradition of the 'freeborn Englishman'). These help shape particular *expressions* of working-class 'agency', but they do not alter the assumption that experiences must converge in *class* experiences.[33]

The 'working class formation paradigm' is a prime example of 'classic' social history's inability to bring structure and agency together. Structure generally meant causal primacy for structure and the de-centring of agency. 'Structure' was most salient ('hard' is a frequently used adjective) in economic institutions and relations of production. Although historians of the working class recognized that there were 'structures' in culture and organization, too, these seemed much less rigid. William H. Sewell has criticized this as 'misplaced materialism'.[34] For it is not the *degree of structuration* that distinguishes between segments of society, but their *specific structural properties.* Finally, social history's de-centring of the 'agent' has resulted in a tendency to make *collectivities* the unquestioned units of analysis, to the extent that they almost appeared capable of acting like people. 'Traditional' social history took group formation for granted, so it was almost impossible to think of social identity in terms of 'difference'. Yet 'difference' became the banner under which the new 'cultural history' assailed social history in the early 1980s.[35]

12.3 'Social history' under attack

Some say that social history first experienced 'crisis' in the late 1970s. In Britain and America this meant the disintegration of what had never really been a coherent field. Social history became a loosely circumscribed territory with room for numerous approaches, even if some seemed mutually exclusive.

Labour history was the first area where a 'history of experience' – *how* people experienced the past – strove to emancipate itself from Thompsonian patronage. This was evident in a new 'micro-history from below' and in claims for the relative autonomy of culture and rejection of economic determinism. History of experience, even when adopting a watered-down 'thick description' derived from

Geertz's anthropology, largely remained within the social history perimeter. It combined minute analyses of symbolic systems with rather conventional descriptions of context.[36] Nevertheless, it initiated a shift in focus from sociology to social (or cultural) anthropology as a theoretical reference point. 'New cultural history' also sought to reverse the traditional privileging of economic causation.[37] Yet this revisionism retained the conceptual framework of materialist social history. Cultural representations still figured as internalizations – if symbolic – of material reality.[38]

Gareth Stedman Jones' view that language decisively shapes past reality was more radical, and opened the way for postmodernism and the 'linguistic turn'.[39] Likewise gender history attacked not only social historians' neglect of sexual difference, but the materialist character of their basic categories. Feminists denounced as 'essentialist' social historians' assumption that the proletariat was male.[40] Michel Foucault's discourse theory influenced most of these revisionists. His linkage of knowledge and power disturbed social historians by distracting attention from economic institutions, social conflict and 'real people'. Social history could deal neither with the alleged centrality of language nor the view that culture was a symbolic system independent of 'real' people. Social historians' representations of the past, their very notion of 'historical reality' and their 'scientific' approach all seemed at stake.

The above critiques all share the view that social categories should be understood in terms of difference. Even in their most conventional understanding, which considers 'difference' central to 'social identity', this poses a momentous challenge to a social history preoccupied with collectivities. For 'difference' is foremost an individual property of acting subjects. Acceptance of this proposition would mean a fundamental rethinking of how collectivities are formed. In the USA, the impact of 'difference' quickly led to expansion of social historical vocabulary, especially in the focus on the trinity of 'class, race and gender'. This did not in itself extend the horizons of social history, but made its stories more complicated.[41] It was more critical that this 'deconstruction' of collectivities threatened the unitary notion of history still favoured, as we have seen, by many social historians. Hence social history's hostility to gender and micro-history.

Only Germany has seen a polarized debate between social and cultural history. On one side is a disciplinary establishment loyal to social history; confronting it are cultural historians, who, if not without disagreements, possess a common sense of purpose. This polarization is due to the unusually strong position acquired by 'social-science history' in the 1970s and early 1980s. Although it does not represent a majority in the historical discipline, and not even all social historians, 'social-science history' had temporarily exerted a sort of discursive hegemony over the field. In other countries new approaches added breadth to an already pluralized field, but in Germany innovators had to fight an uphill battle against a 'new orthodoxy'. In the course of this struggle, German social history became identified with economic determinism, analysis of social structure, anti-hermeneutic structuralism, macro-causal explanations, political social history and the *Sonderweg* synthesis typified by Wehler. In the 1980s 'social-science history' rejected all challengers – whether *Alltagsgeschichte* or women's history. The intention was to taint these leftist threats with the odour of right-wing historism.

'Social-science history' has nevertheless changed and expanded during the last 30 years. Social historians finally started to heed the call for historical comparisons, which had been demanded during the *Sonderweg* debate. These studies transcended national histories, subverted the nationally centred *Sonderweg* model and undermined social history's categories of analysis. In labour history, this led to a critique of the 'working class formation paradigm'.[42] Social-science history's own large-scale project on the history of the bourgeoisie launched in the mid-1980s broadened the object of analysis to include culture, gender relations, value systems and discourses. The German 'bourgeoisie' increasingly appeared as a cultural formation rather than a socio-economic class.

Some proponents of new cultural history still define themselves against a narrowly conceived social history. The manner in which cultural historians bring together concepts usually considered incompatible is a peculiarly German phenomenon, as is the attempt to bring some coherence into cultural history by returning to turn-of-the-century German theories of culture.[43] And, whereas social-science history continues to produce one monumental synthesis of national history after another, cultural historians struggle to present an alternative metanarrative, pitting a story of 'radicalized modernity' against the *Sonderweg* thesis. Thus they remain confined to national history after all.[44] Some cultural historians even demand replacement of 'society' with 'culture' as a more comprehensive focus for synthesis.[45] Playing society off against culture represents another German *Sonderweg* inevitably leading into another dead end.[46]

12.4 What future?

Social history did have its merits. It was social history, after all, that brought up the question of social inequality in the study of the past and introduced the workers and the underprivileged masses to the historical record. It explained the process of industrialization, and of social change and conflict in a broad sense. It pioneered the integration of economic, social and political analysis into the history of entire societies. Social history also became a fertile ground of theoretical debate. Current discussions of various theoretical 'turns' are still capitalizing on this pioneering work.

Yet revisionist challenges have exposed the whole historical discipline's weaknesses, social history included. I have pointed to social history's inability to reconcile structure and agency, to the weaknesses of its 'materialist' conception of the economy and collectivities, its neglect of culture as symbolic practice, and to its intransigent rejection of the notion of the historical construction of difference. The solutions offered by the linguistic turn to the problems of the agency of historical subjects, the cultural meanings of their interaction and the power relations intrinsic to economic, social and political institutions are only partly convincing. Yet cultural historians have posed the right questions. A renewed social history must take on board a whole range of key insights derived from recent debates. Some historians speak of an imminent 'social turn' in the history of culture and society. This must not be a turn *back* to the 'old' structuralist social history, but a step 'beyond the cultural turn'.[47]

We might now be attaining a social history that pays full credit to language, symbols and discourse, but moves on by embedding these in 'social practice'. 'Practice theory' – as associated, for instance, with Pierre Bourdieu and Anthony Giddens – is capable of grasping interaction both as structured by rules and resources and as acted out by the agency of subjects. Starting from the premise that agents interpret their environment in the process of making 'experiences', it can cope with the constructed nature of (historical) reality and multiple identities of actors. I can envisage in the near future a social history that combines the analysis of economic, social, cultural and political institutions from the perspective of the social subjects meaningfully interacting with one another. Collectivities will not be taken for granted, but will be explained in terms of social and cultural practice. This approach might breathe fresh life into research areas largely deserted since the linguistic turn. The histories of work, business enterprises and marketplaces, of social inequality, social movements and political culture, all conceived of as complex fields of interaction, all stand out as potentially innovative research areas in an age of globalization.[48] This will be a self-reflexive social history, beyond the cultural turn, but conscious of its achievements.

Guide to further reading

Michael Bentley, *Modern Historiography. An Introduction* (London, 1999).

Victoria E. Bonnell and Lynn Hunt (eds), *Beyond the Cultural Turn. New Directions in the Study of Society and Culture* (Berkeley, 1999).

Christoph Conrad, 'Social History', in Neil J. Smelser and Peter B. Baltes (eds), *International Encyclopaedia of the Social and Behavioural Sciences*, Vol. 21 (Oxford, 2001), pp. 14299–14306.

Geoff Eley, and Keith Nield, 'Starting Over: The Present, the Postmodern and the Moment of Social History' in Keith Jenkins (ed.), *The Postmodern History Reader* (3rd edn, London, 2001), pp. 366–79.

Anna Green and Kathleen Troup (eds), *The Houses of History. A Critical Reader in 20th-Century History and Theory* (Manchester, 1999).

Peter N. Stearns (ed.), *Encyclopedia of European Social History* (New York, 2001).

Notes

1 Eric J. Hobsbawm, 'From Social History to the History of Society', *Daedalus* 100 (1971), pp. 20–45, esp. p. 43.

2 Tony Judt, 'A Clown in Regal Purple: Social History and the Historians', *History Workshop Journal* 7 (1979), pp. 66–94, esp. pp. 66, 67, 89.

3 Geoff Eley and Keith Nield, 'Starting Over: The Present, the Postmodern and the Moment of Social History', in Keith Jenkins (ed.), *The Postmodern History Reader* (3rd edn, London, 2001), pp. 366–79; Geoff Eley, 'Is All the World a Text? From Social History, to the History of Society Two Decades Later', in Terrence J. McDonald (ed.), *The Historic Turn in the Human Sciences* (Ann Arbor, MI, 1996), pp. 193–243, esp. pp. 216–23.

4 Stefan Berger, 'The Rise and Fall of "Critical" Historiography', *European Review of History* 3 (1996), pp. 213–32.

5 The German journal *Vierteljahrschrift für Sozial- und Wirtschafts-geschichte* was first published in 1893.

6 Lucien Febvre and Marc Bloch founded the *Annales d'histoire économique et sociale* in Strasbourg in 1929. See Chapter 6 in this volume on the *Annales* for further details and elaboration .

7 George Macaulay Trevelyan, *Illustrated English Social History* (London, 1942).

8 Cf. Jürgen Kocka, *Sozialgeschichte. Begriff – Entwicklung – Probleme* (2nd ed., Göttingen, 1986), pp. 48–111.

9 Charles Tilly, *Big Structures, Large Processes, Huge Comparisons* (New York, 1984).

10 Geoff Eley, 'Edward Thompson, Social History and Political Culture: The Making of a Working-Class Public, 1780–1850', in Harvey J. Kaye and Keith McClelland (eds), *E.P. Thompson. Critical Perspectives* (Philadelphia, 1990), pp. 12–49.

11 Michael Kammen (ed.), *The Past Before Us* (Ithaca, 1980).

12 Stephen Thernstorm, *Poverty and Progress. Social Mobility in a 19th-century City* (Cambridge, MA, 1964), and Stephen Thernstorm, *The Other Bostonians. Poverty and Progress in the American Metropolis; 1880–1970* (Cambridge, MA, 1973).

13 The benchmark synthesis of the 'old' labour history was John R. Commons *et al.*, *History of Labor in the United States*, 4 vols (New York, 1918–35).

14 A good example is Alan Dawley, *Class and Community. The Industrial Revolution in Lynn* (Cambridge, MA, 1976).

15 The seminal study is David Montgomery, *The Fall of the House of Labor. The Workplace, the State, and American Labor Activism 1865–1925* (New York, 1987).

16 Harry Braverman, *Labor and Monopoly Capitalism. The Degradation of Work in the 20th century* (New York, London, 1974); Richard C. Edwards, *Contested Terrain. The Transformation of the Workplace in the 20th century* (New York, 1979); David M. Gordon, Richard C. Edwards and Michael Reich, *Segmented Work, Divided Workers. The Historical Transformation of Labor in the United States* (Cambridge, MA, 1982).

17 Werner Conze, *Die Strukturgeschichte des technisch-industriellen Zeitalters als Aufgabe für Forschung und Unterricht* (Köln, 1957).

18 Theodor Schieder, *Geschichte als Wissenschaft. Eine Einführung* (2nd ed., München, 1968), pp. 18–20, 157–94.

19 Hans-Ulrich Wehler, *Geschichte als Historische Sozialwissenschaft* (Frankfurt am Main, 1973).

20 Kocka, *Sozialgeschichte*, p. 73.

21 Thomas Welskopp, 'Die Sozialgeschichte der Väter. Grenzen und Perspektiven der Historischen Sozialwissenschaft', *Geschichte und Gesellschaft* 24 (1998), pp. 169–94.

22 Jürgen Kocka, *Facing Total War. German Society 1914–1918* (Leamington Spa, 1984).

23 Kocka, *Sozialgeschichte,* pp. 76f. For Koselleck's notion of structure, see Reinhart Koselleck, 'Darstellung, Ereignis, Struktur', in Reinhart Koselleck, *Vergangene Zukunft. Zur Semantik geschichtlicher Zeiten* (Frankfurt am Main, 1989), pp. 144–57.

24 Stefan Berger, *The Search for Normality: National Identity and Historical Consciousness in Germany Since 1800* (Oxford, 1997).

25 Hans-Ulrich Wehler, *The German Empire 1871–1918* (Leamington Spa, 1985).

26 See his monumental *Deutsche Gesellschaftsgeschichte*, 3 vols published to date (München, 1987–95). A critical analysis is provided by Thomas Welskopp, 'Westbindung auf dem "Sonderweg". Die deutsche Sozialgeschichte vom Appendix der Wirtschaftsgeschichte zur Historischen Sozialwissenschaft', in Wolfgang Küttler, Jörn Rüsen and Ernst Schulin (eds), *Geschichtsdiskurs*, Vol. 5 (Frankfurt am Main, 1999), pp. 191–237.

27 Hartmut Zwahr, *Zur Konstituierung des Proletariats als Klasse. Strukturuntersuchung des Leipziger Proletariats während der industriellen Revolution* (Berlin (GDR), 1978), and Ira Katznelson, 'Working-Class

Formation: Constructing Cases and Comparisons', in Ira Katznelson and Aristide R. Zolberg (eds), *Working-Class Formation: 19th century Patterns in Western Europe and the United States* (Princeton, 1986), pp. 3–43.

28 Hansjörg Siegenthaler, 'Geschichte und Ökonomie nach der kulturalistischen Wende', *Geschichte und Gesellschaft* 25 (1999), pp. 276–301, esp. p. 280.

29 Jürgen Kocka, 'Problems of Working-Class Formation in Germany: The Early Years, 1800–1875', in Katznelson and Zolberg (eds), *Working-Class Formation*, pp. 279–351, and Jürgen Kocka, *Lohnarbeit und Klassenbildung. Arbeiter und Arbeiterbewegung in Deutschland 1800–1875* (Berlin, 1983).

30 Ibid., p. 283.

31 Ibid., p. 351.

32 Thomas Welskopp, 'Class Structures and the Firm: The Interplay of Workplace and Industrial Relations in Large Capitalist Enterprises', in Paul L. Robertson (ed.), *Authority and Control in Modern Industry. Theoretical and Empirical Perspectives* (London, 1999), pp. 73–119.

33 William H. Sewell, Jr, 'How Classes are Made: Critical Reflections on E. P. Thompson's Theory of Working-Class Formation', in Kaye and McClelland (eds), *E. P. Thompson*, pp. 50–77, esp. pp. 59–66.

34 William H. Sewell, Jr, 'Toward a Post-materialist Rhetoric for Labor History', in Lenard R. Berlanstein (ed.), *Rethinking Labor History. Essays on Discourse and Class Analysis* (Urbana, Chicago, 1993), pp. 16–38.

35 The zenith of German social history can be located around the turn to the 1980s. Cf. the triumphant tone in Wehler's stocktaking essay: Hans-Ulrich Wehler, 'Geschichtswissenschaft heute', in Jürgen Habermas (ed.), *Stichworte zur 'Geistigen Situation der Zeit'*, Vol. 2, *Politik und Kultur* (Frankfurt am Main, 1979), pp. 709–53.

36 For example, Sean Wilentz, *Chants Democratic. New York City and the Rise of the American Working Class, 1788–1850* (New York, 1984).

37 Lynn Hunt, *Politics, Culture, and Class in the French Revolution* (Berkeley, 1986); William H. Sewell, Jr, *Work and Revolution in France: The Language of Labour from the Old Regime to 1848* (Cambridge, 1980); Lynn Hunt (ed.), *The New Cultural History* (Berkeley and Los Angeles, 1989).

38 Miguel A. Cabrera, 'On Language, Culture, and Social Action', *History and Theory* 40 (2001), pp. 82–100, esp. pp. 84–6.

39 Gareth Stedman Jones, *Languages of Class: Studies in English Working-Class History, 1832–1982* (Cambridge, 1983); Patrick Joyce (ed.), *The Historical Meanings of Work* (Cambridge, 1987); Patrick Joyce, *Democratic Subjects. The Self and the Social in 19th-century England* (New York, 1994).

40 Joan W. Scott, *Gender and the Politics of History* (New York, 1988); Joan W. Scott, 'The Evidence of Experience', in James Chandler, Arnold I.

Davidson and Harry Harootunian (eds), *Questions of Evidence. Proof, Practice, and Persuasion across the Disciplines* (Chicago, London, 1994), pp. 363–87.

41 Kathleen Canning, 'Gender and the Politics of Class Formation: Rethinking German Labor History', *American Historical Review* 97 (1992), pp. 736–68.

42 Thomas Welskopp, *Arbeit und Macht im Hüttenwerk. Arbeits- und industrielle Beziehungen in der deutschen und amerikanischen Eisen- und Stahlindustrie von den 1860er bis zu den1930er Jahren* (Bonn, 1994).

43 Ute Daniel, *Kompendium Kulturgeschichte. Theorien, Praxis, Schlüsselwörter* (Frankfurt am Main, 2001).

44 Geoff Eley (ed.), *Society, Culture, and the State in Germany 1870–1930* (Ann Arbor, MI, 1996).

45 Rudolf Vierhaus, 'Die Rekonstruktion historischer Lebenswelten. Probleme moderner Kulturgeschichtsschreibung', in Hartmut Lehmann (ed.), *Wege zu einer neuen Kulturgeschichte* (Göttingen, 1995), pp.6–28; Ute Daniel, '"Kultur" und "Gesellschaft". Überlegungen zum Gegenstandsbereich der Sozialgeschichte', *Geschichte und Gesellschaft* 19 (1993), pp. 69–99.

46 Stefan Berger, 'Social History vs Cultural History', *Theory, Culture and Society* 18 (2001), pp. 145–53.

47 Victoria E. Bonnell and Lynn Hunt (eds), *Beyond the Cultural Turn. New Directions in the Study of Society and Culture* (Berkeley, 1999).

48 Anna Clark, *The Struggle for the Breeches. Gender and the Making of the British Working Class* (Berkeley, 1995); Kathleen Canning, *Languages of Labor and Gender: Female Factory Work in Germany, 1850–1914* (Ithaca, 1996); James Vernon, *Politics and the People. A Study in English Political Culture, c. 1815–1867* (Cambridge, 1993); Robert E. Weir, *Beyond Labor's Veil. The Culture of the Knights of Labor* (University Park, PA, 1996); Margaret L. Anderson, *Practicing Democracy. Elections and Political Culture in Imperial Germany* (Princeton, 2000); Thomas Welskopp, *Das Banner der Brüderlichkeit. Die deutsche Sozialdemokratie vom Vormärz bis zum Sozialistengesetz* (Bonn, 2000).

13

Economic history

Pat Hudson

Economic history is distinctive in terms of subject matter and approach. It is concerned with the material underpinnings of human existence: how people make their livings, how food and goods are produced and distributed and the sorts of societies, ways of life and institutions that different regimes of production and consumption support or encourage. Thus the best economic history is concerned with political, social and cultural as well as economic life. In terms of approach, economic history most often combines the historian's craft and training with the interests, theories and methods of social science, in particular economics. Employing social science concepts and theories in historical research and writing can be enlightening but problems often arise because most social science of the last century has been geared to contemporary issues. The social sciences in general, and economics in particular, are largely present-centred and policy-oriented. They incorporate many assumptions that are only applicable (and even then not always easily applicable) to modern, commercial, capitalistic, usually western, societies. They have a temporal and cultural bias. The dangers in using economics, or any other social science, in history are thus anachronism and ethnocentrism. Economic historians must think carefully about the social, cultural and economic environment of different periods and parts of the globe, and may need to adapt economic and social theory to their purposes or even rethink aspects of economic and social science for themselves to make them more appropriate to the historian's needs.

When asked to define economic history some years ago, Donald Coleman emphasized two aspects that differentiate it from both history and economics. First, economic history seeks to identify and to measure forces normally outside the control of single individual actors. This causes problems for the many historians who reject the idea that forces can be identified as agents that create or condition historical events. Second, Coleman restated the truism that economic phenomena have no existence independent of the social, political, religious and physical environment in which they occur.[1] The embeddedness of economic activity within the social, cultural and personal fabric of everyday life means that the economic historian needs to take a holistic and interdisciplinary approach.

Despite its distinctiveness in these ways, it is the case that the nature and popularity of economic history have always been tied to developments in the parent disciplines of history and social science, particularly economics. In the 1960s and 1970s, for example, there was a widespread appreciation and uptake of social science approaches in history, and a concern for economic structures. This went along with the expansion of social science in universities and the popularity of Marxian ideas that placed emphasis upon the role of the economy in influencing social, cultural and political structures. Furthermore, the social sciences generally, and economics in particular, were more open than is the case today to evidence from the past as well as the present. Today, priorities in history, where they are not focused upon military and political narrative, have turned to cultural phenomena and to the use of literary and dramatic metaphors and methods of analysis rather than using the mechanical or causative reasoning that economists and economic historians generally employ. Textual sources have been increasingly privileged over the quantitative data that was traditionally favoured by economic historians. Some would say that these trends, taken together, have left economic history stranded. But economic history is not just a set of concerns passively waiting around for the right environment in which to flourish. It is able significantly to critique the narrow purview of much contemporary economic theory and also to ambush the many cultural historians who appear to have forgotten what the economy is and why causal analysis is important. Thus, economic history is currently faced with growing opportunities as well as some problems, and perhaps more of the former than the latter.

This chapter considers the ways in which the economy has figured in the work of historians, and at the way various approaches to economics have been used by historians to throw light on the past. It does this by outlining the history of economic history, relating it to broader trends in the development of history and social science. Stress is placed throughout upon different ways of conceptualizing the economic sphere and economic motivation and in questioning the boundaries between economic actions and other forms of social and cultural behaviour.

13.1 Economic theory and history: two sorts of approaches

There are two very different ways in which the use of economic theory in history has come about. The first involves seeing the economy as fundamentally important within an overall explanation of history, underpinning a metanarrative.

It involves acceptance that the nature of the economy has a primary role in conditioning all aspects of society, culture, politics. In its various forms the Marxian approach to history adopts this position, as do some forms of modernization theory. Marxian studies of social, cultural, legal or other aspects of life in the past inevitably involve relating the nature of their subject, and change in their subject over time, to the nature of the economy and shifts in the economic base of society. For example, E. P. Thompson in his classic, *The Making of the English Working Class* (1963), focused on the rise of class solidarity and social protest in the early 19th century, but shifts in technology, manufacturing, competition, work relations and trading are shown to be the forces underlying social change, in the face of which people came together and began to act, and to see themselves, in class terms. John Foster, in his *Class Struggle in the Industrial Revolution* (1974) used the Marxian base/superstructure model to compare the nature of class consciousness in three English towns in the 19th century. By these means he not only explained the revolutionary threat in Oldham in the 1840s, but also the more peaceable nature of the later 19th century, which, he argued (along Marxist-Leninist lines), was brought about by the economic stability of a more mature capitalism resting on the gains from imperialism. Although the Marxian model reached a peak of influence upon western history between the 1940s and the 1970s, and is now very consciously rejected by most historians and social theorists, its influence upon social science runs deep. It is impossible (even if thought desirable) entirely to escape its influence. We are all Marxian now in the sense that non-Marxist and post-Marxist works of history and social science often retain a strong commitment to considering the role of the economy as a major variable (if not a determining one) in analysing aspects of society and culture, past and present.

The second way in which an economic approach to history and the use of economic theory in history occurs is by using a variety of 'middle range' economic theories (which are not metanarratives in any sense) and various concepts and explanatory devices drawn from economic theory. The toolbox is varied. Historians have drawn upon many different strands of economic theory and have used diverse concepts from economic sociology, and from economic and social anthropology as well as from economics. Much can be gained by using first principles of economics, particularly supply and demand theory, to think through the impact of, for example, food shortages or population expansion during periods for which firm evidence is lacking. M. M. Postan's argument about the decline of feudal relations in England rested upon economic reasoning about the impact of the Black Death upon the prices of land, labour and agricultural produce.[2] The dominant paradigm in economics during the last century, and particularly since the 1950s, was based upon formal and mechanical models frequently represented in algebraic or graphical terms and underpinned by the assumption that human beings, in satisfying their material needs, are driven by 'rational' profit-maximizing motives. This neo-classical approach has been very influential in economic history, but its use has varied over time. Such variations are best understood by considering the history of the subject.

13.2 The history of economic history: Origins

For most of the eighteenth and nineteenth centuries, English, Scottish, French and German political economists, and the founding fathers of western social science (figures a diverse as Adam Smith, David Ricardo, John Stuart Mill, Karl Marx, Max Weber, Emile Durkheim and Ferdinand Tonnies), all drew from historical evidence when analysing society. In this sense economic history has a long lineage central to the emergence of social science in Europe. However, it arose more specifically as an academic concern of historians and economists at the end of the 19th century and in the early 20th century. This came as part of a wider rejection of 'drum and trumpet' history – the history of elites, diplomacy and wars – in favour of the history of the mass of the population and of agriculture, industry and trading. This move to study non-elite and 'non-political' history was also the aim of the founders of the *Annales* School in France. It was a history favoured by socialists and social reformers who were addressing the problems arising from industrialization. This encouraged an economic history that looked to the past in order to understand the causes of social dislocation and for evidence of government regulation in the interests of the masses. In England, this approach was exemplified by the work of Sidney and Beatrice Webb, founders of the London School of Economics (LSE), by Arnold Toynbee, Barbara and John Hammond, Charles Beard and many of the first generation of academic writers in economic history. William Ashley was the first British historian to adopt a periodization not derived from political history, an important step in freeing history from the rule of political events.

Economic history also evolved as an academic subject, from the later 19th century, as a branch of economics. Indeed the so-called Historical School represented the dominant approach in economics in the early and mid-19th century. It was highly empirical, statistically orientated and historically attuned. It placed emphasis upon fact gathering (from the past and the present) and induction (the idea that general patterns would emerge, if at all, once all the data had been assembled). Much early economic history was of this kind. Further enthusiastic recruits to economic history as a discipline came from the reaction of many economists against new developments taking place in economics in the 1880s and 1890s (the so-called marginalist or neo-classical revolution). These developments made economics more present-centred, more formal (mechanical, mathematical and graphical) in its methods and more deductive (depending upon the predictive ability of generalizations and statistical inference). This development was not only perceived as a major threat to the older Historical School, which eventually became a minority tradition, but economic history, allied to historical economics, was viewed as an attempt to find an alternative methodology to the growing mainstream in economics, one which would better take account of different time periods and cultures. William Cunningham, who published the first English economic history text in 1882, objected to the idea, dominant in neo-classical economics, of 'economic man' as a rational calculating and maximizing individual whose behaviour could be seen as deriving from an immutable human nature, present in all societies. He favoured the study of societies in their own time and with their own special social and cultural attitudes and motivations.[3] These views came out in his controversies with Alfred Marshall, the leading exponent of the marginalist revolution in Britain. Although Marshall himself saw economics as 'the study of man in the ordinary business of life', the method which he helped to establish encouraged economists to specialize in abstract generalized theorizing. Similar debates between the Historical School and formal, neo-classical economists were going on in Europe, and particularly in Germany, where the *Methodenstreit* ('debates upon method') in economics was most vociferous, partly because of the strength of the Historical School there.

From the outset, economic history as a distinctive academic discipline also included those who wished to take the deductive, formalist approach becoming dominant in economics and apply what was seen as rigorous 'scientific' method to studies of the past and to historical data. This was a very minor strand in economic history before the mid-20th century. Its attraction as a method was the application of those universalist assumptions about economic behaviour that Cunningham, amongst others, had been so keen to reject. This conflict, together with the commitment to economic history from socialists and reformers made for keen debates within economic history about purpose and method from the outset.

13.3 The history of economic history: Expansion and diversity

The subject expanded in the USA and Europe in the 1920s, in Britain with the foundation of the Economic History Society and the *Economic History Review* and with a growing number of university appointments and courses in the subject. Much research appeared that used hitherto untouched historical documents for the first time: for example, the censuses of population and production, overseas trade figures, local municipal records, parliamentary reports and commissions, business archives. This broke new ground because the sources and the concerns which economic and social historians tackled had not traditionally been regarded as a priority for historians or even as a legitimate sphere of their interests. There was also a strong internationalist flavour to many of these early works: a preoccupation with international trade and with the nature of economic development in various parts of the globe. Economic history, in Britain at least, was also noted in this period for the relatively high proportion of female historians who had been attracted to the subject, including Eileen Power, E. M. Carus Wilson, Ivy Pinchbeck and Lilian Knowles. Their research interests helped to shape the scope and preoccupations of the subject, in particular its emphasis upon internationalism, the social impact of change and the experiences of families, women and children as well as men.[4]

Two very different strains were apparent in economic history in Britain by the early 20th century, which spawned further creative tension.[5] The first can be termed the political or moral tradition represented in the work of R. H. Tawney, Barbara and John Hammond, Sidney and Beatrice Webb and G. D. H. Cole. These writers were influenced by varieties of socialist thought (such as Christian socialism, Fabianism, Marxism). They sought connections with other developing fields of the social sciences and attempted to answer big questions of causality such as the causes of the English Revolution or the Industrial Revolution. They also sought answers to contemporary moral and political questions through interrogating the past. Tawney argued against piling up statistics and facts, advocating the need to consider the moral questions and relationships that underlay economic activity. Tawney held the first chair in Economic History at LSE (from 1931). His best-known work *Religion and the Rise of Capitalism* (1926) challenged the Weber thesis that the rise of capitalism in western Europe was spurred by the social and economic values of Calvinism. Tawney argued that Calvinism provided a religious rationale for capitalism and that both Puritanism and capitalism were perversions of Christian values, which favoured social obligation over individualism. Tawney wore his moral position on his sleeve and his interpretation of the capitalist ethic and other subjects was the focus of intense debate over many decades.

A second strain within economic history at this time might be termed the empirical and conservative: characterized by an economic focus, underdeveloped cultural or political context and a disinterest in formulating theories or laws about cause or effect. The approach was also often marked by an interest in collecting and analysing quantitative data. In different ways the works of Sir John Clapham, Herbert Heaton, A. P. Wadsworth and J. de L. Mann fall into this tradition. Clapham produced a three-volume *Economic History of Modern Britain* (1926–38), which used a range of evidence to study sectors of the economy in detail. He rejected the term 'industrial revolution' because he uncovered just how gradual and partial change was at the time. He also challenged the socialist and moral tradition by suggesting that, with the exception of a few dying trades, living conditions improved for the masses during industrialization.

The early 20th century expansion of economic history took place at a time when sociology and anthropology were joining economics in becoming less concerned with historical study and focusing more upon contemporary studies and fieldwork. Economic history expanded to fill the void left by the increasingly present-centred nature of the other social sciences. The subject at this time was generally conceived as a broadly based branch of historical enquiry that took in social as well as strictly economic events and conditions and had a broad definition of the economic sphere. This was also true of the subject in France and Germany, and because of this it had a wide appeal, not just as a university subject, but amongst a lay readership. In Britain it was popular in university extension studies classes and in courses run by the Workers Educational Association. Most economic historians wrote accessible books and pamphlets in a non-technical style and for a popular as well as an academic audience. *Religion and the Rise of Capitalism* had total sales running into six figures and was translated into several languages.

13.4 The history of economic history: The 1950s and 1960s

By the 1950s economic history as an identifiable academic discipline had largely fallen into the hands of the Clapham tradition marked most obviously and perhaps surprisingly by the succession of T. S. Ashton to Tawney's chair at LSE. Ashton was a conservative, not a socialist. His work nevertheless remained accessible and widely read. His bestseller *The Industrial Revolution* (1948) was written for a general readership in the *Oxford Home Library of Knowledge* series. However, the subject was changing in the 1940s and 1950s to incorporate more theoretical insight from contemporary economics, especially economic development and trade cycle theory. This resulted in some classic studies of trade cycles (following a pattern set by N. D. Kondratieff and Joseph Schumpeter in the 1920s and 1930s) and of the composition of GNP in different phases of economic growth (seen most obviously in Britain in the work of Phyllis Deane and W. A. Cole).[6] In addition, many worthy studies of particular industries or sectors of the economy appeared, such as Peter Mathias on brewing and Donald Coleman on paper.[7] There was a growing tendency at this time to see the experiences of western, and specifically British, industrialization as a model that could throw light upon solutions to third-world development problems, illustrated most clearly in the work of W. W. Rostow.[8] The 1950s onwards also saw the development of 'business history'. Large firms commissioned historians to write their histories, and classic works appeared, such as Charles Wilson on Unilever, Donald Coleman on Courtaulds and Theo Barker on Pilkington.[9] This development created a bias in research in favour of successful and wealthy firms and, because the firms themselves had often financed the research, it tended to encourage interpretations favourable to big business.

The moral and socialist tradition also continued strongly, however. The British Marxist historians were at this time writing a parallel theoretically informed set of socio-economic histories, seen in the work of Maurice Dobb, Eric Hobsbawm, Christopher Hill, Rodney Hilton, Edward Thompson, Victor Kiernon and others. Work of great interest and excitement was produced in the 1960s and 1970s, its popularity bolstered by the political climate and youth culture. Many of these books sold thousands of copies outside the realm of academe and they were internationally very important. A succession of books by Eric Hobsbawm about international economic change have sold in their hundreds of thousands across the globe since the 1960s.[10] Stress upon the pivotal role of the economy in impelling change, however strongly mediated by social and cultural factors and by human agency, made the work of Hilton, Hill, Hobsbawm and Thompson required reading on all undergraduate economic history courses. Political cleavages in the subject during these decades created acrimonious and lively debate in the pages of learned academic journals on topics such as the rise of the gentry and the rise of capitalism (debates carried over from Tawney's writings); the standard of living and the threat of political insurrection during the Industrial Revolution; the causes and impact of imperialism. This led many young scholars, including myself, to believe that they had chosen the most exciting subject possible. Partly because of the influence of Marxist social historians, such as E. P. Thompson, but also because of the general expansion of social science in these years, much economic history, Marxian or not, incorporated a great deal of social history and some cultural history, particularly where this had a materialist basis. This was seen particularly in histories of social protest, labour and social conditions, trades unions and class. Much of it was written 'from below' – that is, from the perspective of working people rather than the elites.

13.5 The 'new economic history'

A major turning point in economic history came with the so-called 'new economic history' of the 1960s and 1970s, also referred to as econometric history. Economic history had always had a strong quantitative bent, but this became more sophisticated, using not just tables, graphs and figures better to display the character of data, but also employing statistical analysis to consider trends and the relationship between the movements of different variables. The big change occurred as more historians became convinced of the gains to be delivered by marrying the statistical approach with the formal deductive methods of neo-classical economics and applying these to economic circumstances and choices in the past. This arose first in the United States, where economic history had always retained very close connections with economics, having developed as a university subject largely within economics departments. Economics at this time was becoming more confident and assertive in formal model building, and statistical inference as its cutting-edge method of choice, and many economic historians were infected by this enthusiasm. The most vigorous exponents of econometric history claimed it would eventually provide definitive answers to many of the most fundamental questions asked by economic historians. The implication was that this would put history back upon the objective or scientific path from which it had mistakenly wandered.

The 'new economic history', and quantitative history more generally, were aided by increasing use of computer technology. This not only facilitated the production of graphs, tables and statistical breakdowns, but also enabled more advanced model building, interpolations and simulations such as back-projection, and counterfactual developments. 'Model building' refers to the construction of a simplified and abstracted set of economic relationships intended to represent the functioning of an economy or a sector of the economy. Such models have been used many times in the study of the British and American economies in the nineteenth and twentieth centuries and in studies of sectors such as railways and cotton. 'Back-projection' is the estimation of what growth rates or other measures might have been for periods where figures do not exist, by extrapolating on the basis of later periods where figures do exist. For example, Wrigley and Schofield's study of English population growth projected population figures from the 1851 Census back into the 18th century to calculate the shortfall in parish registrations.[11] Although counterfactual propositions are implicit in many historical arguments, 'counterfactual history' is the most controversial technique in econometric history. It involves calculation of the advantages of an historical innovation by comparing economic growth in the presence of the innovation with economic growth in the absence of the innovation (the latter estimated by building up a counterfactual model of the economy in the absence of the innovation). The groundbreaking work here was R. W. Fogel's *Railways and American Economic Growth* (1964). In this, Fogel constructed a model of what the US economy might have looked like in 1890 if railways had never existed. By comparing this with the actual economy in that year, he demonstrated that the role of railways in American economic growth had been grossly overstated.

13.6 Achievements and problems of econometric history

The major achievements of econometric history in the 1960s and 1970s lay in highlighting new lines of enquiry, creating new data sets and growth indices and in disturbing old impressionistically based assumptions. But there were many problems. The new economic history was usually highly reductive, numerical and laden with jargon, making it difficult for non-specialists to read or understand. This resulted in a group of econometricians writing largely for each other and with little regard for the rest of the historical establishment, a strong contrast with the accessible and popular nature of most branches of economic history in earlier decades.

The first wave of econometric history also frequently failed to be sufficiently critical of the reliability of the quantitative evidence that it used. Historians often got carried away with enthusiasm for the techniques and forgot to pay sufficient attention to the shortcomings of their sources. An additional problem lay in the fact that the models and methods of econometrics involve efforts to quantify (and reduce to a monetary value) things for which this is difficult, if not impossible – for example, changes in opportunities, social conditions and intellectual horizons, the quality of goods, the advantages of increased leisure. This brought much criticism from conventional historians, as did the fact that much of the new economic history made historically dubious assumptions about human behaviour on the basis of the universalist claims of neo-classical economics. Neo-classical models assume that people will always act to optimize their economic position (the so-called rationality postulate) and that prices have the power to convert individual choices into an efficient productive system. But the rationality postulate is impossible to apply to all societies in all times. The possibilities of individual rational choice are affected by many circumstances: by power relationships as well as by the degree of information to which economic agents have access (hence their expectations) and by their cognitive ability in processing such information. Rational choice theory will always be prone to challenge, particularly in analysing societies with poor information flows, devolved power structures, forceful customary arrangements and low levels of literacy and education. In past societies, it may have been more rational for individuals to act to maximize the economic position of the village, the estate or the extended family than the individual or nuclear family, or not to maximize at all. Sufficiency may be more important in cultures and contexts where mortality is high and disease rife and/or where there are few consumer goods available. In such circumstances leisure rather than wealth is likely to be the prized possession.

Furthermore, the efficiency of the price system depends upon a competitive environment and upon the efficient flow of capital, labour, raw materials, finished goods and information. Competitive regimes of production and exchange and the efficient flow of factors, goods and services are much less prevalent in earlier societies and in non-western cultures than they are today in Britain and the United States. The new economic history often erred in applying concepts and models anachronistically and without due regard for different cultural contexts. Furthermore, the econometric models that were constructed in this era were often derisively simplistic and easy to criticize. They depended upon a limited number of variables in relatively straightforward combinations: the first wave of econometric history was insufficiently self-critical and too ambitious to recognize the technical limits of the tools available at the time.

Econometric history was never the dominant approach in Britain, and certainly not in Europe or elsewhere in the world outside of the United States. It did, however, capture the high ground of economic history in the latter, and its proponents were forceful and influential in exporting their product to Europe. They also produced some thought-provoking and controversial work influencing the subject beyond the boundaries of their own techniques. Probably less than one in ten British economic historians were directly involved with econometrics (even fewer in Europe), but the association of economic history with such positivistic and frequently flawed scientific method contributed to a decline in the popularity of the subject. It was responsible for associating economic history with a much narrower set of methods and sphere of interest than had been the case earlier, and a disinterest in broader social, cultural and political issues.

13.7 Economic history since the 1980s: The rejection of Marxian analysis and the challenge of postmodernism and poststructuralism

In the 1970s and 1980s specialized areas of research within social and economic history emerged, or were consolidated, such as urban history, agricultural history, transport history, labour history, business history, medical history, demographic history. This sub-disciplinary specialization produced important results. In business history, for example, the subject broadened out to include work using insurance records, bankruptcy hearings and oral evidence and other sources to look at smaller more typical firms. But specialization was also accompanied by a damaging compartmentalization that hindered understanding of historical processes in the round.[12] The separation of business history from labour history created obstacles to understanding, while urban history and agricultural history encouraged individual case studies rather than attempts to understand overall economic development. In the field of demography groundbreaking work appeared using many new techniques, but demography is generally defined to exclude discussion of sexual behaviour, sexuality or sexual desire! With one or two key exceptions, the need to understand long-term change in a holistic way slipped largely from the agenda and this left economic history vulnerable to criticism.

While the identification of economic history with econometric history had weakened potential interest in the subject, fragmentation into specialized fields undermined the identity of economic history and its integrative role. More importantly, the rejection of Marxian analysis as an underpinning intellectual force in the social sciences and in history also reduced the attraction of studying the economy. Concern to avoid any charge of economic or technological determinism, or any association with what popular opinion now sees as a discredited body of theory, contributed to a general and damaging disinterest in the relationship between the economy and the rest of society.

A further factor in the declining popularity of economic history since the 1980s is the influence of postmodernism, and general scepticism about positivistic historical and social-science explanations. This has been strong in the last two or three decades. The argument that academic disciplines, including history and economics, which purport to explain reality, should be viewed as discursive formations which promote some ideas and also constrain what is written and thought, has naturally undermined respect for approaches that do not much question their own concepts and language or their basic assumptions about an anterior reality. Economics and economic history can be seen as particularly vulnerable to these charges. The rejection of positivism, alongside the related expansion of new forms of cultural history, has involved a growing preference for literary, dramatic, symbolic and linguistic analyses and understandings over the mechanical analogies and structural models that lie at the heart of traditional social science and especially of economics. Linking phenomena to their causes and understanding their impact upon broader systems has been increasingly supplanted by the desire to relate actions to their sense and to study representations rather than 'reality'. Traditional forms of economics and of economic history have little obvious role to play in the new dispensation. But the subject is undergoing change, following innovations in economic theory, rediscovering some of its earlier, holistic preoccupations with society and culture and responding to the intellectual environment of the 21st century in rigorous ways.

13.8 Economics and history in the 21st century

The relationship between economic history and economic theory is shifting because economics is undergoing changes that make it potentially much more useful in historical applications. First, it is becoming a great deal more sophisticated in its assumptions about human motivations and the efficiency of markets, and in modelling the complex and differing circumstances that occur in the 'real world'. These developments are generally referred to as the new institutional economics.[13] Second, and much more radically, there are growing challenges to neo-classical formalism and rational choice theory arising from evolutionary approaches and a revival of the hermeneutic tradition. The preoccupations of economists are thus now more in line than they have been for many decades with those of economic historians. Such concerns include the varieties of market and non-market forms of exchange; gender relations in the formation of household decisions; 'irrational' behaviour; variation in the performance of firms and economies under similar sets of conditions; the structure of trade; the role of trust and reputation, custom and habit; economic horizons in risk taking and decision making; and issues concerning the quality of life as a measure of economic growth.

The importance of institutions and their impact upon contracts and transaction costs is now much more fully recognized than in the past. Institutions are sets of rules and understandings that parties in business and commerce observe in order to act more efficiently. Transaction costs are the expenses incurred in doing business, negotiating a deal and making sure that it is carried out. Historians have long been acutely aware of the importance of these elements, particularly when studying imperfect markets and the importance of customary and inflexible influences upon the adjustment of wages and prices. More attention is also now paid to asymmetric information where one party in a transaction knows more than the other. Such asymmetries are likely to have been more important in the past, especially in trade and in financial transactions. Reinforcing theories of asymmetric information is an acknowledgement of agency problems. Agency theory is concerned with how people get others to do what they want where there is asymmetric information and where incentives and monitoring will be required. Such circumstances characterized economic relationships in earlier times.[14]

The technical limits of economics have also been greatly extended, particularly in time-series analysis and general equilibrium modelling. This allows formal models to cope with many more variables and with more complex interactions. Multiple equilibria models and a much greater use of game theory characterize economic theorizing. Game theory explains the structure and logic of interpersonal inter-reactions and is fast becoming the mainstay of modern economic theory, particularly in relation to contracting and bargaining and in analysing institutions that develop in response to information asymmetries between parties to an exchange. This, together with the greater sophistication of rationality assumptions and the ability to allow for changing tastes and conventions, opens up the possibility of many new uses for economic theory in historical applications.

13.9 Economic history and economics: The challenge of alternative economics

Despite these developments, economists generally start with interests, of a profit-maximizing or 'rational' kind, and then move to take institutions and social behaviour into account, while sociologists, anthropologists and others generally start with society, culture and institutions, explaining how economic behaviour (oriented towards interests or utilities) is 'embedded', and can only be understood, within them. These approaches involve different understandings of human nature as well as different methodologies, and this limits the potential for integration. It is not just a question of deduction versus induction but also of formal mechanical analogies and instrumental reasoning versus hermeneutic understanding. Hermeneutics is the method of the cultural sciences, a method of interpreting human action in a similar way to studying the authenticity of a text. It is based on a dialogical (two-way, reciprocal) process of shared understandings between creator and interpreter. Important minority traditions in economics have always sought to engage with hermeneutics and there is currently a growing revival of alternative economics adopting evolutionary, institutional and cultural approaches, and seeking entirely to reform the purview of economics from within. Unlike the neo-classical paradigm (even in its most sophisticated forms) these alternatives place emphasis upon interpretative understanding of human behaviour and motivations, not upon the predictive success of formal logical models.

Evolutionary economics is very different from neo-classical economics because it sees economic systems to be in constant disequilibrium. This is much more applicable to most historical contexts than the neo-classical idea of economies and markets tending towards equilibrium. Evolutionary theory takes its cue from biological rather than mechanical analogies, and the economic, the social and the cultural are regarded as inseparable elements in an environment that is constantly changing. Evolutionary theory stresses the importance of habits and routines, analogous to memes in socio-biology. These evolve slowly as both the result and the cause of change in the environment. Routines are behaviours (including language use) that are conducted with little explicit thought. They create an institutional structure based upon continuous feedback from experience, which is rarely articulated. Such structures include the complex of socially learned and shared values, norms, beliefs, meanings, symbols, customs and standards that delineate the range of expected and accepted behaviour in a particular context.

Various hermeneutic approaches to economics take this emphasis upon institutions further to suggest that the economic behaviour of individuals cannot be adequately understood (as in conventional economics) as a kind of automatic reaction to objective stimuli; it must instead be understood in terms of an individual's *reading* of prices, opportunities, relative costs and so on. In other words, priority must be given to the social environment and to the inster-subjective ways in which people make sense of the world and its stimuli and communicate that sense one to another. This approach has the potential to revolutionize economics by suggesting that what really counts in economic explanation is not empirical verification or falsification (the traditional approach), but narrative and hermeneutic acceptability. Such an approach to economics gives history a new set of tools that are compatible with the cultural and linguistic turn. Stress upon the importance of the habitual, the everyday and unconscious routines in the material life of individuals, families and communities, is becoming a stronger current in socio-historical research. The habits of mind which are stressed as well as routines, social arrangements and organizations make the 'economic' workable, invest it with meanings, rules, sanctions, and give it both durability and a capacity for change.

13.10 Economic history: Contrasting examples and a conclusion

We finally consider two books that illustrate the enormous contrast in style and method characteristic of economic history and the shifts in approaches to the subject over time. *Time on the Cross: The Economics of American Negro Slavery*, by Robert Fogel and Stanley Engerman, appeared in 1974, at the height of the econometric revolution. It is the best-known example of the new economic history of the period. The work appeared in two volumes, the second given over entirely to statistical evidence and methods.[15] Unlike Fogel's earlier book on the railroads, *Time on the Cross* is not a counter-factual study, but it employs neo-classical models and statistical analysis to demonstrate that slavery was more successful and efficient than the contemporary agricultural system based on free labour. Fogel and Engerman argue that, as a result, slavery provided a high standard of living for all southerners, including slaves. They argue that planters in the mid-19th century were a rational and humane group and that slaves were fairly prosperous and generally well treated. Slaves had both the capacity and the drive for upward social and economic mobility. They worked harder and more efficiently than free farm labourers and adopted a work ethic and style of family life similar to their capitalist employers. Slaves learned to respond to a range of economic incentives, to seek extra income, leisure and occupational advance through cooperation and identification with the economic interests of their masters. Fogel and Engerman call this 'the record of black achievement under adversity'. They also 'prove' that slavery had not ceased to be profitable to owners at the time of the US Civil War, as several historians had previously argued. Their main sources are quantitative: plantation records of trade, slave output, profit and loss, coupled with census schedules for demographic evidence and probate data.

The main claim made by Fogel and Engerman is that traditional historians of slavery had had to rely upon the unsystematic use of fragmentary literary sources. The bulk of quantifiable data was beyond their reach because they had lacked the assistance of computers and the mathematical and statistical training for quantitative analysis. The fact that quantitative data is frequently as unsystematic and fragmentary as any other sort of evidence is swept under the carpet. This point is neatly illustrated in the debate between Fogel and Engerman and their critics on the subject of the whipping of slaves. Fogel and Engerman have a sophisticated argument about the role of punishments vis-à-vis incentives in slave labour discipline, but it is largely based upon quantitative data from just one set of plantation records, which cover a two-year period. Their source is almost certainly unrepresentative but, more importantly, their conclusions ignore the deterrent and fear elements of physical punishments, which are difficult, if not impossible to quantify. This is symptomatic of a wider problem of privileging the importance of quantifiable over non-quantifiable evidence. They also confuse what is from what ought to be, assuming society operated on market principles, and arguing backwards from the outcomes of social and market processes in order to comment upon the motives and actions of individuals who participated in them, whether masters or slaves. There is no place in their analysis for masters who raped or partnered slave women at the risk of upsetting labour discipline, who owned more slaves than they could employ efficiently and who behaved irrationally in other ways such as by abusing slaves for racist rather than efficiency reasons. The most fundamental assumption of the work, and the one that remains a weakness at the heart of the analysis, is whether an economic system that had slavery at its core can justifiably be analysed in the same way as a capitalist economy using free labour. Are concepts such as 'economic exploitation' and 'economic efficiency' appropriate? Can neo-classical analysis really be applied to systems of involuntary servitude? Critics suggested that prejudice had resulted in the selective use of evidence and that the resulting positive view of slavery and the motives of slave owners arose from the desire to make everything fit into a neo-classical model in which 'each and every slave owner regarded slaves solely as productive instruments and used them for a single transcendent purpose: the maximisation of pecuniary gain'.[16] *Time on the Cross* did, however, provoke extensive debate, stimulated new research that considerably advanced our knowledge of slavery, and forced later historians to be much more explicit about theoretical and ideological assumptions, as well as about the nature and use of sources.

Craig Muldrew's, *The Economy of Obligation: The Culture of Credit and Social Relations in Early Modern England* (1998) is an example of recent economic history in which the economic, the social and the cultural meld together. Muldrew's aim is to write a social history of the market, arguing that markets have not been interpreted culturally because of the dominant influence of anachronistic neo-classical economic analysis:

> the relationship between economic theory and history needs to be reversed, so that a thickly researched historiography of the complex motivations and practices of agents – together with an understanding of how they themselves interpreted such actions – [can] inform future theory, rather than the other way round.[17]

Muldrew combines the sources and methods of community history used by social and economic historians with the practices of intellectual history, which look closely at the interactions and interpretations of contemporary texts. His sources include instructional pamphlets on the use of credit, letters, diaries and autobiographies, as well as court records and a range of account books, tax, probate and other evidence, which enables him to describe the trading activities and social structure of King's Lynn (the focus of his research) in some detail. He examines the cultural meaning of credit and how this changed under the impact of the expanding economy of the later 16th century. He places emphasis upon trust and household reputation and the importance of sociability and neighbourliness in understanding the nature of 'economic' transactions. He is interested in the cultural representation of trust and credit in the literature of the period, as well as in social practices. His concern is to examine economic motivation in the terms that contemporaries understood it.

Muldrew analyses the cultural changes that accompanied the expansion of the market and the proliferation of credit based upon personal trust and the reputation of individuals and families. Households became more dependent on one another through complex networks of exchange, credit and obligation. The combination of competition and dependence this involved meant that families and neighbourhoods increasingly had to try to find a balance between hospitality, reciprocity and charity on the one hand, and thrift and profit on the other. Both were needed to keep the economy expanding and thus to ensure the financial security of both households and the wider society. Muldrew demonstrates that the practice of litigation in debt cases reflected the equality embodied in contemporary social theories of bargaining and market exchange. The book concludes by considering the impact of subsequent economic change in altering the way in which the ethics of markets are now understood. By extending his thoughts to the present and by uncovering a complex economy very different from our own, Muldrew raises questions about our contemporary perceptions of the economy. The entire analysis is innovative in considering representations and understandings as well as actions, in combining cultural and economic history, and in using the skills and sources of literary analysis and intellectual history, as well as more conventional economic history. It is no accident that Muldrew did not train as an economic historian but as a social and cultural historian with an interest in economic activity and behaviour. This frees him from the tendency to seek conventional neo-classical explanations. While Fogel and Engerman's work was groundbreaking in showing the limits as well as the possibilities of the application of neo-classical models to historical debates, Muldrew's analysis resonates with the broader approach to the economy and with the political and moral commitment that characterises earlier generations of economic histoians. His work reflects the current move among a wider array of historians to study the economy in diverse and innovative ways.

The future for economic history looks bright because it is able to draw upon a wider and more sophisticated range of economy theory and method than in the past and because it is redefining the economic sphere in broader terms and for its own purposes, eschewing the disciplinary boundaries erected by modernism. It is placing new stress upon the cultural, social and institutional framework of economic activity and it is drawing increasingly upon the tools of anthropology, ethnography and cultural history, alongside economics, to analyse those aspects of material life that conventional economists have rarely reached.

Guide to further reading

D. C. Coleman, *History and the Economic Past: An Account of the Rise and Decline of Economic History in Britain* (London, 1987).

N. F. R. Crafts, 'Cliometrics 1971–86: A Survey', *Journal of Applied Econometrics* 2(1987), pp. 171–92.

S. Cullenberg, J. Ameriglio and D. F. Ruccio (eds), *Postmodernism, Economics and Knowledge* (London, 2001).

G. Hodgson, *Economics and Evolution: Bringing Life Back into Economics* (London, 1993).

G. Hodgson, *How Economics Forgot History: The Problem of Historical Specificity in Social Science* (London, 2001).

Pat Hudson, *History by Numbers* (London, 2000), Chapter 8.

Alon Kadish, *Historians, Economists and Economic History* (London, 1989).

Harvey J. Kaye, *The British Marxist Historians* (London, 1984).

Don Lavoie (ed.), *Economics and Hermeneutics* (London, 1990).

John S. Lyons, Louis P. Cain and Samuel H. Williamson eds, *Reflections on the Cliometrics Revoution.* Conversations with Economic Historians (Routledge, 2008)

J. Maloney, *What's New in Economics?* (Manchester, 1992).

M. Rutherford, *Institutions in Economics* (Cambridge, 1994).

Notes

1 D. C. Coleman, 'What is Economic History?', *History Today* 35(2) (1985), pp. 35–43.
2 M. M. Postan, *The Medieval Economy and Society* (London, 1972).
3 W. Cunningham, *The Growth of English Industry and Commerce* (Cambridge, 1882).
4 M. Berg, 'The First Women Economic Historians', *Economic History Review* 45(2) (1992), pp. 308–29.
5 D. C. Coleman analyses these distinctive strains in a slightly different way in *History and the Economic Past: An Account of the Rise and Decline of Economic History in Britain* (Oxford, 1987).
6 P. Deane and W. A. Cole, *British Economic Growth, 1688–1959* (London, 1969).
7 P. Mathias, *The Brewing Industry in England, 1700–1830* (Cambridge, 1959); D. C. Coleman, *The British Paper Industry 1495–1860: A Study in Industrial Growth* (Oxford, 1958).
8 W. W. Rostow, *The Stages of Economic Growth* (Cambridge, 1960)
9 C. Wilson, *The History of Unilever: A Study of Economic Growth and Social Change* (London, 1954); D. C. Coleman, *Courtaulds: An Economic and Social History*, 3 vols (Oxford, 1969); T. C. Barker, *Pilkington Brothers and the Glass Industry* (London, 1960).
10 Starting with *The Age of Revolution, 1789–1848* (New York, 1962) the sequence includes *Industry and Empire* (London, 1968); *The Age of Capital, 1848–1875* (London, 1975); *the Age of Empire, 1875–1914* (New York, 1987) and *The Age of Extremes: The Short 20th century, 1914–1991* (New York, 1994).
11 E. A. Wrigley and R. Schofield, *The Population History of England, 1541–1871* (Cambridge, 1981).
12 For critiques of this specialization, see Keith Wrightson, 'The Enclosure of English Social History', in A. Wilson (ed.), *Rethinking Social History* (Manchester, 1993); J. D. Marshall, *The Tyranny of the Discreet* (Aldershot, 1997).
13 See O. Williamson, *The Economic Institutions of Capitalism* (New York, 1985). For an example of the potential of some institutional perspectives when applied to long-term economic change, see D. C. North, *Institutional Change and Economic Performance* (Cambridge, 1990); for

indications of their impact upon micro-theory in relation to historical applications, see Avner Grief, 'Micro-theory and Recent Developments in the Study of Economic Institutions through Economic History', in M. Kreps and K. F. Wallis (eds), *Advances in Econometrics and Economics: Theory and Applications*, Vol. 2 (Cambridge, 1997), pp. 79–113.

14 For examples of historical work employing informational asymmetry and agency theory, see A. Carlos and S. Nicholas, 'Agency Problems in Early Chartered Companies: The Case of the Hudson's Bay Company', *Journal of Economic History* 50(4) (1990), pp. 853–75; D. Sunderland, 'Principals and Agents: The Activities of the Crown Agents for the Colonies, 1880–1914', *Economic History Review* 52(2) (1999), pp. 284–306.

15 A second major work was published by Fogel in 1989, partly in response to the wave of criticism that followed *Time on the Cross*. This was accompanied by three companion volumes of technical papers written by various collaborators who had been working with Fogel since 1985.

16 Paul A. David *et al., Reckoning with Slavery. A Critical Study of the Quantitative History of American Negro Slavery* (New York, 1976), p. 341.

17 Craig Muldrew, *The Economy of Obligation: The Culture of Credit and Social Relations in Early Modern England* (London, 1998), pp. 7–8.

14

Intellectual history/history of ideas

Beverley Southgate

14.1 Introduction

The terms 'intellectual history' and 'history of ideas' are here used interchangeably.[1] Either way, the concept is elusive – potentially all-embracing, but perennially in danger of falling between any number of academic stools. Its all-embracing nature derives from its subject matter as the history of thought. That can include the history of philosophy, of science, of religious, political, economic or aesthetic ideas, and indeed the history of anything at all that has ever emerged from the human intellect. But such wide-ranging terrain can prove hazardous: it is hard to confine and locate neatly within the conventional departmental boundaries of academia, or even the regimented shelves of libraries and bookshops. The subject and its practitioners defy the constraints of disciplinary structures.

That defiance is not always approved by those academic frontier guards who strive to keep their sanitized domains free from external intrusions, but it can claim a thoroughly respectable pedigree. Able to trace its ancestry back at least as far as Aristotle, the subject quite properly exemplifies the ancient Greek ideal of universality. For Aristotle himself, philosophy comprised science, politics, ethics, aesthetics, rhetoric, poetry, history – in fact, anything to do with 'wisdom', or anything that might excite our 'wonder'; and historians of ideas can be seen as Aristotle's intellectual heirs in the breadth of their concerns.

Indeed, for the intellectually adventurous, the subject's academic promiscuity can constitute a major attraction, for while retaining its core concern with history and the historical, it is necessarily involved with many other areas, on which it draws both for procedures and for evidence. Literature, for example, whether poetry or prose, provides some of the most important source material for the study of ideas: one cannot study the thought of classical antiquity without reference to Greek tragedy; nor can one exclude Shakespeare from a consideration of ideas in the English Renaissance. Linguistics, too, makes a vital contribution. As the rhetorical and politically infused nature of historical (as of any other) writing is increasingly appreciated, the analysis of language, and its forms and uses and effects, plays an increasingly important role in what is inevitably a largely text-based study; while the 'linguistic turn' encourages reassessments, as it does in all humanities subjects as they come to terms with postmodernity. Other important inputs come from psychology and anthropology, but the history of ideas' most obviously close relation is philosophy. Indeed, while anglophone philosophers (especially in the mid-20th century) focused narrowly on the linguistic aspects of philosophical problems, their chronological contextualization remained the preserve of intellectual historians, and although the history of philosophy has now taken off as a separate subject, there remains considerable overlap of interest.

While historians of ideas may take some credit for injecting more historicity into traditional philosophy, they can also be seen as the vanguard for introducing more explicit conceptualization into conventional history. That has not always been welcomed by social, political, economic or so-called 'proper' historians. These characteristically emphasize the empirical aspects of their discipline, and some have continued determinedly to profess their lack of concern with 'conceptual' or 'theoretical' issues. Geoffrey Elton was one eminent historian who believed that infection from 'the virus' of theory was particularly likely to emanate from the history of ideas, as being a subject that was 'by its very nature ... liable to lose contact with reality'.[2] But such 'reality', of course, is itself culturally determined, and so liable to the flux of fashion, and it is noteworthy that the history of 'mentalities', and intellectual history more generally, are now widely accepted categories within historical study and find a home within university history departments.

14.2 Antecedents and precursors

Paternity of the history of ideas is often attributed to the American Arthur Lovejoy in the 1930s. Lovejoy's approach, of attempting to identify what he called 'unit ideas' and trace their development through time, has long been out of fashion. But his basic aim of uncovering our own foundational ideas, his stress on the psychological factors involved in the acceptance and retention of such ideas, and his interest in the multivocality of language as facilitating intellectual change, remain of continuing relevance; and he can importantly take credit for the foundation in 1940 of the enduring *Journal of the History of Ideas*.

But it is possible, of course, to trace back ancestry almost indefinitely; and in this case the buck certainly does not stop before Aristotle. In the opening to his book entitled *Metaphysics*, Aristotle gave a synopsis of earlier philosophies, before embarking on his own. He thus provided an invaluable source for pre-Socratic thought, but he also incidentally bequeathed a model for much subsequent intellectual history. In the first place, that history was essentially 'whiggish', in the sense of showing a progressive development designed to culminate in the work of Aristotle's own good self. In the second place, it indicated a 'canon' – a measure by which philosophers could be assessed – so that the work of some could be seen as significant in the narrative as proposed, while others were firmly relegated to the role of inconsequential 'minor' figures. 'No-one', Aristotle categorically asserted, 'would think it fit to include Hippo', for example, in a list of significant philosophers, 'because of the paltriness of his thought';[3] and condemned by that unilateral assessment, Hippo's historical fate was effectively sealed. And subsequent histories of ideas – whether philosophical, scientific or political – have often tended to conform to that Aristotelian model, presenting a progressive development, and focusing on those who are supposedly 'truly great', or who conform to the rules of what Nietzsche referred to as the 'permitted sagacity' of any given time.

Histories of ideas have thus often replicated the approach of historiography more generally, and presented a triumphalist, progressive account of intellectual developments, centred on a team of canonical figures, passing the torch of increasing enlightenment 'from hand to hand – from Descartes to Locke, from Locke to Hume, and from Hume to Kant',[4] and so on, as if (in Milan Kundera's analogy) they were all in 'a relay-race in which everyone surpasses his predecessor, only to be surpassed by his successor'.[5]

That approach was, until comparatively recently, particularly evident in the history of science, where the notion of a cumulative progression remains, perhaps, most understandable. From early modernity and the significantly entitled Enlightenment on, the usually preferred narrative projected an ascent – from antiquity, through the darkness of the Middle Ages, up to the Scientific Revolution. Thus, from his vantage point spearheading the new philosophy, Francis Bacon could confidently explain that, in his review of past developments, 'neither the Arabians nor the [mediaeval] Schoolmen need be mentioned'.[6] They were to him, as Hippo had been to Aristotle, irrelevant to his progressive narrative, so could safely be consigned to oblivion.

By the end of the 17th century, Bacon's progressive narrative could be seen to culminate in the intellectual synthesis of Isaac Newton. Whereas previously, in the words of Pope's intended epitaph, 'Nature and Nature's laws lay hid in night,/God said, "Let Newton be!" and all was light.' And, after him, it was just a question of the progressive assimilation of his methods into other intellectual areas – from physics to biology, to psychology and sociology.

That optimistic approach continues in such 19th-century intellectual histories as those of J. W. Draper, who saw progress exemplified by the gradual erosion of religious superstitions at the hands of rationality and science. Even from early Greek intellectual developments, he concludes, 'we learn that there is a definite mode of progress for the mind of man; [and] from the history of later times we shall find that it is ever in the same direction'. A study of history reveals that 'there is a predetermined, a solemn march, in which all must join, ever moving, ever resistlessly advancing'.[7]

For all its imposed tidiness, such a progressive narrative sweep did, however, have its disadvantages. In particular, it took no account of anything that failed to fit its own model of 'rationality' and science; so that whole theories and intellectual movements were relegated, like Hippo and the Arabs, to the historically irrelevant, and individual human beings suffered amputations as they were forced into a Procrustean mould. Thus, for example, the 'vortex theory' of Descartes (his attempted explanation of the universe in terms of atomic particles) was shunted down a siding, as a part of his philosophy that could safely be forgotten; and the more mystical aspects of Newton's thought (including his extensive writings on theology and belief in his own links with an ancient tradition) were ignored, or even more positively suppressed, as being anomalous aberrations and inexplicable in a man of his accepted intellectual stature.

If 19th-century historians (like those of all other periods) tended to reflect the values of their time, they nonetheless left some impressive achievements in the field of intellectual history. Draper's work cited above incorporates a huge range of research, including what we would now refer to as history of the sciences and of technology, history of philosophy, theology and maritime discoveries, and digressions on such subjects as Buddhism, Egyptian medicine and the social condition of America. In his two-volume *History of European Morals from Augustus to Charlemagne*, W. E. H. Lecky similarly sweeps authoritatively over a vast range of historical material, as is indicated in his modestly stated, but hugely ambitious, aim 'simply to trace the action of external circumstances upon morals, to examine what have been the moral types proposed as ideal in different ages, in what degree they have been realized in practice, and by what causes they have been modified, impaired, or destroyed'. With that agenda, Lecky's intellectual history necessarily focuses on developments in philosophy and theology, but the whole is set in a socio-political context; and it concludes with a lengthy and sympathetic discussion of 'The Position of Women', which anticipates by a hundred years the development of more formal 'women's history'. Although currently largely ignored, then, Draper and Lecky can, in a number of ways, be seen as important 19th-century precursors of the history of ideas.

So too can Leslie Stephen, who published his *History of English Thought in the 18th Century* in 1876. Taking the history of philosophy as his starting point, he again ranges widely over the history of thought, noting that such 'intellectual history' (a term he actually uses) cannot be properly studied in isolation but needs to take account of social influences, political applications and literary expressions. The wider breadth implied by the description 'history of thought' is re-emphasized a generation later by J. T. Merz. In his four-volume *A History of European Thought in the 19th Century*, he starts from the history of science, but aspires to answer the much wider question of 'what part … the inner world of Thought [has] played in the history of our [19th] century'. For him, too, thought embraces much more than just philosophy; and he notes how the 'history of philosophy has little to say about Goethe', though the poet expresses 'probably the deepest thought of modern times', with his character of Faust embodying nothing less than 'the classical expression of 19th-century doubts and aspirations'.[8]

That evaluation of Goethe might stand as a challenge even to 21st-century historiography, as does Merz's perceptive observation that, in future times, 'the objectivity on which some … [contemporary historians] pride themselves will be looked upon not as freedom from but as unconsciousness on their part of the preconceived notions which have governed them'.[9] The articulation of such insights, then, long pre-dated postmodernist challenges to historical 'objectivity', and these 19th-century examples confirm that the history of ideas by no means sprang fully formed from the head of Arthur Lovejoy. Numerous historians, biographers and philosophers had contributed to a tradition of intellectual history, or the history of thought (including especially philosophy), from the time of classical antiquity, through the early modern period and into the 20th century.

14.3 Theory 1: Aims and purposes

The theoretical aims and purposes of history of ideas (as of most other humanities subjects) tend to be couched in platitudinous terms. What looms large in such self-justificatory mission-statements is 'understanding', which can be applied to an author or a text, to the wider cultural environment or to the individual self. As Mark Bevir has recently written, 'Historians of ideas want to make intelligible the way someone else has made the world intelligible; they want to *understand* how someone else has understood things.'[10] And that will sometimes involve an attempt to understand how people in the past have 'understood' things very differently from us, embracing beliefs that seem to us 'irrational' or mutually inconsistent (as with Newton and his mystical theories relating to theology and chronology).

'Understanding' of historical texts will be considered in section 14.4, but first let us briefly note the claims that the history of ideas can contribute to a more generalized understanding of our cultural environments, and hence of our own good selves. The very term 'cultural environment' is, of course, hugely problematic. It seems to imply a homogeneous background against which various cultural forms, such as philosophy, literature, art and music, are produced, with the further implication that there will be something shared by all those forms, since they each constitute an expression of something experienced in common. They will all, it has been claimed, express the 'spirit of their time', or provide physical manifestations of that almost mystical, and certainly elusive, entity, the 'zeitgeist'. The quest for that idealized construction has, again, long been out of fashion; but that is not to deny that various cultural manifestations might share some qualities, and that an examination of those qualities might provide some insight into the period in which they were produced.

It might also provide insight into how cultural and intellectual change occurs, so that historians of science, for example, have been concerned to account for such modifications in 'world-view' as that occasioned by the early modern Copernican Revolution in cosmology; while historians of political theory have considered turning points such as that articulated in the works of Machiavelli. In examples of this kind, attention has to be paid to the replacement of one intellectual framework (or 'paradigm', or web of what has become 'customary'), and its associated linguistic structures, by another. The history of ideas thus inevitably broadens out again to encompass a potentially infinite range of study, but can profitably focus on how individuals respond to intellectual challenges and are able (or unable) to adapt and modify and replace their systems of belief.

The point of it all, though, is not to set out in pursuit of some holy grail, or redeeming essence, or even to trace assumed connections in the service of some moral or aesthetic goal. It is rather to demonstrate contingency – to show that it, and therefore we, could have been quite different from what it is and what we are. That is to say, cultural environments and the individuals that inhabit them are to be understood as historical entities (however different from ourselves). They – and we – are derived from earlier forms, and are subject to being succeeded by other later ones; and both those forms themselves and the course of their succession could well have been quite otherwise. We may like to consolidate our own identities by ascribing to them antecedents that make the end result at least seem feasible, but more important is the resultant recognition of our own historicity – of the fact that we are ourselves a part of history, not only a product of past history but also a potential agent for history in the future.

And the history of ideas is an ideal vehicle for promoting such recognition, since it is concerned with the examination not simply of thoughts which have been expressed, but also with those attitudes and presuppositions which we all have, but which are so much a part of us that they may never be consciously formulated. The actual foundations of our thoughts don't need to be expressed:

they are precisely what is accepted as 'obvious', or as 'common-sense' at any given time, and therefore simply taken for granted. So the point of questioning those unarticulated foundations is to enhance our own self-awareness – our awareness of how and why we think (and therefore act and react) as we do. And that self-consciousness is central to what it means to be human. 'The unexamined life is not worth living', insisted Socrates, his mantra derived from the Delphic Oracle's perennially relevant instruction to 'Know thyself!'

Self-knowledge and a recognition of our own contingency can be fostered also through the examination of alternatives: by studying the ideas and beliefs of people in antiquity or the Middle Ages or in other cultures, for example, we are forced to confront situations and structures quite different from our own. So we come to realize that we could have had – and could have – altogether different values and aspirations from the ones we simply take for granted. Viewed from an alternative perspective, our own position no longer appears as inevitable and as the necessary outcome of some predetermined historical process. It is the result of numerous contingencies (of things that, by chance, turned out one way rather than another, and affected further events accordingly), and we can see that, for the future, we actually do have a choice.

Liberation from the constraints of tunnel vision, then, can be seen as an important aim of the history of ideas: the study of the past can be used creatively for the present and the future. Even in practical terms, the key to current problems may be there, awaiting rediscovery. Early modern thinkers, for example, utilized the newly recovered text of the Roman poet Lucretius in their formulation (or reformulation) of atomic theory, which came to underpin the new mechanical philosophy; the rediscovered text of Sextus Empiricus in the 16th century was enormously influential in the development of modern scepticism; and the inventor Barnes Wallis claimed to have got his inspiration for a spinning bomb in the Second World War from a 17th-century account of an attempt to fire a gun round corners. Aspects of the past, often long forgotten and ignored, await imaginative reintegration into our own syntheses.

14.4 Theory 2: Methods

How, then, do we set about attaining intellectual liberation and enlightenment? What methods can realize such ambitious aims?

The history of ideas is essentially a text-based study: its study of the past is centred on texts and their contexts – with varying relative emphasis on those two elements. 'Texts' may include works of art or architecture, or any artefact or even human gesture intended (or not) to express an idea; but for the most part, historians of ideas utilize literary sources, or written texts. They will therefore inevitably be confronted by the whole problematic issue of reading and interpreting and trying to understand those texts in relation to their (no less problematic) contexts.

It has often been assumed that, granted the exercise of due diligence and proper procedures, intellectual historians can penetrate to 'the meaning' of a text; but even the meaning of that 'meaning' has become the subject of dispute. Some literary critics have affirmed the need to ascertain 'intrinsic' meaning, through careful analysis of the text itself as an autonomous entity, without regard to any context; others have concentrated on the meaning as it now appears to us. But historians are primarily concerned with the meaning that the author originally intended the text to convey, so that they come to focus on intention. As Quentin Skinner has affirmed: 'to know what a writer *meant* by a particular work is to know what his primary *intentions* were in writing it'.[11]

To ascertain those intentions, and recover the truth of an author's meaning in its original context, has remained a main motive for historians through the modern era. As recently as 1990, Conrad Russell has written that 'the most important historical skill is that of putting information into context'. He goes on immediately to concede that 'the selection of the right context [sic] is one that requires very considerable knowledge',[12] but one might well ask how, even with an infinite amount of knowledge, an historian could possibly select *the* context that is 'right'. It can only be 'right' within another context, which is to say for a particular purpose; since only a few aspects of any totality can ever be selected, and selection must be based on some criteria. Skinner has suggested that the texts with which intellectual historians are likely to be concerned can be seen as interventions in arguments, as responses to some other text(s); so attempts at contextualization might start there. But those other texts are not necessarily contemporary, but can date to any period; so that again the context may be indefinitely extended. Indeed, the whole concept of 'context' remains highly problematic. Where do we stop? How do we determine the foreground and background (what is more important, and what less)? Is anything ever discrete, and separable from everything else?

Further difficulties, concerning the text itself, derive from considerations of language. Expressing and incorporating, as it must, the intellectual and socio-political power structures of its users, language (and so 'meaning') is itself subject to constant change through time. We may read words from the past, but do they mean the same to us as the author originally intended (assuming, against the odds, that authors succeed in expressing what they mean and intend only a single meaning anyway)? How do we ascertain their 'tone' – whether direct, or metaphoric, or ironic, or whatever? (The raised eyebrow may need to be sensed, if not seen.) What are we to make of words that refer to concepts we no longer even have, or believe in (such as the long-lived Aristotelian 'primum mobile', for instance)? And how are we to recognize and interpret those absences and silences, often more pregnant with meaning than our words, that punctuate our conversations and our texts? Do they denote a deliberate obfuscation, or refusal explicitly to concede an 'unacceptable' position, or a (possibly unconscious) personal indecision about the propriety of certain revelations? No language (neither its actual words, nor the manner of its usage) remains static through time, and any translation from one language to another (including translation from that of the past to that of our own in the present) inevitably involves some loss of meaning and of understanding.

If the 'meaning' of a text itself, together with its context, thus remains, in absolutist terms, impenetrable, we need to find some compromise. As with other forms of intellectual activity, we need to take a pragmatic stand that enables work and life to continue; and in history (as in science) that has generally been thought to imply a need to present tentative hypotheses of varying degrees of probability. While remaining aware of our inability ever to attain to a single 'true' meaning of a text, we might yet ask what it was that the text's author wished to convey. That, after all, is how we contrive to get around in real life, constantly evaluating the authenticity and reliability of witnesses and evidence by which we are confronted. So we can reasonably ask, in other words, what action the author of a text might have intended to be taken, as a result of what was presented (in the form of writing, painting, gesturing, or whatever).

Even that, of course, is by no means easy to answer: signals not infrequently convey ambiguous messages; and messages themselves may be less than decisive or consistent. As Wittgenstein noted, the person waving his arms in the distance may be trying to swat a fly or warn us of a dangerous bull; or, in Stevie Smith's poetic example, may be just waving, or drowning.[13] Or that waver may be signalling numerous other supposed 'meanings' – and not least his own inability to articulate coherently just what it is that he wishes to convey.

However, some knowledge of a context might help us to read the waver's actual intention (on the assumption that there is one). Maybe, for example, there are no bulls in the vicinity; and the swimmer is well within his depth. So, although there may be some residual texts where the recovery of *any* context will remain impossible, and although it will *never* be possible to recover any context in its entirety, it may yet be possible to unearth *some* context which throws light on the object of our study – which might, for instance, clarify that some ascribed intentions are anachronistic or anomalous within the belief structures of the time, while others cohere with contemporary debates. Our knowledge may not be perfect, but it enables us to get around in the world – at least to the extent of appropriately evading bulls and rescuing swimmers in danger of drowning, and reaching some tentative conclusions about the probable meaning of a text.

14.5 Practice 1: Richard H. Popkin, *The History of Scepticism*

Originally published in 1960, Richard H. Popkin's *History of Scepticism from Erasmus to Descartes* was revised and extended to carry on the story to Spinoza in 1979. It has proved to be a seminal work in the history of ideas, and illustrates in practice many of the theoretical points introduced above.

There had, of course, been some earlier recognition of the importance of sceptical philosophies, which had originated in ancient Greece and gained in influence after their recovery and development in the early-modern period. In the 18th century, Pierre Bayle had actually dated modern philosophy from the reintroduction of ancient Greek scepticism; Henry Buckle in 1858 had identified scepticism as the trigger for scientific investigation, religious toleration and political liberty; and Leslie Stephen in 1876 had noted how scepticism, as developed in particular by David Hume, 'marks one of the great turning-points in the history of thought'.[14] But it was still possible in the mid-20th century to write that '17th-century Pyrrhonism [scepticism] is a movement that has been almost completely neglected';[15] and there can be no doubt that Popkin's work stimulated a veritable academic industry, dealing as it did with a subject that can now be seen to have had increasingly obvious relevance in the context of postmodernity.

First, it is worth noting that Popkin early acknowledges his sympathy with the objects of his study – the sceptics: he is effectively on their side of the argument. He writes elsewhere of the sceptical crisis having 'become our permanent heritage', and clearly approves of a philosophy that exposes the absurdity 'of all our intellectual pretensions'. He also writes, significantly, of how 'we need all the insight we can garner from the past, so that we may yet have a future';[16] so it is clear that *The History of Scepticism* is to be a history of something that matters to its author – a history, not of some obscure and passing inconsequential intellectual fad, but of an essential and lasting ingredient of modern thought of which we need to be aware.

Popkin's opening chapter already illustrates further important points about the nature of the history of ideas as he sees it: its essentially interdisciplinary character; its inevitable fusing of the intellectual with the social and political; and its obvious relevance for our self-understanding in the present. By starting with 'the intellectual crisis of the Reformation', Popkin indicates how an intellectual trend can appear in one area of human experience – here theology – and ripple out from that to affect life much more generally. Luther's questioning of the authority of the Pope and Church Councils to arbitrate on matters of religious truth and doctrine constituted a highly significant challenge in its own right; for it raised doubts about the validity of what had for centuries simply been taken for granted, or presupposed as the norm. But the implications of that theological challenge were to prove much more widely unsettling: as Popkin puts it, Luther in 1519 opened a 'Pandora's box that … was to have the most far-reaching consequences, not just in theology but throughout man's entire intellectual realm' (*History of Scepticism*, p. 4).

What escaped from Pandora's box – what was lost for ever – was the confidence that people had in their institutions to validate 'the truth'. For better or worse, Luther's repudiation of theological authority was to leave individuals free to make their own judgements: in the assessment of truth, the sole criterion was to become the individual conscience. And if people were to be left to their own resources in matters of religion, why should not those resources be similarly utilized in the determination of matters moral, social and political?

Theologically induced scepticism could never be tidily confined to Sunday-morning church (nor even to the intellect), especially once its practical force was underpinned by theoretical justification; and Popkin goes on to show how it was just such underpinning that was provided by the rediscovery of (especially) Sextus Empiricus's account of Pyrrho's sceptical philosophy. The exact chronology of that reintroduction of the current of Greek scepticism into the western intellectual mainstream is disputed, and highlights one general difficulty in the history of ideas – namely, that of assigning influence. While the publication dates of such works as that of Sextus (in its various translations) can of course be ascertained, without direct references (in other works, or diaries, or letters), the extent of actual influence is harder to assess.

For there were other reasons for taking an interest in scepticism, and various motivations for prescribing that philosophy. Most importantly, perhaps, and showing again the interaction of ideas with wider cultural experiences, was the cultural relativism to which people were exposed in the wake of contemporary exploration and discovery. Awareness of alternative customs and values permeates the work of such writers as Michel de Montaigne – a man who is seldom included in histories of philosophy, but who is identified by Popkin as playing a prominent part in the transmission of sceptical philosophy; for not only did he read, assimilate and reformulate the thought of Sextus, but he also advocated scepticism as an encouragement to faith in Christianity. When all else is brought into doubt, he believed, one reverts to the certainties of religion.

Montaigne is one of many thinkers cited by Popkin who have never attained the respectability of inclusion in the philosophical canon, as being truly 'significant' in the history of philosophy; and in this respect *The History of Scepticism* shows how the history of ideas includes within its purview many who would slip through a historical net designed to catch only figures now considered 'major'. These lesser-known characters can be particularly difficult to assess, owing not least to the dearth of evidence (and its often contradictory nature) about them; and Popkin himself ponders the sincerity of some in making their sceptical outbursts. Can they, for example, have sincerely professed both to scepticism and to Christianity? Such questions can never be definitively answered, but historians of ideas, such as Popkin in this case, attempt to assess the characters of their subjects in the wider context of their lives, the style of their writings and the examples that they use to make their arguments; and they try (not least post-Foucault) especially to avoid imposing anachronistic categorizations and values on people in the past.

Montaigne himself, at all events, together with his later follower (another underrated thinker whose importance has been emphasized by Popkin) Pierre Bayle, favoured fideism – a lurch into faith as an escape from the torment of doubt. That may sound an unlikely ploy to us, but it becomes, as Popkin shows, one of the main ways in early modernity to circumvent the sceptical crisis and to accommodate seemingly incompatible intellectual demands. The other escape route was initiated by yet another often neglected figure, identified by Popkin as 'one of the most important figures in the history of modern thought', the French Minim monk, Marin Mersenne. At the centre of an intellectual circle embracing such luminaries as Descartes, Gassendi, Galileo and Hobbes, Mersenne was well placed to recognize the virtues of the so-called 'new philosophy' (embracing Copernican cosmology and mechanistic science); and his task became to reconcile these with the seemingly unanswerable arguments of the sceptical philosophy. The result was a form of 'mitigated' or 'constructive' scepticism that conceded the ultimate unknowability of nature's essences, but nonetheless pragmatically allowed some real and useful knowledge of their appearances. As with postmodernism, we may no longer lay claim to certainty based on unshakeable foundations, but we can adopt a common-sense approach which allows us to proceed on the basis of varying degrees of probability. Mersenne's science, like our history, is no description of reality, but a hypothetical structure that allows us to go on living and doing science and history. Subsequent attempts were made, notably by Descartes, to refute scepticism with alternative dogmatisms (and it is noteworthy in this context that the force of Descartes's anti-sceptical arguments has been illuminated by Popkin's work); but it was Mersenne's approach that came to constitute the core of pragmatic modern philosophy and science.

That pragmatism, deriving from a consciousness of our own limitations, is (or should surely be) accompanied by other virtues: namely, the 'Modesty … and Humility' identified by Hume as the necessary 'Result of Scepticism'. Popkin's approval of Hume, then, relates to more than a purely intellectual position. Hume, who contrived in John Leland's words to throw doubt even on 'what is so obvious and apparent to the common sense and reason of mankind',[17] provides a very practical lesson for historians of ideas. Modesty, humility and a questioning of presuppositions remain as virtuous goals for the subject.

Popkin might seem to some to have adopted the position ascribed to Lovejoy – that is, of having selected for study a 'unit idea' (in his case 'scepticism') which can be seen periodically to emerge through his allotted time-scale. But Popkin's approach is actually far more subtle: having identified the sceptical arguments of (especially) Pyrrho, he shows how these were variously accepted, adapted, circumvented and transmitted, and how protagonists often wrestled with the problem of reconciling seemingly incompatible positions (of scepticism with Christian faith, for instance). There are others who might criticize Popkin for his overly intellectualized treatment of ideas, with insufficient attention paid to their wider socio-political contexts. But one cannot do it all at the same time and, despite the current fashion for more synchronic studies, such diachronic surveys as *The History of Scepticism* will always have their place in the history of ideas. This particular example has proved seminal inasmuch as it has acted as a seedbed for much further research; and the importance of its subject matter has become increasingly obvious as scepticism again assumes a dominant position in our own postmodern times.

14.6 Practice 2: Annabel Patterson, *Early Modern Liberalism*

Published in 1997 as part of a series of 'Ideas in Context', Annabel Patterson's *Early Modern Liberalism* is remarkable for being a work of intellectual history that not only takes full cognizance of postmodernity in historical study, but actually succeeds in making of it a positive virtue. That is to say, the author is well aware of her own responsibility in constructing a narrative of past events and actions, weaving a web (as she puts it) of ideas and beliefs. The story she has chosen to tell was not lying there in the past, ready-made; but she has gone to great trouble to select from the past those relics and memories (in the form of various texts, literary and pictorial) that enable her to make a case that she believes to be of contemporary importance.

Thus, Professor Patterson makes it clear at the outset that she does indeed have a case to make: hers is *not*, she proclaims, a disinterested academic investigation of the past. Rather, she readily confesses to being 'in the missionary position', seeking support for a liberal agenda in the present. That immediately sets her apart from the tradition of modernist history, with its insistence on authorial detachment in a subject that denies the propriety of any moral or political connections; but it does, of course, align her with the committed position earlier adopted, as we have seen, by Richard Popkin. Just as 'scepticism' was studied, not only as an intellectual development, but as a philosophy the virtues of which were still to be recommended, so 'liberalism' is to be seen as something that still demands our constant cherishing.

Liberalism (a word not actually used at the period in question) is defined in terms of human beings being naturally equal and having equal rights – rights to such basics as physical and religious freedom, education, justice, political choice and freedom of expression. These are the sorts of thing that many of Patterson's prospective readers are likely to simply take for granted, so that one function of the book is to demonstrate how a liberal tradition did not arise naturally at all. On the contrary, it was something that had to be fought for at enormous cost, something that emerged slowly and precariously in the face of authoritarian vested interests and is by implication something that needs to be carefully tended and maintained.

Patterson argues, then, that liberalism actually arose as a direct response to perceived injustices. Treason trials, for example, in which men were arraigned on charges at the arbitrary whim of monarchs and their advisers, were early seen as an affront to natural justice, and provoked determined resistance. A succession of such trials was initiated in 1553 with that of Sir Nicholas Throckmorton, whose spirited self-defence won acquittal by a jury whose members were themselves then imprisoned and heavily fined. A record of the Throckmorton case was incorporated into his *Chronicles* by Raphael Holinshed, and was thus enabled to act as an inspiration in the following century, when charges of treason were made, by very different political authorities but in not dissimilar ways, against the Leveller John Lilburne in 1649, Sir Henry Vane in 1662 and Algernon Sidney in 1683. Accounts of their trials, and of the gross injustices they suffered, were surreptitiously written and published; and these unofficial or 'secret' histories came to constitute a public memory and tradition of dissent that then gave encouragement in turn to later victims and exponents of liberalism.

Annabel Patterson's work, then, no less than Richard Popkin's, exemplifies in practice a number of the theoretical issues raised in earlier sections; and more particularly it demonstrates how intellectual history might well look in the context of postmodernity. Thus, in the construction of her historical narrative, the author utilizes a wide range of sources – not only such conventional literary texts as official documents, canonical philosophies and court transcripts, but also poetry, engravings and writings of lesser-known people retrieved from previous obscurity. As herself an interloper from a literary background, she clearly has little time for rigid disciplinary distinctions, and she insists on the centrality for her theme of 'literature' – including, for instance, the politically infused works of Andrew Marvell and John Milton. She goes on to examine all her chosen texts with due regard to the underlying motives and intentions of their producers, and to their styles and rhetorical devices. Interested as she is in the diffusion of ideas, and the conveyance of a liberal tradition from England to the American colonies, she has also confronted problems relating to the transmission of ideas and causal influence, producing evidence from known personal contact, direct reference and acknowledged inspiration; and she has explored, not only more 'popular' writings, such as newspapers, pamphlets, diaries and personal correspondence, but a whole alternative intellectual tradition in the form of 'secret histories'.

'Secret histories' are those alternative accounts of people and events that fail to cohere with orthodox narratives. They might, for example, record the sexual misdemeanours of those in power, or the alleged political misdemeanours of those who challenge that power; and they often incorporate 'anecdotes', or particular exemplary episodes of a seemingly private nature. These have often been rejected and disallowed as respectable historical evidence, but it is quite reasonably claimed that they might well throw light on the shady parts of more official histories. Often transmitted to posterity by publicly motivated 'insiders' concerned with open governance, such anecdotes, Patterson argues, provide an 'energetic counterpoint' to conventional history. They can include those who might otherwise remain on the periphery, and provide important evidence of dissident opinion that might otherwise have been suppressed.

Her interest in the *particularity* of anecdotes is but one example of how Patterson emphasizes the very *personal* nature of intellectual history. Far from generalizing about abstract 'ideas' and 'influence', she meticulously reveals how the tradition of liberalism was constructed and conveyed by real people, operating within and constrained by real socio-political pressures. Her argument, as she herself makes clear, depends largely 'on persons – not on extracting thought from its context but on putting it back into the heads of real thinkers and into the causal webs of real lives' (*Early Modern Liberalism*, p. 280). Thus, for instance, John Adams (the second American President) reveals in his diaries how he idolized such representatives of the European liberal tradition as Sidney, Milton and Locke. But he realized that theirs were not just theoretical constructions: they had developed their theories in practical opposition to political tyrannies. And Adams himself was concerned in turn to use that historical insight for his own practical purposes on the other side of the Atlantic.

In that transatlantic transmission of ideas, another major player claimed by Patterson is Thomas Hollis. Indeed, it is with Hollis, as an exporter of liberal ideas to the American colonies in the mid-18th century, that she starts her story, defying the constraints of conventional linear chronology by beginning that story 'not at the beginning, but almost at the end' (*Early Modern Liberalism*, p. 27). As with Richard Popkin on scepticism, she is of course well aware of her theme's classical antecedents, but for her own purposes she cuts into the seamless web of a continuing tradition with Hollis, in order to set up a framework of ideas and arguments and people that helps to clarify and illuminate the chronologically earlier developments in England. Thus, for example, Hollis expressed enormous enthusiasm for Milton, some of whose works he edited, and whose revolutionary tracts he donated to Harvard

University as part of a deliberate commitment to transplant the European tradition of dissent; and it is in the context of Milton's established place in that tradition that Patterson is enabled to analyse diverse interpretations of his sonnets, and reach conclusions of his own ambivalence.

Above all, though, Annabel Patterson's work is characterized by a self-consciousness about its purpose; and that purpose is not only intellectual, in stimulating greater awareness of those presuppositions that we ourselves take for granted, but is also moral and political. By investigating the early-modern roots of liberalism, and showing how, against all odds, these actually took hold and grew, she reminds us of our indebtedness to brave individuals in the past, and alerts us to the tenuousness of our own hold on what we may all too often assume are the naturally given 'rights' of a liberal tradition. Writing of John Locke, she pointedly asks (*Early Modern Liberalism*, p. 250), 'And what of our own prospects for toleration?' She is concerned, that is, through her history to inspire self-conscious liberally orientated action in the future, and she thus provides a very positive model for postmodern historical study.

14.7 Conclusion: The future

History of ideas shares the position of history more generally at the beginning of the 21st century: some sense has to be made of the subject in the context of postmodern challenges. That implies, first, that historians of ideas are bound to proceed in the manner ascribed above to Mersenne – aware of their inability to reach any ultimate 'truth' about the past, but able nonetheless pragmatically to make some headway in practical respects. It is those practical respects with which the second main implication of postmodernism is concerned: just what is the point of it all? And, as we have suggested above, that is not hard to answer. By trying to understand intellectual developments and transformations in the past – the ways that one set of ideas is gradually or more suddenly replaced by another, both at a personal and public level – we may gain some insight into our own thought processes, presuppositions, sometimes inconsistent beliefs, and motivations now. By studying other people at other times and in other cultures, we are confronted by alternatives, and by those who have struggled to assimilate ideas that initially seemed alien. We may, thus, further come to see their (and our own) historicity and contingency, and so be empowered to take some action for the future; and that future will almost certainly require an openness to ideas long since jettisoned from the western intellectual tradition. Annabel Patterson has written (*Early Modern Liberalism*, p. 215) of the need for 'the combined acts of memory and imagination, thinking backwards in order to think forwards'; and that might well set the agenda for historical study in postmodernity.

In that context, we might return to Geoffrey Elton, who described historians of ideas as 'a vociferous minority'. That was not intended as a compliment by a man who readily conceded that 'Good historians are not primarily men of ideas.'[18] But it may suggest a fitting aspiration for intellectual historians in the 21st century?

Guide to further reading

Iain Hampsher-Monk, *A History of Modern Thought: Major Political Thinkers from Hobbes to Marx* (Oxford, 1992).

David Harvey, *The Condition of Postmodernity: An Enquiry into the Origins of Cultural Change* (Oxford, 1989).

John Henry, *The Scientific Revolution and the Origins of Modern Science* (2nd ed., Basingstoke, 2002).

Arthur Koestler, *The Sleepwalkers* (Harmondsworth, 1964).

Carolyn Merchant, *The Death of Nature: Women, Ecology, and the Scientific Revolution* (San Francisco, 1980).

Annabel Patterson, *Early Modern Liberalism* (Cambridge, 1997).

Richard H. Popkin, *The History of Scepticism from Erasmus to Spinoza* (Berkeley and Los Angeles, 1979).

Roy Porter, *The Enlightenment* (2nd ed., Basingstoke, 2001).

Quentin Skinner, *Liberty Before Liberalism* (Cambridge, 1998).

James Tully (ed.), *Meaning and Context: Quentin Skinner and his Critics* (Cambridge, 1988).

Beverley Southgate, *Postmodernism in History* (London, 2003).

Notes

Many thanks to John Ibbett for helpful conversations and constructive comments on an earlier draft.

1 Justification is provided by the fact that the leading academic *Journal of the History of Ideas* has as its subtitle 'an interdisciplinary journal devoted to intellectual history'. For discussion of such terminology, see Maurice Mandelbaum, 'The History of Ideas, Intellectual History, and the History of Philosophy', *History and Theory* 5 (1965), pp. 33–66.

2 Geoffrey Elton, *Return to Essentials* (Cambridge, 1991), p. 27.
3 Aristotle, *Metaphysics*, Book 1, 984a.
4 Leslie Stephen, *History of English Thought in the 18th Century*, 2 vols (London, 1876), Vol. 1, p. 3.
5 Milan Kundera, *Immortality* (London, 1992), p. 136.
6 Francis Bacon, *The New Organon*, ed. F. H. Anderson (Indianapolis, 1960), p. 75.
7 J. W. Draper, *A History of the Intellectual Development of Europe*, 2 vols (London, 1875), Vol. 1, p. 142; Vol. 2, p. 400.
8 J. T. Merz, *A History of European Thought in the 19th Century*, 4 vols (Edinburgh, London, 1896–1914), Vol. 1, pp. 14, 61, 76.
9 Merz, *History*, Vol. 1, p.7.
10 Mark Bevir, *The Logic of the History of Ideas* (Cambridge, 1999), p. 178 (my emphasis); cf. p. 190.
11 Quentin Skinner, 'Motives, Intentions and Interpretations', reprinted in James Tully (ed.), *Meaning and Context: Quentin Skinner and his Critics* (Cambridge, 1988), p. 76 (emphasis added to 'meant' and 'intentions', and removed from 'is').
12 Conrad Russell in Juliet Gardiner (ed.), *The History Debate* (London, 1990), p. 48.
13 For Wittgenstein's example, as for much else in this chapter, I am indebted to Quentin Skinner, whose writings on both the theory and practice of history of ideas has been of the first importance during the last four decades. For Stevie Smith, 'Not Waving but Drowning', see James MacGibbon (ed.) *The Collected Pomes of Stevie Smith* (London, 1985), p. 303.
14 Pierre Bayle, *Dictionary*, art. 'Pyrrhon', cited by Richard H. Popkin, *The History of Scepticism from Erasmus to Spinoza* (Berkeley and Los Angeles, 1979), p. 252, n. 3; Henry Buckle, *History of Civilizations in England*, 2 vols (London, 1858), Vol. 1, pp. 317, 328; Stephen, *History*, Vol. 1, p. 43.
15 R. H. Popkin, 'Berkeley and Pyrrhonism' (1951), reprinted in Myles Burnyeat (ed.), *The Skeptical Tradition* (Berkeley and Los Angeles, 1983), p. 394, n. 21.
16 Popkin, *History*, p. xxi; Richard A. Watson and James E. Force (eds), *The High Road to Pyrrhonism* (San Diego, 1980), pp. 37, 29, 53.
17 David Hume and John Leland, quoted by Popkin, *High Road*, pp. 57–8, 206.
18 Elton, *Essentials*, p. 29; *The Practice of History* (London, 1969), p. 192.

15

From women's history to gender history

Laura Lee Downs

On 18 March 1920, Virginia Woolf reminded readers of the venerable *Times Literary Supplement* that, despite the existence of isolated works on the history of women (one of which she had reviewed that day), the lives and condition of women in history remained shrouded in profound obscurity: 'It has been common knowledge for ages that women exist, bear children, have no beards, and seldom go bald', wrote Woolf with acerbic wit, 'but save in these respects, and in others where they are said to be identical with men, we know little of them and have little sound evidence upon which to base our conclusions. Moreover, we are seldom dispassionate.'[1] And indeed, aside from the work of a few maverick pioneers, to whom the history of women offered fresh and challenging terrain – Mary Beard, Ivy Pinchbeck, Léon Abensour, Alice Clark, Olive Schreiner – women's history continued to languish in the shadows of which Woolf had complained until the 1960s, when the first stirrings of renewed political activism (feminism's much-vaunted 'second wave') turned the sustained attention of historians and activists toward the recovery and analysis of those who remained 'hidden from history'.

The history of women has come a long way since Woolf underscored our astonishing ignorance on the subject, for with the revival of feminist militancy in the late 1960s came a vast outpouring of research on women in both Europe and the United States. Much has already been written on this initial phase of 'primitive accumulation', where scholars and activists devoted themselves to demonstrating in amplitude that women did indeed have a history, and that, moreover, recovering this rich and varied past had the potential to reshape the contours of official, 'male' history. This article will therefore focus on the evolution of historical writing about women since the mid-1980s. It opens with a brief survey of developments across the period 1975–2000, focusing in particular on the emergence of gender history from women's history, and on the way that the poststructuralist challenge has progressively reshaped both the methods and objects of research in the field since the late 1980s. It then turns to a more detailed analysis of two works – Leonore Davidoff and Catherine Hall's *Family Fortunes: Men and Women of the English Middle Class, 1780–1850* and Lyndal Roper's *Oedipus and the Devil: Witchcraft, Sexuality and Religion in Early Modern Europe* – in order to illustrate some of the ways that feminist historians have deployed the concept of gender so as to open out entirely new research domains, while developing new perspectives on existing fields of research.

In the early 1970s, feminist scholars and activists founded the first women's studies courses in universities and adult education programmes across the United States and Europe. '1973: the first course on women at Jussieu,' recalls Michelle Perrot.

> On the 7th of November, Andrée Michel opened fire with a lecture on 'Women and the family in developed societies.' The lecture hall was packed, the atmosphere over-heated by the hostility of leftist (male) students for whom the study of women was but a distraction from the real work of revolution.' [2]

But such resistance merely fuelled feminist scholars' determination to recover their own history, a history that had been unjustly banished from view, a history that could serve to reinforce feminist politics by offering a historically grounded account of women's identity as a group distinct from men. As publications accumulated, feminist historians moved from their initial, hesitant question 'Is it possible to write a history of women?' (and what might it look like?) toward the more confident formulation that to write a history *without* women was a foolhardy endeavour indeed, for it would be to tell barely half the story.[3] Fired by an enthusiasm that was at once political and intellectual, feminist scholars, students and activists engaged in individual and collective projects of research and teaching whose accumulated, and sometimes unexpected results did not always fit smoothly into the existing narratives of history. The problem of integrating the 'women's story' soon prompted feminist scholars to challenge the traditional contours of their discipline by posing a new and difficult question: 'Is women's history merely an "innocuous supplement" to existing narratives, or does the integration of these new stories and perspectives demand that the analytic structures themselves be reshaped?' For if, as the growing body of scholarship on women suggested, gender identity was not a biological given but a social and historical creation, then the task of the historian was no longer merely adding women to an existing narrative whose outlines were familiar. Rather, her task was now to excavate the precise meanings that femininity and masculinity have carried in the past, to demonstrate the evolution of those meanings over time, and so to reveal the historically constructed nature of these concepts in our present world.

From early on, then, feminist scholars were committed not merely to adding new material to the historical record; but to changing the analytic structures of historical practice. Crucial to this ambition was the distinction drawn between biological sex, understood as the material and unchanging ground of one's identity, and the infinitely malleable carapace of gender, a socially constructed series of behaviours that code one as male or female, but that vary across time and space in such a way as to reveal their culturally constructed nature.[4] Women (and men, for that matter) were thus made and not born, and much productive research proceeded on the ground of the sex/gender distinction, as feminist historians smoked out the various ways that gender, understood as a socially constructed system of difference, has operated to shape social relations and understandings of self in societies past.

Women's history was fast transforming itself into a broader history of gender relations, though not without protest from scholars who feared that the turn to gender signalled the abandonment of women's history as a feminist political project.[5] Yet the very move by which women's historians had underscored the constructed nature of male and female roles in society had already destabilized the notion of identity as an essential, natural property. In this sense, gender history was immanent in the very development of women's history, and feminist scholars moved increasingly toward the study of gender as a way to locate the experiences of women in a broader context, while arguing for the gendered nature of all human experience, and not simply that of women.

The shift from women's history to gender history over the course of the 1980s thus had several important consequences, not the least of which was to contribute to the development of an entirely new arena of research: that of masculinity and 'men's' studies, a field that was to expand and develop rapidly during the 1990s. But de-essentializing maleness and femaleness by underscoring their historical construction also met a vital intellectual need of the young sub-discipline, by taking these categories out of the timeless realm of eternal verities, where male dominance and women's subordination were written into the very order of things, and returning them to the stream of history. By the same token, the de-essentializing of the category 'woman' served an equally important political goal, underscoring the historical, and hence changeable, non-necessary content of the category 'woman' as it is deployed in contemporary politics and social policy.

Finally, it was argued that the turn to gender would give feminist scholarship greater impact on the shape of historical discipline itself. For by the mid-1980s, it was clear that women's history on its own had failed to transform the epistemological bases of the historical discipline, despite the conviction of many feminist historians that the integration of the women's story rendered such transformation inevitable. Rather, women's history was being researched and taught alongside the standard narratives of 'real' history without affecting those narratives in any fundamental way. The only way to break out of this intellectual ghetto, it was argued, was to cease focusing exclusively on women and follow instead the mutual construction of masculinities and femininities as they have evolved over time. Drawing heavily from the anthropologist's tool-kit, historians of gender sought to render the study of sexual division an instrument of historical analysis by arguing that such divisions are rooted in a more global sexual division of social, symbolic and political space. Any history worth the name would henceforth have to abandon the pretext that the masculine represents a neutral and universal history of the species, while the feminine remains the particular object of a revendicating identity politics. Rather, historians of any subject, whether military, social, political or diplomatic, would henceforth have to identify the gendered constitution of their object of analysis, to demonstrate how it had been coded masculine or feminine, and then explain what the consequences of that gendering have been for its evolution in time. For gender (unlike women) was everywhere, or so the theory went.

Feminist scholars' desire to render women visible in history thus resulted ultimately in a broader conceptual vision of the social distinction of the sexes; a less militantly woman-centred concept, perhaps, but one which has nonetheless altered historical practice, not only among feminist scholars but among many of their male colleagues as well. Feminist politics and the demands of scholarship thus remained tightly intertwined in the intellectual history of the discipline, even as its practitioners moved outwards from the particulars of women's history to a more universal history of gender, understood as a fundamental aspect of social being and social order.

Throughout this initial phase of its development, women's history had been riding the people's history wave, which, fed by a number of streams (notably the *Annales* school, and the 'new' social history movement) peaked in the 1960s and early 1970s. In this, the golden age of social history, where scholars strove to restore the voices of common people to history, women found their place as a prime example of the generally unheard-from in standard history textbooks. In addition, the link to social history gave women's history a strong orientation toward labour history, an orientation that was reinforced by the conviction, common to 1970s feminists in Europe and the United States, that one key to women's liberation from the patriarchal domination of fathers and husbands lay in their finding paid employment outside the home.

Social and labour history would continue to dominate the emerging fields of women's and gender history until the late 1980s, by which point historians in general, and women's and gender historians in particular, began turning away from social history, with its basis in macro-structural forms of analysis (social and economic structures as determinants of individual behaviour), toward more cultural and discursive forms of analysis, often grounded in more micro-historical contexts. Thanks to their long-standing recourse to the notion of social construction in the study of masculinities and femininities past, feminist historians found themselves on the cutting edge of this larger poststructuralist movement in historical analysis. For at the very moment that feminist critiques of an essentializing women's history were driving the growth and elaboration of gender history, the entire discipline of social history was engaged as a whole in the search for more nuanced ways of addressing the relationships among the social, material and cultural aspects of history. Frustrated by the limits of earlier, social-science-driven and/or Marxist perspectives, scholars across the discipline placed increasing stress on the importance of the play between representation and social reality. Here, the use of the notion of social construction (in this case of sex/gender) became a way to navigate between the two.

At a time when the discipline of social history was pushing up against the limits of earlier models and conceptualizations, then, feminist historians carved out an avant-garde role for themselves as theoretical and methodological innovators, developing fruitful new approaches that were grounded in psychoanalytic understandings of gender identity-formation, and in the insights of radical feminist consciousness-raising groups into the inherently political nature of domestic gender relations, which are, after all, relations of power. The feminist challenge to stable social categories like male and female, achieved through the historical study of gender relations as they have shifted in time, thus preceded the arrival of poststructuralist theory in departments of history, which arrived bearing the chic banner of 'French theory'. Although such theory had blossomed in departments of language and literature since the late 1970s, the message came to history rather late in the day, borne notably by Joan Wallach Scott in her famous essay 'Gender: A Useful Category of Historical Analysis', first published in the *American Historical Review* in 1986.[6]

Feminist historians would thus play a leading role in the theoretical and methodological debates that shook the discipline from the late 1980s through the mid-1990s. As we will see, these debates would upset the epistemological certitudes on which history had confidently rested, notably the idea that textual sources give us a direct window onto the past. At the same time, they challenged the original synthesis of scholarship and politics that had characterized women's and gender history, by casting doubt on the notion that at the core of each individual subject lies a stable and coherent identity. In order to explore more concretely what the turn from women's to gender history, and the subsequent engagement with poststructuralism have meant for the practice of women's and gender history, the next section of this article focuses on the evolution of the field in Britain. I choose to explore this case more closely in part because it provides the specific historiographical context for an analysis of Davidoff and Hall's magisterial study of gender in the making of the English middle class, a key text in the development and deployment of gender as a tool of historical analysis. But I also use this specific case study to demonstrate in detail that the shift from social to cultural history, from the analysis of experience to the analysis of discourse and the construction of social categories, has had important consequences for the shape of the field as a whole, shifting attention from histories based in women's experiences (notably of work) to analyses of the gendered construction of the basic categories that have shaped our perceptions of civil and political life. Of course, this shift had its parallels in the United States, France and Germany, where from about 1990 on, numerous historians turned increasingly away from macro-structural analysis toward more cultural and micro-level studies. But it is only by exploring the particularities of a single historiographical tradition that one can document precisely the effects that the turn from social to cultural and discursive forms of analysis has had on the forms and objects of historical analysis in general, and feminist historical analysis in particular. The article then closes with a brief discussion of Lyndal Roper's deeply searching essays on gender, witchcraft and religious reform in 17th-century Germany. Though written in the early 1990s, when the stormy debate around poststructuralism was at it height, these essays look beyond that moment and set forth a challenging agenda for gender historians that in, my view, has yet to be met.

15.1 Feminist historians and the 'new' social history

The field of women's history in Britain first took shape within the great tradition of social, and socialist, history of working-class life and labour. It was an intellectually and politically vibrant tradition, one that had given rise by the mid-1960s to a 'new' social history that stressed the agency of working-class people in making their own history.[7] The epistemological base of this 'new' social history rested on Edward Palmer Thompson's famous articulation between agency and structure, between experiences (of exploitation), social identity (class consciousness) and politics. Class was thus understood as a dynamic process set in motion by individual agents as much as by material conditions. But it did so thanks to the key, mediating force of inherited cultural tradition. Hence, in the case of Thompson's seminal *Making of the English Working Class*, pre-existing notions of the 'rights of free-born Englishmen' enabled individual (male) artisans to transform their individual experiences of exploitation into a collective identity, based on a shared consciousness of their exploitation as a class.[8] For the new social historians, then, individual experiences, interpreted in the light of inherited cultural tradition, formed the indispensable ground of all political and revolutionary action.

But if the chain binding experience, social identity and politics constituted the epistemological ground of early feminist scholarship, it was the vast, if poorly paid domain of popular and adult education that gave the first generation of feminist historians a precarious institutional anchor. Working outside the four walls of traditional universities, in programmes that were often located in working-class neighbourhoods, socialist historians of both sexes offered courses on the lives and labour of British workers. In so doing, they sought to bind socialist intellectuals more closely to the working-class movement by returning to the people the history of their own class.[9] It was here, in this politically alive, if institutionally somewhat marginalized atmosphere, that feminist scholars of the 1960s and 1970s first began to research and teach the history of women and work as an integral aspect of people's history.

British women's history thus put down its first institutional and epistemological roots in the socialist movement for a people's history, organized around a new social history that, while methodologically innovative on a number of fronts, remained largely a history of men. Dominated by images of barrel-chested miners shouldering their axes, or sooty metalworkers hammering away like devils before the roaring flames of the forge, the initial narratives produced by the new social historians seem to have forgotten that the nation's first industrial proletariat, called to work in the weaving sheds of early 19th-century Lancashire, was predominantly female. Only with the flourishing of feminist-socialist scholarship after 1968 would this picture slowly began to change, as the figures of women, bent over in the fields or standing at the loom, were gradually restored to view.

Over the next ten years or so, the majority of feminist scholars in Britain would continue to work on the margins of the university, teaching history in adult education or neighbourhood women's centres while participating in a flourishing array of autonomous associations that sprang up around the history of women: The Women's Research and Resources Centre in London (which later became the Feminist Library), the Feminist Archive (Bath), The Lesbian Archive (Manchester), numerous informal feminist history groups that met in London, Bristol, Brighton and Manchester (to name but a few), and the Virago Press, dedicated to publishing new work in women's history while reissuing handsome editions of out-of-print works as well. 'The margins can be a very productive terrain', wrote Catherine Hall in 1992, 'a space from which both to challenge establishments and develop our own perspectives, build our own organizations, confirms our own collectivities.'[10] For feminist scholars of the 1970s, this marginality also served to remind them of the overarching political purpose of women's history: to restore women's voices to history while using these discoveries to transform present-day gender relations.

During the 1980s, feminist scholars moved gradually from adult education into the universities. In part, this movement was involuntary, for the severe budget slashing of the Thatcher years forced major cuts in adult education. At the same time, the first interdisciplinary programmes in women's studies appeared in certain of the 'new universities', including Bradford, Essex, Kent, Warwick and York.[11] The need to create interdisciplinary programmes gave rise to fruitful exchanges among feminist scholars across the disciplines, breaking their isolation from one another inside separate departments (where they were often the lone exponents of women's studies) while reinforcing the cross-disciplinary nature of women's and gender history. And yet very few of the participants in these first women's studies programmes were historians, for until the end of the 1980s, the British historical discipline as a whole proved reluctant to concede that women's and gender history might be legitimate fields of research.[12] Numerous key works were thus produced by scholars in sociology (Leonore Davidoff), social policy (Pat Thane), education (Penny Summerfield, Carol Dyehouse) or social science administration (Jane Lewis) – scholars in the social sciences who found that adopting a historical approach was crucial to the success of their enterprise.

A look at two classic works from this period illustrates the shape that feminist historians' overarching preoccupation with the world of labour, and with the often tense relation between socialist feminists and their male comrades, assumed in the guise of history. Jill Liddington and Jill Norris's "*One Hand Tied Behind Us*": The Rise of the women's suffrage movement thus recounts the hitherto untold story of the radical suffrage movement Theory and Practice among women textile workers in turn-of-the-century Lancashire.[13] Both authors were teaching in adult education in Manchester at the time (1978), and their book is the fruit of an enormous labour of research conducted in local archives and through interviews with the surviving daughters and granddaughters of such local activists as Selina Cooper and Doris Chew. Burdened by a double load of domestic and factory labour, these women sought the vote not merely as an end in itself, but as a means to the larger end of improving the conditions of life and labour for working-class men, women and children. Lancashire's radical suffragists thus fought equally hard to gain those social and economic rights which they judged every bit as important as the simple right to vote: equal pay, better educational opportunities, birth control, child allowances and the right to work on an equal footing with men. In order to piece together the tale of this all-but-forgotten movement, Liddington and Norris had to write against the conventional tale of exclusively middle-class heroics first propagated by middle-class and London-based activists such as Sylvia Pankhurst and Rachel Strachey, militant suffragists for whom the social and political activism of women workers was but a distant echo of their own, more narrowly vote-based struggle.[14] Inspired by the convictions of 1970s socialist-feminism, and sustained by the structures of popular education in a region that was heavily populated by retired textile workers, Liddington and Norris used their contacts in the milieu to recover the unwritten tale of a political movement, led by the women workers themselves, in which feminist politics and class struggle were inextricably linked.

Barbara Taylor's *Eve and the New Jerusalem: Socialism and Feminism in the 19th Century* explores the encounter between feminism and Owenite socialism in early

19th-century England in what is, ultimately, a sustained meditation on the often fraught relationship of feminism to socialism. Taylor's richly documented study shows how Owen's moral critique of gender inequality within the family constituted an essential pillar of so-called 'utopian' socialism in the 1820s, 1830s and 1840s. Unlike the 'scientific' socialists of the later 19th century, for whom the struggle for gender equality was always subordinated to class struggle, Owenite socialists placed women's liberation at their heart of their political project to liberate all of humanity from all forms of oppression and inequality, be they class- or gender-based. Once again, one can read the preoccupations, and discontents, of 1970s socialist-feminists in the study of a long-since marginalized movement in which the liberation of women formed an integral part of the larger struggle, and not just a coda, left to the tender (and studiously vague) mercies of 'after the revolution'.

Feminist historians of the 1970s and early 1980s thus privileged working-class history and the study of women's work, sometimes adapting terms and categories of Marxist analysis – 'sex-class', 'sex struggle' and 'patriarchal mode of production' – in order to extend a materialist analysis of women's exploitation from the factory to the family, and so unmask the material basis of male domination. In some instances, patriarchy travelled alone in its relentless exploitation of women's domestic and reproductive labour.[15] More often, however, socialist-feminists analysed patriarchy in its unholy alliance with capitalism, a 'dual system' whose elements had to be analysed simultaneously in order to explain women's double burden of labour (and exploitation) – in the factory, to be sure, but also in the home.[16] The tension that this first generation felt between feminism and socialism, between gender versus class as the privileged category of analysis, expressed itself above all in the long debate over whether patriarchy (understood as a system of relations that is generated entirely outside the workplace) or capitalism should be regarded as the prime source of working women's oppression. While much important work was produced under the sign of this 'dual systems theory', its underlying hermeneutic, in which patriarchy and capitalism are treated as autonomously functioning structures of oppression, would remain unchallenged until the early 1990s, when the history of women's experiences of work was broadened to embrace the study of gender divisions inside the workplace itself. The workplace then revealed itself to be a world in which notions of masculinity and femininity have always played a central role in shaping divisions of labour and hierarchies of authority, a world in which the two structures (patriarchy and capitalism) are in fact inextricably bound together in a single, gendered order of production.[17] The adoption of gender as a central category of analysis would thus resolve certain of the epistemological difficulties that had dogged women's history from its origins – not, however, without raising several new epistemological problems of its own.

15.2 From women's history to gender history

The publication, in 1987, of Leonore Davidoff and Catherine Hall's highly influential book, *Family Fortunes: Men and Women of the English Middle Class, 1780–1850*, marked a decisive moment in the turn to gender history in Britain, and in gender's diffusion outward into historical practice more broadly. The product of nearly ten years' collaboration between the historian (Hall) and the sociologist (Davidoff), *Family Fortunes* recounts in detail the formation of the provincial middle classes in turn-of-the-19th-century England, a process whose roots lie, the authors argue, in the progressive separation of public (male) space from the private and female-dominated realm of the middle-class home. At the heart of the book lies the ambition to analyse the construction of gendered identities within a particular society, with identity conceived as the link between individual psychology and the larger collectivity. In this sense, *Family Fortunes* contributed mightily not only to the broader diffusion of gender as a tool of historical analysis, but also to the turn in the late 1980s toward subjectivity as an object of historical study.

Of course the idea of separate male and female spheres was far from new in 1987, for feminist scholars across Europe and the United States had long deployed the model as a description of middle-class social organization – or at least, of an *ideal* of middle-class social organization – in modern western societies. What was new was Hall and Davidoff's ambition to lay bare and analyse the gendered foundations of large social processes like class formation:

> We wanted not just to put the women back into a history from which they had been left out, but to rewrite that history so that proper recognition would be given to the ways in which gender, as a key axis of power in society, provides a crucial understanding of how any society is structured and organized.

wrote Catherine Hall some five years after the publication of *Family Fortunes*.

> What was the specific relation of women to class structures and how should women's class position be defined? How was class *gendered* …? Do men and women have different class identities? Are their forms of class consciousness and class solidarity the same? … D[o] women have an identity as women which cut across forms of class belonging?[18]

The result is a book that speaks of both men and women, and of the formation of the middle classes during the Industrial Revolution on the basis of a gendered distinction in social space and social function.

This gendered distinction between the moral world of the home, where acts are reciprocal and performed for love, not money, and the competitive, amoral world of business and politics, is one that the authors trace back to the texts and practices of Protestant evangelical religion. To my mind, the exploration of the religious sources of gender distinction constitutes one of the most original aspects of Hall and Davidoff's argument. Among other things, it allows the authors to document in some detail the very particular visions of masculinity and femininity that emerged in this world of middle-class evangelicals; visions that were hardly congruent with those of the landed aristocracy, on the one hand, or of the labouring poor on the other. Evangelical religion thus gave a specific moral meaning to the strict and gendered segregation of space and activity, to the productive activity of men in the world, and to the economic dependence of women, who remained close to the hearth and held aloft the pure flame of domesticity. Here, the pious husband would always find a morally uplifting retreat from the unavoidable sullying of hands and spirit that his implication in the competitive and treacherous worlds of business and politics entailed. Across the decades that *Family Fortunes* covers, gender and class are perpetually constructed and reconstructed in relation to one another and in the context of the gendered separation of public and private. And this, in turn, implies that the class consciousness of both men and women must, of necessity, take gendered forms.

With its uncanny capacity to reveal and analyse the gendered underpinnings of such fundamental social processes as class formation, Hall and Davidoff's book became something of a classic almost overnight. It was widely taught in university courses from the late 1980s onward, and not only in women's studies but in general history classes as well. Yet *Family Fortunes* also drew substantial criticism, often from feminist historians who criticized the separate spheres model for its functionalist logic, as well as for its proximity to the world-view of the very bourgeois whom it purports to analyse. And indeed, there is something deeply disturbing in the peaceful harmony with which the tale of the complementary division of public and private unfolds. It is a tale in which all hint of male domination as a political problem fades behind the comfortable harmonies of gender complementarity. It is a tale that, as Carolyn Steedman astutely observed,

> repeats the imperative of the *Bildungsroman*, which, in its many forms, typically symbolizes the process of socialization, and makes its characters and its readers really want to do what it is that they have to do anyway (be married, have children, clean the stairs ...).[19]

Yet the separate spheres model was seductive, a structure of binary classification that allowed feminist researchers to move beyond social history and to integrate women and gender into more political histories as well, notably into studies of the gendered contours of social and political citizenship. Studies of male–female relations, and of the construction of gendered identities in a wide range of social contexts, began to multiply rapidly, and the history of women and work inexorably lost its privileged position in feminist research.

15.3 Gender history and poststructuralism

The arrival of gender as a tool of historical analysis thus contributed to the displacement of feminist history's attention away from women's experiences (especially of work) and toward the construction of masculine and feminine identities across the social spectrum. This shift in object – from experience to the social construction of gendered identities – would be confirmed and extended by the arrival of poststructuralist theory in departments of women's studies and history all across Britain at the turn of the 1990s.[20] Poststructuralist thinkers (with feminist poststructuralists often leading the way) thus mounted a powerful critique of historical practice, focusing in particular on historians' reliance on written texts ('primary sources') as a guide to events and experiences past. Borrowing various techniques of deconstruction from literary critics, poststructuralist historians analysed historical documents as literary artefacts, placing at the heart of their work an exploration of the internal structure of these texts and the construction of the categories on which their internal logic is based.[21]

Rather than seeking to reconstruct the past 'as it really was', poststructuralist historians preached the analysis of discourses, of representations, and of the (often gendered) construction of social categories. If nothing else, this had the salutary effect of renewing and expanding techniques for the critical reading of sources. But in asking that historians turn their attention to the textual construction of social categories, poststructuralists also called into question the very epistemological base of the new social history, namely the logical chain that bound experience to identity, and from there moved to politics. The relationship between structure and agency that had animated so much of the new social history, including women's and gender history, was thus supplanted by a new concern with the relationship between culture and politics, and the ways that language serves to mediate that relationship.[22] Those scholars who remained faithful to the project of social history would henceforth try to marry their narratives of social and economic structures with new stories of the 'cultures' of work, that is, of the representations and discourses that surround work, and notions of production and the economy more generally. But historians in general and feminist historians in particular would continue to move away from the world of labour, so cherished by the new social history, and toward a newly renovated cultural and political history that focused on such things as the gendered and raced construction of categories like citizenship and of representations of nation and empire.

Feminist historians in Britain became acquainted with poststructuralist thought through a variety of intermediaries, notably the American historian Joan Wallach Scott and the British philosopher and poet Denise Riley, whose widely read works disseminated to a broader public the sustained reflections of poststructuralist feminists on the constructed nature of such fundamental categories as 'woman/women' and 'gender'.[23] As a part of this reflection, poststructuralist feminists took up once again the question of power, though this time (following Michel Foucault on the power/knowledge nexus) the focus was less on the micropolitics of power in the household than on gender as a metaphor for social and political power. Hence, to borrow from Joan Scott's oft-quoted formulation, relations between the sexes constitute a 'primary aspect of social organization' (and not simply of class formation as Hall and Davidoff would have it), for 'the differences between the sexes constitute and are constituted by hierarchical social structures'.[24] Gender thus becomes a 'primary way of signifying relationships of power ... one of the recurrent references by which political power has been conceived, legitimated and criticized'. Moreover, 'gender both refers to and establishes the meaning of the male/female opposition'.[25]

In light of these reflections, 'gender' in its social-historical incarnation (social relations of the sexes, the sexual division of labour) would undergo serious conceptual transformation as poststructuralist feminists displaced the accent from the social to the discursive construction of categories, including gender identities and the category of 'women' as a self-evident collectivity. Henceforth, the goal of gender history would no longer be that of recovering or reconstructing the experiences of women in the past, but rather that of tracing the process by which discourses about masculinity and femininity have been produced over time. The category of experience, on which reposed the narratives of social and gender history, was thus dismissed as part and parcel of a worn-out and positivist social history that had (since 1989) been deprived of all Marxist legitimation. Indeed, for some of the more radical partisans of poststructuralist feminism, experience does not really exist as such. Rather, the notions of experience, and of subjectivity itself, are themselves products of discursive processes that position individuals in relation to discursive formations, and so produce both their experiences and their sense of possessing a 'true' inner self/subjectivity. The real objects of historical research are therefore constituted by the discourses that organize experiences, and not by the experiences themselves.[26]

The turn toward cultural history and discursive modes of analysis met with a sharply divided reaction in the history departments of early 1990s Britain: on the one hand, a defensive rejection of what was perceived by some to be a perverse deconstruction of the entire historical enterprise; on the other hand, considerable enthusiasm from those historians who, since the late 1970s, had been living uneasily with the growing 'crisis' of social history.[27] This crisis was an epistemological one, rooted in historians' increasing discomfort with the determinist vision of the individual-experience-to-social-identity link on which so many narratives of social history rested. After all, it is by no means clear that a particular experience will inevitably give rise in individual consciousness to one social identity and not another. Indeed, once one relinquishes all notion of a fully determined relation between the two, then a troubling explanatory gap opens up between individual self-perception and the 'objective' structures of society and economy. So long as scholars were prepared to presume that the move from inner cognitive process to outward social identification was a fully determined one, no such gap was visible. By the late 1970s, however, historians were no longer so sure, as debates over problems such as 'false consciousness' (a way to account for those workers who, in an apparent failure to grasp the political consequences of their class position, vote Conservative) led scholars increasingly to question the determinist nature of the epistemological chain binding individual consciousness to larger collective identities.

Well before the arrival of poststructuralist theory, then, social historians already entertained serious doubts about the explanatory power of categories like 'experience'. Small wonder that the poststructuralist message found receptive ears in history departments across Britain. Indeed, for some (ex-)social historians, the study of discourse became the sole possible way to do history, a history that focused on the 'discursive aspects of experience', and on analysing the discursive logic within which individual identities were produced.[28]

Feminist historians were likewise divided in the face of the poststructuralist onslaught on the certitudes of experience. Thus, poststructuralists' 'refusal of the real' presented genuine, practical problems for scholars (feminist and non-feminist alike) who had been raised up inside the empiricist traditions that have long shaped British historical research. In addition, many feminist scholars were frankly suspicious of the claim that our understanding of the intersection between gender and power had arisen exclusively from poststructuralist thought. After all, hadn't feminist consciousness-raising groups, with their stress on the personal as political, generated just as much insight into the power/knowledge couplet as had the rarefied debates of poststructuralism? But in the end, it was the profound anti-humanism of poststructuralism's most extreme claims that stirred the sharpest reaction from feminist historians, for whom an approach that preached the analysis of discourse rather than of human activity and consciousness was deeply off-putting. Though powerfully drawn by the prospect of broadening gender's analytic reach to include gendered analyses of the foundations of social and political organization, many feminist scholars remained ambivalent before poststructuralists' radical demand for a complete abandonment of the study of social phenomena and experiences in favour of a kind of cultural history that seemed utterly turned in on itself, circularly self-referential and absorbed by linguistic word play.[29]

Despite these reservations, however, poststructuralism and the crisis around Britain's own 'linguistic turn' have left durable traces in the methods and objects of historical research, placing the analysis of representations and discourses firmly on the agenda while turning historians' eyes from the analysis of social experience *tout court* and toward more cultural histories of political and national identity, of citizenship, and of the multiple (and sometimes competing) forces of race, class and gender in shaping those identities. In the wake of the often violent debates around poststructuralism, feminist historians are thus working on a differently constituted range of subjects, and are drawing their techniques from an increasingly eclectic tool-kit. For if the basic epistemological differences between poststructuralists and anti-poststructuralists have found no real resolution (nor could they, being grounded in fundamentally opposed ontologies), the sound and fury that attended these debates over the period 1988–94 has since abated, leaving historians to continue their work as they may.

Yet even in this more theoretically heterodox era, some of the issues that divided poststructuralist feminists from their non- (or anti)- poststructuralist colleagues continue to find expression, though in less polemical and more historically grounded terms. Hence, those historians of gender who would like to take the more purely constructivist route continue to face some very real epistemological difficulties, notably the fact that gender, understood as a purely discursive construct, cannot in and of itself explain change. If, for example, sexual identities are understood to be produced solely through discursive processes, then how are we to account for changes in said identities over time? Without some way of linking discursive process to social experience, historians cannot account for the changing meanings of masculine and feminine. This is doubtless the most serious problem that the radically constructivist posture – which focuses on the performative, rather than the representational aspect of language – has left to historians of gender.[30] For while endless performativity and subjectivities that are the pure product of discursive positioning pose no *a priori* problem for literary analysis, they are of limited use to historians, who need tools that will allow them to account for change in time. Some scholars have sought to resolve this problem by hooking gender to another, more dynamic category that can explain change (class being the obvious example here). Lyndal Roper proposes a rather different solution, suggesting that we look for some way to understand gender as both discursively constructed *and* as real bodily/psychic experience.

I would therefore like to close with a brief look at Lyndal Roper's work, focusing in particular on her *Oedipus and the Devil* (1994); a most suggestive set of essays that play off of many of the debates around poststructuralism without ever really becoming entangled in their philosophical snares. Rather, Roper hews closely to her historical object, and uses to great effect a broad range of theoretical insights in order to develop fruitful and imaginative approaches to the very new questions that she poses of her material. In so doing, she raises some searching questions about the capacity of gender, in its purely constructivist incarnation, to serve as a tool of historical analysis.

15.4 Gender and history in a post-poststructuralist world

Oedipus and the Devil brings together a series of essays on witchcraft, religion and sexuality in early modern Germany, written over the period 1988–92. When read together, these essays offer a sustained meditation on the role of the irrational and the unconscious in history, on the importance of the body, and on the relation of these two to sexual difference. They do so through a series of case-studies drawn from Reformation and Counter-Reformation Augsburg that involve motherhood, witchcraft, possession, masculinity and sexuality – 'all fields in which gender is at issue, and where the relation of psyche and the body are at stake'.[31] Roper thus proposes no less than a cultural history of that age-old conundrum – the mind–body conjunction, as it was experienced and understood by early modern Germans – but viewed from a startlingly new perspective, one in which gender is not simply an additional line of analysis, but rather lies at the heart of the matter. For as Roper points out, sexual difference, as physiological and psychological fact, and as social construction, is a central and constitutive aspect of human culture. Issues of sexual difference must therefore stand at the heart of cultural history.

Roper's ambition is to grasp the subjectivities of early modern women and men across the period of the Reformation, subjectivities that, in her words, are 'recognizable, evincing patterns with which we are familiar'.[32] Through a series of precise investigations, based on specific kinds of archives that the cultural revolution of religious reform produced in abundance (witchcraft trials, ordinances of discipline), she seeks to illuminate such questions as: how did early modern understandings of the body shift in the context of struggles between a Catholic theology of the body as a vessel of divine (or diabolic) possession, and a Protestant theology that sundered the link between the physical and the spiritual? How did the magical capacities associated with female bodies differ from those associated with male bodies? How did the dilemmas surrounding the psychic identity of womanhood express themselves in accusations of witchcraft? Gender and matters of sexual difference weave themselves through the fabric of the stories she tells, of the deep antagonisms among women that emerged in the trial (1669) of a lying-in maid accused by her (female) clients of harming their young infants through sorcery, or of the generational conflicts among men that expressed themselves in ordinances of discipline intended to control the drunken brawling of village youth. In each case, the dark side of subjectivity comes to the fore: the powerful enmities that can arise when a young mother, anxious about her child's fate and her own ability to nourish it, projects her anxieties onto the person of the older, postmenopausal lying-in maid trusted with its care, when the infant in question fails to thrive; or the political threat that the raw fighting energy of rowdy young men could present to a stable, patriarchal village order. On the one hand, such brute energy, properly channelled, provided the military force necessary to defend the city. But when young (and sometimes not-so-young) men went marauding through tavern and street, beating one another (and at times their own wives) within an inch of their lives, the village council was forced to intervene in order to control the disruptive impact of such excesses of virility. In the end, Roper concludes that '16th-century masculinity drew its psychic strength not from the dignity of the mean but from the rumbustious energy which such discipline was supposedly designed to check.'[33] The uncivilized wildness of 'manly' men was thus the product of civilized society's carefully structured rules.

Throughout these essays, Roper strives to maintain a tension between certain universal aspects of human psychic process, evoked in her working assumption that early modern subjectivities are 'recognizable' to us, and attention to that which changes in time, namely, the particular content with which the categories 'masculine' and feminine' are invested. She thus invites us to see gendered subjectivities as the product of a dialectical relationship between those more labile, socially constructed elements and some notion of an essential self that is located in the fact of having a sexed body:

> Sexual identity can never be satisfactorily understood if we conceive it as a set of discourses about masculinity or femininity. Nor can the individual subject be adequately understood as a container of discourse – a conception which evacuates subjectivity of psychology.[34]

On the one hand, therefore, sexuality comprises elements that run deep and are difficult to change. At another level, we find that 'glittering profusion of sexual identities' that historians have discerned in discourse. In between the two, notes Roper, lies the realm of individual subjectivity, a meeting ground for the social and the psychic that lies at the core of each individual. In order to explore the realm of the psychic, however, historians need a theory of subjectivity that will allow them to account for the tenacious hold of sexual stereotypes (in the present or the past), while explaining the attraction of 'particular rhetorics of gender' at a given historical moment. Moreover, historians need to specify the kinds of connections that arise between social and psychic phenomena, so that they can distinguish that which is historical about our gendered subjectivities from their transhistorical psychic elements. For so long as it lacks an account of the links between the social and the psychic, gender cannot adequately conceptualise change. By linking gender to the social via individual subjectivity, Roper proposes to endow gender with a historical dimension that it necessarily lacks when it is understood as a discursive creation alone.

Roper thus takes her distance from a long-established article of feminist faith, namely the radical constructivist conviction that gender is the pure product of social, cultural and linguistic practices, asserting, rather, that 'sexual difference has its own physiological and psychological reality, and that recognition of this fact must affect the way we write history'.[35] Hence, she astutely identifies one of the fundamental difficulties with both social and linguistic constructionism, namely that each 'short-circuits' the gap between language and subjectivity, as if there were no space there to be bridged. In the constructivist universe, language, by means of its social character, simply 'impresses a social construction of gender upon the wax of the individual psyche'. But bodies are not the mere creations of discourse. And if we already have plenty of histories of discourses about the body, what is sorely lacking is a history that can problematize the relationship between the psychic and the physical (since bodily experience must of necessity be connected with mental life).

Roper attributes the determined constructivism of feminist historians to their long-standing tendency to 'deny' the importance of the body.[36] Though deeply sympathetic to the desire to escape the snares of femininity by fleeing from their bodies and retreating to the 'rational reaches of discourse', Roper is nonetheless convinced that the costs of such flight are too high. After all,

> sexual difference is not purely discursive nor merely social. It is also physical. The cost of the flight from the body and from sexual difference is evident in what much feminist historical writing has found it impossible to speak about; or indeed, in the passionate tone of the theoretical work which insists on the radically constructed nature of sexual difference … We need an understanding of sexual difference which will incorporate, not fight against, the corporeal.[37]

So experience seems to be entering into the equation once again, though this time through the rather different door of bodily and psychic phenomena.

Roper thus asks us to consider how it is we might link discursive constructs like gender to social and psychic experience. It is a question that was hardly posed in the thick of theory wars (which instead tossed experience out with the bathwater). But the epistemological difficulties that a purely constructivist concept of gender present (namely, that gender, conceived as a purely discursive construct, cannot in and of itself explain change) force us to consider this question very seriously. Here, Roper joins Barbara Taylor and Sally Alexander in what Colin Jones and Dror Wahrman have called an 'anticonstructionist backlash: wondering … whether historians have overemphasized the cultural construction of subjectivity to the preclusion of deep historical mechanisms that are a precondition to becoming human'.[38] For both Taylor and Roper, psychoanalysis is one obvious place to look for a way forward through this dilemma, allowing gender historians to come to terms with that which changes in time (the precise content of fantasies of maleness and femaleness) and that which, perhaps, does not (basic psychic process, 'those mechanisms of fantasy formation, particularly identification, that are the precondition of having any sexed subjectivity at all').[39] One may have reservations about a solution that rests on positing a continuity in the underlying structures of the human psyche across time. Indeed, Roper herself would point out just a few years later that psychoanalysis 'raises, but cannot yet convincingly answer the question of how the psyche varies over time and in different cultures'.[40] But the questions that Roper raises about the role of subjectivity and experience in the shaping of gender identity are precisely the questions that need exploring, for it is this kind of enquiry that poststructuralists pushed to one side in their haste to demonstrate the discursive construction of both subjectivity and experience.[41]

Oedipus and the Devil thus offers a searching and sustained engagement with certain of the epistemological questions that the poststructuralist turn to pure constructivism left hanging in the balance, notably the status of gender as a tool of historical analysis, but also the question of whether gender, on its own, acts as a motor for historical change.

Conclusion

In the wake of the struggles that attended history's famous linguistic and cultural turn, women's and gender history can no longer be said to be shaped by one or two dominant approaches, but is, rather, characterized by a kind of theoretical eclecticism in which scholars deploy a range of tools and approaches so that they might better understand the ways that gender, as social/discursive category and as lived experience, has shaped human history. After so much struggle and upheaval, one might reasonably ask where women's and gender history are headed from here? While historians are notoriously bad at predicting future outcomes, I would nonetheless hazard a guess that in the short run, at least, work in the field will continue to be characterized by a great diversity of methodological approaches. I say this in part because there is no way to reconcile the deep epistemological differences that divide poststructuralist from anti-poststructuralist, but also because the arrival of gender as a tool of historical analysis has not displaced the felt need for a specific history of women.

This is perhaps most obvious in the case of the emerging fields of eastern European and Russian women's history, where the institutional precariousness of the field, combined with a not-yet-fully-attained sense of legitimacy in public discourse, creates a situation that in some ways recalls the battles women's history fought simply to have a hearing in 1960s and 1970s western Europe and North America, though one should be wary of pressing the analogy too far. After all, Eastern Europe in the early 21st century is not America or western Europe of yesteryear. An insistence on the centrality of women's history is thus often combined with poststructuralist and postcolonial approaches, for example when studying particular societies within the multi-ethnic empires that for centuries organized these regions politically.[42] Moreover, there is evidence that the history of women may also be making a comeback among a younger generation of students and scholars in North America and western Europe; scholars who, in the words of Ruth Harris, are 'inspired by an undying interest in the lives of women in the past'.[43]

Perhaps we would do best, then, to consider the 'return' of women's history in both East and West as participating in a broader 'return of the social' that historians like Lynn Hunt, Victoria Bonnell and William Sewell Jr have called for over the past ten years.[44] Not the social of the too-often-determinist macro-social analyses of the 1960s and 1970s, but a more culturally situated social that operates on the 'richer and more supple epistemological terrain' opened up by the cultural turn and that seems to be finding an echo in recent historical practice.[45]

If the return of 'herstory' is indeed part and parcel of a larger return of the social, then this provides a salutary reminder that in the early 21st century it will not do to draw hard-and-fast distinctions between women's and gender history, for the forms of women's history that are now developing in formerly inhospitable environments such as Russia or East central Europe, or among a new generation of students and scholars in western Europe and North America are inevitably influenced by the scholarship on gender. In this context, women's history and gender history are not easily uncoupled, nor should we wish for them to be. For, as I have argued elsewhere, the considerable methodological gains that the cultural and linguistic turns have brought to historical practice are nowhere more visible than in the field of gender history.[46] Indeed, gender has been at the forefront of scholarly debate for the past 30 years precisely because it is a tool of critical thinking that allows us to interrogate some of the discipline's most cherished categories of analysis.[47] If this vanguard role seems less obvious today than it did five to ten years ago, I think that is because of the way that gender has become increasingly central to historical analysis.[48] It has done so through its attentiveness to the role of language in shaping subjectivity, its far-reaching critique of traditional notions of agency, its insistence that understandings of sexual difference are key in shaping hierarchies of power, its pioneering use of the idea of social construction – an idea that has since been taken up to great effect by scholars across a broad range of domains: race, nationalism, empire, ethnicity, etc. Most importantly, gender has, from the outset, shown its capacity to effectively critique and unsettle the metanarratives of determinist macro-social analysis.

It is precisely its force as a tool of critical thinking, its demonstrated capacity to refine historical method, that gives gender ongoing relevance in historical scholarship well beyond the fields of women's and gender history. This is perhaps most evident in the importance of gender to historical epistemology in two of the discipline's most cutting-edge fields: transnational history and histories of empire. These are fields in which feminist scholars have played a key role, using gender not only to write women back in to the story but also to transform the approach more broadly. Hence, the feminist insight that gender is a relational concept, and that men and women, masculinity and femininity are historically and discursively constructed in relation to each other, has deeply influenced the way scholars of empire think about the construction of categories like race, sexuality, nation, ethnicity and religion. Similarly, gender history has informed and enriched historians' understanding of the ways in which such categories are constructed and reconstructed not only in relation to each other but also with respect to the dominant formations of the social and political spheres.[49]

By using gender to critically reflect on the categories and concepts that organize research in imperial and transnational history, feminist scholars have been able to make a vital and pioneering contribution to historical analysis more broadly, recasting the political in far larger terms and, in so doing, rethinking state–society relations in new and broader terms.[50] I think that in the future we can expect that more and excellent work will continue to be done along these lines by gender historians and by a host of others who might not identify themselves as such, but whose thinking may be no less deeply marked by the force of gender as a tool of critical analysis. At the same time, it is worth pointing out that the very centrality of gender to so much recent historical scholarship has resulted in a paradox. For if now, more than ever, gender informs how historians go about their work, such work nonetheless tends to deploy gender alongside other tools and categories, a fact which might lead one to conclude that gender has as its vocation to disappear. Paradoxically, then, the operations of gender as a tool of critical analysis have become less visible even as it is being incorporated into ever-wider realms of research. This has led some scholars to worry that gender, rendered banal through overuse, has lost its critical edge.[51]

Yet the success of gender does not necessarily imply that its has 'lost' its critical edge; far from it. A widely diffused tool of historical analysis can always become banal or routine in the hands of scholars who choose to treat gender as an interpretive device that permits the rediscovery of the same old binary oppositions. But scholars who do such a thing are precisely refusing to use gender for explicitly critical purposes, preferring to turn it to normative ends rather than to deploy gender's undimmed power to unsettle comfortable binaries. Such a refusal may tell us much about the scholars in question but says nothing at all about the critical force of gender.

Ultimately, however, the question 'whither women's and gender history' can never be answered in the abstract; indeed, such a question will only be resolved by history's practitioners, rather than by those who merely speculate about how history can and cannot be written.

Guide to further reading

Alison Assiter, *Enlightened Women: Modernist Feminism in a Postmodern Age* (London, 1995).

Lynn Hunt, 'The Challenge of Gender', in Hans Medick and Anne-Charlotte Trepp (eds), *Geschlechtergeschichte und Allgemeine Geschichte* (Goettingen, 1998), 59–97.

Joan Kelly, *Women, History and Theory: The Essays of Joan Kelly* (Chicago, 1984).

David Morgan, 'Men Made Manifest: Histories and Masculinities', *Gender and History* 1 (1989), pp. 87–91.

Linda Nicholson (ed.), *Feminism/Postmodernism* (London, 1990).

Joan W. Scott (ed.), *Feminism and History* (Oxford, 1996).

Notes

1 Virginia Woolf, review of Léonie Villard, *La Femme anglaise au XIXe siècle et son évolution d'après le roman anglais contemporain* (Henry Didier, 1920), first published in the *Times Literary Supplement,* 18 March 1920, cited in Rachel Bowlby (ed.), *Virginia Woolf: A Woman's Essays* (Penguin Books, 1992), 18.

2 Michelle Perrot, *Les Femmes ou les silences de l'histoire* (Paris, 1998), xi–xii.

3 I refer here to the famous pair of conferences in women's history organized by the University of Toulouse-Mirail in 1983 and 1997, titled, respectively, 'Une histoire des femmes est-elle possible?' and 'Une histoire sans les femmes, est-elle possible?'

4 For more on the sex/gender distinction, see Annie Oakley, *Sex, Gender and Society* (London, 1972); Gayle Rubin, 'The Traffic in Women: Notes on the Political Economy of Sex', in Rayna Reiter (ed.), *Towards an Anthropology of Women* (New York, 1975), 157–210; Michèle Barrettt, *Women's Oppression Today: Problems in Marxist-Feminist Analysis* (London, 1980); and Joan W. Scott, 'Gender: A Useful Category of Analysis', *American Historical Review* 91 (1986), 1053–75, reprinted in

Joan W. Scott, *Gender and the Politics of History* (New York, 1988). For a critique of the iron-clad division between biology and culture on which the sex/gender distinction rests, see Mary Midgley, 'On Not Being Afraid of Natural Sex Difference', in Morwenna Griffiths and Margaret Whitford (eds), *Feminist Perspectives in Philosophy* (London, 1988), and Judith Butler, *Gender Trouble: Feminism and the Subversion of Identity* (New York, 1990).

5 Judith Bennett, 'Feminism and History'. *Gender and History* 1(3) (Autumn 1989), 251–71; Joan Hoff, 'Gender as a Postmodern Category of Paralysis', *Women's History Review* 3(2) (1994), 149–68; and Jane Rendall, 'Women's History: Beyond the Cage?', *History* 75 (1990), 63–72.

6 The Subaltern school of history, with its concern for understanding the articulation of nation and class, occupied a similarly advanced position theoretically.

7 Hence, 'Class is defined by men as they live their own history', wrote Edward Thompson in a famous and oft-quoted passage from the introduction to his path-breaking study *The Making of the English Working Class* (London, 1963), 11. The new social history was defined largely by the work of Thompson, Eric Hobsbawm and the young Gareth Stedman Jones, among others. (I refer here to Stedman Jones's early work, notably his *Outcast London: A Study in the Relationship Between Classes in Victorian Society* (Oxford, 1971). Over the next 13 years, Stedman Jones would gradually turn away from the Thompsonian preoccupation with the relationship between structure and agency in favour of exploring the links between culture and politics. See G. Stedman Jones, *Languages of Class: Studies in English Working-Class History, 1832–1982* (Cambridge, 1983).

8 As feminist historian Joan Wallach Scott would later point out, Thompson's artisans relied not only on the freeborn Englishman but on pre-existing ideas about gender, as well. See Joan W. Scott, 'Women in *The Making of the English Working Class*', in Joan W. Scott (ed.), *Gender and the Politics of History* (New York, 1988), 68–90.

9 Adult education in Britain goes back to the University Extension movement, at the end of the 19th century, followed by the Workers' Education Association, which was organized at the turn of the century. See Raphaël Samuel, *People's History and Socialist Theory* (London, 1981), especially the articles by Ken Worpole, 'A Ghostly Pavement: The Political Implications of Local Working-Class History', Jerry White, 'Beyond Autobiography', and Stephen Yeo, 'The Politics of Community Publications'.

10 Catherine Hall, *White, Male and Middle-Class: Explorations in Feminism and History* (Oxford, 1992), 34.

11 The 'new' universities were founded in the aftermath of the Second World War in order to assure higher education to the masses. Elite universities like Oxford and Cambridge would continue to hold themselves aloof from

such Johnny-come-lately disciplines as women's studies until the mid- to late 1990s.

12 A survey of 53 history departments in 1991 Britain revealed that, despite the fact that nearly half the students were women, only 17 per cent of lecturing jobs were held by women, while only 12.7 per cent of senior lecturers, 6.6 per cent of readers and 3 out of 134 professors were women. *Times Literary Supplement*, 7 June 1991, cited in Hall, *White, Male and Middle-Class*, 34.

13 Jill Liddington and Jill Norris, *'One Hand Tied Behind Us': The Rise of the Women's Suffrage Movement* (London, 1978).

14 Sylvia Pankhurst, *The Suffragette* (New York, 1911), and Rachel Strachey, *The Cause* (London, 1978; first published in 1928).

15 Christine Delphy, 'L'Ennemi principale', *Partisans* (1970), 54–5. It is worth noting that those who approached women's history under the sign of the capitalism-versus-patriarchy debate were from the outset struggling with the theoretical difficulties that one particular form of difference among women – that of class – posed for the creation of a unitary feminist approach to historical analysis.

16 See Sylvia Walby's *Patriarchy at Work* (Minneapolis, 1986) for a thorough introduction to the scholarship on theories of patriarchy and women's work. See also Heidi Hartmann, 'The Unhappy Marriage of Marxism and Feminism: Towards a More Progressive Union', in Lydia Sargent (ed.), *Women and Revolution* (Boston, 1981). For an important critique of Hartmann, see Veronica Beechey, *Unequal Work* (London, 1987).

17 See, for example, Sonya Rose, *Limited Livelihoods: Gender and Class in 19th Century England* (Berkeley, 1992); Miriam Glucksmann, *Women Assemble: Women Workers and the New Industries in Interwar Britain* (London, 1990); and Laura Lee Downs, *Manufacturing Inequality: Gender Division in the French and British Metalworking Trades, 1914–1939* (Ithaca, New York, 1995).

18 Hall, *White, Male and Middle Class*, 12–13.

19 Carolyn Steedman, 'Bimbos from Hell', *Social History* 19(1) (January 1994), 57–66, esp. 65. See also Steedman, '"Public" and "Private" in Women's Lives', *Journal of Historical Sociology* 3(3) (1990), 294–304. For an elegant critique of the separate spheres concept, see Amanda Vickery, 'Golden Age to Separate Spheres? A Review of the Categories and Chronology of English Women's History', *Historical Journal* 36(2) (1993), 383–414. For an intelligent and extremely useful exploration of the ways that the widely variable range of individual character and experience constantly threatens to destabilize the binary constructs (such as public and private) that underpin ideologies of gender difference, see Mary Poovey, *Uneven Developments: The Ideological Work of Gender in Mid-Victorian England* (Chicago, 1988).

20 There is an enormous literature on poststructuralist feminist theory. Some useful starting points include Linda Nicholson (ed.), *Feminism/Postmodernism* (London, 1990); Judith Butler and Joan W. Scott (eds), *Feminists Theorize the Political* (London, 1992); Seyla Benhabib and Drucilla Cornell (eds), *Feminism as Critique* (Minneapolis, 1987); and Alison Assiter, *Enlightened Women: Modernist Feminism in a Postmodern Age* (London, 1995).

21 For a more detailed discusson of these points, see Laura Lee Downs, *Writing Gender History* (London, 2004, 2009), and Chapter 7 of this volume.

22 As early as 1983, then, Gareth Stedman Jones argued that it was political language that endowed political behaviour with meaning: 'we cannot therefore decode political language to reach a primal and material expression of interest since it is the discursive structure of political language which conceived and defined interest in the first place'; Gareth Stedman Jones, *Languages of Class: Studies in English Working-class History, 1832–1982* (Cambridge, 1983), 22.

23 Joan Scott, *Gender and the Politics of History* (New York, 1988); Denise Riley, *Am I that Name? Feminism and the Category of Women in History* (Minneapolis, 1988). As I have argued elsewhere, both Scott and Riley explore the internal instabilities that riddle the category 'woman/women'. Riley, however, does so across time, using an approach that is reminiscent of Foucault's genealogical analysis of the 'descent' of words, concepts and identities (see Michel Foucault, 'Nietzsche, Genealogy, History', in D. F. Bouchard and S. Simon (eds and trans.), *Language, Counter-Memory, Practice; Selected Essays and Interviews* (Ithaca, NY, 1977.) Riley's historical-genealogical examination of the category 'woman/women', of the 'sedimented forms of previous characterisations on which new outcroppings flourish', enables us to see gender shape-shift in time; a temporally specific category produced by specific historical relations and 'possessing their full validity only for and within those relations' (Riley, *Am I that Name?*, 166, paraphrasing Marx's *Grundrisse*). See Laura Lee Downs, 'If "Woman" is Just an Empty Category, Then Why Am I Afraid to Walk Alone at Night? Identity Politics Meets the Postmodern Subject', *Comparative Studies in Society and History* (April 1993), 414–37, esp. 416. Riley is also the author of very a fine and subtle history of social policy regarding working mothers in 1940s and 1950s Britain, *War in the Nursery: Theories of the Child and Mother* (London, 1983).

24 Scott, *Gender and the Politics of History*, 25.

25 Scott, *Gender and the Politics of History,* 48–9.

26 In other words, recourse to 'experience' as a category of analysis presupposes the system of signification that must itself be analysed; Scott, 'The Evidence of Experience', *Critical Inquiry* 17(4) (1991), 773–97.

27 See Richard Evans, *In Defense of History* (London, 1997), for a detailed summary of the opposition to poststructuralist 'nihilists'.

28 Patrick Joyce, 'History and Postmodernism', *Past and Present* 133 (November 1991); and Joyce, 'The End of Social History?', *Social History* 20 (1995).

29 See Hall, *White, Male and Middle Class*, 15.

30 See, for example, Judith Butler, *Gender Trouble: Feminism and the Subversion of Identity* (New York, 1990), which argues that identities and differences do not arise from a group's socio-political location but rather are discursively constructed and performatively elaborated through cultural processes. See also Joan Scott, 'Evidence of Experience'.

31 Roper, *Oedipus and the Devil*, 3.

32 Roper, *Oedipus and the Devil*, 227.

33 Roper, *Oedipus and the Devil*, 119–20.

34 Roper, *Oedipus and the Devil*, 26.

35 Roper, *Oedipus and the Devil*, 3.

36 Here I think Roper overstates her claim, leaving to one side the work of such feminist historians as Carolyn Bynum, whose groundbreaking book *Holy Feast and Holy Fast: The Religious Significance of Food to Medieval Women* (Berkeley, 1987) explores (in much the way Roper does) the intersections between religious expression, female subjectivity (in relation to their bodies) and constructions of masculine and feminine in thirteenth- and 14th-century Europe.

37 Roper, *Oedipus and the Devil*, 17, 18.

38 Colin Jones and Dror Wahrman (eds), *The Age of Cultural Revolutions: Britain and France*, 1750–1820 (Berkeley, 2002), 14. Michael Roper has also pursued some of these same points in a fascinating article on subjectivity and emotion in gender history that lays bare the limits of an approach that understands masculinity and femininity as the products of social or cultural construction rather than as aspects of personality. Michael Roper, "Slipping out of view: Subjectivity and emotion in gender history," *History Workship Journal 59, Spring 2005, 57–72.*

39 Barbara Taylor, 'Misogyny and Feminism: The Case of Mary Wollstonecraft', in Jones and Wahrman, *Age of Cultural Revolutions*, pp. 203–17; and Roper, *Oedipus and the Devil*, 13.

40 Lyndal Roper, 'Witchcraft and Fantasy', *History Workshop Journal* 45 (Spring 1998), pp. 265–71, esp. 270.

41 Roper herself admits that psychoanalysis must be deployed alongside other forms of analysis, that the full range of human behaviour cannot be reduced to basic psychic mechanisms. The analysis offered in each of her essays is thus multi-causal, with historical circumstances and contingency playing at least as great a role as psychic conflict. In the end, and to the great benefit of history, Roper's actual historical essays do not grant psychoanalytic explanation the kind of primacy that she preaches in her introductory essay. For a lucid analysis of the issues at stake in historians' adoption of psychoanalytic approaches, see Garthine Walker's contribution to this volume (Chapter 8).

42 For a recent example, see Maria Bucur and Nancy Wingfield (eds), *Gender and War in 20th Century Eastern Europe* (Bloomington, 2006). In western Europe and North America, where the need for a specifically women's history also continues to make itself felt, this need has taken the form of maintaining specific journals that keep the focus on women as a matter of political and intellectual militancy, or of maintaining courses on the particular history of women within the programmes on women's and gender history that have proliferated in universities since the 1970s.
43 Ruth Harris, 'Is Gender Dead?', in Robert Gildea and Anne Simonin (eds), *Writing Contemporary History* (London, 2008) 75.
44 Bonnell and Hunt, *Beyond the Cultural Turn*, p. 11; William Sewell Jr, *Logics of History: Social Theory and Social Transformation* (Chicago, 2005).
45 Sewell, *Logics of History*, 80. See, for example, Silvia Evangelisti, 'Rooms to Share: Convent Cells and Social Relations in Early-Modern Italy', in *The Art of Survival: Gender and History in Europe, 1450–2000, Past & Present*, Supplement 1 (Oxford, 2005).
46 Laura Lee Downs, *Writing Gender History* (2nd ed., London, 2010).
47 Bonnie Smith, *The Gender of History: Men, Women and Historical Practice* (Cambridge, MA, 1998).
48 This phenomenon is beautifully illustrated by Isabel Hull's book *Sexuality, State and Civil Society in Germany, 1700–1815* (Ithaca, 1996), on sexuality and state formation in 18th- and 19th-century Germany.
49 Mrinalini Sinha, *Specters of Mother India; The Global Restructuring of an Empire* (Durham, 2006), 13.
50 I have already mentioned Isabel Hull's work in this regard, but one might also cite Claudia Koonz's classic *Mothers in the Fatherland: Women, the Family and Nazi Politics* (New York, 1987) as well as more recent work that continues to use gender to rethink the political; Tara Zahra, *Kidnapped Souls: National Indifference and the Battle for Children in the Bohemian Lands* (Ithaca, 2008); Kevin Passmore, 'The Gendered Genealogy of Political Religions Theory,' *Gender and History* 20(3) (2008), 644–68; Laura Lee Downs, '"Each and Every One of You Must Become a *Chef*": Towards a Social Politics of Working-Class Childhood on the Extreme Right in 1930s France', *Journal of Modern History* 81, (March 2009), 1–44.
51 Joan Scott, 'Feminism's History', *Journal of Women's History* 16(2) (2004), and Scott, *Gender and the Politics of History*, introduction to the 2nd ed. (New York, 1999).

16

Race, ethnicity and history

Miles Rosenberg

Although theories of race have a long trajectory, the ways in which historians have approached race began to shift rapidly in the 19th century. While scholars of the past had long drawn upon geographic conceptions of peoples, historians increasingly viewed cultures as hierarchical – that is, they ranked peoples with a set of classifications provided by new scientific disciplines. The turn to science served in extending hierarchies of racial difference.

This consideration of the making of race in history requires us to be sceptical of such systems of classification yet aware of the *effects* they have had on the lives, experiences and cultures of people across the world. In other words, we must distinguish the use of *racist* categories to explain history, from the analysis of the ways in which race has been used by historical actors, whether racist, non-, or anti-racist, to make sense of the world. In the former case, race is taken as a self-evident scientific or biological fact that explains the ways in which people see the world and act in it; in the latter, it is a culturally and historically constructed category, and racial attributes are *ascribed* to people. The concept of race in this latter sense is worth studying, as it has pervaded numerous historical texts which sought to render cultural groups different from the writer's own. As a conceptual category, most late 19th-century historians used race to assign fixed quanta of cultural worth; thus, race has served to distribute benefits to those judged 'naturally' well born. Yet, these inequalities have met with resistance across all cultures, from political struggle, to scientific counter-research, to academic scholarship and legal contestation.

In this chapter, we look at historical writing from the late 19th century as a way of understanding how racialized theories informed some of the most prominent works of history. Then, we explore how new theories, and particularly forms of cultural history, have shaped historical works until the present.

16.1 Race, racism and anti-racism in historical explanation before 1920

The revolutions of the 18th century held out promise for colonized peoples – as revolution erupted in the United States, France and then the continent, some revolutionaries advocated the abolition of slavery and the recognition of equality for all peoples. Haiti established independence from France in 1799 – the first time an oppressed people threw off a colonial power. Yet, the coming to power of Napoleon in 1801, the speeding up of trade and industrialization and a renewed imperialism led to the resurgence of strategies of domination.

One of these strategies was the application of new sciences to assert hierarchies, which positioned people of colour as inferior and white peoples as superior. With roots in the Enlightenment, scientists sought to generate a system of classification that would place all human 'species' on a measurable scale. In the early 19th century, the founder of comparative anatomy, Georges Cuvier, forcibly removed a South African woman and took her to France. After she fell ill and died, he and his colleague Henri de Blainville dissected her and put her genitalia on display as a way to prove Africans' 'primitive' status.

At mid-century, Charles Darwin's *On the Origin of Species* outlined the forces of natural selection. As historian Jennifer Terry notes, this theory emphasized 'the dynamics of mating, reproduction, and survival'.[1] As such, it lent itself to 'Social Darwinism', whereby evolutionists extended these theories to take political positions on issues surrounding immigration and reproduction. In 1883, British scientist Francis Galton, a cousin of Charles Darwin, coined the term 'eugenics', which he defined as 'the science of improvement of the human race germ plasm through better breeding'. That is, eugenics appealed to the language of science as a means to limit the births of those deemed 'unfit' (including blacks, Jews, gays, deaf people and the 'feeble-minded') and increase the births of the wealthiest classes. Eugenics became such a powerful system that it traversed national borders – the First International Congress of Eugenics was held in London in 1912, the Second and Third, in 1921 and 1932, respectively, were convened in New York City, drawing participants from Norway, Czechoslovakia, Japan, Venezuela, India and New Zealand.

These assertions of progress through the 'management' of races would shape social policy, anthropology and history. This is clear in the work of Houston Stewart Chamberlain.

Chamberlain, an English-born son of an admiral, travelled to Geneva, where he studied botany, astronomy, anatomy and physiology. After strains on his health, he moved to Dresden and focused his studies on Wagnerian music and philosophy (he would later marry Wagner's daughter). While his first book was a work of art criticism, he shifted back to natural science; after relocating to Vienna, he published a highly regarded botanical study, a treatise on Wagner's dramas and then finally, the controversial *Grundlagen des Neunzehnten Jahrhunderts* (*Foundations of the 19th century*) in 1899.

The *Foundations* was, in an immediate sense, a response to Assyriology, a discipline that had flourished in the universities of Germany. The work addresses a professor Delitzsch, who had recently found evidence of worship of one God among 'the Semitic tribes of Canaan which at the time of Khammurabi, two thousand years before the birth of Christ, flooded Assyria, were worshippers of one God, and that the name of that God was Jahve (Jehovah)'.[2] At issue here was the degree to which scholars could discuss Near Eastern origins or religious commonalities in Germany, a nation experiencing an increasing nationalism in the late 19th century. This nationalist fervour was buttressed by several currents in the academy. As George Mosse has noted, disciplines such as anthropology, ethnology and linguistics, the latter which Frederich Schlegel helped to develop, attempted to draw a line between European and supposed 'lesser' cultures. Schlegel legitimated the notion that India was the foundation for all European languages. While he did not explicitly claim European superiority, he disparaged languages derived from Chinese (including Native American and Slavonic) as random and weak. Through his theory of 'noble' and 'ignoble' languages, Schlegel popularized the concept of 'Aryan' origins.

Chamberlain instead set out to provide a complex account of the rise of Indo-European civilization, the story of what he called 'Der Germane'. Within this appellation, Chamberlain attempted to subsume all Celts, Germans, Slavs and 'all those races of northern Europe', including the white peoples of the United States. While he excluded the French, he claimed Louis XIV as a 'genuine Germane' for having challenged the Papacy. Using this classification, Chamberlain asserted a racial discourse of history.

Chamberlain outlined a sweeping narrative of 'critical knowledge' of the past, a past 'which is still living'. From research on the first eighteen centuries of the 'Christian era', with reference to the ancients, the 19th century would emerge 'clearly shaped', not in encyclopaedic form, 'but as a living 'corporeal' thing' (Chamberlain, *Foundations of the 19th Century*, p. xii). This corporeal history represented a scientific conception of the past.

Foundations was very well received, garnering praise in Germany, Britain and America. Kaiser Wilhelm II thanked Chamberlain by letter:

> Our stifled youth needed a liberator like yourself, one who revealed to us the Indo-German origins which no one knew about. And so it was only at the cost of a hard struggle that the original Germanic Aryanism (das Uranische-Germanische) which slumbered in the depths of my soul was able to assert itself.[3]

Chamberlain's writings assumed that race was *the* underlying category that explained the course of history, determined (or should determine) the behaviour of individuals and groups, and set out Germany's mission in the world. His vision impacted not only historians, but also legislators, scientists and commentators, who saw race as a *problem* to be regulated.

16.2 Race, empires and progress

In the 1930s, historians began to use several theories to explicate the meanings of race. When historians like Chamberlain asserted that their race was superior, they rewrote the ancient past to trace the grand development of a European people. Theirs was a story of progress through the history of race. Ancient cultures have benefited from new readings, including social science research on 'race relations' and histories of ancient languages, to best understand commonalities across cultural difference.

The concept of 'race' is entangled with the notion of 'civilization'. Historians have long seen 'world history' as a successive study of *empires* and the formation of new political identities. Much 19th-century historical writing – from English Whig history to German historism – was concerned with the rise of empires and states, and was concerned to legitimate them historically. Some of these assumptions about necessary historical development survived in social scientific theories such as modernization theory. As such, students of history have considered interactions between different empires; given the West's tendency to locate its origins in Greco-Roman culture, were the encounters between Greco-Roman and African civilizations reciprocally influential? The works considered in this section represent critiques of certain explicitly or tacitly racist ideas of progress – including some versions of the notion of 'modernization'.

Frank Snowden has written two defining works on the links among Mediterranean, Egyptian and Ethiopian civilizations. In *Blacks in Antiquity* (1970), Snowden explored Africans' experiences in Greco-Roman culture from the time of Homer through the rule of Justinian. His task is to trace Greco-Roman views of Ethiopians using diverse evidence: 'literary, epigraphical, papyrological, numismatic, and archaeological' (*Blacks in Antiquity*, p. viii). He demonstrates the African origins of western 'civilization'. Yet, Snowden's use of 'Ethiopian' follows Greek and Roman usage. Both cultures homogenized all African peoples regardless of place under this term. In parallel to the way 'Negro' performs an erasure of African and Caribbean cultural variation, Snowden renders classical depictions of Africans.

His aim in *Before Colour Prejudice* (1983) was to provide a 'comprehensive study of *the image of blacks in the minds of Mediterranean whites* who opposed them in battle or lived with them in peace during the period from the Pharaohs to the Caesars' (*Before Colour Prejudice*, p. vii, my emphasis). Snowden's method is twofold: first, he closely examines the meanings of artists' conceptions of blackness. Second, Snowden draws upon social science research on the origin of colour prejudice – while the ancients accepted slavery as an institution and sometimes made ethnocentric judgements of *other* societies, 'nothing comparable to the virulent colour prejudice of modern times existed in the ancient world' (*Before Colour Prejudice*, p. 63). Blackness was viewed neither as a sign of inferiority nor as a bar to integration. While one finds pejorative statements about blackness, the ancients were aware of varying conceptions of beauty; thus, 'it is questionable whether individuals should be called "racist" because they accept prevailing aesthetic canons in the country' (*Before Colour Prejudice*, p. 63). Still, we must ask about the individual's status, and whether their texts defined social norms, enacted legislation, or were symptomatic of the dominant views of the empire.

The interaction between classical and African cultures is also central to Martin Bernal's two-volume *Black Athena*. This sweeping study tracks the influence of Egypt on Greek culture. Written by a scholar of Chinese studies, Bernal became interested in ancient Jewish history. Around this time, he began to study the Hebrew language and noted many parallels between Hebrew and Greek. Within four years, Bernal had recognized that nearly 90 per cent of the Greek language was comprised of Indo-European, Egyptian and Semitic roots.

Bernal sets out two models of scholarship on the Near East: the 'Ancient' model and the 'Aryan' model. In the former, the dominant view in Greek culture, Greece had arisen from Phoenician origins around 2100 BCE. In contrast, the Aryan model held that an invasion from the north overtook Pre-Hellenic Greece and gave it a fundamentally Indo-European civilization. Drawing upon the work of the historian of science Thomas Kuhn, Bernal points out that this *paradigm* emerged in the last 150 years in the context of European neo-colonialism and anti-Jewish discourse.

Bernal then traces how the Ancient model was gradually displaced in the 18th century by aristocrats, influenced by the Enlightenment, who turned to science for the 'origins' of man. Informed by Romanticism, European scholars from Johann Gottfried von Herder, who fostered the discipline of linguistics, to Johann Winkelman, the founder of art history as a discipline, posited Greece as the foundation of European civilization. These writers would figure 'Egypt' as increasingly backward, and Europe became redefined as the site of 'progress'. While both volumes deal with how racism shaped accounts of European origins, the terms 'race' and 'racism' are only briefly treated; for Bernal, after 1650, racism is 'greatly intensified by the increased colonization of North America, with its twin policies of extermination of the Native Americans and enslavement of Africans'

(*Black Athena* , p. 201–2). In sum, Bernal criticizes the kind of history written by open racists like Chamberlain and the subtly racist implications of certain recent stories of progress.

16.3 Critiquing whiteness: The grammars of race

The texts in this section, informed by currents in literary theory, seek to unravel the 'grammars' of race. Grammars here refer to codes, both linguistic and social, denoting stereotypes, terms or 'small acts', that mark racial hierarchy, difference and contestation.

David Roediger's work marks an important departure in the uses of theory to compose histories of race. Drawing upon writers of colour, especially novelist and literary theorist Toni Morrison, he critiques race as not simply a 'Negro problem', but rather a problem of whites, showing 'working-class "whiteness" and white supremacy as creations, in part, of the white working class itself' (*Wages of Whiteness*, p. 9). In *The Wages of Whiteness* (1990), Roediger tracks the formation of the 'white worker' in Antebellum America. His goal is to find how labourers came to see themselves as white in relation to systems of slavery and the movement for Reconstruction. He explores how Irish immigrants, many of whom had built alliances with African-Americans in unions as well as in social settings, were divided through racist stereotypes. Irish politicians, turning to the Democratic Party, crudely dismissed its opposition through the grammar of race: 'Democratic politicians charged that Republicans and abolitionists had "nigger on the brain"' (*Wages of Whiteness*, p. 154).

While Roediger's work may seem indebted to poststructuralism, it is actually more closely allied with Mikhail Bakhtin's theory of language. Roediger critiques poststructuralism for neglecting interactions between the 'individual' and the 'text' and its assumption that

> each *generation* finds its own different meanings in texts. Bakhtin on the other hand, holds that 'at any given moment … language is stratified not only into linguistic dialects … but also – and for us this is the essential point – into languages which are socio-ideological'.[4]

In other words, Roediger seeks to render the complex production of racial 'grammar' without losing the role of class in language itself. *The Wages of Whiteness* is thus an innovative social history of race and labour.

Examining blackface minstrelsy, Roediger usefully points out that many performers were artisans, mechanics and working-class tradesmen; in sex-segregated spaces, white workers caroused and played out fantasies of racial difference. Interestingly, one can locate a degree of oppositional culture within blackface – masters were often ridiculed, yet many shows supported white supremacist views and mocked civil and women's rights.

While this oppositional element of blackface is significant, it cannot replace histories of raced *experience*. Although the literature on race thus far had sought out every text complicit in the production of *racism*, few had traced either the felt sense or the challenges of race or ethnicity, as told by those resisting racism.

Ronald Takaki's *A Different Mirror* (1993) explores the cross-currents of migration and the contributions of Native Americans, Mexicans, Chinese, Irish, Japanese, Jews and African-Americans to debates about race. Writing in the wake of the Los Angeles riots and demographic projections that white Americans would soon become a minority, Takaki takes as a point of departure the debates over 'multiculturalism' by tracing America's diversity since the first settlement at Jamestown in 1607.

Takaki uses Shakespeare's *The Tempest*, with its monstrous character Caliban, as a parable of colonists' racist conceptions of native peoples and the effects of racism in the New World. Drawing on retheorizations of *The Tempest* by Shakespeare scholar Stephen Greenblatt, Takaki shows how the play illuminated the politics of colonization. The play's title referenced a real incident – in 1609, a ship on its way to 'Virginia' had shipwrecked in Bermuda. Shakespeare knew some of the voyagers and set his play in 'Bermoothes'. Creating 'Caliban' from the word 'Carib', the name for an Indian tribe, Carib became a metonym for New World racist fantasies – it was believed that Caliban could be acculturated; yet, he came from a 'vile race'. His mother, 'Sycorax', was a witch from Africa, giving him dangerous connotations; yet, he was a 'deformed slave'. For Takaki, race is socially constructed, and these constructions considerably affected conditions for minorities in America.

Takaki takes a comparative approach to 'the varied experiences of different racial and ethnic groups … within shared contexts' (*Different Mirror*, p. 10). In tracing Chinese migration, Takaki relocates the formation of 'immigrant' identity to the West Coast, away from the dominant saga of New York's Ellis Island. After Reconstruction, many Southerners sought to use Chinese labour on plantations. Soon, they were demonized in ways similar to blacks, as 'heathen, morally inferior, childlike, and lustful' (*Different Mirror*, p. 205). This transfer of racism was perniciously inscribed into law. During the murder trial of Ling Sing in 1854, the California Supreme Court declared that 'the words "Indian, Negro, Black, and White" were generic terms, designating races', and that therefore 'Chinese and other people not white could not testify against whites' (*Different Mirror*, p. 206). This became the prelude to the federal Chinese Exclusion Act, which closed America's borders in 1882 and, in 1902, was extended indefinitely. Still, despite overwhelming odds, the Chinese formed vibrant communities in California and the Northwest.

In *Race Rebels*, Robin D. G. Kelley (1994) gives a history of working-class blacks from 'way, way down below'. Informed by W. E. B. DuBois's *Black Reconstruction* (1935) and C. L. R. James's *Black Jacobins* (1938) on the overthrow of French colonialism in Haiti, as well as new work in British cultural studies, Kelley traces the small acts of resistance by black labourers and the ways they maintained 'a sense of racial identity and solidarity' (*Race Rebels*, p. 5). While Kelley acknowledges the mid-1960s writings of E. P. Thompson and Eugene Genovese, he draws upon those earlier 'majestic histories of revolution, resistance, and the making of new working classes out of the destruction of slavery [which] anticipated the "new" social historians' efforts to write "history from below"' (*Race Rebels*, p. 5).

Breaking from both labour histories that focused solely on white workers and African-American historiography that posited a generalized 'black community', Kelley tracks the *hidden transcripts*, a concept developed by anthropologist James Scott, of black working-class lives at the margins. From the songs and poems of African-Americans in the Communist Party, to the black volunteers who fought fascism in the Spanish Civil War, to the politics of 'hipness' in the life of young Malcolm X, the politics of black cultural production, vis-à-vis, but not dependent upon racism, becomes visible. Kelley's work, informed by Marxism and by the 'history from below' movement, but not reducible to it, captures the making of radical African-American culture.

16.4 Cultivating race: The poststructuralist and postcolonial turn

Historians have addressed race as not simply the product of individual actors, but as a kind of constantly retold grand fable. Mosse anticipated this method, that of postructuralism, in his discussion of myth. He wrote:

> Racism substituted myth for reality; and the world that it created, with its stereotypes, virtues, and vices, was a fairy-tale world, which dangled a utopia before the eyes of those who longed for a way out of the confusion of modernity and the rush of time. (p. xiii)

In other words, race was constructed as a myth (akin to Foucault's 'discourse'), which, Mosse noted, became a 'foundation for national policy' of the Nazis. Mosse traced this myth through racial iconography, in what appears to be the first anti-racist study to include and critique paintings, political cartoons and propaganda.

Thus, race is not static or fixed – systems of racial classification were profoundly shaped by political dynamics, scientific priorities and the increasing demands of mercantile trade. But race and politics were mutually affected in another way – that of racial 'cultivation'. Racial *cultivation* refers to ways in which social classes figured 'race' as a means to elevate or maintain their status. In the early modern era, aristocrats spoke of race increasingly in terms of primary, 'authentic' stock. Countering royal genealogies asserted by monarchy, aristocratic commentators such as Sir Edward Coke and Boulainvilliers confronted the realities of *sanguinity* – marriages for the purposes of wider political rule – with a 'racial' discourse of aristocratic privilege. Drawing upon poststructuralism, we understand from Foucault that meanings are constructed through language. His *genealogy* in *The History of Sexuality* briefly noted a historical shift from this *deployment of alliance* (that is, the use of marriage alliances to further diplomacy) to the concept of *biopower* (in other words, the role that sciences had in extending power over human life). Foucault asserts that the interchange between these two points is the model of *confession*, which is extended in and through medicine and psychiatry. Whereas confession had been confined to the church, doctors and psychiatrists increasingly adopted it as a means to secure professional authority. What is more ambiguous is how this shift played out, especially in colonial contexts.

Ann Laura Stoler's *Race and the Education of Desire* is a detailed study of racial cultivation. Stoler opens with a careful reading of the 1976 Collège de France lectures of Michel Foucault. Drawing upon archival research, Stoler fills in a major gap in Foucault's work: an engagement with racism. While Foucault had provided stunning critiques of prisons, sexuality[5] and medicine, many Foucauldian scholars who sought to confront race were at a loss. While studies of peasant revolts under colonialism had benefited from structuralism,[6] only a few works combined a tenable critique of imperialism with a nuanced analysis of the forces which gave rise to it. Edward Said's *Orientalism* critiqued European conceptions of a racially homogenous 'Oriental' – whether Arabic, Asian or Indian, travel writers and novelists rendered the 'Oriental' as incompetent and inferior.[7]

Stoler is interested in how Foucault's chronologies have bracketed certain possibilities for colonial studies. She writes (in *Race and the Education of Desire*, pp. 5–6),

> What is striking is how consistently Foucault's own framing of the European bourgeois order has been exempt from the very sorts of criticism that his insistence on the fused regimes of knowledge/power would seem to encourage and allow. Why have we been so willing to accept his story of a 19th-century sexual order that systematically excludes and/or subsumes the fact of colonialism within it?'

In other words, what analytical tools are needed to examine colonial regimes outside of the terms of Western discourse?

Stoler renders Foucault's 7 January 1976 lecture as an 'analytic repositioning' of his earlier work. In subsequent weeks, Foucault would trace a 'war of races'. This discourse saw the formation of law as 'the consequence of massacres, conquests, and domination, not as the embodiment of natural rights' (*Race and the Education of Desire*, p. 65). For Foucault, this discourse did not detach itself from 'rights' – truth is still linked to 'the rights of a family (to property), of a class (to privilege), of a race (to rule)' (*Race and the Education of Desire*, p. 65). As aristocrats challenged royal genealogies, this 'war of races' became one of 'an upper-race and lower-race', with the latter representing the 'reappearance of its own past' (*Race and the Education of Desire*, p. 66). The latter quote may seem cryptic, but means that aristocrats both acknowledged the king's power and vigorously defended themselves as the 'pure' stock and leaders of the realm.

One of Stoler's critical insights is that '19th-century science may have legitimated racial classifications as many have claimed, but it [did] so by drawing on an earlier lexicon, on that of the struggle of races' (*Race and the Education of Desire*, p. 68). In other words, sciences like craniology depended upon earlier racial grammars. Modern racism has its roots in a discourse on 'races', which would become singularly rendered as *race*.

Drawing together a range of analyses, Ruth Roach Pierson and Nupur Chaudhuri's *Nation, Empire, Colony* serves as a key starting point for understanding the histories of women under colonialism and within nation-states. The Introduction builds upon insights of feminists of colour to explore the asymmetries of race and class in the experiences of women. Yet, this analysis does not assume that the categories 'gender' and 'women' are synonymous. Pierson and Chaudhuri note that 'the ways one becomes a woman or a man are much more complex than in simple opposition to members of the other sex' (*Nation, Empire, Colony*, p. 2). Thus, the authors recognize that gender can be 'raced'; put more broadly, social categories are linked within a network of power relations.

This set of essays emerged from a 1995 meeting of the International Federation for Research in Women's History. The Federation advocated international women's history without 'global' pretensions, a term associated with neo-imperialism. In dialogue with Stoler's work, the authors bring research on both the 'metropole' and 'colony' together, 'to dismantle the barriers separating the imperialists' history from that of the imperialized, the colonists' from that of the colonized, the narrative of the nation's core from that of its excluded margins' (*Nation, Empire, Colony*, p. 3).

Rosalyn Terborg-Penn considers the links between the US suffrage movement and parallel activism in the Caribbean. She shows how American women's political work was inflected by neo-Victorian conceptions of womanhood, which figured Caribbean women as 'Other'. Her writing shows that 'successful 20th-century woman suffrage movements appeared first in western nations, which controlled colonies in other areas of the globe, and in white-dominated or white-colonized colonies' (pp. 43–4). Working against the assumption that women of colour had no involvement in the early movement, the author shows how Caribbean women, working-class and well-to-do, lobbied for the right to vote as early as the century's turn. Often, feminist victories in the United States sparked new efforts by working-class Puerto Rican and St Thomian women for suffrage. Combining readings of new work in colonial women's history and her own preliminary research, Terborg-Penn traces how white American suffragettes often expressed racist views of black women.

Gabriela Cano's essay 'The *Porfiriato* and the Mexican Revolution' shows how the Mexican Revolution of the 1890s would affect representations of Mexican identity. In dialogue with work on Indians in Mexico, Cano illuminates the stakes of nationalism. Cano combines two approaches: an analysis of images of the 'Mexican woman' at the turn of the century, and a critique of liberal republicanism, which viewed indigenous peoples as a block to progress. Many writers, influenced by the Social-Darwinism of Auguste Comte and Herbert Spencer, claimed that Mexican women were naturally sentimental, given to domesticity and 'discreet'. Women, nevertheless, gradually called for equality and the proper governing of Mexico. Still, women had to contend with definitions of Mexican femininity as racially impure. Statements from prominent figures like novelist Julio Sesto 'implied that the "Mexican woman" is *mestiza*, that is, a mixture of Spanish and Indian blood in which European physical traits, such as whiteness, have predominated and diluted Indian ones' (p. 110).

After civil war in 1911 broke the power of the *Porfiriato* (the dictatorship of Porfirio Díaz), fears about women's power subsided somewhat in more radical circles and in post-revolutionary governments. Within five years, the military government of the Yucatan was supporting feminist congresses, which challenged the power of Catholicism in Mexico. Thus, women's movements, in their official recognition, were often part of a larger strategy of nationalism and modernization.

In 'Men, Women, and the Community Borders', Sayoko Yoneda portrays the Japanese military 'comfort women' that forced Korean women into prostitution during the Second World War. In an impressive essay that calls attention to a pressing problem of historical memory, Yoneda draws upon recent newspaper accounts of comfort women to excavate how this system depended upon both sexism *and* racism. She notes that in the 1930s, when Japan began to invade China, Japanese prostitutes travelled with soldiers and served in the 'comfort' system – this afforded women a sense of patriotism and allowed them to escape a more haphazard, unregulated system at home. But as the war escalated, the number of Japanese prostitutes was 'insufficient'. At this time, the government began to look toward Korea, which was under Japanese control.

The Japanese government would also extract women from the Philippines, Singapore and Indonesia in the early 1940s. Yoneda also connects the rise of prostitution to 'sex tours' that many businessmen, from Japan and the West, conduct today in the Philippines and Thailand; notably, Thai and Filipino women have been taken to Japan against their will. The Japanese government has continued to deny its involvement in this system or express any remorse to these women.

It is fair to say that poststructuralism is open to the charge of constructing the oppressed as the negative term – the 'Other' – of a binary opposition. Thus, we ought to explore histories of race that show the contestedness of theories of race.

16.5 Race as a contested discourse

Recent histories of slavery, informed by new theoretical developments, have reinvigorated the field. So many pioneering studies of the Atlantic Slave Trade were written during and after the Civil Rights Movement, when the methods of psychohistory and social history predominated. Yet, in the 1980s, many historians began to situate their work in relation to several disciplines, including semiotics and cultural anthropology. Sue Peabody's *There Are No Slaves in France*, located at the intersection of legal history and cultural history, looks at legal cases, edicts and registers to understand the experience of slaves in France and the political culture of the Ancien Régime.

Benefiting from the groundbreaking work of Robert Darnton, the author places lawyers, masters, slaves and royal officials within their historical and legal contexts to give a *micro-history* of 18th-century France. Treating race here in a way that implicitly challenges the narrative of modernization that Mosse had asserted, Peabody tracks the role of the Church in the regulation and potential 'liberation' of slaves within France. For example, baptism, while inscribed into the *Code Noir* (1685) as solely a precondition for slaves upon entering France, actually served as one path to freedom. Some French masters, along with their English counterparts, would 'recognize baptism as a formal act of manumission' (*There Are no Slaves,* p. 80).

Second, Peabody excavates a critical concept in histories of race in France: the 'Freedom Principle', according to which once a slave touched French soil, they were free. While in practice, the French kept servants, as early as the 1570s, the phrase 'There are no slaves in France' resonated in the streets of Paris. This principle would be the basis for many legal challenges to enslavement and detainment of African slaves.

For authors influenced by structuralism, such as Stocking, 'race' is largely the product of declarations by scientists, policymakers and legislators—they construct a *dominant discourse* of the 'Other', an object of scientific, legal and political knowledges. With Peabody, race is *refigured* – dominant discourses by the king, ministers and police are contested by both accounts of free blacks as well as those who *spoke back* to the law in the courts.

Lawyers who defended escaped slaves drew upon legal arguments grounded in the view that early Christianity had helped to undo Roman slavery. Peabody writes of the case of Jean Boucaux vs Bernard Verdelin – Boucaux was the son of two slaves owned by the governor of the French colony, Saint Domingue. When the governor died, his widow married Monsieur Verdelin, and they soon travelled to the island to make arrangements on the estate. In 1728, they returned with two slaves, including Boucaux, who served as Verdelin's cook for nine years. Near the end of that period, Boucaux married a French woman. From then on, Boucaux became the object of Verdelin's hatred; the enmity became so strong that in 1738, 'Verdelin had Boucaux arrested "because he suspected Boucaux of planning an escape and he was afraid to lose him"' (*There Are No Slaves*, p. 25). Boucaux prevailed, providing an important precedent for future legal decisions in the French Admiralty Court.

Students interested in how both racism and anti-slavery discourse shaped law will find much insight here. Peabody traces how the *Code Noir* (literally 'Black Code') of 1685 met increasing legal challenges throughout the 18th century. Notably, the grammar of the *Code Noir* appeared 150 years later in the United States, where 'black codes' enforced common law segregation throughout the United States. This critical point demands further research – how did racial discourses travel? What forces allowed racism to move within and across specific geographic domains? In order to confront this issue, we must consider how race has operated through *political* spheres. As we further explore the history of colonized subjects under slavery, we begin to find the traffic of regulations between 'home' country and colony.

Matthew Frye Jacobson's book *Whiteness of a Different Colour* (1998) is attentive to the ways in which language serves in the fabrication of race. He opens with a 'Note on Usage' that discusses the author's decision not to put the word 'race' in undermining quotation marks. A stylistic and practical move, Jacobson found that nearly every sentence would have been rife with quotation marks. Still, he included the word 'race', as well as 'Teutons', 'Nordics', 'Hebrews' and other appellations in quotation marks when an author actually used this punctuation.

First, Jacobson's decision is incisive – to understand historical meanings around race, we must consider not only how critical theories shape current writing, but also how authors of the past problematized or deployed race. Sometimes, authors did so strategically to challenge dominant conceptions of race; at others, those dedicated to segregation used scare quotes to further a white supremacist agenda.

Second, this is a rare opportunity to meditate upon the composing of scholarship on race. While he originally tended to put words such as 'Anglo-Saxon' and 'racial' in quotes, terms such as 'white' or 'black' received less consideration. Bidding the reader to consider their own linguistic desires, he writes,

> I wonder about the unexamined racial certainty that this denotes, too. *All these designations belong on the same epistemological footing*, and so they appear before you now without any stylistic marker to separate archaic fabrications from current ones. *If you are inclined to supply your own as you go, I only invite you, too, to note the patterns of your own choices.* A principled consistency on this score is rendered very difficult by the culture within which we operate. (*Whiteness of a Different Colour*, p. x, my emphasis)

Jacobson makes a claim here that must be unpacked. If all classifications of race are *equally* problematic, then what does it mean for cultural groups to redefine insults or reclaim domains from which blacks were historically marginalized? For example, hip-hop artists sometimes speak of 'droppin' science'; artists depend on and *transvalue* the *power* of science to establish the 'truth' of their rhymes. Thus, over time, certain terms are reappropriated by sub-cultures to create very different epistemologies. We need new histories that consider the *specific* valences which each racial concept carries.

The construction of whiteness is a central theme in Jacobson's work. Combining archival research in immigration law, demography and stunningly perceptive readings of literature, Jacobson carefully traces the racialized landscape for European immigrants to America. Rather than assume that race has a fixed meaning, he critiques works which confuse race with colour.

In other words, Jacobson's goal is

> to map the significance of the racial designations that have framed the history of European immigration – white and Caucasian on the one hand, and narrower distinctions such as Anglo-Saxon, Celt, Hebrew, Slav, Mediterranean, or Nordic on the other – in order to make sense of pervasive racial articulations that scholars have too conveniently passed over simply as misuses of the word 'race'. (*Whiteness of a Different Colour*, p. 6)

The historical, experiential specificity of *race* is crucial here. Some African-American scholars, such as W. E. B. DuBois, were not ready to simply discard the term 'race', as they understood its significance *within* black culture. For Jewish, Irish, Mediterranean and Slavic emigrants, the ways in which one became 'white' were not given – their transmutation into 'Caucasians' was a complex, non-linear process. Jacobson periodizes this gradual shift into three eras: 1790 to 1840, 1840 to 1924 and 1924 to 1965. The first era was marked by the rise of the designation 'free white male inhabitants' in several state constitutions. Concomitantly, legislators rendered specific restrictions against blacks, who were defined as 'dependents'. This highlighted a paternalist racism – blacks held the same political status as women and children.

While Jacobson acknowledges Roediger's work, he differs with Roediger's focus upon class formation. If white workers solely benefited from what W. E. B. DuBois called the 'public and psychological wage' of esteem from political institutions, then how do we explain nativist stereotypes directed at Celtic, Slavic and Italian peoples? How is possible that Irish people were once viewed as 'savages'?

Between 1840 and 1924, America was rapidly transformed by the second wave of industrialization with mines, chemical plants and steel mills. Thus, the republican ideology of 'independence' confronted the reality of emigrants who sought religious freedoms and new opportunities. Republicanism, Jacobson shows, was marked by the shifting boundaries of racism. He notes that, while before the 1840s 'whiteness' depended upon its opposition to 'non-whiteness', the latter half of the century witnessed the construction of scientific hierarchies of racial difference.

Readers seeking to understand the rise of American eugenics will find much wisdom here. Jacobson critiques assumptions of the most prominent, conservative commentators of this era, including Harry Laughlin and Madison Grant. Also useful are examples of the ways in which writers, both emigrant and non-emigrant, offered snapshots of racial meanings. From the works of Hugh Henry Brackenridge, to the turn-of-the century writings of Charles Chestnutt, to Arthur Miller's politically acute novel *Focus* (1945), Jacobson intersperses how authors understood the boundaries of race. This is not so much a recuperative effort as a theorization – Jacobson outlines how scientific theories of race infused literary texts, and what they articulated about the politics of race.

Racial assumptions of difference underwrote even anti-racist efforts in the 1930s and 1940s. The liberal focus on the 'Negro Question' would posit new dichotomies (white/coloured, white/Negro), erasing Asians and Latinos from public discourse. Anthropologists only bolstered these notions, asserting the 'three great divisions of mankind': 'Caucasian', 'Mongoloid' and 'Negroid'. Jacobson captures how 'ethnic' writers negotiated these systems.

16.6 Conclusion

Historians are in a unique position to subvert dominant debates about the meanings of race. Recently, after an interminable silence on race from the profession, historians have begun to apply knowledges in the public sphere. For example, Eric Foner called upon the state of New York to recognize its participation in the slave system. Encouraging projects that would educate citizens, he identified corporations that benefited from slavery.[8]

Given the legacy of discrimination, histories of race can open up dialogue and initiate the process of redressing the violences that racism has wrought. The need for cultural understanding, across all (supposed) racial and ethnic boundaries, will lead to promising futures.

Coda

While race has marked US political culture since its founding, in this current election season, a certain discourse around both campaigns has been inflected with racial grammar. Take, for example, the Weblink for senator Barack Obama's campaign, which reads 'Welcome to Obama for America'. The subtle meaning implies, vis-à-vis Conservative doubts about Obama's father's birth outside of the United States, or his son's partly Muslim upbringing, that Obama is proactively *for* America (and not, say, holding allegiance to another nation or for 'More Foreign Oil', as one of McCain's negative campaigns ads claimed). Compare this to senator John McCain's site, which reads, 'JohnMcCain.com'. Moreover, John McCain claimed that Obama played the 'race card' with Obama's famous comment that he 'doesn't look like all those other presidents on the dollar bills'.[9] Obama has campaigned, in this author's humble estimation, by applying the highest of ethical standards. In the face of an older white generation's obsession over his 'eloquence', Obama has directly addressed key national security, economic and social issues. What is historic is that, in the post-civil rights era, Obama can be a front-runner in the campaign for America's highest office.

Guide to further reading

Martin Bernal, *Black Athena: The Afroasiatic Roots of Classical Civilization*, 2 vols (London, 1987; New Brunswick, 1991).

N. Chaudhuri and R. R. Pierson (eds), *Nation, Empire, Colony: Historicizing Race and Gender* (Bloomington, 1998).

Matthew Frye Jacobson, *Whiteness of a Different Colour: European Immigrants and the Alchemy of Race* (Cambridge, MA, 1998).

Robin D. G. Kelley, *Race Rebels: Culture, Politics, and the Black Working Class* (New York, 1994).

Sue Peabody, *'There Are No Slaves in France': The Political Culture of Race and Slavery in the Ancien Régime* (New York, 1996).

David Roediger, *The Wages of Whiteness: Race and the Making of the American Working Class* (London, 1991).

Frank M. Snowden, Jr, *Blacks in Antiquity: Ethiopians in the Greco-Roman Experience* (Cambridge, MA, 1970).

Frank M. Snowden, Jr, *Before Colour Prejudice: The Ancient View of Blacks* (Cambridge, MA, 1983).

George W. Stocking, Jr, *Race, Culture, and Evolution: Essays in the History of Anthropology* (New York, 1968).

Ann Laura Stoler, *Race and the Education of Desire: Foucault's History of Sexuality and the Colonial Order of Things* (Durham, NC, 1995).

Notes

I would like to thank Jennifer Terry, David Horn, C. L. Cole, Dale Van Kley and Melissa Orlie for dialoguing with me and fostering my interests across the disciplinary terrain covered here. Much appreciation goes to Kevin Passmore for his encouragement and careful reading of this essay.

1 Jennifer Terry, *An American Obsession; Science, Medicine, and Homosexuality in Modern Society* (Chicago, 1999), pp. 36–7.
2 John Lees 'Introduction', p. ix, in Houston Stewart Chamberlain, *Foundations of the 19th century*, trans. John Lees (New York, 1914, first published 1901).
3 Léon Poliakov, *The Aryan Myth: A History of Racist and Nationalist Ideas in Europe*, trans. Edmund Howard (New York, 1974; first published 1971), p. 319.
4 Quoted in David Roediger, *The Wages of Whiteness: Race and the Making of the American Working Class* (London, 1991), p. 15.
5 For the ways in which scientific discourses of race shaped homosexuality, consult Terry's *An American Obsession*. For racism and figurations of gay sexuality in late 19th-century film and literature, see Siobhan B. Somerville, *Queering the Colour Line: Race and the Invention of Homosexuality in American Culture* (Durham, NC, 2000).
6 Ranajit Guha (ed.), *Subaltern Studies: Writings on South Asian History and Society* (Delhi, 1982).
7 Edward W. Said, *Orientalism* (New York, 1979). Although Oriental studies, as a discipline, once took aim at both Muslims and Jews, Said shows that the Israeli military and rightist parties have demonized Palestinians as 'irrational' and incapable of self-government.
8 'Slavery's Fellow Travelers', *New York Times*, 14 July 2000. Foner notes that in the 19th century, New York's merchant class controlled the South's cotton trade, thereby challenging the still persistent notion that the North was somehow 'less' racist.
9 Quoted in Steven Walters, 'McCain Says Obama Made Race an Issue', 31 July 2008, *Milwaukee Journal-Sentinel* (online edition), http://www.jsonline.com/story/index.aspx?id=778794, accessed 4 October 2008.

17

Voices from below: Doing people's history in Cardiff Docklands

Glenn Jordan

History, in the hands of the professional historian, is apt to present itself as an esoteric form of knowledge. It fetishizes archive-based research, as it has done since the Rankean revolution – or counter-revolution – in scholarship. When matters of interpretation are in dispute, disagreement may turn on such apparently arcane questions as the wordings of a coronation oath, the dating of a royal portrait or the correlation of harvest yields with fluctuations in peasant nuptuality. Argument is embedded in dense thickets of footnotage, and lay readers who attempt to unravel it find themselves enmeshed in a cabbala of acronyms, abbreviations and signs ...
Popular memory is on the face of it the very antithesis of written history.

Raphael Samuel[1]

Who produces history? Whose side is history on? What is the relationship between history and cultural democracy? One of the most interesting developments in the practice of academic and public history since the early or mid-20th century (depending on where one wishes to assign the point of 'origins') has been the 'recovery' of marginalized memories, voices and experiences – of the working-classes, women, black people and other subordinate groups. Whether based in academic institutions or in community settings, 'people's history' has transformed the practice of history writing in a range of contexts, from books to exhibitions to media programmes. When it has been rooted in cultural democracy – i.e. in practices that ensure the active involvement of a broad public, including marginalized groups – 'people's history' has sometimes transformed people's lives.

This chapter is a case study of one attempt to practise cultural democracy, including people's history, community education and community art, over a period of some 20 years in one of Britain's oldest multi-ethnic, working-class communities. The paper reflects on that practice and seeks to relate it to larger issues having to do with unofficial knowledge, engaged intellectual work and the project of history from below. The organization is Butetown History & Arts Centre; the location is Cardiff docklands, specifically, the famous, often maligned, community known as Butetown, or 'Tiger Bay'.

17.1 The context

From the mid-1800s to the 1990s, Butetown linked the port of Cardiff with the city centre. From the 1840s to the redevelopment of the 1960s, this small, mile-long district housed one of Britain's largest immigrant and minority communities. It was home to people from more than 50 nations, from virtually all over the world: Welsh, Irish, English and Scots; Greeks, Turks and Cypriots; Spanish, Italians, Portuguese and Maltese; Cape Verdeans and other colonial Portuguese; Yemeni, Egyptians and Somalis; Nigerians, Sierra Leoneans and other West Africans; West Indians; French and Colonial French; Chinese and Malays; Indians (i.e. people from what is now India, Pakistan and Bangladesh); Poles, Ukranians and eastern European Jews; Estonians, Latvians and Lithuanians; Germans, Norwegians, Swedes, Finns and Danes; North, South and Central Americans; and a few more.

Most of the immigrants in Cardiff docklands were Merchant Navy men, who transported Welsh coal around the world. Most of the women with whom they formed relationships and married were local, resulting in the development of the community as not only multi-ethnic but as thoroughly racially and culturally mixed. (Given this legacy, the history that Butetown History & Arts Centre produces – whether in our exhibitions and books or our bottle openers and key chains – problematizes any notion of Welshness or Britishness that is mono-cultural or white.)

For a century, beginning in the 1850s, Butetown included a thriving commercial sector and part of a notorious 'Sailor Town' – with prostitution, gambling, and numerous legal and illegal drinking establishments. Its 'dens of vice' were the frequent target of Victorian moralist campaigns; its alleged activities inspired a series of moral panics – over TB, venereal disease and mixed-race relationships.[2] Throughout most of its history, the area was physically isolated – an 'island' bounded by (now filled-in) canals, railway tracks and the sea, whose geographical separateness helped to naturalize its Otherness.[3]

Today, Butetown sits surrounded by a massive docklands regeneration scheme involving some 2700 acres and featuring a huge artificial lake, leisure complexes, luxury hotels, restaurants, galleries and other attractions catering primarily for tourists and the middle classes. The scheme is billed as 'Europe's Most Exciting Waterfront Development'.

This chapter explores the work of an initiative – Butetown Community History Project and its successor, Butetown History & Arts Centre – that is positioned in the heart of this development. The discussion weaves between the particular and the general, locating our case in a broader context of (a) the politics of history writing, (b) people's history and (c) cultural democracy.

The chapter makes considerable use of dialogue with three individuals who have been associated with this initiative over a long period of time: Glenn Jordan, the Centre's co-founder and Director; Marcia Brahim Barry, co-founder and long-term member of the Centre's board of directors; and Professor Chris Weedon, who has served as Chair of the organization since the mid-1990s.[4] The interviews with Marcia and Chris were conducted in 1996 by Karen Gehrke, an Erasmus student from Germany, for an undergraduate dissertation (supervised by Glenn Jordan) at the University of Glamorgan.[5]

17.2 'History from below'

What is the role of historical knowledge in society? Does it play in favour of, or against, the existing social order? Is it an elitist product that descends from the specialists to the 'consumers' of history by way of books, television and tourism? Or is it rooted, from the outset, in a collective need, an active relationship to the past . . .?

Jean Chesneaux[6]

Oral history . . . can be a means for transforming both the content and the purpose of history.

Paul Thompson[7]

Grassroots history, history seen from below or the history of the common people . . . no longer needs commercials.

Eric Hobsbawm[8]

Movements towards the development of *people's history* – i.e. history grounded in radical politics that explores and celebrates the lives and struggles of working class and marginalized groups – have a long history. Determining origins is usually, if not always, fraught with difficulties. As far as 'people's history' – or 'history from below' – is concerned, one can locate the starting point in many different contexts depending on the country concerned and one's criteria for defining 'people's history'. For example, to take the case of the USA, one could say that it began in the 1930s with the WPA interviews of ex-slaves or more recently in the public history and oral history movements.[9] Whatever birth date one wishes to assign, it is the case that 'people's history', like many other radical cultural initiatives, has become especially significant after '1968'.

One of the most useful periodizations is provided in a seminal intervention by members of the Centre for Contemporary Cultural Studies at the University of Birmingham.[10] They identified six different phases or traditions in the development of people's history (in Britain): (1) the early work of John and Barbara Hammond, two radical liberals, on working-class culture;[11] (2) the Communist Party Historians' Group of the early post-war period, which included a number of people who later became leading historians – such as Christopher Hill, Rodney Hilton, Eric Hobsbawm, Dorothy Thompson, E. P. Thompson and George Rudé; (3) the historical research and political practice of E. P. Thompson, especially his *The Making of the English Working Class* (1968);[12] (4) the more recent oral history or 'popular memory' movement, which began in the 1970s and has now achieved considerable international success;[13] (5) radical community history, which often involves 'the people' not just as the object of history but as researchers, writers and publishers of history;[14] and (6) feminist history writing from the 1970s onwards.

As will become apparent from the following discussion, the work of Butetown History & Arts Centre, since its inception in 1987/8, resonates with the core concerns of movements for people's history and cultural democracy – both in Britain and elsewhere in the world.

17.3 Butetown History & Arts Centre

So history is a political battleground. The sanction of the past is sought by those committed to upholding authority and by those intent on subverting it, and both are assured of finding plenty of ammunition.

John Tosh[15]

Oral history . . . makes a much fairer trial possible: witnesses can now also be called from the under-classes, the unprivileged, and the defeated ...

Paul Thompson[16]

Butetown History & Arts Centre (www.bhac.org) currently occupies some 3000 square feet of ground-floor space and 1000 square feet of first-floor space in a

Victorian office block in the heart of Cardiff Docklands. The Centre includes (1) an image, sound and video archive; (2) gallery spaces; (3) a small viewing room; (4) an educational space for young people; (5) a classroom for adult education that doubles as a meeting room; and (6) a small shop. Our current budget is about £150,000 ($270,000) per year. Most of our income comes from grants, usually project grants lasting from one to three years – from sources such as the Home Office, the Arts Council of Wales, the Community Fund (formerly the Charities Lottery), Cardiff County Council and foundations. We also currently generate about £25,000 ($40,000) per year from the selling of books, photographs, cards and other products in our gallery shop; from the educational services that we offer to school groups; and by providing television and other media companies with images from our archive.

In partnership with local people, we collect, preserve and utilize oral histories, old photographs and other documents. We are a multi-ethnic, multi-racial team, including full-time workers, part-time workers and volunteers. The number of paid staff varies considerably – depending on the level and nature of grant funding at any given time. Under ideal circumstances, our paid staff occupies the equivalent of six or seven posts: a Centre Director (me, part-time), an Administrator, an Archivist/Picture Researcher, an Exhibitions Officer and Graphic Designer, an Education Officer (whose specialities include history, geography and the National Curriculum), an Arts Education Officer (part-time), a Community Outreach Officer/Community Historian and a Marketing Officer (part-time). Our dozen or so volunteers include gallery workers, typists and research assistants. The participation of volunteers precedes that of paid staff and has always been central to our success.

Ours is history with a social purpose, a conscious attempt to link *historical knowledge* to *social practices,* including critical, interventionist practices. Our work transgresses the boundaries between *social history*, the study of social relations, institutions and practices, and *cultural history*, the study of meanings and values.[17] The *problem of representation* – of past and present relations among dominant, subordinate, marginal and contested *images, discourses* and *narratives* – lies at the core of our engagements.

Our goals are: to ensure that the social and cultural history of Cardiff Docklands and multi-ethnic Wales is carefully collected and preserved for posterity with the active involvement of local residents; to offer opportunities for all members of the local community – across the broadest spectrum of social backgrounds, cultural backgrounds and age ranges – to engage in creative practice; to produce educational materials, exhibitions, performances and other cultural products grounded in local history and experience; and to facilitate understanding and respect between people of different class, racial and cultural backgrounds. Our long-term aim is to create a Bay People's Museum & Arts Centre – with a major archive, permanent galleries, changing exhibitions, classrooms, a performance space, a café and a gift shop. The challenge is to realize this goal while remaining true to our founding principles and ethos.

17.4 Groundings

If history was thought of as an activity rather than a profession, then the number of its practitioners would be legion.

Raphael Samuel[18]

But history is far too important a matter to be left to the historians!

Jean Chesneaux[19]

Founded in 1987/8 by a black American anthropologist and half a dozen local residents, Butetown History & Arts Centre is an intervention on the terrain of culture and power. It began as a serious attempt to develop a group of locally based indigenous researchers – working-class, *organic intellectuals* – and to create a space for the production of *alternative histories, identities and representations* of life in Cardiff Docklands. Our work, especially in the early phases, shares the ethos of other emancipatory intellectual projects – such as feminist history, as Catherine Hall explains:

> Feminist history as first conceptualized in the early 1970s was about the recovery of women's history. We needed to fill out the enormous gaps in our historical knowledge which were a direct result of the male domination of historical work.[20]

And British labour and working-class history – as John Tosh explains:

> The purpose of much labour history written by politically committed historians is to sharpen the social awareness of the workers, to confirm their commitment to political action, and to reassure them that history is 'on their side'… In Britain this approach is reflected in the History Workshop movement . . . which began in the late 1960s; for them, the historical reconstruction of working people's experience serves as 'a source of inspiration and understanding' – to use a phrase from the first editorial in the *History Workshop Journal*.'[21]

'Recovering' marginalised experience, *'filling in the gaps'* and *subverting dominant constructions*; using history as a means of *sharpening social awareness*, *increasing*

understanding and *inspiring action* – all of this is consistent with the practice of Butetown History & Arts Centre. Listen to Marcia Brahim Barry, a founder member of the project:

> We knew that we had a unique history but we hadn't realised how unique it was until someone [a Black American anthropologist called Glenn Jordan] came in and said, 'You are history and if we don't do something about it, it will be lost.' So in a way, for me, it became a crusade . . . I suddenly realised that everything around us was changing – we could actually see it – and that the elderly people were dying and lots of residents had moved away through the 'slum clearance' of the 1950s and 1960s, so the community had depleted and from I believe about 5000 in the 1950s, we're now down to two and a half thousand . . . We realised that we had to start to do something about it.[22]

The anthropologist/oral historian, an activist-intellectual who had largely abandoned the ivory towers of the academy, confirmed what the Butetown community already knew but the dominant culture seemed constantly to deny. Whatever his intentions, one of the effects of his intervention was to affirm the importance of their history, to validate key aspects of locally based *popular memory* and *unofficial knowledge*. Through dialogue with an Other, their *self-recognition* was facilitated.

For people in the Butetown community (i.e. in 'Tiger Bay' and 'The Docks'), Butetown Community History Project offered a space in which they could contribute to an oppositional history, to a culturally democratic practice of research and writing that sought to challenge and subvert hegemonic constructions. For generations, people in and from this community have encountered images and stories about themselves in newpapers[23] and magazines, in fiction and autobiographical books, in academic studies, in the common-sense rhetoric of everyday conversation. For some 150 years, since the 1850s, their community has been recurrently represented in negative terms – as dirty, violent, diseased and immoral; and in romantic terms – as primitive, exotic and fascinating. As one local resident explains:

> Whatever the origin of the name [i.e. 'Tiger Bay'], ever since the dawn of its people, a negative mythology has surrounded it. Disparaging second-hand hearsay remarks – such as 'You wouldn't walk down the streets in Tiger Bay!', 'It was dangerous there!', 'Harm would come to you there!', 'They carry knives and all kinds of weapons down the Bay!', 'It was a terrible place. People gambled openly in the street!', etc. – can still be heard today from people who, on the whole, never set foot in Tiger Bay.[24]

The most famous representation is that produced by Howard Spring (1889–1965), the Welsh popular writer, in his autobiography:

> [T]here was a fascination in the walk through Tiger Bay. Chinks and Dagos, Lascars and Levantines, slippered about the faintly evil by-ways that ran off from Bute Street . . . Children of the strangest colours, fruit of frightful misalliances, staggered half-naked about the streets; and the shop windows were decorated with names that were the epitome of all the clans and classes under the sun . . . It was a dirty, rotten and romantic district, an offence and an inspiration, and I loved it.[25]

People from this community are deeply offended by such constructions.

When Butetown Community History Project was born, it was necessarily always-already positioned within a long-established field of representations.[26] The ethnographer/oral historian who co-founded the project was partially aware of this fact; local people were fully aware of it. Thus, for them, at least as much as for him, this initiative was, from the very beginning, a dialogic, cultural-political intervention. It was not so much a matter of finding out about a community that had been 'hidden from history' (to use the phrase made famous by Sheila Rowbotham).[27] Rather, it was that of studying a community that was hyper-visible in the sense that they are always-already written about, yet simultaneously invisible in that key dimensions of their experience have been hidden – mostly because those who represented them rarely bothered ask them for their stories or points of view.

Butetown Community History Project, certainly from the point of view of the anthropologist/oral historian, sought to achieve empowerment through practical education and demystification of the research process.[28] The following is from an interview in which Marcia Brahim Barry describes our practice in the early years of 1988–90. The activity being described is part of the work we did in our first community education initiative, a weekly course/workshop begun in February 1988. The interviewer, as before, is Karen Gehrke.

> ***MB:*** I don't know whether you know the old library. Well . . . Glenn wanted us to start to learn to do research and we all went up there and it was the summer holidays and so we did a few stints . . . [with] people just looking in old newspapers and things. It was quite fascinating because people were beginning to learn to do research. And yet because we were all together, it wasn't like doing some sort of painful task . . . In fact, we got involved in looking up the papers and found them really fascinating. And you could actually see what he was trying to tell you ...

> [H]e used to stress that we actually could write our own history, that we could write the history that we saw, not the history that people thought was our history, so that we actually had a voice ...[29]

The effort was not simply to get people to collect and tell their own stories but also to encourage them to engage with what had already been written and said about them: the project always involved an element of critical engagement with hegemonic discourses, e.g. local discourses of racial and cultural difference. To this end, we began by studying old newspapers. The intent was also to read accounts by social scientists and (other) fiction writers.

The course title was 'The Way We Were: Life Stories from Tiger Bay'. The first session attracted 42 people. This sort of turnout was unheard of: the local authority had been trying to get adult education classes going in Butetown for a few years with very little success.

In terms of funding and other material resources, we began our weekly sessions with virtually nothing. Our only possessions, purchased thanks to a small grant of £350 from the county Community Education Service, were minimal level broadcast-quality equipment – a Marantz CP430 cassette recorder and two good microphones – and a small supply of audiotapes. One consequence of the lack of resources was that it helped to bond the group together through collective responsibility:

> ***MB:*** We didn't have any money so we had the Butetown Community Centre for nothing on Tuesday nights . . . I used to bring the kettle from home. Molly and Rita or Olwen or any of us – we all pooled our money and we bought biscuits and tea and coffee.[30]

The point of the sessions was twofold: for local residents to learn how to do oral history and for the group to begin systematically collecting life stories on audiotape. The idea was for the anthropologist/oral historian to mediate the process of knowledge acquisition, eventually making his presence unnecessary. The emphasis was not simply on training (practical demonstration of techniques in interviewing, use of the microphones, etc.) but on education (critical discussion of themes and issues in research, oral history and cultural democracy):

> ***MB:*** The first half of the sessions would be for us to learn interviewing techniques, and so we used a book by Paul Thompson [*The Voice of the Past*] . . . Glenn got a stack of them. We were all supposed to pay him but I don't think anybody did. In the end he gave us all a book. So we used to talk about oral history and we used to think of questions and themes and we used to read passages out of the books . . . I don't think we realised what was happening to us, but we were actually developing [knowledge and] skills.

The sessions were intended to run for 32 weeks, but ended up running for three years. About half of those who regularly attended those sessions are still actively involved in the Centre today. Obviously, our sessions had some significant, lasting effect. Alessandro Portelli has observed:

> [W]hen the encounter takes place [on the basis] of equality, not only the observer, but also the 'observed', may be stimulated to think new thoughts about themselves. This throws a new light on an old problem: the observer's interference on the observed reality. The positivistic fetish of non-interference has developed outlandish techniques to bypass or remove this problem. I believe we ought to turn the question on its head, and consider the changes that our presence may cause as some of the most important results of our field work.[31]

17.5 Keeping cultural democracy alive

Perhaps after reading the foregoing discussion about cultural democracy in our early years, the reader may imagine that it has been easy to maintain. Nothing could be further from the truth, as the following dialogue between Karen Gehrke and Chris Weedon makes clear:

> ***KG:*** You mentioned once that an idea behind the Centre was also to real um ... to realise the idea of cultural democracy.
>
> ***CW:*** Yes, . . . the whole project, even when it was in its early phases of a community history project, was an exercise in cultural democracy in the sense that rather than having someone from the outside come and do it, the idea was that people should collect their own history, should interview each other, collect their photographs, archive them and all the rest of it. And that every decision... and all the objectives should be discussed by the group. And it should be a collective thing that went forward, which everybody was involved in irrespective of their background, education or whatever ...
>
> Now obviously since those early days it's got bigger, but I think those principles are still important. It's just that it's more diverse now, so people choose to work in different areas. Everybody can't do everything because there are too many things going on, but certainly the idea that it should be people doing it for themselves and it should be empowering . . . is still there.
>
> ***KG:*** So you think from your point of view it worked out so far?
>
> ***CW:*** I wouldn't say it was a 100 per cent success, I think it's an ongoing battle. I think cultural democracy is very difficult because [it] rests on the

> notion that people really want to take responsibility and I think one of the things that this project has shown is often people don't actually want to take responsibility. I mean they want to feel like they're involved and they want to have a say but they don't always want to do all the other things that come beyond that, to actually realise it.
>
> There are limits to how much they are willing to do, or what areas they are willing to get involved in . . . I think it's an ongoing struggle, cultural democracy.[32]

With regard to taking responsibility, it is still the case that almost all of the audiotaped life-history interviews in our archive were done more than a decade ago by two volunteers (the anthropologist and Marcia Barry) in the first few years of our existence. Despite the community's deeply felt view that their history needs to be preserved, not many local people have been willing to go out and ensure that it is done – even though the necessary equipment and expertise is readily available to them.

17.6 What do we do with voices?[33]

There is no reason why those who use oral evidence should be on the defensive when faces with the issue of the respective value of documentary and oral sources.[34]

Our oral history archive now includes about 1000 hours of audio-recorded interviews and a dozen hours of video (the latter made in collaboration with two local video groups). We have not yet been able to make substantial use of this material – except for short, digitally recorded interviews that we have recently done. Because of the resources required, transforming audio-recorded interviews into a form that can be shared with a public audience of readers or listeners can pose serious difficulties for groups such as ours.

We have made use of oral testimony on radio – and, in the future, this will probably increasingly involve the medium of community radio. Our most notable achievements with the media were our central involvement in the production of *Cymru Ddu*, a three-part television programme on the history of black people in Wales (with accompanying book), which was broadcast in Welsh with English subtitles in 2005, and in the production of *Bay People*, two half-hour programmes, narrated by Glenn Jordan and broadcast on BBC Radio Wales in October 2001. Most of the voices in the programmes are of people, from varying ethnic backgrounds, who we recommended; and many of the interviews were recorded in our centre. These developments suggest important shifts in the politics of representation.

Producing books from audiotapes is a long, tedious and costly business. From our early days we have intended to produce two volumes of life histories, *Women's Lives from Tiger Bay* and *Men's Lives from Tiger Bay*. More generally, we planned to produce publications, including children's books, that would make extensive use of oral history. To date, that has not happened: indeed, as it turns out, all of the life stories/community histories that we have published – except for short extracts for our exhibition panels or our (previously existing) newsletter – have been by people who have typed their texts on to computer, i.e. into a form that could be easily read, discussed and edited. This has ironic consequences: those whose voices are most marginalized within this community have only rarely appeared in print – despite our lofty, culturally democratic aims.[35]

17.7 The people write back

This is not the story of my life. It is simply a record of memories of a childhood spent 'Down the Docks' in Cardiff. Some of the sights and sounds, the smells, the feelings.

Phyllis Grogan Chappell[36]

A number of community-based groups have produced and published working-class writing, including community histories and life stories. In the UK perhaps the most successful is Centreprise, based in the Hackney district of London.

> Centreprise began publishing working-class writing in 1972 . . . From its beginnings as a local history project, Centreprise publishing has expanded to include, alongside history, a wide range of other work by local people. Publications include: writing by young people; local autobiographies of working-class life; local history materials; writing by literacy students; Black writing; and the poetry and stories produced by the writers' workshops.
>
> In its first few years (1972–5) Centreprise produced 25 titles, each of which sold between 450 and 5,000 copies. Subsequently it continued to publish several titles each year and in 1992 had a list of 34 titles in print.[37]

The publishing programme of Butetown History & Arts Centre has not been nearly as successful as Centreprise. Our efforts, however, are guided by similar principles and practices – except we do not place as much emphasis on literary work. To date, our publications include 15 books (we co-produced one other) and two booklets.[38]

From the very beginning, we established a series entitled 'Life Stories from Tiger Bay' in which local people would be encouraged to publish. Thus far, four titles have been published in the series: Neil Sinclair, *The Tiger Bay Story* (140 pages, 1993); Phyllis Grogan Chappell, *A Tiger Bay Childhood: Growing Up in the 1930s* (80 pages, 1994); Harry 'Shipmate' Cooke, *How I Saw It: A Stroll thro' Old Cardiff Bay* (112 pages, 1995); and Neil Sinclair, *Endangered Tiger: A Community under Threat* (196 pages, 2003). We are currently working on our fifth and sixth titles: Olwen Blackman Watkins, *A Family Affair: Three Generations in Tiger Bay*, and Patti Flynn, *Under the Bridge and Down the Bay*.

The books in our 'Life Stories' series are user-friendly: the size is A5 (approximately 150 × 210 mm) and the length is usually considerably less than 200 pages. The shortest book, Phyllis Chappell's *A Tiger Bay Childhood*, is only 80 pages. I kept pushing her to write more until we had enough text to produce a book rather than a booklet. There is a serious point here, which has to do with the politics of visibility: if working-class writing is to be noticed, one needs to be able to see the title on the spine.

What is the motivation to write these books? Alessandro Portelli has observed, 'The telling of a story preserves the teller from oblivion.'[39] In the case of our writers from Tiger Bay, the desire seems more to proclaim 'WE WERE!' rather than affirm 'I AM!' These writers privilege family and, especially, community history – not autobiography.[40] The desire to tell their personal stories is superseded by a quest to write insider accounts about a maligned community that they know and, usually, love.

Their sources are not research reports or maps or census books. They are shared memories and stories preserved across generations through traditions of storytelling and in the interactions of daily life – the sort of memory and knowledge discussed in the following passage by the CCCS (Centre for Contemporary Cultural Studies) Popular Memory Group:

> A knowledge of past and present is also produced in the course of everyday life . . . Such knowledge may circulate, usually without amplification, in everyday talk and in personal . . . narratives. It may even be recorded in certain intimate cultural forms: letters, diaries, photograph albums and collections of things with past associations. It may be encapsulated in anecdotes that acquire the force and generality of myth . . . Usually this history is . . . not only unrecorded, but actually silenced. It is not offered the occasion to speak.[41]

Such memory is the object of much of our work.

It is sometimes said that oral history and life stories are inevitably *partial* – both in the sense that they are incomplete (i.e. they are often fragmented or bitty and do not provide a sufficiently broad-based account) and that they are partisan (i.e. they are not 'objective' or 'neutral' but take up a position, often that of defending their community and/or their past). The writers in our 'Life Stories from Tiger Bay' series are well aware of this, and regard their moral stance as a positive one.

The role of the anthropologist/oral historian in the production of the books in the series is that of facilitator. Sometimes he has rearranged disparate bits of the text to form more coherent sections and chapters; edited sentences for grammatical reasons; or suggested names for chapters. However, his editing does not extend to matters of 'truth': he does not challenge 'the facts' that the locals present. He also tends to relinquish the power to name: most of the books' titles were chosen by their authors, sometimes over the editor's objections. The key concern in the editing process has been preserving the author's voice – such that local people who know the author could literally hear him or her speaking if they read the text. The mode of writing is popular, rather than academic.[42]

The merit of our 'Life Stories' books does not simply lie in their motivations, sources and style. Perhaps their greatest contribution lies in the detailed accounts they provide – i.e. the specific information that can trigger local memories, and can also serve the student or scholar as a guide to further investigation.

Since 2000, our publishing programme has considerably increased, this time with the anthropologist/oral historian often assuming the role of 'editor' or 'author'. This does not signal an abandonment of our commitment to cultural democracy but a decision to produce a more diverse range of publications, including children's books and educational packs and books that privilege visual imagery – in particular, photographs.[43]

17.9 History, memory and the visual

Why photographs? Because of their power – to trigger emotions; to bring together individual and collective memory; to convince the viewer that what they see did indeed exist. Marita Sturken explains:

> The photograph of personal value is a talisman . . . It evokes both memory and loss, both a trace of life and the prospect of death . . . [I]t is a mechanism through which the past can be constructed and situated within the present. Images have the capacity to create, interfere with, and trouble the memories we hold as individuals and as a culture. They lend shape to personal stories and truth claims, and function as technologies of memory, producing both memory and forgetting.[44]

Our turn to photographs seems to have happened by accident. In 1989, Butetown Community History Project was commissioned by an organization called NewEmploy Wales to prepare a permanent exhibition for their new office in Cardiff Bay, which was to be a training centre for local young people.

The exhibition was co-curated by the anthropologist and Olwen Blackman Watkins, one of the most highly respected residents of Butetown and recently retired schoolteacher. Using her large personal collection of family and community photographs as a starting point, we collected hundreds of photographs dating from near the turn of the century to the redevelopment (so-called 'slum clearance') of the area in the 1960s. The images were copied, enlarged and professionally framed. The exhibition consisted of some 90 images: most of them were 12 × 16, 16 × 20 or 20 × 24 inches; six or seven of them were very large, perhaps around 48 inches in width.

The exhibition opened on a hot Sunday afternoon in July 1989. The response was phenomenal. 400 people showed up. The building was literally jam-packed. As past and present residents of Butetown encountered the images, they seemed to not quite believe it. They pointed to people in the group photographs and argued over their names. They laughed and cried as they recognized themselves, their friends, their place. Some even went home and brought back some of their own photographs to share with the group. The joy of recognition, the validation of popular memory, the pain of loss – that is the experience many local people had upon seeing those images.

We knew that photographs were important, but we had not realized how important. From that moment, we resolved to collect photographic images. Unlike the museum, we have not especially sought to collect original photographs – we think people should keep their personal and family photographs – although sometimes such images have been donated to us for safe keeping. Our archive now includes nearly 5000 images.[45]

The exhibition at NewEmploy Wales remained in place for more than ten years, until that organization ceased to exist. Despite the fact that the pictures did not change, people still came to see them. The exhibition became a site of memory. Why? Because, to echo Roland Barthes, those photographs reminded local viewers that what they saw – their friends, their streets, their community, their selves – was no longer but 'has indeed been'.[46]

In 1997, after holding a few temporary exhibitions in other buildings in Cardiff Docklands, Butetown History & Arts Centre developed its own gallery.[47] Our gallery is committed to cultural democracy – to producing and presenting images, text, sound and moving images that are accessible and meaningful to ordinary people. Most of our exhibitions engage with issues of local people's history, cultural politics and everyday life, exploring themes such as immigration, identity, community, popular culture, urban regeneration, refugees' lives and media representations of racial and cultural difference. Common sources for our self-generated exhibitions include photographs by street photographers, photographs from personal and family albums, and images from newspapers and other popular media.

Although we seek to reach 'non-traditional viewers' – i.e. people who rarely, if ever, attend museums or galleries – we do not assume that they are unintelligent or unsophisticated. We wish to produce exhibitions that are visually interesting and intellectually rigorous. Thus, for example, our exhibitions are becoming increasingly polyvocal: they may incorporate competing conceptions of the past or they may both praise and problematize the images they contain.[48] Our exhibitions are also making increasing use of large photographic portraits with the subjects' life stories.

To accompany our exhibitions, we now produce substantial exhibition catalogues, exploring issues such as the *poetics and politics of representation*[49] and usually designed so they can have a life after the exhibitions.[50]

As I write this (October 2008), we are our preparing our sixth image-based book: *Mothers and Daughters: Portraits from Multi-ethnic Wales*. This book, like the major exhibition that it will accompany, will include 100 portraits and life stories of women of diverse ethnic backgrounds from throughout Wales. The exhibition portraits are one metre in size and are intended to address the viewer directly – contesting hegemonic notions of Welshness, Britishness and old age.

One of our most interesting image-based books is the smallest one: *Fractured Horizon: A Landscape of Memory*.[51] This small, beautiful and disturbing book is the result of a project done in 2001 by Mathew Manning, then a student studying photography and media studies at the University of Glamorgan, and Patti Flynn, a singer-writer whose family has deep roots in that place that is now called Cardiff Bay. Together, through pictures and words, they confront the past and present of Cardiff Docklands:

> Over a period of several weeks, the writer and the photographer walk together around the shoreline of the area that is being reinvented as Cardiff Bay . . . In order to guide the photographer, the narrator draws upon a personal and collective archive of stored impressions. To find what she remembers, to repossess fragments of her past, the narrator takes the photographer to the edges, the margins, the not-yet-completed spaces of the redevelopment. There, among the time-ravaged and the eroded, the used and the abandoned, she manages almost to be at home.
>
> . . . These are photographs of the present, imprinted with traces of the past.[52]

Catherine Belsey has stated, 'The kind of cultural history I am putting forward is a history of representation.'[53] This is close to the project we pursue in our exhibitions and related activity. People's history, as we practise it, includes ways of seeing – i.e. an engagement with images that goes beyond any assumption that they simply provide 'evidence' or a 'window on to reality'.

Fractured Horizon, the exhibition and the book, signals an engagement with the visual that is very different from that usually practised by historians, including those producing 'people's history': image and text exist in a dialogic relationship in which neither is privileged. Raphael Samuel has perceptively observed:

> 'History from below' . . . stopped short of any engagement with graphics. Caught up in the cultural revolution of the 1960s *it nevertheless remained wedded to quite traditional forms of writing, teaching and research.* E. P. Thompson's *The Making of the English Working Class* (1963) has not a single print to leaven the 800 pages of narrative which covers some of the most brilliant years of English political caricature. Nor has Peter Laslett's *The World We Have Lost* (1965) . . . 'New-wave' social history did take photographs on board . . . but it was for their reality content rather their pictorial value or interest – in short because they were thought of as being of a piece of documentary truth.

He continues,

> It seems possible that history's new-found interest in 'representation', and its belated recognition of the deconstructive turn in contemporary thought, will allow for, and even force, a more central engagement with graphics . . . Photographs, if in the spirit of postmodernism they are dissevered from any notion of the real, might be studied for the theatricality of social appearances, rather than as likenesses of everyday life.[54]

'Postmodernism' is a term rarely used at Butetown History & Arts Centre. Nonetheless, some of our practices are informed by mild doses of poststructuralist and postmodernist ideas.

17.9 Concluding reflections

This chapter has raised various issues having to do with people's history and cultural democracy through a discussion of a project that has existed for some 20 years in the docklands area of Cardiff. It has explored how Butetown Community History Project began, and the ethos and practices – of oral history, collaborative research, community-based education, community publishing and exhibiting – that it and its successor (Butetown History & Arts Centre) have sought to maintain. The chapter has repeatedly demonstrated the centrality of history to cultural democracy and the persistence of community.

I would like to conclude by reflecting on two challenges – that of doing radical intellectual work and that of achieving cultural democracy. Consider the following statement from Stuart Hall, the cultural theorist and activist- intellectual:

> I come back to the deadly seriousness of intellectual work. It is a deadly serious matter. I come back to the critical distinction between intellectual work and academic work: they overlap, they abut with one another, they feed off one another, the one provides you with the means to the other. But they are not the same thing. I come back to the difficulty of instituting a genuine cultural and critical practice, which is intended to produce some kind of organic intellectual political work . . . I come back to theory and politics, the politics of theory. Not theory as the will to truth, but theory as a set of contested, localized, conjunctural knowledges, which have to be debated in a dialogical way. But also as a practice which always thinks about its intervention in a world in which it would make some difference, in which it would have some effect. Finally, a practice which understands the need for intellectual modesty.[55]

From the perspective of Butetown History & Arts Centre, as for Stuart Hall, radical intellectual work is serious business, involving localized intervention and long-term engagement. It also implies a commitment to collective work and shared responsibility. However, this is not always easy to achieve: people have different skills and motivations and, as indicated earlier, they sometimes do not wish to take significant responsibility for ensuring that the organization succeeds.

Finally, in our view, doing radical intellectual work includes a commitment to writing in a form that is both intellectually rigorous and – in terms of vocabulary, syntax and mode of presentation – accessible to a broad audience, including people who have had no higher education. In the case of this chapter, this position means that whatever is written here should, in principle, be accessible to members of our organization or the local community who might wish to read it.

Writing in this way poses real challenges. I do not claim to have always met them.

Guide to further reading

Kate Darian-Smith and Paul Hamilton (eds), *Memory and History in 20th-Century Australia* (Oxford, 1994).

Michael Frisch, *A Shared Authority: Essays on the Craft and Meaning of Oral and Public History* (Albany, 1990).

Eric Hobsbawn, 'On History from Below', in *On History* (London, 1997), pp. 201–16.

Stephen Humphries, *Hooligans or Rebels? An Oral History of Working-Class Childhood and Youth 1889–1939* (Oxford, 1981).

Glenn Jordan, "'We Never Really Noticed You Were Coloured': Postcolonialist Reflections on Immigrants and Minorities in Wales', in Jane Aaron and Chris Williams (eds), *Postcolonial Wales* (Cardiff, 2005), pp. 55–81.

Glenn Jordan and Chris Weedon, 'Whose History Is It? Class, Cultural Democracy and Constructions of the Past', in Jordan and Weedon, *Cultural Politics* (Oxford, 1995), pp. 112–73.

Robert Perks and Alistair Thomson (eds), *The Oral History Reader* (London, 2006).

Popular Memory Group, 'Popular Memory: Theory, Politics, Method', in Centre for Contemporary Cultural Studies, *Making Histories: Studies in History-writing and Politics* (London, 1982), pp. 205–52.

Alessandro Portelli, *The Death of Luigi Trastulli and Other Stories: Form and Meaning in Oral History* (Albany, 1991).

Alessandro Portelli, *The Order Has Been Carried Out: History, Memory, and Meaning of a Nazi Massacre in Rome* (New York, 2003).

Peter Read, 'Presenting Voices in Different Media: Print, Radio and CD-ROM', in Robert Perks and Alistair Thomson, *The Oral History Reader* (London: Routledge, 1998), pp. 414–20.

Richard Price, *First-Time: The Historical Vision of an Afro-American People* (Baltimore, 1993).

Marita Sturken, 'The Image as Memorial: Personal Photographs in Cultural Memory', in Marianne Hirsch (ed.), *The Familial Gaze* (Hanover and London, 1999), pp. 178–95.

Paul Thompson, *The Voice of the Past: Oral History* (Oxford, 2000).

Notes

1 Raphael Samuel, 'Unofficial Knowledge', Vol. 1 of *Theatres of Memory* (London, 1994), pp. 3, 6.
2 Not all of Cardiff's Sailor Town was in Tiger Bay and not all of Tiger Bay was in the Sailor Town. This fact is often overlooked.
3 On stereotyping and the racializing of 'Others', see Stuart Hall, 'The Spectacle of the Other' in Hall (ed.), *Representation* (London, 1997), pp. 223–90.
4 Chris Weedon is best known as a feminist cultural theorist. Her doctoral thesis, however, is on the cultural politics of British working-class writing, see Christine M. Weedon, 'Aspects of the Politics of Literature and Working-class Writing in Interwar Britain' (PhD thesis, Centre for Contemporary Cultural Studies, University of Birmingham, 1984).

5 Karen Gehrke, 'Struggling For Cultural Democracy: A Case Study of Butetown History & Arts Centre' (BA dissertation, Communication Studies, University of Glamorgan, 1996).
6 Jean Chesneaux, *Past and Futures: Or What Is History For?* (London, 1978), p. 1.
7 Paul Thompson, *The Voice of the Past: Oral History* (Oxford, 2000), p. 3.
8 Eric Hobsbawm, 'On History from Below', in Frederick Krantz (ed.), *History from Below: Studies in Popular Protest and Popular Ideology* (Oxford, 1988), pp. 13–28.
9 George P. Rawick (ed.), *The American Slave: A Composite Autobiography*, Vols. 1–19 (Westport, CT, 1972).
10 Centre for Contemporary Cultural Studies, *Making Histories: Studies in History-Writing and Politics* (London, 1982).
11 John Hammond and Barbara Hammond, *The Village Labourer* (London, 1911); *The Town Labourer* (London, 1917); and *The Skilled Labourer* (London, 1919).
12 E. P. Thompson, *The Making of the English Working Class* (London, 1968).
13 For an excellent introduction to developments in oral history, see Robert Perks and Alistair Thomson (eds), *The Oral History Reader* (London, 1998). The 'classic text' in the field arguably remains Thompson's *Voice of the Past*.
14 This work tends to be published by small, local publishers, e.g. in Britain, by groups belonging to the Federation of Worker Writers and Community Publishers (FWWCP).
15 John Tosh, *The Pursuit of History* (London, 1984), p. 8.
16 Thompson, *Voice of the Past*, p.7.
17 One might wonder why the two fields do not more often come together, since practices signify and meanings are reproduced in and through practices.
18 Samuel, 'Unofficial Knowledge', p. 17.
19 Chesneaux, *Past and Futures*, p. 9.
20 Catherine Hall, *White, Male and Middle Class: Explorations in Feminism and History* (Cambridge, 1992), p. 5. A classic work from this early 1970s period of feminist history-writing is Sheila Rowbotham's *Hidden from History* (London, 1973).
21 Tosh, *The Pursuit of History*, p. 6.
22 Marcia Brahim Barry, interview document, transcript of interview conducted by Karen Gerhke, 1 March 1996. All quotations from Marcia Barry are from this document.
23 There have been innumerable articles in local newspapers on 'Tiger Bay'. In the 1800s and early 1900s the *Cardiff Times* and *South Wales Daily News* regularly provided their readers with long, juicy accounts. In the 1920s and 1930s the *Western Mail* periodically launched viciously racist tirades against 'coloured seamen'. Since then, the *South Wales Echo* has provided many a romantic, mythological contribution.

24 Neil Sinclair, *The Tiger Bay Story* (Cardiff, 1993), p. 3.

25 Howard Spring, *Heaven Lies About Us: A Fragment of Infancy* (London, 1939), p. 33.

26 For an analysis of Spring's discourse, see Glenn Jordan, 'Images of Tiger Bay: Did Howard Spring Tell the Truth?', *Llafur: Journal of the Society for Welsh Labour History* 5(1) (1988), pp. 53–9. The rhetoric of 'insider' accounts is explored in Glenn Jordan and Chris Weedon, 'When the Subaltern Speak, What Do They Say?', in Paul Gilroy, Lawrence Grossberg and Angela McRobbie (eds), *Without Guarantees: In Honour of Stuart Hall* (London, 2000).

27 Rowbotham, *Hidden from History*. Often women's history is literally hidden. When we were working on our first exhibition we went through the local history collection in Cardiff Central Library in search of images of women at work. We found virtually nothing.

28 Over the decades, the area has literally become a social laboratory – without any consent from the community. Every year perhaps a few dozen students from Cardiff University descend on what is left of Tiger Bay. Local people, with very few exceptions, have grown very tired of them – so tired that they often send the students to us, i.e. to the official 'experts' on their community.

29 The anthropologist was already an experienced researcher – with an interesting connection to Butetown. As an undergraduate and graduate student at Stanford University in California (1970–6), he was a research assistant to Professor St Clair Drake, an African-American scholar who, like Kenneth Little, did anthropological fieldwork in Tiger Bay in the 1940s. See St Clair Drake, 'Values, Social Structure and Race Relations in the British Isles' (PhD thesis, Department of Anthropology, University of Chicago, 1954).

30 Marcia Barry, interview document, 1 March 1996.

31 Alessandro Portelli, 'Research as an Experiment in Equality', in Portelli, *The Death of Luigi Trastulli and Other Stories: Form and Meaning in Oral History* (Albany, 1991), pp. 43–4.

32 Chris Weedon, interview document: transcript of interview conducted by Karen Gerhke, 2 March 1996.

33 For an excellent discussion of practical problems involved in making use of audiotaped oral history, see Peter Read, 'Presenting Voices in Different Media: Print, Radio and CD-ROM', in Perks and Thomson, *The Oral History Reader*, pp. 414–20.

34 Trevor Lummis, *Listening to History* (London, 1987), p. 12. One of the most successful attempts to combine oral testimony and written documents is Richard Price's remarkable book *First-Time: The Historical Vision of an Afro-American People* (Baltimore, 1983), which provides a dialogic and polyvocal account of the history of the Saramaka maroons of Surinam.

35 Perhaps BHAC's most ambitious use of oral history to date in an academic publication is Glenn Jordan, '"We Never Really Noticed You Were Coloured": Postcolonialist Reflections on Immigrants and Minorities in Wales', in Jane Aaron and Chris Williams (eds), *Postcolonial Wales* (Cardiff, 2005), pp. 55–81.

36 Phyllis Grogan Chappell, preface to *A Tiger Bay Childhood* (Cardiff, 1994), p. 1.

37 Glenn Jordan and Chris Weedon, *Cultural Politics* (Oxford, 1995), p. 133. Centreprise's 'People's Autobiography' project in the 1970s had an ethos very similar to ours; see, for example, *A People's Autobiography of Hackney, Working Lives: Hackney,* Vol. 1, *1900–1945* (London, 1977).

38 The two booklets are *Prejudice & Pride* (BHAC, 2001), which accompanied an exhibition on Afro-Caribbean people in post-war Britain; and *Windrush: A Sense of Belonging* (BHAC, 2001), a selection of poetry by children from a local Saturday school.

39 Portelli, '"The Time of My Life": Functions of Time in Oral History', in *The Death of Luigi Trastulli and Other Stories*, p. 59.

40 One of these books, Harry Cooke's *How I Saw It*, does not include family history. Harry grew up in Liverpool, not Cardiff.

41 Popular Memory Group, 'Popular Memory: Theory, Politics, Method' in *Making Histories*, p. 210.

42 That is, except on those occasions where the author's themselves, perhaps imagining their audience, shift into an assumed 'academic' register – as in parts of the preface to Neil Sinclair's *The Tiger Bay Story*.

43 Our children's books series includes one book thus far: *Sian: Traveller in Time* (Cardiff, 2003). A Welsh translation of *Sian* is forthcoming, as is a book on *Cardiff Docklands at War*. These volumes are illustrated by local artist Leon Balen and they all employ a comic-book format, while drawing on oral history and archival research. They are part of our effort to make history interesting and pleasurable to young people.

44 Marita Sturken, 'The Image as Memorial: Personal Photographs in Cultural Memory' in Marianne Hirsch (ed.), *The Familial Gaze* (Hanover, 1999), p. 178.

45 The development of our image archive has made an impact. Most recent television programmes made in Britain about old Cardiff docklands and/or about immigrants and minorities in Wales include images from our archive. A number of our photographs are on the BBC Wales website; now, unlike before, Wales appears as a multi-ethnic nation.

46 Roland Barthes, *Camera Lucida: Reflections on Photography* (London, 1984), p. 115.

47 Opening our gallery was made possible by a grant from the European Regional Development Fund (ERDF) to develop a 'visitor attraction', i.e. to facilitate economic and cultural development in the new Cardiff Bay.

48 This was the case for an exhibition held in May–July 2002. *One Island, Many Faiths: 100 Years of Diverse Religions in Tiger Bay* explored the competing discourses and practices of the many religious organizations that have sought to establish a foothold in Butetown: Baptists, Catholics, Church-in-Wales, Greek Orthodox, Lutheran, Methodists, Muslims, Quakers and the Salvation Army.

49 I borrow this term from Stuart Hall (ed.), *Representation* (London, 1997), and from James Clifford and George E. Marcus, *Writing Culture: The Poetics and Politics of Ethnography* (Berkeley, 1986).

50 These new publications include Glenn Jordan (ed.), *'Down the Bay': 'Picture Post', Humanist Photography and Images of 1950s Cardiff* (Cardiff, 2001); Glenn Jordan, *Tramp Steamers, Seamen and Sailor Town: Jack Sullivan's Paintings of Old Cardiff Docklands* (Cardiff, 2002); Matthew Manning, Patti Flynn and Glenn Jordan, *Fractured Horizon: A Landscape of Memory/Gorwel Briwedig: Tirlun Atgof* (Cardiff, 2003); Glenn Jordan with Akli Ahmed and Abdikarim Adan, *Somali Elders: Portraits from Wales/Odeyada Soomaalida: Muuqaalo ka yimid Welishka* (in English and Somali) (Cardiff, 2004); and Glenn Jordan, Liz Taylor and Phil Cope, *It's Already in the Wood: The Afro-Welsh Sculpture of Raymond Charles Taylor* (Cardiff, 2006).

51 BHAC received a publishing grant from the Arts Council of Wales to subsidize the publication of *Fractured Horizon*. I mention this fact because we have often had difficulties convincing the art establishment that we do *art* – as we may have difficulties convincing some readers that we do *history*.

52 Glenn Jordan, 'Tortured Journey: Cardiff Bay, Photography and the Landscape of Memory', introduction to Patti Flynn, Mathew Manning and Glenn Jordan, *Fractured Horizon: A Landscape of Memory* (Cardiff, 2003), pp. 11–2.

53 Catherine Belsey, 'Reading Cultural History' in Tasmin Spargo (ed.), *Reading the Past* (Houndmills, 2000), p. 106.

54 Raphael Samuel, 'Unofficial Knowledge', in *Theatres of Memory*, pp. 38–9; emphasis added.

55 Stuart Hall, 'Cultural Studies and Its Theoretical Legacies', in Lawrence Grossberg, Cary Nelson and Paula Treichler (eds), *Cultural Studies* (London, 1992), p. 286.

Glossary

Agency. The capacity of an individual or group to act consciously towards a particular end.

Determinism. In history refers usually to the notion that historical processes conform to certain patterns or laws which (a) are beyond our control and (b) make a particular course of events necessary or inevitable. The opposite belief is the notion of free will. (*see also Agency and Teleology*).

Discourse. Used generally to refer to communication in speech or writing, or to a lengthy spoken or written treatment of a subject. Discourse is used in a special sense by poststructuralists, and refers to the relationship between language and its context – as a means of both producing and organizing meaning in social contexts. As such it is related to social power.

Empiricism. The doctrine that knowledge should be founded upon experience, observation and perhaps experiment.

Epistemology. The theory of knowledge, its validity and foundations.

Hegemony. A dominant group's rule by ideological consent (non-coercive means); the dominant group achieves power and control over other groups in society by successfully representing to them that the existing state of affairs is in their best interest.

Hermeneutic. In history usually means the interpretation of sources, often to uncover the intentions and ideas of their authors.

Heuristic. A concept or other device that serves to discover or learn something.

Historism. A historical doctrine associated particularly with Leopold von Ranke in which all actions, categories, truths and values are explicable in terms of particular historical conditions, and in consequence can be understood only by examining particular historical contexts, in detachment from present-day attitudes. Historists often focus on political history and great men. The term 'historicism' is also used to designate this type of historiography, but we have preferred 'historism' in this volume because 'historicism' is also used to designate the doctrine that particular events can only be understood in terms of 'historical laws'. Historism as we have defined it rejects this contention on the grounds that historical events are always unique.

Metanarrative. A theory which purports to be comprehensive and to be able to explain all particular instances (also known as grandnarrative, master narrative, grand theory).

Metaphysical. Used generally to designate or abstract, perhaps speculative, reasoning. Used by Derrida in a different sense – to designate the illusionary quest for underlying realities.

Ontology. The study of the nature of being, of what it is to be in the world.

Positivism. A doctrine contending that sense perceptions are the only admissible basis of human knowledge and precise thought. Positivists hold that historical laws – if there are any – must be derived from observation. Positivists often attacked metaphysics as abstract speculation.

Relativism: The doctrine that knowledge is not absolute, but depends upon point of view.

Subject: Can designate the ability of an individual or a group to make sense of the world and choose particular course of action (*see Agency*) or, in contrast, it can mean subjection to linguistic or social structures. Some theories attempt to reconcile these two meanings of the term.

Teleology: The notion that history moves towards a predetermined end – socialism, capitalism, the rule of God, the realization of the nation-state, for example.

Universalism/universalist. Concepts, ideas or theories that are considered to be generally applicable – not just to particular categories of people, nations or societies.

Index

Index